PATHWAYS OUT OF POVERTY

PATHWAYS
OUT OF POVERTY

INNOVATIONS IN MICROFINANCE FOR THE POOREST FAMILIES

Edited by Sam Daley-Harris

Kumarian
Press, Inc

Pathways Out of Poverty: Innovations in Microfinance for the Poorest Families

Published 2002 in the United States of America by Kumarian Press, Inc.,
1294 Blue Hills Avenue, Bloomfield, Connecticut 06002 USA.

Copyediting and design by Nicholas A. Kosar.
Proofreading by Jody El-Assadi. Index by Robert Swanson.
The text of this book is set in Adobe Sabon 10.5/13.5.

Printed in Canada on acid-free paper by
Transcontinental Printing Book Group
Text printed with vegetable oil-based ink.
∞ The paper used in this publication meets the minimum requirements
of the American National Standard for Information Sciences—Permanence of
Paper for Printed Library Materials, ANSI Z39.48–1984.

Library of Congress Cataloging-in-Publication Data
Daley-Harris, Sam, 1946–
    Pathways out of poverty: innovations in microfinance for the poorest families /
Sam Daley-Harris.
        p.   cm.
    Includes bibliographical references and index.
    ISBN 1-56549-159-9
    1. Microfinance—Developing countries.   2. Financial institutions—Developing
countries.   3. Poor—Developing countries.   I. Title.
    HG178.33.D44 D354 2002
    332—dc21   2002014809

    11 10 09 08 07 06 05 04 03 02   10 9 8 7 6 5 4 3 2 1

First Printing 2002

Contents

Acknowledgments

This book has benefited from many contributors. The ideas for these chapters were suggested by members of the Microcredit Summit Campaign in evaluation forms completed at various global and regional meetings, and they were improved upon through feedback to various e-mail questionnaires. The Campaign Executive Committee provided the final reflection and approval that set the commissioning of each chapter in motion. Of course, primary thanks go to the authors, who generously gave of their time and intellectual energy to write several drafts of their chapters during the development of the book.

In chapter 1, "Ensuring Impact," Anton Simanowitz has done a brilliant job of showing how microcredit is playing an important role and could play an even greater role in cutting absolute poverty in half by 2015. We are delighted with the result and with his contribution to the field.

An excellent literature review and analysis of the effects of microfinance on poverty reduction conducted for the Canadian International Development Agency (CIDA) by Jonathan Morduch and Barbara Haley, on behalf of RESULTS Canada, was an important underpinning of this chapter. It supported the findings from the case studies reviewed for this section with more generalized evidence, giving a detailed and comprehensive review of a huge range of literature and presenting the key issues and an analysis based on the literature reviewed.

We are grateful to the ImpAct program for allowing Anton the time to write this chapter. Many of the ideas and material in the chapter have been developed as part of the ImpAct thematic group, Microfinance for the Very Poor. Alice Walter, who analyzed materials on the case study MFIs, also gave significant input to this chapter. We are grateful for the efforts of Syed Hashemi of the Consultative Group to Assist the Poorest (CGAP) for facilitating the poverty assessments of the case studies. Funds for the poverty assessment were generously provided by CGAP. Funds for the rating of CRECER (Crédito con Educación Rural) were provided through CGAP's rating fund, Caisse des Depots et Consignations (France), and the Microcredit Summit Campaign. We extend our appreciation to PlaNet Rating for its work on CRECER's rating for this chapter. While completed prior to the conception of this paper, the work of Micro-Credit Ratings and Guarantees India Ltd. and The Credit Rating Information Services of India Limited (CRISIL) on the ratings of Share Microfin Limited were also very important. Of course the question of impact is paramount, and this chapter has had the benefit of the work of Helen Todd and the CASHPOR Network who shared the preliminary findings from their impact assessment of SHARE. In addition, the analysis of CRECER greatly benefited from an impact evaluation conducted by Freedom from Hunger. We would also like to thank Udaia Kumar of SHARE and Evelyn Grandi of CRECER for their invaluable input. This chapter was partially funded through a grant from the ILO.

The materials were provided too late for the African case study, Nyesigiso in Mali, to be included in this chapter. They will, however, be made available on the Microcredit Summit Campaign Web site.

The ideas raised in chapter 2, "Building Better Lives," are promoted in three other chapters of this book. It is out of a commitment to building better lives that tens of millions of clients and hundreds of thousands of staff work tirelessly in this field. For their insights and contribution to the advancement of thinking in this area, we owe a special debt of gratitude to Chris Dunford, the author, and to those responsible for the case studies: BRAC in Bangladesh, FUCEC-Togo, and Pro Mujer in Bolivia. Portions of this chapter were based on drafts by Barbara MkNelly, Christian Loupeda, Beth Porter, Bob Richards, Kathleen Stack, Didier Thys and Ellen Vor der Bruegge of Freedom from Hunger and by staff of BRAC, FUCEC-Togo, and Pro Mujer. This chapter was partially funded through a grant from UNESCO.

John Hatch, with important assistance from Sara R. Levine and Amanda Penn, has done a remarkable job of highlighting dozens of innovations from around the world in his chapter, "Innovations from the Field." He has received critical support from Jeff Ashe, Barbara Weber, Kim Wilson, Kate McKee, and Barry Lennon.

Thank you to Susy Cheston and Lisa Kuhn of Opportunity International for showing us what is being done and what more can be done in chapter 4, "Empowering Women through Microfinance." They received important assistance from the following individuals and institutions: Elisabeth Fosterm, Michael Walsh, Gems of Hope USA, Morrow Charitable Trust, Women's Opportunity Fund, United Nations Fund for Women (UNIFEM), Nicole Zdrojewski, Jennifer Krueger, Linda Valentine, and Yeling Tan. This chapter was partially funded through a grant from UNIFEM.

David Gibbons and Jennifer Meehan have made significant contributions to the Microcredit Summit Campaign through an earlier paper they were commissioned to write and through chapter 5, "Financing Microfinance for Poverty Reduction." They discussed the ideas in this chapter with many people and are especially appreciative for the thoughtful contributions of the following individuals: staff of the Canadian International Development Agency (CIDA), Ramesh Bellamkonda, Brigit Helms, Dushyant Kapoor, John Lewis, Benji Monetmayer, Helen Todd, and participants in the CASHPOR-PHILNET workshop, Financing Microfinance for Poverty Reduction, which took place in Manila from June 5 to 7, 2002. We are grateful to Deutsche Bank for underwriting this chapter.

Chapter 6 on policy and regulation in microfinance was prepared by the Women's World Banking (WWB) global team. Kathryn Imboden and Nancy Barry were the primary authors, with contributions made by Nicola Armacost and Cecile Zacarias of WWB, and by Harihar Dev Pant, General Manager of Nirdhan Uttan Bank Limited in Nepal. The chapter is based on the leadership of the WWB network in policy change and performance standards over the last eight years, at global and local levels. Since 1995, WWB has convened leading microfinance practitioners, policymakers, and international funders to create consensus on the key elements of financial systems that work for the poor majority, and on the key performance indicators in microfinance. WWB has worked with network members, local microfinance networks, and policymakers to build policies for microfinance in several countries, including India, the Philippines, Russia, Colombia, the Dominican Republic, South Africa, and Ghana.

The ideas in this book are vital to the expansion of microcredit for the very poor and are intended to further the learning agenda of the Microcredit Summit Campaign. The opinions expressed, however, are those of the authors and do not necessarily reflect the views of the Campaign or of any other organization.

Within the Microcredit Summit Campaign, no one has played a greater role in shepherding this book from conception to completion than Anna Awimbo, the Campaign's research director. For more than a year, she has worked with the authors, case studies, and other resource persons to bring this work together. Abbey Gonter played a critical role in completing a style edit of each chapter. Other assistance came from Kate Druschel, Nathanael Goldberg, Katrina Mustoe, Alyssa Boxhill, Anna Oman, Cristina Sanchez, Katie Cafferty, Nicole Jacobs, Rebecca Smart, and Ruth Moreno.

Krishna Sondhi and her team at Kumarian Press have made an exceptional contribution to the field of development through the books they have published. They have been a pleasure to work with, and it is an honor to be among their team of authors.

There are so many others who have had a hand in shaping the final result. To those we have not mentioned, we extend our heartfelt gratitude.

Preface

We live in a world where more than 100 million children of primary school age have never stepped inside a classroom, where some 29,000 children die each day from largely preventable malnutrition and disease, and where 1.2 billion people live on less than $1 a day.

In this same world there are millions of women like Saraswathi Krishnan who lives in India. "When my children cried at night from hunger, I felt like dying," Saraswathi recalled. Her husband, an unskilled wage laborer, earned very little and often squandered what little he made on alcohol. Eventually, when the roof of their tiny hut was about to collapse, having no jewelry or other assets to pledge for a loan to repair it, Saraswathi sold her seven-year-old daughter into bonded labor to a local merchant for 2,000 Indian rupees (about US$40).

"My little girl complained to me daily that the merchant abused her. His family would eat food in front of her and give her none," she remembered. Five years later Saraswathi joined Working Women's Forum, a women's self-help and microcredit program based in Madras, India. With her first loan she paid off her debt to the merchant, freeing her daughter, who now attends school, and began a small vegetable-selling business.

With a second loan she bought her sixteen-year-old son a loom. Previously he would bring home around $5 per month doing odd jobs for wealthy families. With the loom, he can weave two saris per month, earning him $25 per month.

Now Saraswathi's vegetable business is thriving as well, thanks to her hard work and the training she has received from the program. She is glad to be able to "give her children opportunities," she explained. With the family's new sources of income, Saraswathi has a sense of pride and security she never before experienced. "I will never mortgage my children again; they will be educated. Now I see to it that my husband is good and does not beat me anymore."

Inspired by women like Saraswathi Krishnan and in response to the plight of hundreds of millions of very poor women without access to financial services, more than 2,900 people from 137 countries gathered in February

1997 at the Microcredit Summit. At the Summit they launched a nine-year campaign to reach 100 million of the world's poorest families, especially the women of those families, with credit for self-employment and other financial and business services by the year 2005.

Over the last five years the Microcredit Summit Campaign has been guided by four core themes: 1) reaching the poorest, 2) reaching and empowering women, 3) building financially self-sufficient institutions, and 4) ensuring a positive measurable impact on the lives of the clients and their families.

The journey has not been easy. At the time of the Microcredit Summit five years ago the microfinance field was speeding toward a vision that placed financial performance above all else. Many in the field contended that the poorest families in a community were too costly to identify and motivate and their inclusion would keep a program from becoming financially self-sufficient.

They further asserted that if a program was somehow able to reach clients who were very poor and yet be financially strong, the institution would only be adding a debt burden to those very poor families who needed handouts instead of small loans.

The conventional wisdom also held that measuring impact brought unjustified costs, another drag on an institution's financial performance, and warned against trying to add cost-effective educational components in the areas of child survival, reproductive health, HIV/AIDS prevention, and business development services.

These arguments, which were so pervasive five years ago, are a central reason why those who lead the effort to cut absolute poverty in half by 2015 ill advisedly exclude microfinance from being one of the pivotal interventions.

Over the last five years, however, these arguments have been answered by the Microcredit Summit Campaign and others who see that the microfinance industry has the ability to stay true to its roots—to work with very poor women and offer them the services they need to move themselves and their families out of poverty.

We know that microcredit institutions *can* reach the poorest. The Consultative Group to Assist the Poorest (CGAP), the consortium of twenty-nine donor agencies focused on microfinance, has developed a Poverty Assessment Tool that was initially used with seven institutions in as many countries. CGAP concluded that in several of the programs, 50 to 60 percent of the entering clients were in the bottom third of their community when they started with the program and even more were living on less than $1 a day.

Microcredit institutions reaching the poorest *can* become financially self-sufficient. CGAP CEO Elizabeth Littlefield has said: ". . . thankfully we have encouraging evidence on the ground that Microfinance Institutions (MFIs) can do both [reach the poorest and be financially self-sufficient] . . . ." Further evidence can be found in the paper "The Microcredit Summit's Challenge: Building Financially Self-Sufficient Institutions While Maintaining a Commitment to Serving the Poorest Families" (www.microcreditsummit.org/papers/challengespaper.htm).

And of course, microcredit *is* one key intervention in helping families move out of poverty. Shahidur Khandker of the World Bank conducted an exhaustive study of BRAC, Grameen Bank, and RD-12, three Bangladeshi microcredit institutions, the latter a government-run program. Grameen and BRAC alone were reaching 5.3 million families by the end of 2000 or more than 25 million family members. Shahidur Khandker's study, published by Oxford University Press in 1998, concludes, "Poverty in Bangladesh is largely a matter of not having enough to eat. Microcredit programs attack poverty at its source by increasing the household consumption expenditure of participants. Borrowing from a program is estimated to reduce moderate poverty among participants by as much as 20 percent and extreme poverty by as much as 22 percent. This means that as much as 5 percent of program-participating households should be able to lift their families out of poverty every year by borrowing from a microcredit program."

The chapters in this book were prepared for the Microcredit Summit +5, held November 10–13, 2002, in New York City. In addition to advancing the learning agenda of the Microcredit Summit Campaign, they serve as a roadmap for world leaders who are committed to achieving the Millennium Development Goals, especially that of cutting absolute poverty in half by 2015. This book is also a cry for more commitment from world leaders to sustainable microfinance for the very poor—a commitment that is essential if we are to achieve the Millennium Development Goals.

The first chapter, "Ensuring Impact," by Anton Simanowitz of ImpAct, features two institutions (SHARE in India and CRECER in Bolivia) that have undergone externally administered poverty assessments, financial ratings, and impact assessments. The paper shows that these two institutions on two continents are reaching very poor clients, are financially strong, and are showing that their clients are moving out of poverty.

In the chapter "Building Better Lives," Chris Dunford of Freedom from Hunger illustrates how microfinance can be cost-effectively integrated with education in child survival, reproductive health, and HIV/AIDS prevention to enhance impact.

The chapter "Financing Microfinance for Poverty Reduction," by David Gibbons and Jennifer Meehan of CASHPOR Technical Services, shows how innovative financing can speed the growth of small institutions with the vision and ability to reach the very poor while maintaining strong financial performance.

The "Innovations" chapter by John Hatch of FINCA International outlines dozens of innovations that are improving the implementation and quality of microfinance programs worldwide.

In their chapter "Empowering Women Through Microfinance," Susy Cheston and Lisa Kuhn of Opportunity International show what can be done to more fully empower women. When the lives of women are transformed, their families are transformed too.

Finally, Women's World Banking shows how commercialization can push institutions away from working with the very poor because of excessive capital and reporting requirements and what can be done to avoid that.

In 2000 and 2001 I closed the Africa, Asia, and Latin America regional meetings of the Microcredit Summit by reading a quote from retired U.S. Senator Mark Hatfield, a Republican from Oregon. Eighteen years ago Senator Hatfield said, "We stand by as children starve by the millions because we lack the will to eliminate hunger. Yet we have found the will to develop missiles capable of flying over the polar cap and landing within a few hundred feet of their target. This is not innovation. It is a profound distortion of humanity's purpose on earth."

This book and the actions it describes are part of a growing movement to correct that distortion of humanity's purpose on earth and so this book is dedicated to the tens of millions of clients and their families and the hundreds of thousands of staff who are blazing a pathway out of poverty each and every day.

Sam Daley-Harris
August 9, 2002

Acronyms

ACCION	Americans for Community Co-operation in Other Nations, International
ACLAM	Action Contre La Misère (Haiti)
ADAPTE	Asociación de Ayuda al Pequeño Trabajador y Empresario (Costa Rica)
ADEMCOL	Asociación para el Desarrollo Empresarial Colombiano (Colombia)
ADOPEM	Asociación Dominicana para el Desarrollo de la Mujer (Dominican Republic)
AFMIN	The Africa Microfinance Network (Côte d'Ivoire)
AGAPE	Asociación General para Asesorar Pequeñas Empresas (Colombia)
AIMS	Assessing the Impact of Microfinance Services
AMFIU	Association of Microenterprise Finance Institutions of Uganda
ARDCI	Agricultural and Rural Development for Catanduanes, Inc. (Philippines)
ASA	Association for Social Advancement (Bangladesh)
ASPIRE	Asociación para la Inversión y Empleo (Dominican Republic)
BRAC	Bangladesh Rural Advancement Committee
CASHPOR	Credit and Savings for the Hard-Core Poor
CBD	Community-based distributor
CETZAM	Christian Enterprise Trust of Zambia
CFC	Commercial Finance Corporation
CFTS	CASHPOR Financial & Technical Services Limited
CGAP	Consultative Group to Assist the Poorest
CIDA	Canadian International Development Agency
CRECER	Credito con Educacion Rural (Bolivia)
CRISIL	The Credit Rating Information Services of India Limited

CRS	Catholic Relief Services
CSD	Centre for Self-Help Development (Nepal)
CSRA	Consejo de Salud Rural Andino (Bolivia)
CUES	Credit Union Empowerment and Strengthening (Philippines)
DFID	Department for International Development (UK)
EQ2	Equity equivalent
FECECAM	Fédération des Caisses d'Epargne et de Crédit Agricole Mutuel (Benin)
FFH	Freedom from Hunger
FINCA	Foundation for International Community Assistance
FOCCAS	Foundation for Credit and Community Assistance (Uganda)
FORA	Fund for the Support of Small Entrepreneurship (Russia)
FUCEC	Fédération des Unions Coopérative Epargne et Crédit (Togo)
FWWB	Friends of Women's World Banking (India)
GB	Grameen Bank
GIRAFE	PlaNet Finance's rating methodology: Governance and decision-making process; Information and management tools; Risks: analysis and control; Activities and loan portfolio; Funding: equity and liabilities; Efficiency and profitability
HDI	Human Development Initiatives (Nigeria)
HIVOS	Humanistisch Instituut voor Ontwikkelingssamenwerking (Netherlands)
ICDDR,B	International Centre for Diarrhoeral Disease Research (Bangladesh)
IDB	Inter-American Development Bank
IDH	Instituto para el Desarrollo Hondureño (Honduras)
IFAD	International Fund for Agricultural Development
IFPRI	International Food Policy Research Institute
IFS	Institutional financial self-sufficiency
IGVGD	Income Generation for Vulnerable Groups Development
ILO	International Labour Organisation
INAFI	International Network of Alternative Financial Institutions (Bangladesh)
MBB	Microbanking Bulletin

M-CRIL	Micro-Credit Ratings and Guarantees India Ltd.
MDI	Microfinance Deposit Taking Institution
MFI	Microfinance institution
MSC	Microcredit Summit Campaign
NABARD	National Bank for Agriculture and Rural Development (India)
NGO	Nongovernmental organization
OI	Opportunity International
OSS	Operational Self-Sufficiency
PKSF	Palli Karma Sahayak Foundation (Bangladesh)
PVO	Private and voluntary organization
RMDC	Rural Microfinance Development Centre Ltd. (Nepal)
ROSCA	Rotating Savings and Credit Association
RWMN	Russia Women's Microfinance Network
SAT	Sinapi Aba Trust (Ghana)
SDR	Special Drawing Rights
SEDP	Small Enterprise Development Program (Bangladesh)
SEEP	Small Enterprise and Education Promotion Network (USA)
SEF	Small Enterprise Foundation (South Africa)
SEWA	Self-Employed Women's Association (India)
SHARE	Share Microfin Limited (India)
SHG	Self-help group
SIDBI	Small Industries Development Bank of India
SIM	SHARE India MACS (Mutually Aided Cooperative Society)
SNEHA	Social Need Education and Human Awareness (India)
SUM	Special Unit for Microfinance
TIAVO	Tahiry Ifamonjena mombariny Vola Caisse Woccu (Madagascar)
TSPI	Tulay Sa Pag-Unlad, Inc. (Philippines)
UNCDF	United Nations Capital Development Fund
UNDP	United Nations Development Programme
UNESCO	United Nations Educational, Scientific and Cultural Organisation
UNFPA	United Nations Population Fund
UNIFEM	United Nations Development Fund for Women
USAID	United States Agency for International Development
VAT	Value-added tax
VAWA	Village Alive Women's Association (Nigeria)

WEDTF	Women's Entrepreneurship Development Trust Fund (Tanzania)
WKP	Wahana Kria Putri (Indonesia)
WOCCU	World Council of Credit Unions
WOTR	Watershed Organization Trust (India)
WWF	Working Women's Forum (India)

1

Ensuring Impact:
Reaching the Poorest while Building
Financially Self-Sufficient Institutions, and
Showing Improvement in the Lives of the Poorest
Women and Their Families

Anton Simanowitz
with Alice Walter

This chapter is about microfinance and its contribution to the eradication of poverty for millions of the world's poorest people. It also recognizes that microfinance is not a panacea and that expectations should not be built up so high that it is bound to fail. Microfinance is reaching and having an impact on millions of poor people, predominantly women, but the boundaries of who microfinance can reach, and in what ways, have still to be explored. Many millions more can benefit. It is not the poverty level of potential clients that determines access and impact, but the design of the services provided. Not all people need microfinance, but most groups can benefit.

The Millennium Development Goals, agreed to at the United Nations Millennium Summit, set a critical challenge of halving absolute poverty in the world by 2015.[1] Governments and donors around the world responded with plans to work towards the realization of these goals. Given the success of the microfinance industry in reducing the poverty of millions of people, it is surprising that there has not been a greater focus on microfinance in the Millennium Development strategies developed by donors.[2] In this chapter I present evidence of the important contribution of microfinance to the eradication of poverty, particularly through the empowerment of poor people to choose when and how to access other development services such as health and education, and reduction in vulnerability. Donors should be investing in poverty-focused microfinance as a key element in their strategies to achieve their Millennium commitments.

> **Box 1.1**
> **Defining Poverty:**
> **A Note on Terminology**
>
> *[handwritten margin notes: "vulnerable non-poor — POVERTY LINE — Moderate poor — 50%, Extreme poor — 10-50, Destitute — 10%", "MS = poorest = CGAP = very poor = 7$1?"]*
>
> There are a number of definitions of the concept of poverty and how this should be measured. Sebstad and Cohen separate those living above and below the poverty line—poor and non-poor. The category of poor are further divided into *destitute* (bottom 10 percent below the poverty-line), *extreme poor* (those in the bottom 10 to 50 percentile of households below the poverty line), and *moderate poor* (the top 50 percent of households living below the poverty line). A further category of *vulnerable non-poor* is also recognized.
>
> In this chapter, I look broadly at poverty, but I focus particularly on those people living below half the national poverty line or living on less than US$1 per day. This group, which includes the extreme poor and destitute, is defined by the Microcredit Summit as the *poorest* and by the Consultative Group to Assist the Poorest (CGAP) as *very poor*. I use both terms, choosing the term *poorest* to emphasize the need not to automatically exclude anyone from microfinance—even the poorest person.

As the Microcredit Summit campaign passes its halfway point, it moves on from promoting the goal of sustainable microfinance that results in significant positive change in the lives of the poorest women, to reviewing the evidence of its efforts and concluding that these objectives are more than worthy aims—they are being achieved by organizations around the world.

Goals and Structure of the Chapter

This work draws on a range of literature and experience. Two case studies illustrate and support the ideas and arguments presented, but the chapter is based on wider influences and learning from the larger microfinance field. My aim is to frame key questions, to explore and challenge conventional wisdom, and perhaps most importantly to suggest practical and promising ways forward. Given the scale of this task it is not possible to discuss many issues in as much detail as might be desired, nor to present the supporting evidence in full. Three core pieces of work have been used to support this work, and readers are referred to these for more detailed evidence and discussion:

- Two case studies prepared by Alice Walter analyze the available data on the case study organizations SHARE and CRECER.[3] For each organization these include a poverty assessment, an impact assessment, and a rating. No primary research was conducted for this chapter. The case studies provide clear evidence for performance in poverty outreach, impact and financial performance, as well as some details of how each organization has succeeded in achieving these goals, and in balancing the different priorities and challenges that necessarily face a poverty-focused microfinance institution (MFI).

- A comprehensive literature review of microfinance and poverty reduction was prepared by Jonathan Morduch and Barbara Haley in November 2001. This provides compelling evidence for the impact of microfinance on six out of seven of the Millennium goals, especially halving absolute poverty, through its impact on income poverty and vulnerability, and to a lesser degree through impacts on health, nutrition, and schooling. The review concludes there is strong evidence that microfinance can be effective for a broad group of clients, including the very poor or poorest. It also concludes that financial performance of poverty-targeted MFIs can be comparable to those that do not reach the poorest.

- A study by USAID's AIMS project prepared for the World Development Report 2000-2001 looks at microfinance, risk management, and poverty.[4] It examines non-income dimensions of poverty, focusing on the impacts of microfinance on risk, vulnerability, and assets, in helping to protect against risk ahead of time, and managing losses following a shock or economic stress event. This analysis provides great insight into the mechanisms by which the services offered by MFIs relate to poor people's lives. It is important both in broadening the scope of the consideration of impacts beyond income poverty, and in terms of the implications on the design and delivery of microfinance services.

This chapter is divided into three parts:

- *Part One: Evidence for Sustainable Microfinance for the Poorest*

  This part examines the evidence for sustainable microfinance reaching and having an impact on very poor people, particularly women. It examines the challenges and limitations for the realization of these goals. Evidence from two case studies is cited to demonstrate that microfinance can reach very poor women, that it can have a significant impact on their poverty levels, and that it can be delivered by sustainable organizations.

- *Part Two: Design and Delivery of Microfinance for the Poorest*

  This part is a wide-ranging discussion of critical operational issues which determine the effectiveness of microfinance for the poorest. "Including the Poorest: Overcoming Exclusion" looks at both the deliberate and inadvertent mechanisms that act to exclude the poorest, and suggests ways in which these can be overcome. "Design and Delivery of Microfinance for the Poorest" discusses how the effectiveness of microfinance in supporting income growth and reducing vulnerability can be improved, as an active and managed strategy. Central to this is the creation of a culture of impact assessment and poverty outreach within MFIs.

- *Part Three: Implications for the Microfinance Industry*

  This part draws conclusions and presents practical suggestions for practitioners and policymakers. What should the industry realistically be striving for? How can information about performance and achievement of goals be collected and used? What role can donors and policymakers play in realigning the industry towards a greater focus on achieving positive impacts for very poor people?

The Success of the Microfinance Movement to Date[5]

The microfinance movement was founded on the belief that microfinance can be a powerful tool in combating poverty. The realization of the Microcredit Summit Campaign's target of reaching 100 million of the world's poorest families with credit for self-employment and other financial and business services offers a significant contribution to the Millennium Development goals.

To date, a successful microfinance industry has been built that is effective in reaching millions of poor people, in providing them with financial services, and in reducing their poverty. Strong and replicable models of microfinance have been developed and adapted throughout the world, and implemented by increasingly professionalized and commercialized organizations. To achieve these goals practitioners have had to make many compromises and trade-offs. The imperative to develop viable and sustainable institutions has placed great pressure on organizational productivity and efficiency, but this has had to be balanced against social objectives. The goal of combating poverty in the most effective way has also necessarily been compromised, as it is clear that MFIs seeking to become financially sustainable cannot spend the time and resources with clients that more holistic development organizations might. Nevertheless, the achievements in terms of financial performance and impact on poverty have been impressive.

In this chapter I take the position that microfinance has been too cautious and that the compromise has been too much on the side of financial and institutional performance, and not enough on the possibilities for maximizing poverty impact and client performance. The microfinance industry has demonstrated what can be achieved; it has not demonstrated what cannot be achieved. The fact that most MFIs do not reach large numbers of very poor people does not mean that they cannot reach them, or that very poor people cannot benefit. It is now time to innovate and design microfinance services that maintain the high standards of financial performance, but which set new standards in poverty impact. There are costs and benefits in working with very poor clients, and the challenge is to push the frontiers of microfinance so that it better serves its developmental goals.

Microfinance has tended to exclude those that cannot use the one-size-fits-all services provided. The services that have been developed tend to meet the needs of a particular segment of the client market, and have led to the exclusion of those that cannot use or pay for these services. Increasingly it is being recognized that the poor are not an homogenous group and that products and their delivery need to be better tailored to the needs of different groups of clients. Organizations need to be more flexible and to provide services that are appropriate for a range of client markets, not just the middle poor. In doing so, they expand the scope of their market. Services that are better tailored to the needs of clients lead to better performance and sustainability amongst clients, which in turn will lead to higher performance and sustainability for the MFI. This is a time of opportunity, and a time for

---

Box 1.2

"Like many other development tools [microfinance] has insufficiently penetrated the poorer strata of society. The poorest form the vast majority of those without access to primary health care and basic education; similarly, they are the majority of those without access to microfinance."

Source: Jonathan Morduch and Barbara Haley, *Analysis of the Effects of Microfinance on Poverty Reduction*, RESULTS Canada for CIDA (2001), 1.

a renewed commitment to developing services that reach a much greater range of clients, including the very poor.

A symbolic milestone has been reached in the recent announcement of Grameen II.[6] This new approach of the Grameen Bank encompasses lessons learned from twenty-five years of practice, and recognizes that the previous model incorporated a number of elements that limited the ability of many potential clients to benefit, particularly the poorest sections of the community. Grameen II emphasizes the need to focus on the poorest in order to be able to serve their needs. Central to the new model is increased flexibility of products to allow for loans and savings services to fit better with client livelihoods and experience.

The Case Study Organizations

CRECER, Bolivia (Village banking model incorporating Credit with Education)[7]

CRECER provides integrated financial and educational services to very poor women and their families in the rural and marginal urban areas of Bolivia, in order to support their autonomous actions to improve their health, nutrition, and family income. Two thirds of Bolivia's population live below the national poverty line. As of December 2001, CRECER had 30,989 total members in approximately 1,700 village banks, in five of Bolivia's nine departments.

CRECER's methodology follows the village bank model, with self-selected solidarity groups of five to eight women forming village banks of fifteen to thirty. Loans are made to the village bank and then distributed to members. Loan sizes are small (starting at Bs.500/US$71), and are made at an interest rate of 3.5 percent per month flat. No collateral is required; instead clients undertake to jointly guarantee each other. Local CRECER staff, called promoters, visit each village bank for their weekly or bi-weekly meeting, at which the members make repayments of interest and principal in equal installments over four to six months. These meetings are mandatory, and include an educational component in healthcare, nutrition, self-esteem, and management of small businesses.

Loan use is registered for statistical purposes, but is the free choice of each member. CRECER does not carry out loan use checks or income-generating capacity checks. Clients must maintain 10 to 15 percent of the loan amount on deposit, which can be withdrawn at the end of each cycle. No interest is paid on savings, but dividends from the internal account are paid

Table 1.1   SHARE Loan Products

TYPE OF LOANS	DURATION	ELIGIBILITY
General Loan	One year (50 weeks)	From first year
Seasonal Loan	One Year (25-50 weeks)	From second year
Sanitary Loans	One Year (50 weeks)	From second year
Housing Loans	Four Years (200 weeks)	From third year
Supplementary Loans	Six months (25 weeks)	From first year after six months
Small Enterprise Loans	Two Years (100 weeks)	From first year

based on a member's savings and external loan. Each village bank has an internal account, from which borrowers can also take loans, at a slightly higher interest rate, simultaneously to the program loan. The size and term of these loans is decided by the women themselves, but internal loans must be repaid before a program loan cycle can end.

SHARE, India (Grameen model)

SHARE Microfin Limited (SHARE)[8] provides financial services to poor women in the state of Andhra Pradesh, India, for viable productive income-generating enterprises, to help them reduce their poverty and improve their quality of life. Thirty-five percent of the population live below the national poverty line in India.[9] As of March 2002, SHARE was working in thirteen districts with 109,484 active clients in 21,897 centers.

SHARE implements a Grameen methodology, lending to poor women through groups of seven to eight which come together into centers of thirty-five to forty members. SHARE's average loan size is approximately US$85 and the interest rate is 20 percent per annum for loans repayable over fifty weeks. Screening of clients takes place through a means-based client profile format, and pre-lending training is followed by a Group Recognition Test to ensure that members have understood the program's rules and regulations. Various loan products are accessible to members.

Savings, which were compulsory until 1999, are now voluntary, with members pledging to try to save a fixed amount per week into an offshoot savings cooperative. SHARE has access to a proportion of these savings, and interest is paid according to amount and term. SHARE has a culture of

Table 1.2   Reaching the Poorest

	CRECER	SHARE
% clients living at or below US$1/day	41.0%	72.5%
% clients living below national poverty line	73.0%	60.0%
% of entering clients poorest third	38.6%	58.0%
% of entering clients middle third	39.6%	38.5%
% of entering clients least poor third	21.8%	3.5%
% of clients women	99.0%	100.0%
Poverty focus: Design, Geography, Targeting, Screening, Motivation, Culture of organization	D, G, M, C	D, T, M, C
Average loan size	US$128	US$85

Table 1.3   Impact

	CRECER	SHARE
% all clients experience reduction in economic poverty	66%	76%
% very poor clients experience reduction in economic poverty	Not available	89%
% client experiencing increase in savings	86%	84%
Dropout rate for very poor	Not available	Lower than overall rate
Overall dropout rate	Not available	17%

strict credit discipline and close supervision, emphasizing the productive use of loans, and visiting clients to check their loan use. It focuses on financial services, and does not provide many client support services.

Tables 1.1 through 1.4 give basic information about each of the case-study MFIs with respect to their poverty outreach, impact, and financial performance.

Table 1.4 Financial Performance — FY 2001

	CRECER	SHARE
Date of establishment	1990 (as MFI)	1990[a]
Rating	Investment grade[b]	Investment grade[c]
No. clients	30,989	109,484[d]
No. of staff	139	688[d]
Staff productivity (clients per loan officer)	223	343
Portfolio at risk (>30 days)	0.26%	Nil[d]
Outstanding loan portfolio (US$)	3,979,737	6,280,076[d]
Operational self-sufficiency	102%	105%[d]
Financial self-sufficiency	100%	100%[d]
Cost per unit of money lent	0.17	0.07
Return on average performing assets	1%	30%
Administrative efficiency	39%	25%
Financial cost ratio[e]	4.65%	7.9%

a. SHARE Microfin Ltd. from 1992.
b. From PlaNet Finance.
c. From M-CRIL.
d. March 2002.
e. Interest and fee expense on funding liabilities divided by average gross loan portfolio.

PART ONE:
EVIDENCE FOR SUSTAINABLE
MICROFINANCE FOR THE POOREST

Banking the Unbankable

The microcredit[10] movement started with the vision that the poor are bankable. Conventional wisdom—as expressed by the formal banking sector and many in the donor community—told us that poor people (let alone the poorest) could not use credit, and even if they could, the costs of providing credit to them would be prohibitively high. Therefore it would be foolhardy to try, as poor people were bound to fail to use the credit well and would be bad risks.

Some years later we have witnessed a revolution. Millions of poor people now have access to credit and other financial services, and there is no doubt that these services can be delivered in a financially sustainable way, and that they are effectively used. The conviction and innovation of the industry has proved the skeptics wrong.

Now, ironically, we hear the former conventional wisdom being repeated in terms of the *poorest*—in other words, they are unbankable. Very poor people cannot use credit, and even if they could, the costs of providing credit to them would be prohibitively high. Therefore it would be foolhardy to try, as very poor people are bound to fail to use the credit well and would be bad risks.

There is a lack of progress in reaching the poorest, which is leading many to conclude that microfinance cannot reach the very poor or is not an appropriate intervention for most very poor people. For example, the United Kingdom's Department for International Development (DFID), despite a

---

Box 1.3

"International microfinance experience indicates that microcredit is not a suitable tool to assist the chronically poor. Instead, savings can assist them to ride out crises by strengthening their economic security. In Russia, MFIs are currently not able to mobilise savings, thus, this option for assisting the poorest, DFID's primary target group, is currently not an option."

Source: DFID, "Maximising the Outreach of Microfinance in Russia," *Research and Impact Assessment; Terms of Reference for FORA* (London: DFID, 2001).

mandate to working with the poorest, seems to demonstrate a lack of commitment to the use of microcredit in its poverty reduction strategy.

Like the conventional wisdom of the bankers, this message is based on perceptions rather than evidence. There is no evidence to say that *in general* the poorest are unbankable. The "failures" of MFIs to reach very poor clients result not from failure of the very poor to benefit from microfinance, but from failures to design programs to meet their needs.

This chapter is written with the conviction, based on evidence from two case study MFIs and experience from many more, that the poorest *are* bankable. The limiting factor is not the potential of very poor clients, but the ability of microfinance organizations to deliver the right services, in a manner that is cost-effective, and can lead to sustainable organizations and sustainable long-term changes in clients' lives. The microfinance industry needs to rise to this challenge rather than concluding that because the poorest are not being reached, this means they cannot be reached.

The following sections examine this challenge in three parts:

- "The Challenge of Reaching the Poorest" focuses on the practical challenge of identifying large numbers of very poor clients.
- "Impact: What Role for Microfinance in Poverty Eradication?" looks at the role of microfinance in poverty alleviation and how effective microfinance can be in reducing poverty, and whether very poor clients generally benefit from participating.
- "Can MFIs Reach and Impact on the Poorest and Be Financially Sustainable?" examines the issue of financial self-sufficiency and whether a poverty focus is compatible with this aim.

The Challenge of Reaching the Poorest

Can MFIs Reach Very Poor Clients?

Microfinance does serve very poor clients, although in general they do not participate in large numbers.[11] Although very poor people are present in most programs, the majority of clients are from the moderately poor and vulnerable non-poor categories, that is, those just below and above the poverty line. Evidence from poverty assessments conducted by the Consultative Group to Assist the Poorest (CGAP)[12] on a number of MFIs indicates that although all those surveyed were reaching some very poor clients (defined as those in the bottom third of the population), few were reaching large numbers from this group. Most MFIs were biased towards less-poor clients, or

Figure 1.1   Comparison of Poverty-Focused (TCP) and Mainstream Microfinance (MCP) Programs of the Small Enterprise Foundation, South Africa

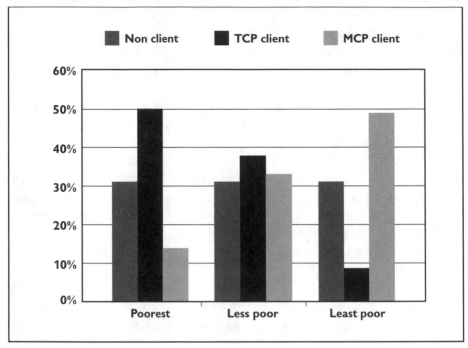

Source: van de Ruit et al.

at best reflected the general population distribution.

The CGAP experience demonstrates that MFIs do not automatically reach large numbers of very poor clients by using conventional design features, such as small loan sizes. It is striking that of the organizations assessed, the four that have analyzed and designed their programs to focus on the needs of the very poor are the only ones with significant depth of poverty outreach.[13] Those that use active poverty targeting are especially effective in biasing their outreach towards the poor and very poor.

Two examples, the Small Enterprise Foundation (SEF) in South Africa and Caisses Feminines in Madagascar are particularly interesting. Both organizations have two programs, the first designed along the lines of conventional non-poverty focused wisdom, the second designed with the needs of the very poor explicitly in mind and with active poverty targeting. There is a remarkable contrast between the poverty profiles of these two programs, with both poverty-focused programs significantly biased towards the poor and very poor, and the non-targeted program biased towards the middle poor and non-poor. Figure one presents the results from a poverty assessment of SEF. The graphs demonstrate a huge gap in poverty outreach between SEF's TCP Project, which predominantly reaches the poorest people and has very few clients in the least poor third, and SEF's MCP Project, which predominantly reaches clients from the least poor group and has few clients from amongst the poorest third.

Reaching the Poorest: Evidence from the Case Studies

Absolute or Relative Poverty?

Poverty outreach can be seen both in absolute and relative terms. Three levels can be defined:

- Those people who are very poor compared to their neighbors. The CGAP poverty assessment looks at the poverty level of *incoming* clients and divides the population in an MFI's operational area into thirds, and defines the bottom-third as very poor, the middle as poor, and the top third as non-poor. This definition does not take into account the relative poverty of the MFI's operational areas compared to the rest of the country.

Box 1.4

SHARE and CRECER work with the poorest clients by international, national, and local definitions:

- By *international standards* 72.5% of SHARE and 41% of CRECER clients are living in *absolute* poverty, as defined by living below US$1/day (purchasing power parity).

- By *national standards* 60% of SHARE and 73% of CRECER clients live below their national poverty line.

- By *local standards* SHARE and CRECER reach the poorest people in the communities in which they operate. 58% of SHARE clients and 38.6% of CRECER clients are amongst the poorest third of people in their communities.

- SHARE and CRECER achieve very high *depth of outreach*. 32.5% of SHARE and 19.8% of CRECER clients are amongst the *poorest 20%* in their own communities.

- Using a national definition of poverty, the poorest are defined as those people living at below half the national poverty line. This definition allows for accurate comparisons within a country, but does not capture how poor the country is on an international comparison.

- *Absolute poverty* (the poorest) is defined internationally as those living at or below US$1/day per person (adjusted for the purchasing power of the local currency).

These definitions are important, since if we are to ask whether MFIs reach very poor clients, we need to understand how this is defined. In a poor country, such as Bangladesh, the majority of clients reached by MFIs are living below the international US$/day absolute poverty line. However, this does not mean that they necessarily include large numbers of the poorest clients relative to national poverty. In a richer country where the national poverty line is higher in terms of US$ levels, an MFI may be very successful in reaching some of the poorest people in terms of their local context, but this would not be reflected in US$/day poverty definitions. The key operational point for MFIs is to focus on who is excluded and for what reasons. Achieving good poverty outreach is about providing the right products and services as far down the poverty scale as is possible. For this to take place two key measures of poverty outreach are important—working in the poorest areas of the country and working with the poorest people relative to the population in an MFI's operational area.

Poverty Outreach Compared to Operational Area and Nationally

CRECER and SHARE are effective in reaching very poor clients relative to the national poverty line and relative to the population in their operational areas. The CGAP poverty assessments and other poverty research demonstrates that they are reaching significant numbers of very poor clients, and are biased towards poorer clients when compared to the general population within the areas in which they work. Both organizations reach large numbers of clients from the poorest 20 percent of the communities in which they operate (SHARE—32.5 percent; CRECER—19.8 percent). Both organizations are working with large numbers of people below their countries' national poverty line (SHARE—60 percent; CRECER—73 percent).

Figure 1.2 shows the profile of *incoming* CRECER clients compared to non-clients in CRECER's operational areas. It demonstrates that CRECER has both an overall poverty bias, and is effective at reaching the poorest. While CRECER includes clients from the full range of poverty levels, it is striking that it reaches down to the poorest 10 percent of people in the

Figure 1.2   Poverty Outreach of CRECER

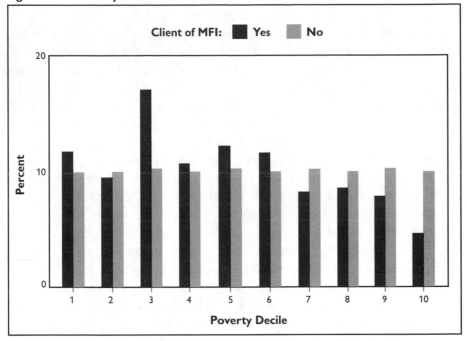

Figure 1.3   SHARE Poverty Assessment (Breakdown of Poverty Levels by Client Group)

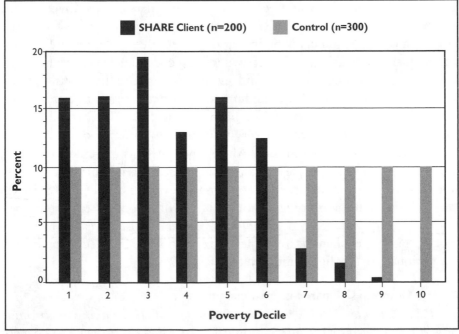

Source: CGAP analysis of poverty assessment data

communities in which it works, and is biased towards the very poor and moderately poor. Poverty indicators demonstrate that incoming CRECER clients are significantly worse off than non-clients in terms of education levels, asset value, per person expenditure on clothes and shoes, and housing. CRECER uses geographic targeting, using a number of UNDP benchmark measures and indices and national statistics to identify the poorer Departments in the country. The CGAP poverty assessment found that "CRECER operations are consistently located in those more deprived areas, and in those *Departamentos* with the lowest Vulnerable Social Index."[14] Approximately 70 to 75 percent of CRECER clients live below the national poverty line. The national data combined with the data on relative poverty outreach in CRECER's operational areas confirm that CRECER is effective at targeting the poorest people in Bolivia.

CRECER has made a practical decision to work in both peri-urban and rural areas, even though rural areas are poorer, so as to allow for cross-subsidization of more costly rural areas by more profitable peri-urban areas. Comparison of the poverty assessment results between these two areas demonstrates that CRECER reaches *relatively* poorer people in the peri-urban areas, although these clients in terms of *absolute* poverty are less poor than those in the rural areas.

Figure 1.3 shows the same figures for SHARE. In this case there is a very strong pro-poor bias, with very few clients from the upper 40 percent of poverty levels, and high numbers of very poor clients right down to the poorest decile. Incoming SHARE clients display greater levels of poverty than non-clients in indicator-by-indicator comparisons relating to food security, quality of housing, and asset ownership, consuming fewer meals, fewer luxury foods, owning less land, and living in poorer quality housing with fewer household goods. Only characteristics such as literacy rates and educational attainment are similar for both groups. SHARE clearly achieves significant outreach towards the very poor and moderately poor, with little inclusion of its non-target groups. Although SHARE is extremely effective at reaching the poorest people in its operational area, it is notable that SHARE does not use geographic targeting to the same extent as CRECER. SHARE works in one of the poorer regions of India (the fifth poorest state), but does not implement a detailed process of identifying the poorest areas in which to work. This may explain the lower percentage of clients reached living below the national poverty line compared to CRECER.

Poverty Outreach Compared to National Indicators

CRECER and SHARE reach large numbers of clients living in absolute poverty as defined by the international US$ per day comparison (72.5 per-

cent of SHARE and 41 percent of CRECER clients). These figures reflect the greater level of poverty overall in India compared to Bolivia. Thus while CRECER reaches a greater proportion of very poor clients according to national poverty line estimates, in terms of international comparisons, SHARE's proportion is much greater.

Impact: What Role for Microfinance in Poverty Eradication?

The previous section demonstrates that MFIs can bring very poor clients into their programs. But to achieve significant impact on poverty, inclusion is a necessary but insufficient goal. High levels of client dropout, and the push to give larger loans to more successful clients, suggest that very often the poorest clients enter programs that are not designed specifically to meet their needs. In some cases this may not matter and very poor clients may succeed or fail in similar numbers to other participants. However, inappropriate services can result in very poor clients experiencing difficulties and not benefiting as much as other clients, or even experiencing negative impacts.

The Case for Poverty-Focused Microfinance

Why a Market-Based Approach Is Inadequate

Many people in the microfinance industry adopt the financial systems approach—they see the primary goal of MFIs as developing strong institutions that can sustainably meet the needs of the market they choose to serve. They argue that the main test of success should be client demand for the service. If clients continue to take loans and deposit savings, then the market is demonstrating that there is value in the services being offered. Steps to limit access—through eligibility criteria or targeting—raise the cost of operations and distort the market. Instead, microfinance can offer appropriate market-based approaches to deliver the right services to the right people. They argue that the increased costs incurred by poverty-focused MFIs undermine their financial performance, and result in services that are inappropriate to the market needs. The very poor should be recipients of government or donor-funded development services, not microcredit.

These arguments have some logic, but viewed through a social rather than banking lens they break down. For a poverty alleviation objective, we need to look at how best to provide financial services to both poor and very poor clients in a sustainable way. Market-led approaches tend to serve the most profitable markets first. Thus the more easily accessible urban and peri-urban areas will be selected before the more remote rural areas; clients

Box 1.5

"Most MFIs have far to go in finding ways of reaching extremely poor households. Too often this is excused in statements such as 'the very poor can only be benefited through welfare' or that 'program sustainability is incompatible with the inclusion of the very poor.' This possibly belies a lack of understanding of the dynamics of poverty and the opportunities that exist for the provision of financial services to the extremely poor. To date there has been inadequate exploration of financial products and low-cost service delivery mechanisms that would allow MFIs to include extremely poor households without compromising their sustainability objectives."

Source: Robert Hickson, "Financial Services for the Very Poor—Thinking Outside the Box," *Small Enterprise Development* 12, no.2 (2001).

with previous business experience will be selected before those without experience; less-poor clients who can take relatively large loans will be selected before very poor clients who need very small loans.

It is not good enough to wait for the market to serve the poor and very poor. There is a strong case for poverty-focused microfinance that actively seeks to work with poor and very poor clients, that seeks to understand their needs and design services specifically for them, and that monitors and assesses the success of the programs in meeting these needs and reducing poverty. This is not to say that all microfinance should be implemented in this way, since there is clearly a strong case for achieving poverty reduction through working with the moderately poor and vulnerable non-poor.[15] But where poverty reduction is a key objective, design and monitoring of program depth of outreach and impact should be central.

Is the Impact of Microfinance Dependent on Level of Poverty?

From a developmental perspective many people view microfinance as inadequate on its own to combat poverty. Particularly prevalent is the view that *credit* is not an appropriate service for the poorest. Much of the work looking at risk and vulnerability points to the important role of savings and other financial services for the livelihoods of the very poor.[16] This work does not negate the role of credit, but redresses the past overemphasis on credit. Unfortunately, it is often cited to support arguments that credit is inappropriate for the very poor, or that the needs of the very poor are separate from mainstream microcredit.

Figure 1.4   Poverty Toolkit

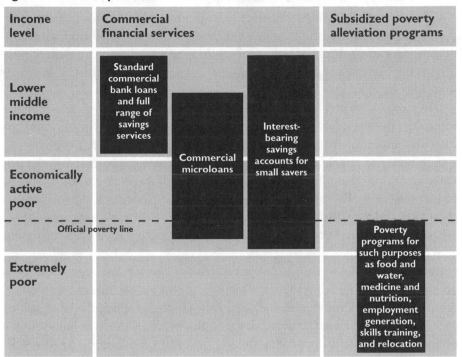

Income level	Commercial financial services			Subsidized poverty alleviation programs
Lower middle income	Standard commercial bank loans and full range of savings services	Commercial microloans	Interest-bearing savings accounts for small savers	
Economically active poor				
Official poverty line				Poverty programs for such purposes as food and water, medicine and nutrition, employment generation, skills training, and relocation
Extremely poor				

Source: Reproduced from Robinson, 2001, p. 21.

Savings vs. Credit — what is more beneficial?

Robinson,[17] for example, argues that savings are better able to reach poorer people than credit, and that the extreme poor, whom she defines as the majority of those below the poverty line, need subsidized poverty alleviation programs, not financial services (see Figure 1.4).

In this chapter I argue against this perspective and demonstrate that millions of people living below the poverty line and indeed below half the poverty line can and do effectively use credit, savings and other financial services. Both CRECER and SHARE, for example, are working with large numbers of clients in Robinson's "extremely poor" category. I take the position that the full range of financial services may or may not be appropriate for different people at different times. Poverty level is not a determinant of this, but does create a challenge for MFIs to deliver appropriate services. Working with the very poor is difficult, but there are a number of frontiers in poverty-focused microfinance which need to be explored, and old models adapted or new ones developed. The challenge then is to systematically look at what is appropriate in what contexts, rather than to accept what is becoming a status quo created by accepted wisdom.

Understanding Poverty and Its Relationship to Financial Services

To understand poverty holistically, it is important to move beyond the economic and include the fulfilment of basic needs (food, shelter, clothing, health, education, and psychological well-being), the means to achieve welfare in the present and future, social networks and empowerment, and vulnerability to risk.

In order to better understand the role that microfinance can play in reducing poverty, it is important to understand conceptually the mechanisms by which financial services can affect poor peoples' lives. Poor people live in a high risk and changeable environment. They need to be able to take advantage of opportunities that lead to improving income or economic status, to protect themselves against the risks of crises or shocks, and to cope with these when they arise.[18] Poverty reduction then is in part a process of increasing income and economic stability, which leads to improved fulfilment of basic needs and access to services. The empowerment of women can facilitate control over resources which allows for this improved access. It is also about developing a range of assets that will reduce household vulnerability to physical, economic, and social shocks. Sebstad and Cohen[19] define these assets as: financial (income size, regularity and security, savings, loans or gifts), human (skills and knowledge, ability to labor, good health, self-esteem, bargaining power, autonomy, and control over decisions), physical (housing, land, productive and non-productive possessions, and so on), and social (networks, group membership, relations of trust, access to wider institutions of society, and freedom from violence).

Most MFIs work with poor clients and there is ample evidence to show that the impacts of microfinance are overwhelmingly positive, particularly through increasing income, reducing risk and vulnerability, and empowering women.[20] However, it is important to be realistic about the changes that can be brought about by financial services *alone*. By itself, microfinance cannot eliminate poverty, or transform social relations and the structural causes of poverty. If we are to push the frontiers of the effectiveness of microfinance then we need to explore and innovate and find where the limitations are in each context.

Financial services can contribute by helping stabilize, diversify, smooth, and increase incomes. Rutherford[21] outlines how the biggest financial need for people (poor or otherwise) is to assemble lump sums of money that can be used to cope with opportunities or demands. "Despite their small incomes, the poor are faced, surprisingly often, with expenditure needs which are large in relation to the sums of money that are immediately available to them."[22] These lump sums can be acquired either through credit or saving. Understanding why lump sums are needed by poor people provides an un-

Box 1.6
Impact on Poverty:
Evidence from the Case Studies[23] and Literature

It is clear that both CRECER and SHARE achieve significant positive impacts on the lives of the majority of their clients. Impact assessments were conducted with each of the case study MFIs. A range of approaches were used which were able to produce credible results describing the range and extent of impacts experienced by the MFI clients.

The complexity of poverty means that the impacts measured in the assessments depend to a large extent on how each organization has conceptualized poverty, its operational design, and the choice of what was measured. Since each organization has different objectives, each impact assessment is different. Therefore it is not easy simply to compare the results, but still there are clear/common impacts on poverty.[a] These are summarized below:

- SHARE is achieving remarkable levels of impact on the incomes, well-being, and business skills of large numbers of very poor clients. SHARE is a minimalist organization and aims to reduce poverty by providing financial and support services to poor women. Although SHARE does not focus much attention on social development, clients do increase their business skills and autonomy of decision-making. But social activism is not part of SHARE's objectives, and community level empowerment is not taking place.

- CRECER achieves positive impact on both economic and social poverty, of a cross section of clients, including a large proportion of the very poor. CRECER has a much broader and more explicit social objective than SHARE. Its methodology is based on the assumption that improved nutritional status of children and household food security requires first improvement in women's economic capacity, empowerment, knowledge, and practice.

a. The lack of commonality between impact assessment results was also observed in the three studies conducted as part of the AIMS project (Snodgrass and Sebstad, 2002, p. vi).

derstanding of how financial services may be useful and what impacts (positive and negative) these may have on poor people's lives.

There are four areas where the need for lump sums may create hardship or problems and where a poor person's livelihood may be strengthened by credit, savings, or other financial services:

Opportunities: Poor people need lump sums in order to invest in opportunities—economic or social. Money may be invested as working capital or as productive assets for an income-generating activity. Other opportunities may not be related to economic returns.

Consumption: There is often a difference between people's consumption patterns and their income. Household consumption patterns, for example, may require regular small purchases or occasional large ones, for example for clothes, buying food in bulk, or housing. Income may be evenly spread through the year, or may be erratic. In both cases money may not be available when it is needed and this may lead to inefficient management of household finances.

Life Cycle Needs: All people have major predictable occurrences throughout their lives, such as birth, marriage, death, school fees, retirement, and so forth. These all require relatively large sums of money.

Crises and Emergencies: Unpredictable events such as illness, death, accident, fire, weather, and crime are common for all people, and more common for the very poor, who are also more vulnerable to their negative impacts.

Microfinance Impacts Directly and Significantly on Economic Poverty[24]

Credit invested in an income-generating enterprise as working capital or for productive assets leads to establishment of a new enterprise or growth of an existing one. Profit from the enterprise provides increased income, and a general strengthening of income sources.

The extent to which income increases occur varies considerably between organizations and between clients, since they are primarily related to the investment of credit in an income-generating activity. The AIMS longitudinal studies, for example, found that increases in household income were driven largely by increases in microenterprise revenues. Clients from programs that did not focus specifically on microenterprise development therefore experienced little or no net income gains.

Both CRECER and SHARE provide credit for enterprise development, and reported income increases for a majority of their clients. The primary source of income increase was through investment of loans into income-generating enterprises.

- *SHARE achieved an unambiguous positive impact on the economic poverty of its clients*. SHARE uses a composite "poverty index" in its impact assessment study. This combines a number of proxy variables

Table 1.5   Economic Poverty Reduction at SHARE

POVERTY STATUS	UPON JOINING (%) N = 125	MARCH 2001 (%) N = 125
Very Poor	64	7.2
Moderately Poor	36	56.8
No Longer Poor	0	36
TOTALS	100	100

Income increase most w investmt in income generally activity.

for income (sources of income, productive assets, and quality of housing) and an independent variable, the household dependency ratio. The poverty index demonstrates that 76% of SHARE's mature clients[26] have experienced significant reduction in their economic poverty, and one third are no longer poor.

- *CRECER clients achieved significant increases in income.* Increased income was reported by 66 percent of clients, but only 1 percent reported large increases. Participants most commonly attributed this improvement to the expansion of their income-generating activity, reduced input costs as a result of buying in bulk or with cash, or the new activities or products made possible by access to credit and selling in new markets.

Microfinance Leads to Stabilization of Income and Expenditure Smoothing

The establishment of a reliable and regular income can create significant impacts in terms of ability to access food, healthcare, education, and other services, and can reduce the negative effects of debt cycles. Similar economic benefits are gained from consumption smoothing, where savings or credit allows for small regular payments to be made, rather than cash having to be found for a larger lump sum. Again this can help with avoiding indebtedness and/or enabling day-to-day payments to be made, for example by avoiding the need to sell assets, cut back on expenditure such as education, or take usurious loans from money-lenders. These impacts are particularly important for very poor clients who may be less able to respond to opportunities to invest in and expand a microenterprise.

The impact assessments of both CRECER and SHARE reported significant changes in terms of the major income sources of clients, and consumption smoothing benefits.

- *SHARE clients experienced a very large change in main income sources* from lower-end occupations, such as temporary laborer work, where wages are low and paid by the day and work is irregular, to self-employment in small business activities (72 percent new clients, compared to 9 percent mature clients). Participation in the program also led to diversification of income sources and to an increase in the number of income earners.

- *CRECER clients experienced benefits through household consumption smoothing.* Thirty percent of clients declared using at least part of their last loan (as opposed to profit) on food or other household necessities. Particularly important was the bulk-buying of food.

Microfinance Leads to Increased Physical Asset Accumulation

A key impact of microfinance is to help clients accumulate or retain physical assets.[27] Assets are increased either through direct loan use, as a benefit of income smoothing, or through the use of profits generated through the investment of a loan. Clients can also protect existing assets, for example through the investment in vaccinations for livestock, or by using savings or credit to cope with shocks when they occur. Poor households invest in physical assets for three main reasons:

- household assets which primarily contribute to quality of life, and may also provide security and possible income in the case of future need

- household assets which are primarily held as savings-in-kind, such as livestock

- productive assets which are used to generate income, such as land or houses for rent or equipment for a business

CRECER and SHARE both report asset accumulation as an important benefit for their clients.

- *SHARE: The strongest impact on poverty status was increased asset ownership.* The majority (59 percent) of mature clients were classified as non-poor in terms of productive asset ownership with assets worth over Rs10,000 (US$200), whereas 81 percent of new clients rank as "very poor" with assets worth less than Rs5,000 (US$100). Mature clients are also more likely to live in bigger houses made of more permanent materials than new clients. Using a housing index that classifies poverty in terms of housing size, materials, and condition, 40 percent of new clients compared with 23 percent of mature clients are classified as "very poor," while 33 percent of mature clients compared to 6 percent of new clients are classified as "non-poor."

- *CRECER*: Clients' diversified loan-use strategies suggest the program allowed participants to augment household assets. Forty-one percent experienced an increase, chiefly in the purchase of animals.

Impact on Basic Needs and Capabilities

Key to the impact of microfinance on poverty is the enabling effect of economic improvements. Increased income and economic security can give clients access to improvements in many aspects of their well-being and basic-needs. Morduch and Haley[28] link improvements in income and empowerment generated through microfinance to improvements in education, healthcare, family planning, nutrition, water and sanitation, coping with HIV/AIDS, and shelter. These are often not direct impacts and may result from the combination of microfinance with other services, or be context specific. However, there is convincing documented evidence for impacts in all of these areas. These indirect benefits are not automatic since they depend on the availability of services and commodities, the knowledge to prioritize these expenditures, and the power to make appropriate decisions for expenditure. One of the motivations for focusing on women rather than men is the evidence that economic improvements experienced and controlled by women will lead to greater improvements in overall household well-being, particularly when they are accompanied by increased empowerment of women. Microfinance allows households to improve their human capital, which allows for improvements in their capabilities to maintain and raise their standard of living in the present and in the future.[29]

Clients of both CRECER and SHARE have experienced positive changes in fulfilment of basic needs. The impacts seem greater in CRECER, where there is an explicit education component that encourages clients to use their economic gains to improve their nutrition and use of health services.

- *SHARE clients were more likely to attend higher quality private clinics*. Household members of mature clients were more likely to go to a private, higher-quality clinic than those of new clients (84 percent vs. 69 percent). Improved access is primarily a result of increased savings and therefore availability of ready cash to pay for unexpected needs. Participation in the program did not reveal any change in behavior regarding children's education.

- *CRECER clients were better able to cope with periods of food stress than non-clients*. They could purchase foods in bulk using CRECER loans, internal village bank loans, or savings. However, there was no evidence of impact on household food security. The education component of CRECER led to increased knowledge of critical health and nutrition behaviors and practices. Increases in *knowledge* of better child healthcare and nutrition practices were clear for all participants; the extent to which this knowledge was put into practice was found to be less dramatic. CRECER clients were also more likely to have spent money on expenses such as medical costs and clothing. These impacts can be attributed partly to the internal loan feature of the methodology which permits emergency spending, but also to improved cash flow associated with trade-based activities, as well as the regular generation, and access to, household savings.

Social Impacts

While the motivation for many MFIs to target women is often instrumental, based on women being more compliant, reliable, and easier to reach, there are also important motivations based on the need to impact on poverty. The evidence is that women are generally more disadvantaged, marginalized, and poorer than men. There is a large body of literature examining the building of women's social assets or capital and their empowerment through microfinance. Sebstad and Cohen[30] review this literature and conclude that microfinance does strengthen social assets and some aspects of women's empowerment. The evidence for these impacts is variable and in some cases contentious, and is often dependent on the manner in which microfinance services are delivered. The role of microfinance in empowering women is also discussed by Cheston and Kuhn in chapter 4 of this book.

Economic and well-being changes impact on the social relations and sense of well-being and confidence of MFI clients. Impacts may also result through the *process* of participating in a microfinance program and the way in which an MFI delivers its services and combines financial with nonfinancial services. Economic changes may lead to women being able to make more economic decisions within the household, participating more widely in community activities, or engaging with authorities outside of the community. The skills and experiences gained through participation in a microfinance program, particularly those that emphasize group work, may lead to changes in poor peoples' self-perception and ability to interact with other people within the household (such as having an impact on gender relations), within the community, or in wider political and social structures. The ability of

MFI clients to engage more as equals with other people in their community may strengthen their social networks.

CRECER and SHARE exclusively target women. Both are effective in achieving social impacts and empowering women, but the degree of empowerment is very much dependent on the way the program is implemented.

- *CRECER clients were empowered through participating in the program.* Changes took place at both household and community levels. An empowerment score looked at women's status and social networks in the community. On average clients scored 4.2 (7 being the maximum) while non-clients and controls only scored 2.6 and 2.8 respectively. At the household level, positive effects were notable in decision-making on expenditures usually associated with men, such as house repairs. Few impacts were evident in women's intra-household bargaining power or work responsibilities. At the community level, participants were more likely to be members of a community group, to give advice on health or nutrition matters, or income-generating activities.

- *SHARE clients experienced increased feelings of confidence and self-esteem, but community-level empowerment remained weak.*[31] Small changes have taken place at a household level, with eleven out of twenty-four clients reporting joint decisions with their spouses about the use of the loan and profits. Forty percent of women report making small personal choices for themselves, although these remain limited. At a community level, the impact on women's empowerment is conspicuous by its absence. Social activism is not part of SHARE's objectives and the program displays no evidence of change to clients' social vulnerability.

Impact on Risk and Vulnerability

Recent studies of the impact of microfinance have placed a much greater emphasis on the role of financial services in reducing client risk and vulnerability.[32] Financial services have the capacity to interact with many aspects of clients' lives, not just to develop a microenterprise. Microfinance is thus an important enabling input. It has a potential to impact on poverty in a holistic way, supporting client livelihoods, reducing vulnerability, fostering social and economic empowerment, and releasing people's potential to achieve their goals.

Even where there are no net gains in income, significant impacts in terms of reduced vulnerability can be achieved through the establishment of more regular, reliable, diversified, and resilient income sources, consumption smoothing, increased savings and assets, expanding options for credit, and improving household money management.[33] The combined effect of these changes reduces the risk of crises and emergencies occurring, and increases the ability of clients to cope if they do occur. Diversified incomes, managed by MFI clients with increased skills, are less likely to fail due to mismanagement or as a result of an external shock. Savings reduce vulnerability, allow for planning and management of household finances, consumption smoothing, and accommodating predictable life-cycle needs as well as for coping with unpredictable negative events, and responding to opportunities. Insurance can provide lump sums that can be used to pay for unexpected needs. Increased investment in such items as food, health, housing, and education lead to healthier, more skilled people living in more secure environments, who are also better equipped to deal with problems. The social networks developed through group-based interaction may mean there are more people to assist in the case of a crisis. Empowerment in turn improves poor peoples' ability to seek outside support and demand the services and support they may be entitled to.

These changes in risk and vulnerability are central to the achievement of poverty reduction, not just in terms of short-term income or food intake, but in many of the long-term structural factors that lead to generation after generation of people remaining in poverty. Snodgrass and Sebstad[34] conclude that the "three AIMS assessments firmly establish the 'protective' role of microfinance . . . Microfinance reduces vulnerability." Indeed Sebstad and Cohen[35] conclude that the impact of microfinance on vulnerability is more generalized and less conditional than impacts on income poverty.

Although CRECER and SHARE are not achieving all of the potential impacts outlined above, it is clear that they impact on a number of areas that combine to reduce the vulnerability of their clients. In particular increased and diversified income, increased savings and improved financial and business management skills reduce vulnerability and increase the ability of clients to pay for life-cycle needs from their increased incomes, savings, or loans.

- *SHARE*: Clients experienced changes to more rewarding and diversified income sources, an increase in the number of earners, expenditure smoothing, and the accumulation of savings. Mature client households were found to have a greater number of income earners and more diversified sources than new clients. Over half of clients interviewed used the profit of their investments on family events, thus avoiding the indebtedness often associated with these events. One third had used all or a major part of a loan for these purposes without suffering any terminal repayment problems. An interesting feature of SHARE's program is that making savings voluntary has not damaged that component, instead it has been revived and 67 percent of clients now cite savings as their favorite aspect of the program, with 84 percent having increased their savings balances during the previous year.

- *CRECER*: Eighty-six percent of clients felt that their savings had increased. The bulk of those are "new savers." Seventy-eight percent of CRECER clients previously had no savings. This was a significant impact in terms of vulnerability reduction, and its success was partly due to the internal fund mechanism, which increased the motivation to save as clients received dividends based on their savings. The impact assessment also found participants were less likely to sell off animals in times of food stress, and more likely to use their business profits or assume debt. Although the majority of households in all groups regularly suffered hardship in the hungry season, only 22 percent of CRECER clients resorted to selling animals (compared to 45 percent for the control group). This helped them protect their productive assets in times of economic hardship. CRECER's impact on these coping strategies was dependent on a number of factors: encouraging diversification (through a financial product most suited to non-farm activities and business training); permitting access to emergency cash from means other than selling assets such as animals; lowering of food expenditure and insecurity by permitting bulk-buying of food at appropriate times; and improving the general cash flow of the household through improved profits, access to emergency loans, and savings.

Impacts of Nonfinancial Services

There is clear evidence of strong potential synergies between microfinance and other poverty reduction interventions—"the benefits derived from microfinance, basic education, and primary health are interconnected, and programs have found that the impact of each can increase when they are delivered together."[36] The challenge for most MFIs is how these additional services can be provided without compromising their core functions and strengths. Gulli[37] concludes for example, "Commercial MFIs are likely to be less effective when they expand into new non-financial activities." Most MFIs do not attempt to provide additional services, although they may play a facilitating role and act to link clients to other organizations or government services. A significant minority, such as SHARE and other Grameen Bank replicants, do provide specific and limited nonfinancial services such

as workshops on business and finance management or on social development issues such as health and nutrition practices. Others, such as CRECER
and other Freedom from Hunger affiliates, provide more integrated education services. A small number of specialized microfinance organizations attempt to provide a more holistic range of services, but these, with the notable exception of BRAC in Bangladesh, are rarely financially sustainable.
In addition there is a wide range of development organizations that have as
their primary objective poverty reduction, women's empowerment, or the
promotion of community-based organizations. These organizations may not
necessarily conform to microfinance best practices, particularly in terms of
financial sustainability, but do demonstrate the important synergies between
microfinance and other development interventions.

CRECER makes a conscious effort to integrate education services into
its work. This is done specifically to link with the financial services and to
increase the range and the extent of positive impacts. In an integrated program such as CRECER's it is difficult to attribute specific impacts to specific
parts of the program. However, it is clear that CRECER does achieve far
greater social impacts than SHARE, particularly in terms of knowledge and
practice in health and nutrition. CRECER's ultimate goal is to impact on
nutritional status and food security. Although positive impacts were not
measured on maternal nutritional status, there is evidence that children's
weight-for-age was positively associated with the quality of the education
services provided.

Impact on the Poorest

One of the key tenets of this chapter is the need to focus on the role of
microfinance in addressing the needs of the poorest. Although Morduch
and Haley[38] report that "the poorest can definitely benefit from
microfinance," Snodgrass and Sebstad[39] find that there are only "modest
impacts experienced by poorer households in the study," which suggests
"scope for improving the relevance of products and services for this group."
Reviewing the evidence from the case study organizations which actively
focus on the needs of the poorest, only SHARE provides impact data that
indicates whether impacts are experienced differently by non-poor, poor,
and very poor clients. CRECER's impact assessment looks at the whole client group, therefore it is not possible to see if, for example, the 34 percent of
CRECER clients who did not experience income increases are disproportionately from one poverty level.[40]

The evidence we have from SHARE demonstrates clearly that very poor
clients are benefiting from their services. In fact, the impact on the poorest is
significantly greater than for less-poor clients. *Eighty-nine percent of very*

poor clients experienced positive change compared to 76 percent of all clients. Sixty percent had moved from very poor to moderately poor, while 28 percent moved from being very poor to being non-poor. Very poor clients were not more likely to exit than less-poor, therefore SHARE is not only effective in reaching very poor people, but ensures that they remain as program members long enough to experience positive impacts.

Client Exit and Negative Impacts

Credit is debt and therefore has the potential to lead to substantial negative impacts. There is much literature on cases of negative impact—business failure, indebtedness, increasing vulnerability, and increasing social and intra-household tensions and negative impacts on women's empowerment. These effects do occur but do not generally seem to be widespread, and most impact assessments predominantly report positive or neutral findings. The AIMS assessments for example found that "there was limited evidence that participation in microfinance programs has a negative impact on these [poor] households."[41] Research conducted for the World Development Report similarly shows generally positive impacts.[42] However, most impact assessments look at existing clients only. Where there is a high rate of exit, there are large numbers of former clients who are eliminated from the impact assessment. Common reasons for client exit include negative experiences of business failure, increased work burden for women, conflict in the family or program, and debt problems.[43] High rates of exit may therefore be an indication of negative impacts.[44]

SHARE has a high rate of client exit (17 percent, calculated on an annual basis), and it was therefore important to include a large number of interviews with former clients in its impact assessment. CRECER has a very low exit rate[45] and therefore did not include former clients in its sample. Interviews that look specifically at negative impact indicate that this does occur, but it is seldom severe, and affects very small numbers of clients.

- *SHARE had very little negative impact on mature clients, but large numbers of former clients have not benefited.* Just 1.6 percent of interviewed SHARE clients had experienced a negative change in poverty level. However, large numbers are not benefiting from reduced poverty level because they leave the program. SHARE had an exit rate of 17 percent, with 41 percent of former clients citing failed ventures as a key reason for leaving, and 33 percent reporting their incomes had stayed the same or decreased. However, only 6 percent reported that they had experienced no benefit through their participation in the program.

- *CRECER: Few clients experienced negative impacts.* Seven percent of clients reported a decrease in income, but there is almost no delinquency and a very low exit rate.

Can MFIs Reach and Impact on the Poorest and Be Financially Sustainable?

The previous sections demonstrate that MFIs can and do reach very poor clients; that very poor clients can benefit from the full range of financial services; and that microfinance should be a central part of poverty-reduction strategies. I now move on to the critical question of whether poverty-focused MFIs that are designed to reach and impact on very poor clients are also able to grow to reach large numbers of clients and achieve institutional financial self-sufficiency (IFS).

Achieving Poverty Outreach and Financial Self-sufficiency

At the heart of this question is a fundamental difference of opinion as to whether microfinance should be orientated to build institutions for those commonly excluded from the formal banking sector, or should provide financial services to help reduce poverty. Advocates of the latter approach contend that "large-scale sustainable microfinance can be achieved *only* with the financial systems approach."[46]

To be able to reach large numbers of clients MFIs need to achieve self-sufficiency, but this should not be attained at the expense of the benefits to these clients in terms of poverty impact. The Microcredit Summit Campaign is founded on the belief that it is possible for MFIs to serve very poor clients and achieve self-sufficiency. A paper commissioned for the Campaign presents evidence from the academic literature and detailed case studies of three MFIs that are achieving this objective.[47] It concludes that there is no inevitable trade-off between poverty impact and the rapid growth of MFIs to serve large numbers of clients. Full self-sufficiency can be reached by organizations serving very poor clients. "Thus it is not the clientele served that determines an MFI's potential for IFS, but the degree to which its financial services program is well-designed and managed."[48] Further recent evidence has been documented which supports this conclusion. For example, an analysis of 114 MFIs in the *MicroBanking Bulletin* concluded that there is no evidence that sustainable MFIs cannot work with very poor clients—"The data suggest that it is possible to provide very small loans and be financially self-sufficient . . . Low-end organizations also target women more effectively than sustainable programs that provide larger loans."[49]

The two case studies reported here both demonstrate that MFIs can achieve excellent performance in the combined objectives of poverty impact and self-sufficiency. SHARE and CRECER have both achieved 100 percent financial self-sufficiency, and are rated investment grade by internationally recognized rating agencies.

CRECER achieves excellent financial performance, with an investment grade rating G4, the third-best grade on a ten-grade scale, by PlaNet Finance[50]:

- *Operationally and financially self-sufficient* (102 and 100 percent respectively).

- *Good lending performance:* CRECER's portfolio quality is rated as very good, with a Portfolio at Risk (>30 days) at 0.26 percent. Its lending methodology promotes ownership and deters delinquency by giving clients the opportunity to generate profit from internal loans, which in turn supports the high client retention rate.

- *Encouraging long-term prospects for efficiency and profitability:* CRECER's profitability has greatly improved in 2001, leading to a positive Return on Equity (ROE) before adjustments; after adjustments it was still not profitable in 2001. Administrative efficiency has improved due to the increase in lending activities between 2000 and 2001 and to a policy change reducing meeting frequency between promoters and village banks to biweekly. At 39 percent CRECER is rated as a little less efficient than its peers, but this is due to its dual mission (finance and social), as well as to the fact that it targets rural areas. CRECER *thus appears to be on a positive path towards greater profitability and maintaining self-sufficiency, providing it continues to increase its lending activities while containing its operating costs.*

- *A strong commitment to financing activities with commercial funds:* CRECER has built up good relations with commercial banks. Its limited dependence on the donor sector has allowed it to follow clear strategies of increasing self-sufficiency.

- *Governance and alliance advantages:* CRECER has a strong governance structure based on a competent management team and an involved and skilled board of directors.

- *A key support role for CRECER's international partner:* Freedom from Hunger continues to give significant inputs in terms of guaranteeing of commercial loans, providing technical assistance, and strong research and development expertise.[51]

SHARE achieves excellent financial performance, with an alpha plus investment grade rating by M-CRIL[52] and "mfR3" rating (on a scale from mfR1 (highest) to mfR10 (lowest)) by CRISIL.[53]

- *Operationally and financially self-sufficient* (107 and 100 percent respectively).

- *An excellent lending performance, with a repayment rate of 100 percent*: SHARE has a Portfolio at Risk (>30 days) of 0 percent, made possible by the strong organizational culture of zero tolerance, which is instilled among clients during the pre-loan phase of group formation and training. Other factors which account for this excellent performance are the close supervision by field staff (including their responsibility for record-keeping), small weekly repayments, and the policy of removal of problem members from groups, or closure of whole groups in some cases.

- *Good mobilization of funds and capital structure*: SHARE succeeds in accessing members' savings by having set up an offshoot cooperative, SIM. It has also been mobilizing share capital from its members, and as of March 2001, paid-up capital had reached over US$1 million, of which 99 percent is owned by SHARE clients. SHARE has mobilized significant external loan funds from donors and banks, borrowing approximately US$3 million from eight lenders as of March 2001.

- *Increasing efficiency*: SHARE's efficiency at institutional and administrative levels is increasing; the number of total clients per field staff rose from 134 to 343 in the year leading up to March 2001, and loan portfolio per field staff also rose from US$6,455 to US$19,987. Administrative efficiency improved from 25 to 19 percent, but rose to 25 percent as of April 2002. The cost per unit of money lent has been decreasing steadily since 1999, and was at 0.07 in November 2001. Keys to this financial health can be seen in SHARE's strategy of building up solid systems before the expansion it undertook in 1997, in its emphasis on discipline, but also in its minimalist approach to financial services provision.

Costs and Benefits of Working with the Poorest: Balancing the Goals of Impact, Poverty Outreach, and Self-sufficiency

SHARE and CRECER are remarkable organizations. They are successfully achieving the difficult balance of excellent financial performance, outreach to the poorest people in their countries, and significant positive impacts on the lives of their clients. Poverty-focused MFIs clearly can achieve excellent financial performance. However it is likely that the process of striving toward these goals will involve trade-offs between the social and financial objectives. The nature of these trade-offs will vary in different contexts and there is little research exploring them. This section aims to give some pointers as to where the trade-offs and benefits might lie.

Costs of Poverty Focus

A poverty focus can create costs in a number of areas. The process of understanding the needs of and targeting very poor clients demands staff time. Active poverty targeting, if used, demands development and management and staff time. Poorer people often live in more remote, inaccessible, or less densely populated areas, which creates additional supervision and operational costs. Once very poor people are reached they are likely to take smaller loans which generate less income and need greater levels of support. Increasing the flexibility of financial services and adding nonfinancial services can increase the effectiveness of an MFI in poverty outreach and impact. However, these may be costly and complicated to implement.

Minimizing the Costs of a Poverty Focus

Poverty-focused MFIs adopt a number of mechanisms aimed at reducing the additional costs imposed by a poverty focus. CRECER and other organizations using the Credit with Education methodology provide an important example of how a specialized nonfinancial service can be integrated into operations, without imposing huge costs (this is explored in detail in chapter 2 by Dunford). CRECER's education component is made sustainable by embedding its costs in the interest rate, with the educational component representing approximately 6 percent of total operational expenses. The additional marginal costs are kept low since the same field agent provides the education and financial services at the same regular village bank meeting. CRECER works primarily in remote rural areas, but cross-subsidizes this by also working in some high density, accessible, peri-urban areas. It preserves its poverty focus by setting a 70 to 30 percent ratio for rural-to-urban borrowers. Cross-subsidizing through individual loans is also planned.

Benefits of a Poverty Focus

Although a poverty focus undoubtedly creates costs, these are balanced to some extent by benefits created by this focus. For example, the industry has embraced the goal of targeting women as it is recognized that this creates positive financial and social benefits.

One of the most obvious but unquantifiable benefits comes with offering services that are appropriate for the market. MFIs that do not differentiate according to the needs of different client groups are inefficient, and they will find that clients do not perform as well as they might otherwise. Thus a simple first step that can be taken by all MFIs is to better understand their market, and ensure they are offering the right products and services for the clients they wish to reach. CRECER, for example, by providing services that meet the needs of poorer clients and working in more remote communities, is able to find a market niche where few other MFIs are operating, and is often the first to enter a market. Thus, in the context of high market penetration and competition CRECER is able to achieve high rates of growth—for example, increasing its portfolio outstanding by 25 percent in 2001 compared to 2000. CRECER has achieved this growth during a period when many Bolivian MFIs have experienced crisis due to debtors' associations and massive default.

Organizations that work with very poor clients depend to a large degree on the success of these clients. To begin with, very poor clients take small loans, repay little interest, and need a lot of support. However, they use their limited resources effectively and are adept at making the most of few resources. If an MFI can succeed in supporting the poorest in overcoming their vulnerability and in coping with shocks as they occur, then there is a good chance the clients will improve their position, and as they do so, develop an increasing need and capacity for financial services. They will be more likely to save more, take larger loans, and experience fewer problems, thereby requiring less staff input. This in turn will lead to the financial success of the MFI. There is anecdotal evidence that very poor clients are more committed to the MFI and less likely to default. CRECER, for example, reports that there is a very low delinquency rate for very poor clients, pointing to the benefits of working with poor people "for whom ancient moral values of duty and honesty are still a reality," reflected in a high retention and low delinquency rate. This may mean that once they have reached a more stable position they are less costly to the MFI. Higher initial costs may be partly balanced by lower costs at a later stage. What is clear is that MFI sustainability very much depends on the sustainability of its clients. A focus with much more attention to client needs is therefore required.

The experience of SEF in South Africa raises a number of interesting points, many of which support CRECER's experience. Figures 1.5 and 1.6 present data from SEF's two programs: MCP, a Grameen replication adapted to the South African context and reaching clients from a range of poverty levels, but on average less poor than the general population; and TCP, a poverty-focused program using a similar methodology to MCP but with

Figure 1.5 SEF, Comparison of Average Loan Sizes

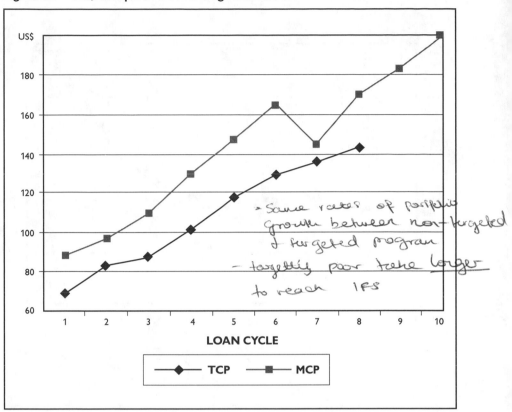

Note: TCP = Poverty-focused program; MCP = Non-targeted program
Source: Presentation given to Imp-Act Global Meeting, April 2002

active poverty-targeting, loan terms, and sizes tailored to the needs of very poor clients, and greater support provided by field staff.[54]

Figure 1.5 shows that the average loan size of TCP is lower than that of MCP and therefore income per client is lower (assuming the same interest rates). However, although TCP clients initially take substantially smaller loans than clients in MCP, the *rate of growth* of average loan size is approximately the same in both programs.[55] There is an effective lag of two loan cycles with TCP loans on the third cycle approximately the same size as those in MCP on the first loan cycle. The similarities in rates of growth mean that although TCP would take longer to reach IFS than MCP, it is feasible for this to be achieved. Figure 1.6 looks at one of the benefits of TCP's poverty focus and charts significant and consistently lower exit rates in TCP compared to MCP.[56] These lower exit rates contribute to the financial performance of TCP and would go some way to balancing the higher

Figure 1.6   SEF, Comparison of Dropout Rates

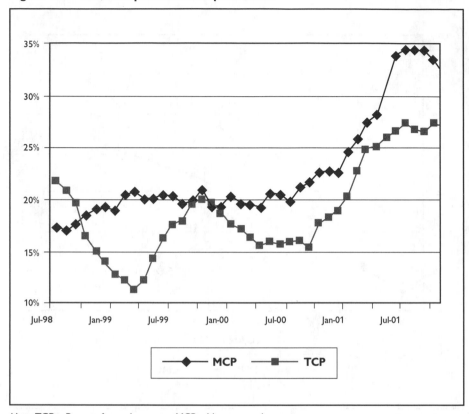

Note: TCP = Poverty-focused program; MCP = Non-targeted program
Source: Presentation given to Imp-Act Global Meeting, April 2002

costs of the poverty-focused program. Anecdotal evidence from SEF, supported by reports from other MFIs, suggests that poorer clients are less likely to leave than less-poor clients. The greater levels of support given to TCP clients are also likely to be a contributing factor to lower exit rates.

PART TWO:
GOOD PRACTICE FOR BANKING
WITH THE POOREST[57]

In part one ("Evidence for Sustainable Microfinance for the Poorest"), I demonstrated that microfinance can and does reach very poor people, impacts positively and sustainably on their lives, and does so through financially sustainable organizations. I challenge the commonly held view that there is a relationship between poverty level and financial or nonfinancial services that are appropriate. Further, the case study examples challenge the notion that poverty-focused MFIs cannot also achieve excellent financial performance and reach scale.

In part two I move on to examine the design and delivery of poverty-focused microfinance using the experience from the case studies and other MFIs. The selection of the case studies necessarily biases this chapter towards large-scale institutionalized microfinance and group-based methodologies. However, I draw on the experience of other approaches, and discuss issues that are relevant to a wide range of organizations. There are a number of frontiers where innovation and research can lead to improved practice. In particular I look at the mechanisms which act to exclude a large number of the poorest, ways in which barriers can be removed, how services can be designed to be more appropriate, and how very poor people can be encouraged to participate.

Including the Poorest: Overcoming Exclusion

The first challenge for any MFI that wishes to impact on very poor clients is to attract the right people into the program. This is in part about designing services that are attractive to the poorest, but it is also about understanding who is reached by a program and why some people are excluded. The most commonly used—and much criticized—proxy for depth of poverty outreach is loan size. This is likely to give very misleading conclusions—large loan size is certainly a good indicator that very poor clients are *not* being served, but it does not follow that small loan size implies very poor clients *are* being served. Dunford concludes for example, "Loan size is often much more a reflection of the institution offering the loan than of the characteristics of the borrower."[59] In light of the weakness of this proxy and the desire of some MFIs to actively target very poor clients, a number of low-cost practitioner tools have been developed to give reliable poverty outreach information.[60]

My starting point for this section is to look at how very poor people are actively or passively excluded from microfinance programs and how this can be overcome.

Mechanisms of Exclusion

There are norms in society that lead to the poorest being regarded as inadequate and incapable of achieving. This is reflected in self-perceptions by the poorest, perceptions by the wider community, perceptions by MFI field staff, and perceptions in MFI management and the microfinance industry. By not adopting a specific poorest focus, MFIs tend to reflect these patterns that lead to marginalization. Outlined below are the deliberate and inadvertent processes that operate to exclude the very poor.

1. *Formal Exclusion by MFI:* MFIs may take a decision to provide services only to a specific group of clients. For example, many MFIs only provide loans to clients with an established microenterprise.

2. *Informal Exclusion by clients:* While the MFI may have a commitment to reaching the very poor, these people may both choose not to join or be prevented by other members. This is often a particular problem where there is a mix of very poor and less-poor clients.

- *Self-exclusion:* Poor people's lack of confidence constrains their capacity to believe that microfinance can be beneficial or gives them the perception that the services provided by MFIs are not intended for them. An example of this is seen in Nyèsigiso, a cooperative in Mali where the very poor self-exclude most often because of "the poverty of their household" or "lack of experience or means for starting an income-generating activity; fear of tainting their reputation or the trust of others if they can't repay and pressure to meet immediate consumption needs such as food and clothing."[61]

- *Exclusion by other members:* In group-based lending (solidarity groups, self-help groups, villages banking, cooperatives) there is a tendency for stronger people in the community to exclude those who are poorer. There is often a negative perception by the community of the very poor (useless, lazy, unlikely to be able to repay a loan) resulting in other members not wanting them in their group. This is particularly apparent where group liability is operated, and group members are encouraged to exclude any person who may be a bad credit risk.

3. *Client Exit:* Where policies are not orientated to the needs of the very poor it is likely that they will experience a greater proportion of problems, and therefore be more likely to choose to leave the program, or to be pushed out by other members.

4. *Informal Exclusion by MFI:* While intending to reach a defined set of clients the MFI unintentionally excludes people who should not be formally excluded. This is a result of a complex interplay of factors at all levels of the organization.

Table 1.6   Mechanisms for Exclusion of the Very Poor from MFIs

ACTION	BY WHOM AND WHY
Formal Exclusion by MFIs	
• e.g., eligibility criteria	• Deliberate and considered MFI policy
Informal Exclusion by Clients	
• Self-exclusion of very poor people	• Lack of confidence and perceptions of MFIs by potential clients
• Other clients prevent very poor joining	• Self-interest of existing clients: to exclude "weak" people, for example
Exit of Clients	
• Self-selection	• Decisions by clients due to perceived lack of benefits
• Pushed out by other clients	• Exclusion of "problem" clients by others
Informal Exclusion by MFIs	
Staff	• Response by staff at all levels to job priorities, mission, and incentives
• Active exclusion by staff assumptions/practices	• Unexpected side effects of MFI
Design	policy and practice
• Inappropriate products/services	

- *Exclusion by staff:* Loan officers may have explicit or implicit incentives to exclude the poorest. This may be based on a perception that the poorest are problematic and will create an increased work burden. This can be exacerbated by an organizational culture and incentive schemes that emphasize financial targets above the need to work effectively with the poorest. This will encourage loan officers to focus on achieving greater productivity, increasing portfolio outstanding, and reaching larger numbers of clients, rather than achieving greater poverty impact.

- *Exclusion by design:* Many aspects of the methodology design of a microfinance program may deliberately or inadvertently exclude the poorest. These may include entry fees, rules that exclude people who do not have an existing business, inappropriate or inflexible loan terms, automatic loan size increases, inaccessible or compulsory savings, group liability rules, providing services from central offices rather than in community-based situations, or locating the program in accessible rather than remote areas. Other aspects of program design may not exclude the poorest, but may be biased towards the less-poor. These are discussed in the section entitled, "Design and Delivery of Microfinance."

Overcoming Exclusion: Understanding Client Needs and Wants

Each MFI needs to understand what processes of exclusion are taking place within their own organization. The products and services, and the way in which they are delivered, can then be modified to overcome this. As microfinance in general becomes more client-driven and responsive to differing client needs, it is vital that we hear the voices of the poorest. MFIs may undertake market research to understand their client or potential client needs, but without careful attention they will hear the needs of the less-poor and not the poorest. The poorest by definition are the least vocal and least likely to express their needs within program structures or through market research.

At the African Microcredit Summit meeting of Councils, I gave an example from the experience of SEF, South Africa: "At SEF, we heard from clients, 'we need larger loans, we need shorter loan terms. We need these different products.' What we were hearing was not the voices of the very poor; we were hearing the voices of less-poor people in the program ... The organization which is listening to the demand of the clients becomes a demand-driven organization; but the demand that you're listening to is not the demand of the very poor."[62]

Services need to be designed to address the perceived needs and wants of clients. If this is done properly, clients will then use and pay for these needs and wants, resulting in good financial performance for the MFI. In addition, MFIs should understand the underlying needs of the poorest so that the services will reduce their vulnerability and poverty. At times there may be a contradiction between these two priorities and the demands of clients may not be the same as the MFI's analysis of what would most impact on poverty. It is a controversial point, but clients do not always know best. People do make decisions that are not in their long-term best interest. For example, many MFIs that insist on regular weekly loan repayments are asked by their clients to move to monthly repayments and meetings. Some organizations that have heeded this call have found that this change leads to loan installments that are unmanageable and increased problems of business failure, arrears, and default.[63]

Market research should then be contextualized in a deeper and broader understanding of poverty. To make a sustainable impact on poverty, MFIs need to see their work holistically, and understand how their intervention fits with the patterns of their clients' livelihoods and the changes that are necessary to reduce their level of poverty. Local conceptions and experience of poverty are important in this.

This is not to say that MFIs should expect to tackle the multiple dimensions of poverty themselves—simply that they should know where the provision of financial services fits into the bigger picture. In many cases credit and savings can act as a key contribution transforming clients' lives. In others there may be other constraints that make it difficult for clients to utilize these services, or may even result in negative impacts.

Overcoming Exclusion: Poverty Targeting

The case studies demonstrate that careful poverty-focused program design, which includes geographical targeting, can go a long way to overcoming barriers to participation. CRECER and SHARE both design their programs around an understanding of the needs of the very poor and have established an ethos of poverty focus. This creates a culture that both promotes the participation of the poorest, and provides support to ensure that the vulnerability of the poorest does not lead to their experiencing problems and leaving. CRECER targets the poorest areas in Bolivia to work in, but does not further target clients within these local areas, yet is able to reach significant numbers of very poor people. CRECER is able to achieve such good depth of outreach through a number of active mechanisms:

- *Geographic targeting:* CRECER employs a rigorous process of identification of the poorest areas in Bolivia, and sets specific targets in terms of the balance between rural and peri-urban areas. Data is used from two sources which give detailed poverty data according to a range of poverty indicators. For example, CRECER only works in those areas classified as very low and low on the United Nations Human Development Index.

- *Active program promotion:* CRECER uses promoters from the same villages as clients. These promoters have a good understanding of the local conditions, and knowledge of the local area, and have a sense of helping their own people.

- *Staff commitment:* There is a strong organizational culture of poverty focus, which is reflected in staff commitment to work with the poorest women. This is supported through management, particularly at the level of branch coordinator, staff training, incentives, and through the experience of staff that very poor people are generally easier to work with and more committed to their village bank.

- *Product design:* CRECER has minimized the obstacles to very poor people joining the program. The banks are easily accessible, and the group-based methodology encourages more reticent women to join in.

It is noteworthy, however, that SHARE's depth of poverty outreach is significantly greater than CRECER's, and that SHARE's client profile is much more biased towards the poor and very poor (see "The Challenge of Reaching the Poorest"). The difference is that SHARE actively targets the poorest people within poor areas. This is also the experience of SEF and Caisses Feminines, both of which successfully use a poverty-targeting tool, and suggests that poverty-targeting at the client level is an important part of program design for MFIs that wish to reach *predominantly* very poor clients.[64] Active targeting is important since it allows an organization to identify a clearly defined group of potential clients, and enables these people to be motivated to join. SHARE, for example, stresses the use of both active client targeting and motivation. SHARE uses a targeting tool based on household assets and per capita income. It sees this tool as an investment rather than a cost, gaining client data which feeds into its management information system and enhances management's access to timely and high-quality information. Through this targeting, SHARE lays the ground for good client monitoring and can tailor services to its clients' changing needs so as to maximize impact.

Each organization must choose whether to focus exclusively on specific clients or not, but needs to be aware of who is reached and who is excluded, and for what reasons. As a minimum, poverty-focused MFIs should work in areas identified as having high concentrations of very poor people. This may not always be practicable due to remoteness and low population density of some very poor rural areas, but in these cases there needs to be a conscious decision not to work in these areas, and an awareness of the exclusion process taking place. Where targeting is used it is important that the system allows for the dynamic nature of poverty whereby people move in and out of poverty.

Design and Delivery of Microfinance for the Poorest

Working with the Poorest and Most Vulnerable

Few MFIs are specifically designed to meet the needs of the poorest. As understanding about the range of client needs increases, the design of poverty-focused microfinance is changing. Previously the focus was on designing products that would be unattractive to the less-poor—small loans, weekly meetings, group liability, and high interest rates. These were delivered with little or no flexibility, and very often these same design characteristics made the services less than ideal for the poor. In a non-competitive environment poor people (and many less-poor people) made the choice that a less than ideal service was better than no service. As the market becomes more competitive, and there is increasing focus on impact, there is much greater pressure for MFIs to deliver flexible services that meet the needs of different groups of clients.

Earlier sections of this chapter outlined the nature of the vulnerability that constitutes the livelihoods of the very poor. This shapes the way in which financial services need to be provided. SEF in South Africa provides a useful example of an organization that has two distinct client groups in separate programs (MCP and TCP), and has analyzed and developed different approaches suitable to these two groups. Figure 1.7 summarizes the differences between these programs and sets the background for the discussion in this section, which looks at how MFIs can overcome the factors that act to exclude the poorest, and design and deliver services that meet their needs. Within the confines of this chapter it is not possible to explore the range of financial services available in detail. I will highlight key areas where the poorest are disadvantaged and look at alternatives for improvements. These relate particularly to the delivery of credit, since there is much excellent work highlighting the role of other financial services, particularly savings.[65]

Access to Credit: The Myth of the Economically Active

Exclusion of Those without an Existing Business

The concept of economically active poor is often used to describe those poor people who are likely to benefit from credit. For example, CGAP[66] states, "For microcredit to be appropriate, a pre-existing level of ongoing economic activity, entrepreneurial capacity and managerial talent is needed. If not, then clients may not be able to benefit from credit, and will simply be pushed into debt." This is then translated into policies that require borrowers to have an existing microenterprise to qualify for a loan. However, experience of many MFIs has demonstrated the economic activity of very poor people particularly through their ability to save.[67] Others successfully lend to people without an existing microenterprise by ensuring careful supervision of the productive use of loans.

The concepts of "economically active" and "entrepreneurial capacity" need to be challenged. The reality is that the majority of the poorest do not have an existing enterprise but *are* economically active—they are by definition otherwise they would not survive—and have considerable experience of some kind of self-employment or income-generating activity.[68] Very poor people survive—individually or collectively—by undertaking a number of economic activities that together create an inadequate and erratic livelihood. The majority are not *entrepreneurs*, but run small businesses or other activities as part of their overall household activities. Their aim is to secure a

Figure 1.7 Meeting the Needs of Very Poor Clients: Experience from SEF, South Africa

	MCP: POOR AND VULNERABLE NON-POOR	TCP: VERY POOR
Vulnerability	Either not quite able to meet their families' essential needs or are just managing to do so. Have more confidence (probably have a life experience that has shown them that they can succeed). Currently less vulnerable in all meanings of this word but are certainly in danger of being thrown into poverty by a financial shock. With opportunities to improve their income they could not only protect themselves from being thrown into far more dire circumstances but they could do a lot better.	In many ways they have the opposite characteristics to MCP clients. They do not meet basic needs (including food and clothing) and are very vulnerable in all senses of the word. Have very low self-confidence; previously have not had life experiences that say life can be different.
Current income source	Have an existing enterprise; often have someone else in the household who brings in wage income.	Often have no existing enterprise; no regular wage employment in the household. Rely on irregular casual work and often beg for food.
Access to and ability to repay credit	Can take on some debt based on their existing household income flows. Will respond to appropriate financial services —they will "access" financial services; have a strong potential to employ others (even though these may be family members).	Often will not access financial services even if they are available. It is very risky for these households to take on debt based on their existing household income flows. They must take on debt based on future income from a future microenterprise.

Source: John de Wit, e-mail correspondence

reliable and sufficient income for their household needs, rather than to develop a business. Their strategies are therefore generally low-risk, focusing on traditional activities with which they are familiar, and certainly in the early stages not venturing into new unexplored markets. Many clients do become more entrepreneurial over time, particularly as their incomes are stabilized and they have more scope for undertaking other activities.

How Do the Very Poor Repay Loans?

Clients will often use loans and savings as they see fit, rather than as the MFI hopes. This creates a specific problem when lending to very poor people without an existing enterprise and low level of skills—in other words, with weak ability to repay a loan. Very poor people can often use credit productively, but programs need to be more cautious and supportive, and to ensure that their products and services are flexible enough to meet the needs of the poorest. Two questions need to be asked:

- What capacity do the very poor have to repay the loan—is it to be repaid from existing income sources or from the profits generated by the loan?
- How can the risk of the loan be lowered so that if a crisis does take place it does not create an unacceptable burden?

Understanding household cash flow and the mechanism by which clients repay a loan is fundamental to understanding how credit can be delivered in an appropriate and supportive way. Many people argue that very poor people cannot take loans as they do not have the income streams with which to repay. There are two possible repayment mechanisms to overcome this, each of which leads to very different strategies of credit delivery.

Repayment from Future Savings Made from Existing Income Streams

Work by Rutherford[69] and others has demonstrated that virtually all people are able to save. Even the poorest have some income from which they are able to make small payments—either installments on a loan, or savings. Most microfinance models assume that repayments will be made from savings from existing income sources, and not necessarily through productive returns on the loan. Clients demonstrate their ability to save, and to take loans based on this saving. Where a client saves regularly for several months or years before taking a loan, she demonstrates the capacity of the household to save over an extended period of time. There is a good chance that this level of saving can continue as repayment of loan installments in the future. In addition the client will have built up a significant amount of savings that can be used to repay the loan should a crisis take place. Increasing levels of savings demonstrate increased capacity to manage debt and entitle clients to a larger loan. Very poor people with erratic incomes and savings will take some time to build up the required levels of savings. They are thus more likely to access loans less frequently—not to mention loans which are smaller, compared to less-poor clients. This is a low-risk approach to working with the poorest, and is successfully applied to many MFIs.

Repayment from Income Generated by the Loan

In many cases very poor people can use credit to invest in a microenterprise, and use the *profits* from this investment to repay the loan. The loan can be given based on the capacity of the client's business to create a surplus that can be used to repay the loan, rather than existing household income streams to cover the loan installments. Lending to very poor clients starting up a new business is very different than lending to moderately poor people with a reasonably secure income with which to repay the loan. If the client fails, then she will have few resources to fall back on. The lending methodology therefore needs to ensure that clients maximize their chances of succeeding and minimize the risk of suffering negative consequences.

Lowering the Risk of Credit

Given the high vulnerability of the very poor, it is important that MFIs design and deliver credit in a way that minimizes the risks to clients, and does not create an unacceptable burden if a crisis occurs. A number of features can be considered.

Participation Should Not Be Linked to Taking a Loan

Many credit-led MFIs define participation in terms of taking a loan, and provide little room for clients to remain if they do not wish to borrow. This clearly does not fit in with current understanding of poor people's livelihoods and the usefulness of credit and other financial services. Life-cycle and seasonality factors may determine when in the year is an appropriate time to take a loan, and inflexible and immediate repeat loans lead to less than optimal timing of loans. This can be both damaging for poor people's livelihoods, and serve to exclude the poorest.

Linking Loan Size and Installments to Clients' Needs and Ability to Repay

For very poor households with erratic and unreliable incomes, it is essential to make sure there is a good chance that the loan can be repaid without creating hardship for the client. Each MFI must work out what combination of loan term, loan size, and consequent installments suit which clients, and balance this against the capacity of the MFI and its staff to manage a range of loan products. "Matching the variable nature of clients' multiple income streams with appropriate repayment amounts and cycles may improve a client's capacity to repay and borrow over the long term and thereby reduce the risk of borrowing for them, as well as reduce the risk of lending for the MFI."[70]

- CRECER's loan products are designed to attract and retain the very poor, and permit slow build-up of income increases: small initial loan sizes; small increments with successive loans; frequent repayments; joint feasibility assessments of loan applications; compulsory but accessible savings; internal lending[71]; and free use of the loans are all methodological features which ensure that CRECER attracts, retains, and impacts on very poor clients.

- SHARE's loan products are designed to make loan management as easy as possible for clients. Initial loan sizes are kept small (6000 Rs in the first year; US$150). Subsequent loan ceilings are set at appropriate levels to enable income source diversification without scaring the very poor away. Weekly repayments over fifty weeks (for the general loan) ensure installments are small.

Loan Sizes Should Not Automatically Increase   An important example of loans that are not linked to ability to repay is the common practice of automatically increasing the size of repeat loans if the repayment record for the previous loan is good. MFIs that do so risk undermining clients' livelihoods. Where the client does not demonstrate an increasing ability to save or increased productive capacity, increasing loan size results in a narrowing gap between the client's capacity to repay and her loan installment. Installments will become increasingly difficult to manage, and this increases her risk and makes her more vulnerable to the negative consequences of shocks. Increasing loan size can also create an incentive for clients to borrow from informal sources or other MFIs to repay loans, in the knowledge that they can repay this from the next loan from the MFI. This can create dangerous situations of indebtedness. For less poor clients with diverse income sources this is unlikely to be problematic—at least not until loans grow quite large. However for very poor clients with limited existing income sources automatic loan increases can rapidly create problems.

Flexibility of Loan Use   There is much debate about the fungibility of money and the resulting inappropriateness in insisting that a loan is used for productive purposes.[72] Many MFIs, such as CRECER, encourage clients to invest in productive activities but accept that clients will use loans for different purposes at different times, and do not attempt to monitor how they are used. Thirty percent of CRECER clients in the impact study reported that they had used all or part of their previous loan for consumption (almost a quarter of participants reporting having used some or all of their most recent loan to buy food for the family). To safeguard its members against over-indebting themselves through excessive non-productive use of loans, CRECER emphasizes business education and the members' own feasibility assessments of each other's proposed activities. Sebstad and Cohen state that "in many cases, credit used for consumption serves as a temporary substitute for another source of income (or expected income) . . . In most cases, *especially when multiple sources of income exist . . .* or when other resources are available to draw upon, this loan use does not endanger the client's ability to repay."[73] However, if the loan is based on repayment from business profits, and particularly in the case of the very poor, then there is a strong case for encouraging the productive use of loans. Very poor clients report that in the context of competing household demands, the discipline of regular fixed loan repayment and loan use supervision encourages them to spend time on their business, and to reinvest profits. In addition to encouraging productive use of credit it is also helpful to provide a range of alternative loan products such as emergency loans or housing loans. SHARE, for example, uses loan utilization checks and visits to encourage clients to invest in microentreprises, and so ensures that very poor clients are able to generate a surplus with which to repay the loan. SHARE also makes available a range of non-productive loans for housing, sanitation, and seasonal loans.

Appropriate Loan Term   Loan products are often inflexible and this can create problems for or lead to the exclusion of very poor clients. This has been exacerbated by the trend to provide working capital loans to businesses with fast turnover which in turn has led to shorter loan terms without accompanying reductions in loan size, resulting in larger installments. Because of their erratic and unreliable incomes, it is very difficult for poor people to conform to the strict credit discipline that requires regular repayments and savings. For example, a poverty outreach study of Nyèsigiso found that lack of flexibility in loan term and coercion in repayment creates problems for very poor clients in terms of management and adds to negative community perceptions that prevent very poor people from joining the program.[74] Flexibility is needed to ensure that when other household needs demand money there is not a conflict between the need to repay the loan and

Box 1.8

"Seen from this perspective, one can perhaps better understand why the pressure of weekly repayment, particularly as it increases with larger loan sizes, becomes more acute over time. The implication is to base loan cycles and repayment schedules on a household's capacity to repay rather than assume clients are managing a specific enterprise that has the capacity to absorb larger amounts of working capital and generate ever increasing regular weekly returns."

Source: Nteziyaremye and MkNelly, "Mali," 60.

these other needs.

Flexibility is also important in terms of the provision of a range of savings and credit products that are accessible as and when necessary by clients. Emergency loans, for example, are often important in assisting clients to recover from a shock and avoid the use of negative coping mechanisms such as taking a loan from a money lender or selling off assets. This flexibility of course needs to be balanced against institutional needs and capacity, as it can impose pressure on management, information systems, and internal controls.

Repayment from Future Savings: Where repayment is being made from existing income sources, clients should be allowed maximum flexibility (within the capacity of the MFI to administer) to make repayments or to save as and when they want to do so. Savings-led models of microfinance such as SafeSave in Bangladesh advocate high levels of flexibility in the repayment of loans and taking of savings. Clients are allowed to make larger or smaller payments (or no payments) according to the cash flow situation in their household. Very poor people are therefore not excluded or negatively affected due to their erratic incomes.

Repayment from Business Profits: For productive loans, very poor clients need an installment that will not create too much of a burden should the business fail, and the anticipated income not materialize. Loans should be timely with small, manageable repayments, and with a regular installment that helps with cash management, but with the option of greater flexibility if a crisis takes place. Grameen II, for example, has a mainstream program that continues with the traditional strict "credit discipline," but with an opt-out "slow stream" that allows for complete flexibility in repayments.[75] A loan term that is too long leads to an increasing chance that the client will have to divert funds away from their business for other uses, which may lead to business collapse. If the loan term is too short this encourages dependency and does not allow for growth of the business. A very poor client may take several loans before she establishes a reliable business and is able to make repayments without problems. Provided the loan term is relatively short and loan size is small, then the risk is low, and even where a client has problems she can return for a new loan and try again without having been damaged in the process.

Providing Other Support Services

The risk of credit to very poor clients can be reduced by providing support services that serve to increase the chances of successful productive use of a loan, and decrease the risk of a shock occurring. For example, where credit is given to very poor clients with little or no previous business experience, and without an existing business, the chances of failure due to inexperience or mismanagement are high. Pressure of loan repayment and supervision of the productive use of the loan can help to focus the client on the business. In addition, MFIs need to ensure appropriate support for clients in gaining the skills needed to run their businesses. This support can come from other clients through the group structures, from field staff, from formal business skills training, or a combination of the three.

Additional inputs may take other forms of support to the income-generating activity. BRAC's microfinance program, for example, is notable in its ability to lower the risk of credit for its borrowers, through the provision of an integrated range of inputs from product ideas, training, veterinary inputs, marketing, and retail outlets. BRAC also provides insurance should the enterprise fail.

Supporting Livelihoods and Reducing Vulnerability

As discussed in part one, reducing poverty is much more than increasing income. The design and delivery of microfinance programs can have a major impact on their effectiveness in reducing client vulnerability and strengthening livelihoods. This section outlines a number of areas where MFI practice can be improved.

Products and Services   Part one outlined the mechanisms by which microfinance can act to support clients' livelihoods and reduce their vulnerability. However, the erratic nature of many very poor people's livelihoods may make it difficult for them to participate in a microfinance program, particularly to take the risk of a loan. MFIs need to consider providing a range of products and services in addition to credit that act to help stabilize and increase income, and are based on an understanding of how financial services are used by very poor people.

Savings: Savings are particularly important for the poor, in terms of reducing vulnerability. Saving needs to be easily accessible, private, and not linked to borrowing. SHARE, for example, switched to voluntary rather than obligatory savings. By doing so, SHARE is reducing the instances of loans being used non-productively, which in turn helps to maintain financial effectiveness and improves chances of positive impact.

Insurance: Recent developments have led to new microinsurance products that may have an important role to play in the ability of very poor people to cope with crises and to reduce their vulnerability. However, "the delivery of insurance services is complex and may be beyond the capacity of most MFIs to provide directly."[76]

Other financial service products: There are a range of products that MFIs develop in response to specific needs of their clients. These may include loans for emergencies, housing, education, consumption, or a variety of savings products. CRECER, for example, has internal group loans which help clients cope with economic vulnerability such as food insecurity, the uncertainty of having sufficient income for repayments—particularly where these are not coming from the activity in which the loan is invested, if this is a longer-term yield activity—and other shocks that make demands on family cash flow and affect socioeconomic well-being.

Grants: Programs such as BRAC's Income Generation for Vulnerable Group Development program (IGVGD) provide grants or food for a fixed period of time. When carefully managed, these can help stabilize the incomes of clients. IGVGD clients are then able to join BRAC's mainstream program to access credit to establish an income-generating activity, with a much lower risk of poverty leading to economic demands that undermine the viability of the business.

Creating a Supportive Environment and Retaining Clients with the Program

Financial services can go a long way to reducing client vulnerability, but for the poorest and most vulnerable clients, it needs to be recognized that problems are almost certain to occur at some stage. These can lead to negative impacts and their leaving the program. Once clients have left, there is no opportunity for the program to achieve positive impacts. MFIs therefore, as well as delivering the right products, need to engage in an active process of identifying who are the people most likely to experience problems and to target support to these clients. Many MFIs use their first loan as a testing loan whereby so-called problematic clients are weeded out. When working with the poorest, it is the first loan where inexperienced clients are likely to have problems and leave the program. The challenge is to retain and support the very poor, not to weed them out.

Minimalist MFIs are not well set up to support clients when problems do occur. Some organizations opt to include a number of social elements in their design, but obviously this increases costs. The approach of the MFI in terms of how it views client problems can go a long way to allowing clients the space they need to be able to recover. Group-based programs, for example, have opportunities for creating supportive networks amongst clients, but those must be actively pursued rather than assumed. The approach of staff therefore needs to be less a focus on credit discipline and ensuring repayment, but rather more supportive, facilitating the solving of problems and development of skills that will prevent clients from not being disciplined. Sebstad and Cohen[77] suggest that "maintaining access to credit is an important risk management strategy for the poor." Clients are very aware of what they have to lose if they leave the program, and are likely to make every effort to repay their loans, even to the extent of making drastic cutbacks in household consumption.

A culture of strict credit discipline may ensure that clients are kept motivated and on the right path, with difficulties highlighted before they have the time to grow into insurmountable problems or indebtedness, but the lack of flexibility can create problems which may, for example, be a cause of SHARE's relatively high exit rate (17 percent for 2000). In the light of this it is important for MFI staff not to be coercive but to create a supportive environment where problems are understood and clients collectively take responsibility for sorting them out, facilitated by MFI staff. Repayment policies also need to allow sufficient flexibility to deal with repayment problems in a more humane way. Grameen II, for example, has moved away from the policy of strict "credit discipline" and is based on the belief that poor people always pay back their loans. "There is no reason . . . to get uptight because a borrower could not pay back the entire amount of a loan on a date fixed at the beginning of the disbursement of the loan. Many things can go wrong for a poor person during the loan period . . . We see no reason why the sky should fall on anybody's head because a borrower took longer time to pay back her loan."[78]

Box 1.9

"Sometimes, we have to give up on some family expenses (food, other social events) in order to repay each week. Even if your husband is starving, you first have to assemble all the money needed to make the payment in order to leave the meeting place. . . . Some women cry when they can't manage to come up with the amount they need for payments."

Source: Nyèsigiso members quoted in: Ntezigyaremye and MkNelly, "Mali,"58.

Improving the Social and Empowerment Impact of Microfinance[79]

Microfinance has an important role in women's empowerment. However, this impact depends to a large degree on how the program is designed and delivered. Activist organizations such as PRADAN in India that work through self-help groups put primary emphasis on the empowerment of small groups of women. Financial services are part of this empowerment process, but not the primary objective. Sustainability for PRADAN and similar organizations is based on the sustainable functioning of the group as an independent unit, and there is no long-term commercial role for the organization. MFIs that seek to deliver financial services directly to clients need to operate in a different manner from organizations with a primary goal of empowerment. However, there are many lessons that can be learned from a range of approaches used by formal microfinance organizations, development organizations, and community organizations.

Groups have the potential to facilitate skills development, building of confidence, and social networks. Group liability conditions often serve to undermine this positive potential of groups and lead to a more coercive and conflictual environment that discourages the participation of the very poor. Moving to individual loans risks losing the potential empowering role of the groups. While the group guarantee can be problematic, when it works well, it does serve to create cohesion and encourage clients to take responsibility for others in their group, ensuring that appropriate loans are taken, and that support is given to members who experience problems. Group liability lending thus has the potential to bring many benefits that act to support the needs of very poor clients. The achievement of these benefits is not automatic and needs active facilitation by the staff of the MFI.

Linking Microfinance to Other Development Services

A holistic view of poverty leads to the question of whether MFIs should be developing an integrated range of services. For some organizations such as the SEWA bank in India or BRAC in Bangladesh, this is the path that they have taken. In many cases paths out of poverty may be constrained by factors beyond the usefulness of financial services, or may even prevent people from accessing the financial services available. In these cases there may be a strong argument for interventions other than microfinance, or to supplement financial services with other inputs such as health education, training, market support services, and so forth. BRAC, for example, argues that in their context the poorest often cannot productively use credit, and need to be given a jump start whereby grants are given to get them up to a level where they can operate sustainably in the market.

But recognizing that poverty is multifaceted does not mean that MFIs should be trying to do everything. MFIs succeed through being focused and by doing what they do well! There is a real danger of MFIs trying to do other things because they feel they "should," doing it badly, and damaging their effectiveness in providing financial services. The history of development interventions is littered with failed integrated development programs that attempt a comprehensive analysis of poverty, and then try to deliver all components necessary to change this. Microfinance takes a very different approach in providing minimal inputs in a sustainable way, allowing clients to make decisions as to how resources should be used.

There is clearly great potential to enhance the impact of microfinance through linkages to other development services, such as the inclusion of education and training components in CRECER and other Credit with Education programs.[80] MFIs can also use their existing structures and contacts with clients to create linkages with other service providers. Decisions about creating linkages by integrating other services into microfinance need to be based on a clear conceptual understanding of poverty in the context of capacity and resources, and the trade-offs between the benefits and the costs to the financial performance and focus.[81]

Managing for Outreach and Impact

A poverty focus requires a deliberate effort. Successful poverty-focused organizations succeed in two areas—vision and systems. The establishment of an organizational "culture of poverty" is central to ensuring that staff and clients at all levels make decisions that are centered on improving depth of poverty outreach and impact. Both CRECER and SHARE demonstrate that organizational vision, mission, and commitment from board and senior management are essential ingredients to an effective poverty-focused orga-

> # Box 1.10
>
> "Programs that make poverty reduction an explicit goal and make it a part of their organizational culture are far more effective at reaching poor households than those that value finance above all else."
>
> Source: Morduch and Haley, *Analysis*, 1.

nization. The message is heard by staff at all levels and by clients, and is a significant factor motivating and focusing the MFI's work. The vision helps guide the systems to meet the needs of the poorest, which are implemented and monitored with this focus at the forefront. The right systems cannot work in an organization that does not have the vision and commitment to work with the poorest. Similarly, vision is not enough by itself, and must guide innovation and the development of appropriate systems.

Organizational Culture

A *culture of impact* should be created that promotes support for the very poor both within the organization and by clients. As MFIs pursue financial sustainability, they have been effective in creating organizational cultures that emphasize efficiency and productivity, and have reinforced this culture with staff incentive schemes. If MFIs are serious about their poverty focus, they need to build a similar culture and incentives for this. Achieving the commitment and understanding of front-line staff is key to organizational effectiveness in poverty outreach and impact. Central to this is designing incentive systems that motivate staff to be effective and efficient in terms of impact and poverty outreach, as well as financial performance. CRECER, for example, bases its staff incentive scheme on a mixture of traditional indicators—loan portfolio size and quality, and the quality of educational services delivered. Poverty outreach is emphasized, with a weighting given to clients included from more difficult-to-reach areas.[82] This serves to back up the organizational culture of cost-effective delivery of financial services combined with the social side of the educational services.

Given the active involvement of clients in supporting one another, or in expelling problematic members, it is important that clients feel this culture too. This raises questions about how clients are involved in organizational processes in general, and how much the organizational objectives reflect the priorities of the people they seek to serve. More participatory processes to

Box 1.11

Grameen II has instituted a "five star" system of staff incentives based on branch and staff performance. For each performance area where targets are met a colored star is awarded which can be worn by staff. Stars can also be earned by individual staff member performance. Performance stars are awarded for a mixture of outreach, impact and financial/operational objectives: 100% repayment record; profitability; savings deposits; school attendance and completion of primary school; borrowers crossing the poverty line.

Source: Yunus, Grameen Bank II.

involve clients in organizational governance and decision-making may be one way to address these questions. There is little experience of these issues in practice, and this is an area for future innovation.

Gender as Part of Program Practice

An understanding of gender issues and the possible positive and negative impacts of microfinance need to be integrated into organizational culture and practice. Programs need to work with women to assess and discuss their constraints rather than leaving them unspoken and then devise strategies to address them. This needs to take place at two levels. First, there should be an awareness of how gender issues operate in the clients' lives and the potential for women's increased decision-making and financial responsibility to have both positive and negative impacts on intra-household dynamics. Second, staff interaction with clients is hugely important in addressing gender inequalities. If they act as positive role models, challenge inequalities, and educate, they can help to redress inequalities within the community. However, if their attitudes and behavior mirror conventional societal norms, then they will serve to reinforce inequalities. The organizational commitment to challenging inequalities *within the organization* will be key to developing good practice among field staff within communities.

For example, the dynamics of groups favored by most poverty-focused methodologies have the potential to influence social networks and support given between people in the community. This influence can be positive, for example by fostering a culture of support, or negative, such as by exacerbating tensions and creating conflict over group guarantees or support. The impact assessment of CRECER found that positive impact on women's empowerment is in part due to the program exclusively targeting women, but is also associated with a number of village bank methodological features: women running their own bank, making decisions on feasibility of each other's proposed activities, electing their leaders, or setting the terms and conditions of internal loans. The concept of solidarity is also built upon through the group structure. Furthermore, regular meetings imposed by CRECER develop the women's links and knowledge about one another, and the education received also helps boost self-esteem.

Organizational Learning and Innovation

Poverty-focused MFIs need to be innovative and responsive to the needs of their clients. Internal learning systems should allow for monitoring of client performance through listening to clients' experiences and views, particularly those of the very poor. Monitoring systems therefore need to be set up in a way that gives information about the poverty level of clients. The MFI also needs to be flexible enough to make changes in response to this learning.

PART THREE:
LESSONS AND CONCLUSIONS

Implications for the Microfinance Industry

This concluding section summarizes the main implications of the discussions of parts one and two for the practitioners who deliver microfinance, and for the donors and policymakers who support them. It is clear that we have moved away from blueprint models that can be replicated, and need to apply general principles of practice and performance instead.

The Importance of Microfinance in Poverty Eradication

I started this chapter by questioning the lack of emphasis placed on microfinance in donor strategies for the realization of the Millennium Development Goals. This chapter has demonstrated the fallacy that microfinance cannot be an appropriate strategy for the poorest. Conceptual analysis and detailed impact assessment studies of the work of the case study organizations show clear pathways for both economic and social impact. These lead to direct impacts on the first Millennium goal of halving absolute poverty and hunger, and potential indirect impacts on most of the other goals.

Box 1.12

"The literature confirms that most microfinance programs do not serve the poorest. However, there are some institutions that do, and the evidence indicates that the poorest can definitely benefit from microfinance in terms of increased incomes and reduced vulnerability."

Source: Morduch and Haley, Analysis, 6.

Design of Poverty-Focused Microfinance

Poverty outreach and impact are not automatic. Conventional microfinance acts through both deliberate and unintentional mechanisms which exclude the poorest. Programs therefore need to be designed to include the poorest, and to facilitate mechanisms that will lead to poverty impacts.

There is a spectrum of organizations and there is no blueprint for success. Some choose to commit themselves fully to a poverty focus, others remain broad-based. All MFIs, however, need seriously to consider the position of the poorest in their organizations. Most MFIs do include some of the poorest as their clients. Some may well have negative impacts on these clients. Through increasing their understanding of poverty, and who is included or excluded and for what reasons, MFIs can take simple steps to improve their outreach and their effectiveness for the poorest.

Improving Outreach to the Poorest

The main challenge is to ensure that the poorest are not artificially excluded from services. "There needs to be sustained, proactive effort at trying to reach poorer people. Conventional microfinance does not automatically push itself deeper."[83]

- MFIs need to improve their contextual understanding of poverty and the needs of the very poor.
- Market research that takes active measures to overcome the exclusion of the poorest can lead to an understanding of their needs.
- MFIs should work in areas with high numbers of very poor people (geographical targeting).
- Rather than putting up barriers to less-poor people, programs should be designed with an understanding of client needs. This can be effec-

tive in encouraging participation of the very poor.

- Active targeting of clients is necessary if an MFI wants to *exclusively* focus on the very poor and the poor.

Appropriate Products

Very poor clients need a range of financial services that fit in with their erratic income and expenditure patterns and help them cope with unexpected demands for money.

- Both credit and savings are important for the very poor to allow for income stabilization and smoothing, investment in income-generation, and reduced vulnerability.

- Design of products should be based on their potential to reduce poverty, risk, and vulnerability, not just in terms of their attractiveness to clients.

- Where loan repayment is made *from existing income sources* there is a need for flexibility in savings and loan repayments. Savings in particular should be easily accessible, both for deposits and withdrawals. Loans do not need to be tied to a particular activity.

- Where repayment is made *from profits from an income-generating activity*, regular repayments and pressure from the MFI are important to encourage focus on the business activity and to develop business management skills.

- Where an overwhelming crisis or emergency occurs, clients should be able to move out of the rigid repayment cycle of enterprise loans, and move to a more flexible schedule.

- A range of other products, such as emergency loans and insurance, can help clients cope with emergencies, smooth consumption, and generally reduce their risk and vulnerability.

Client need for flexibility and a range of products needs to be balanced with an MFI's capacity to manage an increasingly complex and diverse portfolio.

Delivery

Services need to be delivered in a way that recognizes the vulnerability of very poor clients, and seeks to help them stay in the program if they experience problems.

- There should be no compulsion to take a loan.

- Access to increased levels of credit should be linked to ability to re-pay—either through demonstrating savings capacity or business per-formance.

- Client problems and failure should be expected, and the client should be supported rather than being expelled from the program—support-ive, not coercive, relationships should be developed.

- Group liability can exclude the poorest: this can be overcome by re-moving liability from groups, facilitating group functioning, or giving individual loans.

- A culture of poverty focus and impact in an MFI is key to achieving positive impact.

- Client support and skills-sharing should be encouraged. There is a lot to learn from community-based organizations and other models of microfinance, such as self-help groups.

- Gender awareness should be integrated into program practice at the level of field staff–client relations, and within organizations' proce-dures and culture.

Trade-offs and Balances

With no social objectives, MFIs could achieve faster growth and greater profits. With no financial objectives, MFIs could work intensively with small numbers of people, ensuring that few of the target group are excluded and that dedicated staff spend long hours with individual clients to ensure their success. Microfinance is a compromise where the social and financial objec-tives must be balanced. The challenge is to marry the best practice of pov-erty outreach, impact, and self-sufficiency in order to work out compro-mises that allow for an achievable mix of these three goals. The key chal-lenges are:

- To better understand the trade-offs and benefits. What are the positive effects of a poverty focus? To understand this there is a need for better comparative information about MFI operating ratios such as staff sala-ries compared to average loan sizes, or population density compared to number of clients per loan officer.

- To be able to innovate to make poverty-focused microfinance more cost-effective. How important is a focus on the success and sustainability of clients in this?

Box 1.13

"Currently the majority of MFIs neither determine the composition of the clientele upon intake nor evaluate the effectiveness of their program in terms of poverty reduction. The development and use of the new tools for market analysis and evaluation suggests that failure to monitor and evaluate can cut costs in the short-run at the expense of achieving long-term social and economic goals."

Source: Morduch and Haley, Analysis, 2.

- To innovate to improve the impact of microfinance, for example through cost-effective opportunities to improve impact through provision of or linkages with additional services.
- To set realistic performance targets for organizations with these objectives.

Measuring Performance

The microfinance industry has established clear best practices for measuring and reporting on financial performance. We are still a long way from establishing comparable standards for performance in depth of poverty outreach and impact.

There is clearly a need to broaden the concept of best practice to take account of the balance between different objectives that MFIs must achieve. Performance needs to be measured in terms of effectiveness as well as efficiency. The social objectives of poverty outreach and impact need to be given higher prominence and systems developed to allow for transparent reporting of such data.

Measurement and Reporting of Poverty Outreach

In an industry that is heavily subsidized by donors on the basis of its poverty impact, there is a strong case for conditions to be imposed requiring MFIs to report on poverty outreach using credible indicators. This is a particularly contentious issue in the United States at present, where the Microfinance for Self-Reliance Act mandates that 50 percent of the U.S. Agency for International Development (USAID) funding for microenterprise development should be directed towards the very poor and that poverty targeting tools be developed and used, in order to encourage practitioner

Box 1.14

"Average loan size is an easy but inadequate indicator for depth of outreach. Minimal extra effort in data collection can yield much richer information for marketing and evaluation."

Source: Morduch and Haley, *Analysis*, 1.

innovation to serve this market and to ensure that the poverty mandate is being implemented.

The key operational point for MFIs is to focus on who is excluded and for what reasons. Achieving good poverty outreach is about providing the right products and services as far down the poverty scale as is possible. For this to take place two key measures of poverty outreach are important—working in the poorest areas of the country and working with the poorest people relative to the population in an MFI's operational area.

Poverty assessment tools are available to both practitioners and donors that can provide poverty outreach data. These tools provide excellent information about poverty relative to local conditions, but can be improved to allow better comparisons to be made at national and international levels. There needs to be widespread acceptance of the importance of MFIs reporting on this basic performance data.

Basic poverty outreach data should be based on the following:

- Loan size is an inadequate indicator of poverty outreach.
- MFIs should monitor and report on the poverty level of new clients, as well as who they are not reaching. This data should be relative to the local context, but should also be comparable to national and international poverty line calculations.

Measuring and Reporting on Impact Performance

Impact performance is difficult to measure in a cost-effective way, and few would call for all microfinance organizations to undertake detailed impact assessment studies. However, basic impact information is needed for program design to ensure effective management towards improved impact on the poorest. There are two areas to be emphasized in monitoring and reporting on impact performance:

- *Client monitoring and organizational learning systems* can be developed that give basic, regular information about a small number of proxy indicators for impact[84], and which collect detailed qualitative information from clients. These could form the basis of industry-wide indicators that can be reported on, with the credibility of data being determined by the manner in which it has been collected.

- *Poverty auditing:* The establishment of standards of good practice in terms of design and delivery of poverty-focused microfinance can create a basis for monitoring whether MFIs are likely, given their approach, to impact positively on poverty. The CGAP Poverty Audit is an excellent framework that looks at the overall organizational approach to poverty impact, conceptual understanding of poverty, organizational culture and commitment to a poverty focus, staff-client interface, design features which serve to improve its outreach and impact to the poorest, and organizational learning and impact monitoring processes. Together these do not measure poverty impact, but give a good performance measure of the organizational commitment, design, and monitoring to achieve it.

Basic proxies for impact that should be monitored include the following:

- Reporting on who does not join and who leaves the program and why, disaggregated by poverty level.

- Disaggregation of client loan and/or savings performance by poverty level.

- Reporting on penetration rate—the concentration of poor people reached in an area.

Creating Space for Innovation—The Role of Donors

In this chapter I have demonstrated that there are many lessons for practice and many pointers as to how the microfinance industry can improve its social impact without compromising the necessity to establish sustainable organizations. This is now a time for innovation and experimentation. Existing tested models of microfinance can be adapted, new approaches developed, and lessons learned from approaches outside the mainstream of microfinance, from organizations that do not conform to the primacy of IFS as a goal. For example, many development organizations use microfinance as a tool to achieve poverty reduction and empowerment goals. These organizations incorporate financial service components into their existing activities, and do not necessarily seek to achieve sustainability. They are clearly not an alternative to mainstream microfinance since they rely on continuing subsidies and are limited in their scale. However, they are innovating and expanding the experience of the effectiveness of microfinance in poverty alleviation, and there is scope to feed lessons from their experience into mainstream microfinance.

Donors can play a positive role in this process in three ways:

1. Providing financial incentives towards the achievement of certain goals, such as depth of poverty outreach. This is not an argument for greater subsidies for poverty-focused MFIs, rather a call for targeted financial incentives to promote a process of experimentation and innovation in the areas outlined in this chapter.

2. Creating space for MFIs to improve their effectiveness. Rigid performance requirements based on financial best-practice standards push MFIs into a narrow path of chasing financial self-sufficiency. Different pathways need to be explored, and perhaps different timeframes for donor finances to allow them to reach the point of financial self-sufficiency. This needs to be linked to the establishment of clearer industry standards for good practice in poverty-focused microfinance and to much greater transparency in terms of reporting on poverty outreach and impact. However, balance needs to be struck between providing greater space for innovation, for example, by allowing pilot phases in MFI development, and ensuring that innovation is not used as an excuse for poor practice and inefficiency.

3. Development of industry standards and reporting guidelines based on performance measures that take into account both efficiency and effectiveness measures. The performance standards may well vary according to the objectives of the MFI to take into account trade-offs between the financial performance and poverty impact objectives. Much more research is needed to be able to determine at what levels these performance standards would be set.

The Way Forward

In this chapter I have presented evidence of the need and possibilities for a microfinance industry that includes as a major objective the eradication of poverty through the delivery of a range of financial services to very poor people. The case studies demonstrate that this is taking place, but the industry must rise to the challenge of expanding the boundaries of microfinance and innovating to develop more effective and more cost-effective services for the poorest. Too often conclusions are being reached based on false assumptions.

For poverty-focused microfinance to move forward, there is a need for more transparent reporting of achievements, and development of standards. This includes:

- Incentives from donors in funding policies for MFIs to reach the poorest.

- Demonstrated poverty outreach and impact should be included in donor criteria for MFI support.

- A need for transparency in reporting on who is being reached, who stays in the program and for how long, and basic indicators of impact.

- A need for better indicators and tools for measurement of poverty outreach—loan size is inadequate.

- A need for development of good practice guidelines for poverty-focused microfinance.

Microfinance should be given greater prominence in all strategies that seek to integrate a range of approaches to combat poverty. This work is a call to the microfinance community to apply their expertise and explore the potential of microfinance in all its forms to impact on the lives of the poorest. It is a call to give equal weight to the goals of poverty outreach and impact, rather than letting them be subsumed by the overarching goal of sustainability.

Annex: US$/Day Poverty Level of SHARE Clients[85]

According to the Indian national poverty line, based on minimum caloric intake, in 1994, 35 percent (rural—37 percent) of the people were below the poverty line. The World Bank estimates that in 1997, 44 percent of the people were living on less than a dollar a day (PPP adjusted). Given that there are no indications of any serious deterioration of poverty levels between 1994 and 1997, it would seem that the Indian national poverty line is set substantially lower than the $1 a day level of the international absolute poverty level.

Since the national poverty line is based on minimum caloric requirement, we can assume that going without a meal would constitute a caloric

Annex Table 1.1   Number of Meals Served in Last Two Days

No. of meals	Frequency	Percent	Cumulative Percent
1	1	.5	.5
2	7	3.5	4.0
3	14	7.0	11.0
4	56	28.0	39.0
5	41	20.5	59.5
6	81	40.5	100.0
Total	200	100.0	

Annex Table 1.2   Number of Days Rice/Roti with Only Chilli Served in Last Seven Days

No. of meals	Frequency	Percent	Cumulative Percent
0	36	44.4	44.4
1	19	23.5	67.9
2	14	17.3	85.2
3	7	8.6	93.8
4	4	4.9	98.8
5	1	1.2	100.0
Total	81	100.0	

intake of less than the poverty line figure. If we look at SHARE data for clients, we find that 60 percent of the households missed at least one meal in the last two days preceding the survey (see Annex Table 1.1)

Further, out of the eighty-one households which did have six meals in the last two days, twenty-six were reported to have spent at least two days having meals of rice or bread (roti) without *any* vegetables or pulses. In other words, these people were subsisting only on a bowl of rice or a couple of rotis. We assume that these people, while probably consuming the minimum caloric intake, would not have been able to afford other nutritional requirements. We classify these people as above the national poverty line but below the $1 a day line. Adding this figure to the figure above provides us with a total of 145 SHARE clients (out of 200) or 72.5 percent, who would be below absolute poverty levels of $1 a day.

Notes

1. Absolute poverty is defined as families living on less than $1 a day, purchasing power parity (PPP).

2. A Microcredit Summit July 2002 review of Web sites of leading donor agencies such as the United Nations Development Program (UNDP), USAID, DFID, and the World Bank found no reference to microfinance in the agencies' strategy papers on the Millennium Development Goal of cutting absolute poverty in half by 2015.

3. Copies of these case studies are available from the Microcredit Summit at www.microcreditsummit.org.

4. Jennefer Sebstad and Monique Cohen, "Microfinance, Risk Management, and Poverty," AIMS Paper (Washington, D.C.: Office of Microenterprise Development, 2000).

5. In this chapter I use the term microfinance rather than microcredit. Microfinance refers to credit, savings, and a range of other financial services offered to the poor. The Microcredit Summit uses the term *microcredit*, but also defines this term as including savings and other financial services for the poor and poorest.

6. Muhammad Yunus, *Grameen Bank II: Designed to Open New Possibilities* (Grameen Foundation USA, 2002). www.gfusa.org/monthly/june/news/shtml.

7. CRECER was set up as a Credit with Education program of Freedom from Hunger, and was registered as a Bolivian NGO in October 1999.

8. Share Microfin Limited (SHARE) is a community-owned MFI, with two offshoot cooperatives: SHARE India MACS Limited (SIM) for savings mobilization from members, and SNEHA, another cooperative set up to provide microfinance in one particular district. All come under SHARE Group, also including SHARE, the Society, which continues to administer two branches but will have a support role mainly (training, technical, and capacity building services). In this chapter the term SHARE is used to refer to SML.

9. It does seem that the national poverty line is set very low in India (see discussion in Annex).

10. In this section I focus deliberately on the use of *credit*. This is not to down play the importance of other financial services, but to emphasize that need for credit is not linked to poverty level. This chapter seeks to challenge the orthodoxy that very poor people cannot productively use credit but rather need savings, insurance, and other services instead.

11. Jonathan Morduch and Barbara Haley, *Analysis of the Effects of Microfinance on Poverty Reduction*, RESULTS Cananda for CIDA, November 2001; Sebstad and Cohen, "Microfinance."

12. For further information about the CGAP Poverty Assessment Tool and its effectiveness see Simanowitz (2002) and the Poverty Targeting Centre on the Microfinance Gateway, www.microfinancegateway.org/poverty/index.htm.

13. SEF, SHARE, OTIV-Desjardins (Caisses Feminines), and CRECER. SEF operates a modified Grameen solidarity group methodology. Caisses Feminines is a Credit with Education program operating a village banking approach similar to CRECER. It

was initiated by OTIV through a partnership with Freedom from Hunger and CRS Madagascar.

14. Miguel Jimenez, *A Poverty Assessment of Micro-finance CRECER, Bolivia on Behalf of the Consultative Group Assist the Poorest*, Unpublished Draft (2002), 13.

15. Sebstad and Cohen, "Microfinance."

16. Stuart Rutherford, *The Poor and Their Money* (New Delhi, India: Oxford University Press, 1999); Graham Wright, "Examining the Impact of Microfinance Services—Increasing Income or Reducing Poverty?" *Small Enterprise Development* 10, no. 1 (1999); Sebstad and Cohen, "Microfinance."

17. Marguerite Robinson, *The Microfinance Revolution: Sustainable Finance for the Poor* (Washington, D.C.: The World Bank, 2001), 21.

18. Sebstad and Cohen, "Microfinance," 33; describes risk as follows: "the chance of a loss or a loss itself, *risk* has many sources—(1) structural factors such as seasonality, inflation or . . . weather; 2) unanticipated crises and emergencies, such as sickness or death of a family member, loss of employment, fires and theft; and 3) the high costs associated with life cycle events such as marriage, funerals, and educating children. Likewise, risks are associate with 4) operating an enterprise and with 5) taking a loan."

19. Sebstad and Cohen, "Microfinance," 12.

20. Morduch and Haley, *Analysis*.

21. Rutherford, *The Poor*.

22. Stuart Rutherford, quoted in Carlos Ani, *State of Microfinance in Bangladesh* (2002), 2.

23. CASHPOR-Philnet conducted an assessment of SHARE using a modified AIMS methodology. Changes were analyzed using both longitudinal data from a base-line created from member in-take data, and cross-sectional data using a control group of pipe-line clients. Freedom from Hunger conducted an impact evaluation of CRECER. A rigorous quantitative methodology was used collecting base-line data in 1994/5 with follow-up in 1997.

24. Morduch and Haley, *Analysis*.

25. Donald Snodgrass and Jennefer Sebstad, *Clients in Context: The Impacts of Microfinance in Three Countries*, AIMS Synthesis Report (Washington, D.C.: Office of Microenterprise Development, USAID, 2002). www.mip.org.

26. A mature client is defined as a client who has remained with the program for three years or more.

27. Sebstad and Cohen, "Microfinance."

28. Morduch and Haley, *Analysis*.

29. Snodgrass and Sebstad, *Clients*, 68.

30. Sebstad and Cohen, "Microfinance," 98–100.

31. A recent study of women's empowerment reputedly demonstrates significant impact on women's empowerment. Unfortunately the report from this study was not available at the time of writing this chapter.

32. Sebstad and Cohen, "Microfinance"; Snodgrass and Sebstad, *Clients*; Wright, "Ex-

amining the Impact."

33. Snodgrass and Sebstad, *Clients*.

34. Snodgrass and Sebstad, *Clients*, 68.

35. Sebstad and Cohen, "Microfinance."

36. Morduch and Haley, *Analysis*, 2.

37. Hege Gulli, *Microfinance and Poverty: Questioning the Conventional Wisdom* (Washington, D.C.: Inter-American Development Bank, 1998) 78.

38. Morduch and Haley, *Analysis*, 6.

39. Snodgrass and Sebstad, *Clients*, x.

40. This is a speculative comment used for illustration and is not based on any evidence that this is a plausible association.

41. Snodgrass and Sebstad, *Clients*, 54.

42. Sebstad and Cohen, "Microfinance."

43. Anton Simanowitz, "Client Exit Surveys: A Tool for Understanding Client 'Drop-Out,'" *Journal of Microfinance* 2, no. 1 (2000); David Hulme, *Client Exits (Drop-outs) from East African Micro-Finance Institutions* (Kampala: MicroSave-Africa, 1999).

44. Note, not all client exit is for negative reasons or programmatic reasons. Successful clients can graduate to other sources of financial services; clients can also leave because they move away from the operational area or move to a competitor.

45. As reported by the PlaNet Finance rating. However CRECER is not systematically tracking exit rates, and it is therefore possible that the rating figures for client exit are inaccurate.

46. Robinson, *The Microfinance Revolution*, 2, emphasis added.

47. David Gibbons and Jennifer Meehan, *The Microcredit Summit's Challenge: Working Toward Institutional Financial Self-Sufficiency while Maintaining a Commitment to Serving the Poorest Families* (Washington, D.C.: The Microcredit Summit Campaign, 2000). www.microcreditsummit.org/papers/challengespaper.htm.

48. Gibbons and Meehan, *The Microcredit Summit's Challenge*, 4.

49. Craig Churchill, "Bulletin Highlights and Tables—Reaching the Poor," *MicroBanking Bulletin* 5 (2000): 10.

50. PlaNet Rating is a branch of PlaNet Finance, an international non-profit organization based in Paris. PlaNet uses the GIRAFE methodology, and has been recognized by CGAP to provide ratings under the CGAP Rating Fund. Note the investment grade rating for CRECER was only the fourth awarded by PlaNet out of twenty-nine ratings conducted.

51. As is common practice, these inputs have not been adjusted for in the PlaNet Rating.

52. M-CRIL is a microfinance capacity assessment division of EDA Rural Systems, Delhi. M-CRIL has been recognized by CGAP to provide ratings under the CGAP Rating Fund.

53. CRISIL is one of the mainstream-rating agencies in India, which is recognized by the Reserve Bank of India. CRISIL has been recognized by CGAP to provide ratings under the CGAP Rating Fund.

54. A detailed discussion of these two programs and their effectiveness in poverty outreach is presented in the report from the CGAP poverty assessment of SEF (van de Ruit et al., 2001).

55. This is not so clear for the seventh and eighth loan cycle in TCP, but the sample size is very small for these loans. Since loan size growth is linked to business performance, this represents a real growth in clients' ability to use credit, rather than a policy by the MFI to grant increasing loan size.

56. Client dropout or exit is defined as the percentage of clients finishing one loan cycle not taking a repeat loan within one month. Many drop-outs do subsequently return, but they are not captured in these figures.

57. This section is informed by a workshop of the *Imp-Act* Thematic Group "Microfinance for the Very Poor," hosted by the Small Enterprise Foundation in South Africa, 26–29 November 2001. For more information see www.Imp-Act.org.

58. Chris Dunford, *What's Wrong with Loan Size?* (Davis, Calif.: Freedom from Hunger, 2002), 6. www.ffhtechnical.org/publications/summary/loansize0302.html.

59. This chapter discusses the problems of the use of loan size as a proxy for poverty outreach.

60. See: Anton Simanowitz, Ben Nkuna, and Sukor Kassim, *Overcoming the Obstacles to Identifying the Poorest Families: Using Participatory Wealth Ranking (PWR), the CASHPOR House Index (CHI), and Other Measurements to Identify and Encourage the Participation of the Poorest Families, Especially the Women of Those Families* (Washington, D.C.: The Microcredit Summit Campaign, 2000).

61. Anastase Ntezigyaremye and Barbara MkNelly, "Mali Poverty Outreach Study of Kafo Jiginew and Nyèsigiso Credit and Savings with Education Programs," *Freedom from Hunger Research Paper no. 7* (Davis, Calif.: Freedom from Hunger, 2001), 2–3.

62. Anton Simanowitz, quoted in: Microcredit Summit Campaign, *State of the Campaign Report 2001* (Washington, D.C.; Microcredit Summit, 2001), 4.

63. Reported during discussion at *Imp-Act* global meeting.

64. It is important to distinguish between assessment, screening, and targeting: *Assessment* involves analyzing the existing poverty outreach of an MFI and presenting these figures; *Screening* involves assessing the poverty status of people who apply to join the program to determine eligibility; *Targeting* is an active process to identify *all* people who would qualify to join the program, so as to allow active motivation of these people to join.

65. For example: Rutherford, *The Poor*.

66. CGAP, *The Poverty Audit: Guidelines for Determining the Depth of Outreach and Poverty Impact of Microfinance Institutions*, Draft (Washington, D.C.: CGAP, 2001), 2.

67. Rutherford, The Poor.

68. Obviously there are a small number of dependent people in each community who cannot engage in economic activities—for example, those who are severely physically and mentally disabled.

69. Rutherford, *The Poor*.

70. Sebstad and Cohen, "Microfinance," 111.
71. The internal loans seem to be a highly valued and useful feature of CRECER's services. They give people greater flexibility within a relatively rigid lending methodology.
72. For example: Sebstad and Cohen, "Microfinance."
73. Sebstad and Cohen, "Microfinance," 83; emphasis added.
74. Ntezigyaremye and MkNelly, "Mali."
75. Yunus, *Grameen Bank II*.
76. Snodgrass and Sebstad, *Clients*, 69.
77. Sebstad and Cohen, "Microfinance," 108.
78. Yunus, *Grameen Bank II*, 2.
79. For a more detailed discussion of the role of microfinance in the empowerment of women see Cheston and Kuhn in chapter 4.
80. For detailed discussion of these issues, see chapter 2.
81. Examples of synergistic combinations are given in: Morduch and Haley, *Analysis*, 86–91.
82. Areas are divided into low, high, or extreme difficulty in terms of operating conditions and remoteness. CRECER's incentive scheme is currently being redeveloped to include poverty outreach as well as improved impact indicators.
83. Elizabeth Littlefield, presenting institutional view of CGAP, email correspondence, 14 February 2002.
84. Poverty-sensitive impact monitoring should include: information about who (poverty level and characteristics) the program is reaching, not reaching, and who exits, and changes in this over time; information about the penetration rate; indicators that measure changes in livelihood (such as income sources, food security and quality, housing, clothing expenditure, land and asset ownership); gender differences in poverty characteristics and changes.
85. Syed Hashemi, CGAP, 15 August, 2002.

2

Building Better Lives: Sustainable Integration of Microfinance with Education in Child Survival, Reproductive Health, and HIV/AIDS Prevention for the Poorest Entrepreneurs

Christopher Dunford

It is widely acknowledged that the very poor need more than microfinance to address the causes and conditions of their poverty. Ideally, the poor would have access to a coordinated combination of microfinance services and other development services to improve business, income and assets, health, nutrition, family planning, education of children, social support networks, and so on. The question is how to ensure a "coordinated combination" of appropriate services, especially in rural communities and other communities where multiple services are simply unavailable.

Microfinance practitioners are often motivated to provide nonfinancial services to their clients, because they recognize the need and hear the demand. However, the legitimate concern for sustainability, interpreted as the financial viability of the microfinance service as a business, has made practitioners very cautious about nonfinancial add-ons. They believe that add-ons can only be a drag on the drive for sustainability. Where other, nonfinancial service organizations can provide these add-ons for the same clients, some microfinance practitioners have fostered referrals and common points of service with their nonfinancial counterparts. But most microfinance institutions feel compelled or prefer to focus on the financial needs of their clients and do not attempt to meet their nonfinancial needs.

On the other hand, group-based microfinance provides a good opportunity to provide low-cost education services needed by the poor, if only to improve their performance as microfinance clients. This is especially true for village banking and related delivery systems that bring large groups of relatively poor clients together in regular meetings. Good, informal adult education techniques can be used effectively at the regular meetings to promote changes in personal behavior and in child-care practices and also to promote awareness of and confidence in whatever good-quality health services are available locally. Such education technologies can also improve business skills that enable clients to put their loans to more productive use and generate more profit and savings. A variety of education topics can be covered effectively.

One purpose of this chapter is to provide diverse examples of microfinance institutions that have responded successfully to the challenge of integrating microfinance with education, without compromising the sustainability of their microfinance and overall operations. Special attention is given to integration of microfinance with health education for very poor women. They and their children are very vulnerable to health and nutrition problems that threaten women's abilities to contribute economically to their households, even families' abilities to survive. There is critical need for innovative integration of microfinance with promotion of family planning and HIV/AIDS prevention. Pioneering examples are described.

Some institutions create integration by providing microfinance and education as *parallel* services, delivered to the same groups of clients by *different* staff, each specializing in one or the other service. BRAC in Bangladesh and Pro Mujer in Bolivia are described as detailed cases to illustrate this parallel service delivery approach. Both institutions depend on revenues other than their financial margin on credit operations to maintain their educational staffs and related expenses, though they can provide some cross-subsidy from microfinance to education.

This chapter also illustrates the feasibility and effectiveness of a *unified* approach in which microfinance and education services are delivered to village banks by the *same* staff. The overall cost of unified delivery of the two services is considerably less, for the simple reason that one staff in the unified model does the jobs of two different staffs in the parallel model. FUCEC-Togo, FOCCAS Uganda, and CRECER (Crédito con Educación Rural) in Bolivia are described in detail to illustrate the unified model in action. They (and similarly designed unified delivery systems) have achieved, or are likely to achieve in the near future, full recovery of their operating and financial costs for the unified service. The cross-subsidy from microfinance to education is or can be sufficient to sustain the education. Unification with education adds only 6 to 10 percent to the cost of village banking alone. In some cases, at least, the education also seems to give these institutions some competitive advantage with clients over microfinance-only institutions.

For the sake of efficiency (to achieve sustainability), the unified approach delivers microfinance and education as a single package to village banks.

The education is designed to meet prominent local needs and demand, but clients are not given the choice to reject the education component of the package. Some observers have questioned the ethics of not allowing choice, yet there is considerable evidence that the education is appreciated by clients and even that they opt for the unified service when given the chance to switch to microfinance-only institutions.

Certain impacts can be expected from microfinance without education and vice versa. Their combination yields a greater range of impacts and possibly even some synergy of impact. Definitive, direct comparison of unified delivery with parallel delivery or microfinance alone or education alone is yet to be successfully carried out, due to considerable methodological challenges. However, several careful studies of economic, health, nutrition, and empowerment impacts of the unified service demonstrate no less impact than was found in similar studies of microfinance or education alone. There has been concern about diminished impacts due to poorer quality of services delivered by generalists rather than specialists in those services. But the results of the impact studies indicate that the quality of the two services does not have to be compromised when delivered by one and the same person to a village bank.

The multi-sectoral tasking of service delivery staff gives unified-service providers a major advantage for achieving sustainability of both education and microfinance. But it is also a critical challenge to an institution. The self-sustaining unified approach cannot deliver as broad a range of services to the poor as parallel delivery systems with access to long-term external funding. For unified delivery, it can be difficult to maintain balance between the quality of the two types of service in the recruitment, training, and supervision of staff. Field staff and their managers have to respond to different demands and expectations from two different sectors of development (or more than two, depending on the range of education topics). Donors and other stakeholders tend to hold up one sector as more important than the other. Management information systems overemphasize the importance of financial performance of the institution vs. economic and social impact for the clients. These internal stresses and contradictions can be very difficult to manage. The will to unify service delivery, whether it comes from commitment to a philosophy of development or simply lack of other options, or both, is essential for success.

There exist ample and promising opportunities for microfinance providers to create integration with other development services, through either parallel or unified delivery of services from different sectors of development. In terms of impacts for the poor, neither delivery option is inherently superior. In terms of institutional issues, each has its advantages, especially the potential range of services for parallel delivery and potential financial sustainability for unified delivery, and its disadvantages, especially the financing and coordination challenges for parallel delivery and the management and staffing challenges for unified delivery. The best choice depends on local options for providing diverse services and the institutional will to provide more than microfinance.

Integrating Microcredit with Other Development Services

The Challenge

The problems of the poor go well beyond money or things. They suffer a broader syndrome of disadvantage. Access to financial services is powerful because it offers people opportunity—a greater range of options to change their lives. But credit, even combined with other financial services, addresses only one factor of many constraining the poor—lack of liquidity. Just as they have been bypassed by formal banking and other financial institutions, the poor have little or no access to education, health, and other services to build their "human capacity."

The diversity of needs of the poor are reflected in the seven distinct but interlocking goals of international development[1] established by the agreements and resolutions of the world conferences organized by the United Nations in the first half of the 1990s:

1. Reduce the proportion of people living in extreme poverty by half between 1990 and 2015.

2. Enroll all children in primary school by 2015.

3. Make progress towards gender equality and empowering women by eliminating gender disparities in primary and secondary education by 2005.

4. Reduce infant and child mortality rates by two-thirds between 1990 and 2015.

5. Reduce maternal mortality ratios by three-quarters between 1990 and 2015.

6. Provide access for all who need reproductive health services by 2015.

7. Implement national strategies for sustainable development by 2005 so as to reverse the loss of environmental resources by 2015.

All seven contribute "toward a world free of poverty and the misery it breeds." All recognize the need to provide greater support to women in their productive and reproductive roles, both as key beneficiaries of development services and as central players in using them to build human (physical and mental) capacity in their families and communities.

Very poor women—especially in rural areas—face tremendous obstacles: social and geographic isolation, illiteracy, lack of self-confidence, limited entrepreneurial experience, and major health and nutrition problems for themselves and their families. Addressing these obstacles, if only to cultivate better financial-service clients, requires improving people's social support networks and their personal and communal knowledge, skills and health practices, as well as access to good-quality services to support good health, food production, cash income, and asset accumulation. Public health researchers have long appreciated that increasing income and assets alone is a relatively slow and insufficient strategy for combating many serious ills, such as child malnutrition, the spread of HIV/AIDS, and women's lack of choice in determining the number and timing of pregnancies.[2]

Education can be a powerful partner of financial services, particularly if education engages individuals as decision-makers in their own learning—for personal and communal change and for informed use of whatever good-quality services are available. Group-based lending/saving services in particular provide an unusual opportunity to provide transformative educational experiences along with financial services.

Integration: Opportunities for "Economy of Scope"

There should be efficiencies in operations and even synergies of benefits to be gained by integrating different services intended for the same people. Perhaps another service or two can be delivered along with microcredit, perhaps by the same person. Among microcredit practitioners and donors, however, there is a strong bias against such integration. This is a reaction to the history of problems in "integrated rural development" programs and other idealistic models of multiple-intervention responses to the interlocking needs of poor communities. Drawing on the perspective of the for-profit business world, the microcredit community holds that specialization in one type of development service is necessary for development effectiveness, service efficiency and institutional sustainability. "Let bankers be bankers," says one commentator, and let others with different skills and experience take care of the other needs and wants of a community. Why should those setting out to create a microcredit program, or more broadly a microfinance institution, feel compelled to offer services other than those that microfinance specialists know well how to offer? The question is logical, and the logic can appear persuasive.

Microfinance is not alone in this logic. Other sectors may be less adamant but are no less uncomfortable about trying to be "all things to all people" and all their problems. This is the perspective of professionals seeking to focus on what they have been trained to do best. There is a different and broader perspective, however: that of the program designer who gives priority to a development objective, such as alleviating the burdens of poverty on women and children. This designer is not satisfied with planning for economies of scale for a single service, because there is obvious need, even consumer demand, for multiple services. The designer is trying to achieve "economies of scope"—packaging two or more services together to minimize delivery and management support costs and to maximize the variety of benefits for people's multiple needs and wants.

There are three common scenarios for integrating microcredit with other services:

- *Linked service delivery by two or more independent organizations operating in the same area.* Financial services are offered by a specialist microfinance institution at the same time as nonfinancial services (possibly for health and other sectors) are offered by one or more independent specialist or generalist organizations—to the same people in need. When there are several development service providers in a target area, as in many urban and peri-urban areas, an organization reasonably may choose to specialize as a business-like microfinance service provider. Ideally, different services offered by different organizations would coordinate their marketing, including delivery at common points of service and mutual referrals, as clients' needs for other services arise. Many specialist microfinance institutions fall into this scenario; few reach for the "ideal" of coordinated marketing with nonfinancial service providers. One long-standing example is the close coordination of BRAC's Rural Development Program (microfinance provider) with Government of Bangladesh (and World Food Program) food distribution to the "hardcore" poor. The relationship is mediated through the intermediary IGVGD (Income Generation for Vulnerable Groups Development) program, jointly administered by BRAC and the Government of Bangladesh.[3]

- *Parallel service delivery by two or more programs of the same organization operating in the same area.* A generalist or multi-purpose organization (often a grant-mobilizing local, national, or international private development organization) offers microfinance services through a specialist microcredit program staff at the same time as offering other sector services through different program staff of the same organization—to the same people in need. If there are few available services in an area and an organization can afford a long-term commitment to provide two or more services with different specialist staff, then it makes sense to deliver a variety of complementary services in parallel. BRAC again provides a good example of this scenario in action (see "Three Case Studies" in Appendix A). The Grameen Family of Companies is another good example.

- *Unified service delivery by one organization, one program, one staff.* The same staff of the same organization offers both microcredit and other sector services—to the same people in need. When the people in need have access to few, if any, other development services, as in many rural communities, and the organization cannot afford a long-term commitment to provide two or more services with different specialist staff, it reasonably may choose to field only one set of staff tasked to provide microcredit with another service. The organization even may seek to hold its costs to a level it can sustain with revenue generated by the unified service itself. Credit with Education[4] providers are good examples (see details in the next section of this chapter and the case of FUCEC-Togo in Appendix A).

Of course, there can be hybrids of these scenarios. For example, a unified, multi-sectoral service can be linked with other complementary services. One emerging example in Bolivia (around Lake Titicaca) is the joint planning and coordination of services offered by Crédito con Educación Rural (CRECER), a provider of Credit with Education and Consejo de Salud Rural Andino (CSRA), a rural health service provider.

The unified *and self-financing* scenario is the most promising for sustainable delivery of multiple services, but it is also the most demanding. The designer is attempting to build—or fit into—a sustainable, business-like institution that can support the unified-service delivery system for many years to come. Subject to the hard constraints of sustainable institution-building, the designer is trying to get more development "bang" for the development "buck." The assumption is that the same staff can deliver two or more different sector services, with greater overall efficiency and without compromising the individual effectiveness of the services.

Is this unified, self-financing model possible? Is it feasible? The answers appear to be yes to both questions when applied to microcredit and education delivered together. (Credit with Education illustrates this scenario in action.) But only certain types of microcredit and certain types of education offer this opportunity for unification. Is this unified, self-financing approach recommended for everyone providing suitable microcredit services? The answer is no. This approach is only for those whose objectives call for providing multi-sectoral services to address multiple needs/wants of the very poor. It is also only for those committed to long-term dependence only on the revenue generated by the unified service itself—that is, independence from operating grants. In other words, those committed to self-sustaining "poverty lending" (reaching out to the poor with financial services) *and more* will find this unified approach worthy of their consideration.

The first purpose of the rest of this chapter is to provide evidence of the feasibility and effectiveness of the unified, self-financing model for integrating different sector services. The evidence comes almost solely from integration of microcredit with health-related education. Other types of education— for example, for business management, leadership development, community action, self-confidence building, and other topics—are integrated successfully with microcredit through similar application of the unified, self-financing model. Much of what has been discovered regarding feasibility of integrated microcredit and health education services applies to any sort of microcredit-education integration. However, in-depth research studies of impact have been carried out only for health/nutrition education integrated with microcredit.

The second purpose of this chapter is to explore common challenges to the unified, self-financing model for integrating different sector services. The intention is not to promote this model, but to offer balanced information about strengths and weaknesses and thereby allow an informed choice by those whose commitment to multiple sectors of service to the poor leads them to seriously consider this model for their own organizations to implement.

Integrating Education with Group-Based Lending

Group-Based Lending: An Opportunity for Educating the Poor

"Poverty lending" is a form of microcredit characterized by its clientele: the subsistence-level, pre-entrepreneurial, but economically active poor, usually women. These are the very people who most need information and support, as well as money, to improve their lives. Experience seems to show that *group-based lending* mechanisms are usually the most effective and efficient means to deliver financial services to this clientele while minimizing transaction costs and risk to the provider.

Group-based lending also provides a good forum for education. The borrowers' meetings provide an opportunity for regular face-to-face contact with an educator. The solidarity structure and joint guarantee mechanism foster a supportive atmosphere of collective self-interest. Women's successful management of the loans is likely to boost their confidence and thereby their willingness to try new practices for better health and other benefits.

An additional service, such as education, imposes additional delivery costs. However, the marginal cost of the education can be reduced when the regular (weekly, biweekly, monthly) repayment meetings of poverty-lending programs serve as the forum for the education. Moreover, the marginal cost can be made quite small when the same field staff delivers both financial and educational services at the same regular meetings (the unified model).

The Grameen Bank, with its famous "Sixteen Decisions," may have invented the unified delivery model.[5] Grameen's integration of financial services with social change promotion has inspired a variety of integrated-delivery systems whose common bond is *a determination to make education work—cost-effectively—within the context of group-based lending to the poor.* They share the conviction that group-based lending models have social as well as economic potential and that this dual potential must be realized in order to have significant impact on poverty.

A 1999 survey[6] of practitioner organizations (see Box 2.1) revealed that at least thirty-five practitioners around the world were committed to integrating education with group-based microcredit through either parallel or unified delivery within the same organization. Two-thirds of these organizations were operating in Africa. BRAC alone swamps the other respondents with its membership of 3.5 million. Among many others not included in this survey for various reasons, Grameen Bank should be counted as a provider of unified microcredit and education to millions of clients. Clearly, there is a great deal of experience with integration, and even with unified delivery, among a variety of practitioners serving, in aggregate, a large number of relatively poor people, mostly women.

The most common kind of group-based lending integrated with education is "village banking." First developed for Latin America by the Foundation for International Community Assistance (FINCA) in the 1980s, village banking is, in effect, a generic version of Grameen Bank's approach to microcredit, with a more decentralized management structure adapted to more dispersed populations than those in Bangladesh. In the 1990s, a large number of nongovernmental organizations adapted village banking to varied conditions all over the developing world.[7]

Where village banking services are made available by a local organization, anybody wanting a loan to invest in an income-earning activity may

Box 2.1
Practitioners Linking Education with Group-Based Lending

Twenty-four practitioners (not including BRAC) reported detailed statistics (as of December 1999) regarding their programs that integrate education with group-based microcredit.

- In aggregate, these 24 practitioners were providing integrated services to 210,008 individual clients, approximately 95 percent women and 41 percent living in rural communities with less than 10,000 inhabitants.

- Seventeen of the organizations used the village banking model of group-based microcredit (typically 20 to 40 clients per group), and seven used the solidarity group model, averaging five clients per group.

- Twenty-three organizations deliver education sessions at the same meetings where financial transactions occur.

- All 24 require their clients to participate in education as a condition for receiving loans.

- Only six of the organizations require clients to take loans in every "loan cycle" as a condition for group membership and access to education.

- Thirty-eight percent of the organizations responding to the question report their group meetings last from 60 to 90 minutes; 48 percent report meetings take 90 to 120 minutes.

- In 38 percent of the organizations responding to the question, education is delivered exclusively by the same field staff who deliver financial services. In 29 percent, education is done exclusively by group members trained for this purpose. The balance of the organizations use a mix of credit staff and group members, or they use staff assigned solely to deliver education.

- In order of frequency cited, organizations deliver education in the following topics: children's health (96%), children's nutrition (78%), family planning (74%), women's health (70%), calculating profit and accounting for business revenues and expenses (65%), group management skills (65%), marketing goods or services (61%), and selecting an appropriate income-generating activity (52%).

come together with trusted peers to form a "village bank" (different organizations use different names, like "community bank" or "trust bank" or "credit association"). The number of members cannot be too few (otherwise the group cannot be served economically) or too many (making it impractical for all members to participate in oversight and decision-making). Typically, village banks have twenty to forty members, mostly or all women.

After training the new members to manage their own village bank within specified rules, the local organization makes a loan (normally for four to six months) to the village bank as a joint-liability group. The members then break the large loan into small loans (initially about $50 to $100 each) to the individual members for investment in their individual microenterprises. The members guarantee repayment of each other's loans, so they must all agree that each borrower is capable of making a sufficient profit from the proposed income-generating activity to repay the village bank with interest. If the village bank pays its entire loan back to the local organization, on time and with interest, it becomes eligible immediately to receive a new, usually larger, group loan. In most village banking programs, individual members may increase their borrowing incrementally up to a maximum of about $300 per loan.

Borrowers usually invest their loans in activities in which they are already skilled and need no technical assistance, such as food processing and selling, raising chickens, operating a small shop, and making or buying and selling clothing. It is crucial that each borrower earn enough cash to pay back her loan with interest, deposit some personal savings, and have enough money left to purchase food and other necessities for the family. Village bank members meet regularly—typically weekly, biweekly, or monthly—to manage the affairs of their group, including making regular installment payments of principal and interest on their loans and regular deposits of personal savings.

Reinforced by their successful use of credit and their solidarity with others in their village bank, which is an educational experience in itself, the poor expand their awareness of the possibility of improvements in their lives. They become more ready to learn more and change more. And *the regular meetings of the village banks can respond to the learning readiness of the members by giving them new information and support for change.*

Unified Delivery of Village Banking and Health Education— A Detailed Case

The most common model for unified delivery of education with village banking is Credit with Education.[8] A part of each regular meeting, preferably twenty to thirty minutes, is set aside for a "learning session." The Credit with Education field agent—usually a moderately educated person from the local area—is responsible for recruiting new village banks, training the members to manage their own affairs as an informal cooperative, and attending the regular, usually weekly, meetings to oversee and assist the financial transactions of the group and to facilitate the learning session.

The field agent's role in education is to introduce a topic, help participants understand its relevance to issues in their lives, offer basic information about practical changes they can make, identify obstacles to such change, encourage any participants who have mastered these obstacles to share their successful experiences, and promote solidarity to help each other persist in their efforts to change. The field agents are not experts in the education topics. Their training focuses on techniques for presenting simple information messages and on facilitation skills for drawing the participants into learning from each other as much as from the field agent.

Effective education of adults goes beyond simply imparting information. It builds on their wealth of life experiences. It helps them see new ideas in the context of what they already know or believe. Village bank members can identify poverty-related problems they confront in their daily lives and become motivated to develop and use locally appropriate solutions. Field agents have to be carefully recruited, trained, and supervised for the specific purpose of becoming effective facilitators of adult learning.

The topics addressed in learning sessions range from village bank management to the basics of microenterprise management to the improvement of health and nutrition of women and children. Each Credit with Education practitioner organization promotes a different mix of topics in its village bank meetings. Choice of topics depends on organizational objectives, local needs and demand, availability of training and support for delivering the topic (such as family planning), and availability of good-quality local services (such as immunization and primary health clinics), the use of which can be promoted by the education. Typically, during a loan period of four to six months, one or two topics are explored in depth in a series of learning sessions, each building on the last. Several practitioners alternate between two topics, a learning session on a health topic, the next on microbusiness and group management, then back to health, from one meeting to the next over the loan period.

Each Credit with Education practitioner develops its own operational system for self-financing, unified delivery of microfinance, and education to poor women. The FUCEC-Togo case in Appendix A offers a specific example of Credit with Education in the institutional context of credit unions. This credit union federation and its member credit unions offer Credit with Education as one of several financial service products. Credit with Educa-

Figure 2.1   The Original Credit with Education Design

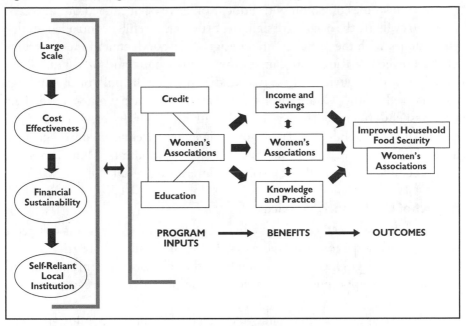

tion gives the FUCEC-Togo credit unions the opportunity for outreach to serve people that otherwise could not join a credit union, specifically poorer women in more remote rural communities.

Evidence of Impacts on Clients and Institutions

Impact Studies of Credit with Education

In its original design, the education component of Credit with Education aimed to improve health and nutrition of children under five years of age, as well as income and assets of poor families (see Figure 2.1). The assumption was that women would borrow capital at affordable rates, build their productive assets, accumulate savings, and build their self-confidence. These outcomes and impacts are the same as those expected from any well-designed and well-implemented microcredit program. In addition, the education would help improve child health and nutrition to an extent not expected from pure microcredit programming. Potentially, the credit and education components would reinforce each other by addressing both the informational and economic obstacles to better health and nutrition. In addition, as Figure 2.1 also indicates, these impacts are intended to be achieved through a cost-effective delivery system that local institutions can bring to scale and financially sustain.

Several studies of Credit with Education have been carried out in recent years[9] to evaluate the original design. In particular, carefully controlled, multi-year studies with the same research design were conducted in the programs of the Lower Pra Rural Bank in southwestern Ghana and of CRECER on the *altiplano* of Bolivia.[10] These two studies provide the bulk of the findings summarized below. Comparisons were made between women (and their youngest children up to three years old) with one to three years of participation in Credit with Education and women in either baseline or control groups. Several other studies, in Burkina Faso, Ecuador, Honduras, Mali, Tanzania, Thailand, and Uganda, also contributed interesting results.

Impact of the Financial Services

Similar to studies[11] of microcredit-only programs, evaluations of Credit with Education demonstrate increased levels of livelihood security among clients—more regular earnings throughout the year, asset accumulation, and consumption-smoothing. Here are some examples of impact evidence:

- Nonfarm Income. In Ghana, between the baseline and follow-up periods, Credit with Education clients enjoyed a significantly greater increase in monthly nonfarm earnings—almost double—as compared to nonparticipants in the same communities or residents living in control communities. Clients most commonly attributed their increased incomes to business expansion, reduced input costs as a result of buying in bulk or with cash rather than on credit, and new activities or products made possible by access to loans.

- Assets. In Burkina Faso, after approximately three years, borrowers increased the scale of their income-generating activities by an average of 80 percent, and roughly one-third of the respondents more than doubled the scale of their activity. Many women were found to have made significant investments in increasing or improving their productive capacity by buying fixed assets, such as aluminum and clay cooking pots, and by establishing regular market sites.

- Shocks. In Mali, program participation enhanced households' ability to reduce risk and deal with periods of crisis or economic difficulty. Clients participating for one and two years were significantly less likely than incoming clients to have experienced a period of acute food insecurity or to have been unable to conduct their enterprise due to a lack of money in the preceding twelve months.

One should expect these impacts on women's economic capacity in any well-designed and well-implemented microcredit program, regardless of the addition or lack of extra education. The addition of education does not appear to diminish the ability of village banking to produce these significant impacts sought in all poverty-oriented microcredit programming.

Impact of the Education Services

Similar to studies[12] of stand-alone health/nutrition education programs, the findings from Credit with Education programs demonstrate positive changes in clients' health knowledge, self-reported practice, and some health outcomes. Here are some examples of impact evidence:

- Breastfeeding. In Ghana, between the baseline and follow-up periods, there was a significant and positive increase among participants in giving their newborns the first antibody-rich milk, colostrum, rather than discarding it, relative to the two nonparticipant groups. Mothers in the program also exclusively breastfed their babies longer—closer to six months—and thus did not unnecessarily expose them to contaminants found in food or liquids other than breastmilk. And, despite their involvement in loan-financed activities, clients did not stop breastfeeding their children earlier than did nonparticipants, and they were even significantly less likely to use feeding bottles.

- Complementary Feeding. In Burkina Faso, women participants learned how to prepare a thicker porridge and when to begin feeding it to their young children. In the recent past, a child could easily go without food besides breastmilk until two years of age; women in the program were more likely to prepare special porridge and entice the child to eat solid food earlier.

- Diarrhea Treatment. In Bolivia, the baseline research indicated a key topic for the education component was the need for rehydration of children suffering bouts of diarrhea. Many mothers explained that when children had diarrhea they withheld or reduced liquids, thinking they would only exacerbate the problem. They gave dry food, such as bread, instead. Between the baseline and follow-up, a significant and positive difference was found in the percentage of clients reporting they gave children with diarrhea "more liquid than usual" (liquids of any kind, including breastmilk) as compared to nonparticipants.

- Immunization. Also in Bolivia, participants' one-year-old children showed significant and positive improvement in the percentage having the DPT3 vaccination relative to nonparticipants' children. This is particularly noteworthy because there is typically a drop-off in immunization coverage for those vaccinations given later in the series. This difference may indicate a positive effect of the program by encouraging mothers to have their children complete the full immunization series and in some cases by inviting health workers to provide these immunizations at the borrower groups' regular meetings.

One should expect such impacts on mothers' knowledge, practices, and outcomes in any well-designed and well-implemented health/nutrition education program, whether or not it is piggy-backed on a microcredit-service delivery system. It appears that unification with village banking does not have to diminish the power of adult education. The Ghana study also showed that health/nutrition behavior-change promotion from multiple sources can be mutually reinforcing when coordinated and focused on the same population. Mothers reported that reinforcement from several trusted sources—local health center staff, the Credit with Education field agent, as well as the other Credit Association members—led them to try exclusively breastfeeding their babies for a longer period. This change represented a radical departure from the common practice of giving newborns water and other drinks in their first days and weeks of life.

Combined Impact of Financial and Education Services

Ideally, the possibility of a synergistic effect of offering credit and education together would be evaluated with a research design comparing the relative impacts of stand-alone credit and education interventions versus parallel or unified delivery strategies. Unfortunately, few research efforts have taken on the considerable practical challenges of this ideal design.[13] Some of the impacts evident in evaluations of Credit with Education programs might be the effect of either the financial or education components or both working together. Here are some examples of evidence of possible synergistic impacts:

- Women's Empowerment. Building on the work of Schuler and Hashemi,[14] Freedom from Hunger defined women's empowerment in terms of 1) women's self-confidence and vision of the future; 2) their status and bargaining power within the household; and 3) their status and networks in the community. In both Ghana and Bolivia, there was evidence that access to the financial and education services had positively impacted women's self-confidence and status in the community. Participants in Ghana rated themselves significantly more confident (than did nonparticipants) that they would earn more in the future and that they could prevent their children from getting diarrhea and other illnesses. In terms of involvement in community life, participants in Ghana were taking on more active roles in community ceremonies, such as funerals, and participants in Bolivia were running for and holding offices in local governing bodies. In both countries, participants were significantly more likely to have given others advice both about practices for good health/nutrition and better business. There was little evidence, however, of women's increased bargaining power within the household; there was no significant increase in influence on a number of household investment decisions, with the exception in Bolivia of spending on house repairs and in Ghana on whether or not children went to school. One to three years of program participation by women may be too little to change deeply embedded power relationships and expectations within households.

• Children's Diet. Researchers from the Noguchi Memorial Medical Institute in Ghana conducted a dietary intake study of children of Credit with Education members and also nonparticipants. They found that the dietary quality of the foods given to participants' children was relatively higher. Also, the estimated caloric intake was significantly higher.[15]

• Children's Nutritional Status. Measurements of the same children in Ghana showed the nutritional status of participants' one-year-olds—both weight-for-age and height-for-age—also significantly improved relative to the children of residents in control communities. For example, the percentage of participants' children categorized as malnourished, based on height-for-age, decreased by eight percentage points between the baseline and follow-up periods, while the percentage of malnourished actually increased in control communities.

Impact on Client Satisfaction and Demand

Client satisfaction with Credit with Education has received less systematic attention. When asked if they do or do not like Credit with Education, clients overwhelming say they do. Without reference to alternatives to Credit with Education (other than no services at all), it is difficult to assess the degree of satisfaction, except in terms of successful repayment and repeat borrowing over time, which are both relatively high in Credit with Education programs.[16]

There are some useful anecdotes indicating women are satisfied with the unified services received, even when opportunities or social pressures might persuade them otherwise. In Bolivia, during the recent "renunciation of debt" in which microcredit borrowers were politically organized to purposely default *en masse* to protest the high interest rates and repayment requirements of local microfinance institutions, CRECER clients remained loyal to CRECER and continued their on-time repayment. When asked why, many clients told CRECER staff, "CRECER cares about us. They are not just here to collect our loans. They talk with us and give us education."

In some locations in eastern Uganda, women can now choose from two or more microcredit providers. The clients of the local Credit with Education provider, FOCCAS Uganda (Foundation for Credit and Community Assistance), have chosen to stay with FOCCAS. They told FOCCAS staff this is "because of the education."

In Burkina Faso, the RCPB (Réseau des Caisses Populaires du Burkina) provides Credit with Education as one of several services or products offered by this network of credit unions. RCPB management believes that providing education with its village banking service gives it a competitive advantage over a national organization that provides village banking alone to the same communities.

All three examples reflect not just overall satisfaction with the unified service but specific appreciation of the education. The degree of satisfaction with the education was investigated in the impact studies[17] in Bolivia and Ghana, but with only one question: "How useful have you found the information in the health/nutrition education sessions to be?" Of seventy-one respondents in Bolivia, 61 percent said, "Very useful," and 37 percent said, "Useful." Only one said, "Not very useful" and one didn't know. In Ghana, 67 percent of 101 respondents replied, "Very useful," and 27 percent replied, "Useful."

Several lines of evidence allow assessment of the relative value that clients place on the separate components of the Credit with Education service package—group dynamics, loans, savings, health and nutrition education, and better business education. Although clients are initially most attracted by the loans, over time they increasingly value the education. For example, when asked what they liked best about the Kafo Jiginew Credit with Education program in Mali, as many two-year clients mentioned the education as mentioned the loans.[18]

A more recent study[19] of the Kafo Jiginew and Nyèsigiso credit union federations in Mali surveyed new members of eight credit unions that had been providing Credit with Education services for four years. This period was considered long enough for Credit with Education members to "graduate" to traditional individual credit union membership. (As Credit with Education members, they are only associate members of the credit union, through the group's membership, and do not have access to the other credit union services.) The survey determined which new individual members of credit unions were coming from Credit with Education groups and whether or not they had left those groups upon joining the credit union directly. Of the 207 new women members surveyed, 35 percent had come from Credit with Education groups, 24 percent choosing to maintain their participation in those groups and 11 percent having left those groups.

They were asked why they chose to continue participating in their Credit with Education groups as well as become individual members of the credit union, or why not. Here are the most frequently cited reasons for continuing participation in Credit with Education:

- Like the solidarity provided by the group   96%
- Like the education   91%
- Like the opportunity for more than one loan at a time   89%
- Want to save with their group   85%
- Want other Credit with Education services   34%

Those who left their groups as they joined the credit unions directly (twenty-one respondents) mostly cited their desire for financial services and products better adapted to their needs, such as larger, longer-term loans at a lower interest rate with less frequent repayments. Only 10 percent cited dislike of the frequent meetings or difficulties with other group members. None mentioned problems with the education.

Freedom from Hunger offers new Credit with Education providers a "first cycle assessment" after repayment of the provider's first round of loans and education to village banks. These assessments include systematic group interviews with village bank members to determine why they joined the program, what they liked best about the services offered, what they liked least and what should be changed and how. For example:

- In Bénin (March 2001), the most frequent response of new clients of Credit with Education offered by FECECAM (Fédération des Caisses d'Epargne et de Crédit Agricole Mutuel du Bénin) was that they chose to participate "because of the education." After the first loan period, what the clients most appreciated about the service was "the education received." Other answers included access to loans, savings opportunities, and solidarity among group members.

- For FITSE Karonga Microfinance (August 2000) in Malawi and OIC Guinea (September 2000), education was cited frequently, but not the most frequently, as the aspect of the program the women liked most.

- For TIAVO, a small network of credit unions in Madagascar, responses of women were concentrated around the appropriateness and applicability of the education to their daily lives. They felt that they could and had already used what they had learned to prevent and deal with sickness in their children and to manage better their loans and businesses. Moreover, some of them spontaneously claimed they could advise other women in the community about what they had learned (January 2000).

- The members of another Credit with Education provider in Madagascar, Haingonala, also frequently cited the education and its practical relevance to their lives and those of other women in the community. They also valued the exchange of ideas with other members on how to address some of the problems they confronted (January 2000).

- Women members of Credit with Education offered by ACLAM (Action Contre La Misère) in Haiti were asked what they most appreciated about the education sessions. They cited not only their ability to adopt better health practices at home, but also the reduced expenses from fewer trips to the hospital due to their better prevention and management of illness (January 2001).

These assessments of client satisfaction show real appreciation of the value of the education relative to other components of Credit with Education. They also are instructive regarding how to improve client satisfaction with education, as well as the other components. Occasionally, women object to the length of the learning sessions, usually in the context of more general objections to the frequency and duration of their village bank meetings, because of the time taken away from their business activities. Most often, however, clients express their desire for *more* education covering a wider range of health and business topics.

Satisfaction with education relative to credit and savings opportunities does not necessarily translate to "demand," in the sense of willingness to pay for the educational services—or how much they would be willing to pay. Demand-related research has not been done, except in a minor way in Tanzania (see Box 2.3), where Credit with Education clients said they would pay extra for education, on top of a high interest rate for loans.

Some influential voices in the microfinance community have challenged the providers of education unified with microcredit to charge an extra fee for the education service. They say that if microcredit clients truly value the extra impacts offered through extra education, they will pay the real cost of the additional service. Yet Credit with Education providers have not sought to recover the additional cost of extra education by charging more for the unified service than would be charged for village banking alone. In part, providers have not wanted to, and in part they have not needed to charge extra. There are important philosophical issues involved in the decision not to charge extra for education. These issues are explored in Appendix B.

Impact on the Financial Bottom Line

The impacts reported were all achieved by Credit with Education programs committed to financial self-sufficiency. The follow-up round of the impact evaluation research in Ghana was conducted in 1996, when the Lower Pra Rural Bank, using entirely its own loan capital, had been offering Credit with Education for about four years. At that time, the program had an operating self-sufficiency ratio of 81 percent, meaning that the interest paid by borrowers covered 81 percent of the Lower Pra Rural Bank's costs of delivering Credit with Education as one of its several services to surrounding communities. These operating costs included financial costs, including interest on debt but not loan-loss reserve. As of June 2000, the program's reported operating self-sufficiency was 130 percent. CRECER, the Credit with Education provider in Bolivia, was one of three microcredit institutions profiled by David Gibbons and Jennifer Meehan in "The Microcredit Summit's Challenge: Working Towards Institutional Financial Self-Sufficiency while Maintaining a Commitment to Serving the Poorest Families."[20] CRECER's efficiency and sustainability ratios were comparable to, some better than, the other two institutions, which offered very little or no education in addition to financial services. At the end of 2000, CRECER's operating self-sufficiency ratio, including interest on debt and loan-loss reserve, was 106 percent.

Vor der Bruegge, Dickey, and Dunford[21] have done a cost-accounting analysis of three years of expenditure data from each of four different Credit with Education programs[22] to estimate the cost of education in addition to the cost of village banking. The analysis treats Credit with Education as a form of village banking with "extra education" beyond the education that village banking programs must provide members to help them form and manage their own village banks. Even without "extra education," village banking field agents are involved in several sessions of start-up training and then are present and providing guidance at most of the regular meetings of the village bank. Time and expenses for field agents (and their managers and trainers) to provide education in health, nutrition, family planning, and business management topics at the regular meetings were allocated to "extra education." These allocated costs represent a percentage of the time and expenses of local program staff spent in training, supervision, and administrative tasks and for technical assistance and training activities conducted in-country by U.S.-based technical and management advisors/trainers.

The three-year average "cost increase for extra education" varied from 5.9 percent in Bolivia to 9.6 percent in Burkina Faso, with intermediate values in Mali and Togo. For example, the annual cost per client served in Bolivia was $63.82. The cost analysis suggests that eliminating the "extra education" could save $3.51 per client per annum. Smith and Jain[23] report a Project HOPE estimate of 6 percent for extra education in its integrated microcredit-education programs in Ecuador and Honduras.

It is unlikely that eliminating the extra education would have significant impact on the costs of staff and capital equipment. The same numbers of field staff and vehicles seem to be required to maintain a village banking program even without the extra education. That is because the time saved by field staff not facilitating learning sessions at the regular meetings is insufficient to allow them, especially those serving dispersed rural communities, to serve more village banks, and thereby produce more revenue. The program manager of FOCCAS Uganda, a Credit with Education provider not included in this cost analysis, says, "Even without education, our field agents could not do more than the four [village banks] per day that they currently target." However, it is likely that eliminating the extra education could significantly reduce time and cost for internal supervision, training, and paperwork and for external technical assistance and training to support extra education (for an overall savings for the program of up to 10 percent).

The extra satisfaction and impact experienced by clients and their families and communities seem to justify this additional cost of extra education. Yet these four unified service programs in the cost analysis charge borrowers no more for the unified service than other group-based microcredit programs in the same countries charge for just credit and savings services. The philosophical rationale is discussed in Appendix B. The practical reason for not charging extra is that it has not been necessary for achieving financial sustainability. All four programs in the cost analysis were rapidly approaching operational self-sufficiency in their Credit with Education operations, and FUCEC-Togo and CRECER in Bolivia are currently very near or surpassing this goal. This means that all costs of unified operations and portfolio financing and reserve set-asides were nearly fully covered by interest revenue from the credit operations.

When we compare village banking with and without extra education, in terms of administrative and salary expense ratios, the providers of education do as well—even better in some respects. Woller[24] compared various performance indicators for nine of the best performing village banking programs reporting data to the *Microbanking Bulletin*, including three which provide extra education: Kafo Jiginew, CRECER, and Pro Mujer. The three integrated programs had the lowest administrative expense and salary expense ratios of the nine institutions. This indicates that the volume of lending in relationship to basic staffing and administrative expenses was relatively more efficient than for the other six village banking programs exclusively focused on microfinance. For the cost-per-borrower ratio, the three organizations placed first, fourth, and sixth, indicating the cost structure relative to the number of borrowers was as good or better than for village banking operations without extra education. The integrated service providers placed first, fourth, and seventh in terms of the staff productivity ratio, or the number of clients served per total staff.

Compared to all 22 village banking institutions reporting to the *Microbanking Bulletin*, all three integrated service providers out-perform the norm (average) for the administrative expense and salary expense ratios, and two of the three organizations out-perform the norm for the cost per borrower and staff productivity ratio. While education might add 6 to 10 percent to the administrative cost ratio, it is offset by the productivity gains made in the portfolio, which actually lead to lower administrative expense ratios.

These ratios can offer more insight than the operational or financial self-sufficiency ratios, since the latter are determined to a great extent by pricing of loans. For instance, Compartamos, a large-scale Mexican provider of village banking services without extra education, is currently 143.7 percent financially self-sufficient, but it has an administrative expense ratio of 62.6 percent, which is very high compared to CRECER's 36.4 percent and Pro Mujer's 37.8 percent. The reason that CRECER and Pro Mujer are not as financially self-sufficient is that they do not charge as much for their services to the poor—not that they are less efficient due to the education.

New High-Priority Applications

Microcredit as Vehicle for Promotion of Family Planning and HIV/AIDS Prevention

Credit with Education seems to offer great potential for large-scale, self-financing delivery of microfinance and education together in one efficient and effective service package. Beyond health and nutrition education, such unified service delivery strategies can and already do serve a wide variety of educational agendas. However, staying focused on public health education, there is growing interest but little documented experience in harnessing the potential of self-financing, unified service delivery to address two of the greatest public health challenges of our time: family planning and HIV/AIDS prevention.

Multiple, closely spaced pregnancies and HIV infection pose widespread and serious challenges to individuals, families, and society, especially in developing countries. Not only are the health and economy of the poor affected, often disastrously, these problems pose threats to the not-so-poor, who are highly vulnerable to financial setbacks due to broken health and death in the family. Too-frequent child-bearing and -caring by poorly nourished women often result in high levels of morbidity and mortality among mothers as well as infants and children. As HIV spreads relentlessly, adults in the prime of their productive and reproductive years grow ill and die due to HIV/AIDS or are dragged down by the unusual financial and time demands of illness and death in their extended families and their communities.

Microcredit institutions increasingly recognize their dependence on the health of their clients and their clients' families. Many acknowledge the challenging circumstances for clients playing the triple roles of wife, mother, and businesswoman. Local public health officials confirm that much of the risk to clients and microcredit institutions alike could be greatly reduced with the use of effective family planning methods. In some countries, the HIV/AIDS epidemic is so severe that it threatens microcredit institutions through reduced loan portfolio growth, decreased client retention, increased portfolio delinquency and increased draw-down from savings deposits, as well as death of experienced staff or the burdens on them of caring for dying relatives. In such environments, many microcredit institutions are asking how they can better serve their clients. It is within the managerial and financial capability of many microcredit institutions to provide an education service that builds on the enhanced self-confidence of borrowers in order to promote use of family planning methods, especially those that prevent transmission of HIV, and other relevant, healthful values and practices.

CRECER Provides Family Planning Education With Contraceptive Distribution in Bolivia

CRECER (Crédito con Educación Rural) provides Credit with Education services (as described in the preceding section, "Evidence of Impacts on Clients and Institutions," and the FUCEC-Togo case in Appendix A) to 24,692 clients, as of December 31, 2000—mostly women in mostly rural areas in five departments of Bolivia. Unlike the great majority of Credit with Education providers, CRECER was created specifically to provide Credit with Education, and to become financially self-sustaining in the process. It is now an unregulated Bolivian "financial NGO," unregulated because the Bolivian banking supervision agency effectively prohibits regulated financial institutions from delivering services other than *financial* services. In the future, CRECER is likely to diversify its services, but for now, Credit with Education is its sole service offering.

The general topics of CRECER's education component are similar to those in other Credit with Education programs worldwide. However, while most programs have long offered family planning education, CRECER was held back by the Bolivian government. Then, in the mid-1990s, new legislation launched the promotion of family planning and introduced modern contraceptives into the government's reproductive health services. CRECER used this opportunity to offer members of its village banks information on the most up-to-date options for family planning. In the normal learning sessions of village bank meetings, the CRECER field agent helps members consider how to use the information to make choices that will improve their lives. The sessions cover the male and female reproductive systems, clear and complete information on each of the methods approved by the Ministry of Health, and the benefits and possible side effects to consider. Members are encouraged to seek additional information and services from health service providers.

Like other Credit with Education providers, CRECER has restricted its nonfinancial services to group-based education, in order to minimize expenses beyond the costs of the village banking service. Providing additional services that require specialized staff and supplies can drive total program cost up sharply. However, with due regard for this caution, CRECER is now experimenting with a system for community-based distribution of contraceptives, because access to contraceptives is very limited for CRECER's mostly rural clients.

One member is identified in the village bank to receive additional training about the use of certain contraceptives. Once trained, this woman is authorized as a community-based distributor (CBD) to sell approved contraceptives to appropriate customers in her community. Her stock of contraceptives is provided at cost by CRECER (which buys them at subsidized prices from local providers) and replenished by the field agent as the CBD sells her stock. Government health regulations limit the items in the CBD's stock to condoms and vaginal spermicide. However, the CBD is given additional training that prepares her to offer counseling in the use of and contraindications for a broader range of methods that couples might want to consider. She is also linked to a local family planning service provider through a referral system. This referral system expands the range of methods the CBD can "offer" to clients.

Of 329 CBDs trained by September 2000, 260 remained active as CBDs in about one-third of the communities served by CRECER. A recent assessment of this CBD experiment found that CRECER trainers do conduct in-service workshops for the CBDs, that the CBDs do talk effectively and accurately about the methods they know, and that the CBDs do refer cases to the formal health system. The participatory education by CBDs appears to be desensitizing the topic of family planning and thereby creating a breakthrough in women's willingness to talk about reproductive health issues. The assessment also found that CBDs are the leading sellers of contraceptives in the rural areas they serve. Even so, the volume of sales is very low, in part because the two types of contraceptives the CBDs can sell are in low demand (the spermicide tablets are preferred over condoms), despite the education provided. Nonetheless, the credibility of the CBDs as family planning educators seems to be enhanced by their ability to sell contraceptives and to counsel and refer people to good-quality reproductive health services.

CRECER's objective was to make the CBD system a self-financing service. The marginal costs of supporting CBDs amount to less than 0.5 percent of CRECER's total operating expenses, but the low volume of sales and a government ceiling on contraceptive prices make it unlikely the CBD service can become financially self-sustaining. Nonetheless, motivated by its members' response to the CBD service, CRECER is committed to bear the costs that cannot be covered through sales of contraceptives. Primarily external grants for this purpose, rather than the interest paid by all borrowers, is likely to be CRECER's strategy to cover costs for the service that can directly benefit only a subset of CRECER members.

FOCCAS Uganda Provides Education for Family Planning and Prevention of HIV Infection

FOCCAS Uganda (Foundation for Credit and Community Assistance) is an unregulated Ugandan microcredit institution founded for the initial purpose of providing Credit with Education. FOCCAS currently offers village banking together with health, nutrition, family planning, and better business education to 13,048 women living, as of December 31, 2000, in rural and peri-urban areas of four districts of eastern Uganda.

Like CRECER, FOCCAS is providing family planning education to its women members and linking them to services provided by others. When the FOCCAS field agent has nearly completed the education module on family planning, field staff from Marie Stopes (a U.K.-based family planning support organization) attend the next regular group meeting. They again review the various family planning methods and answer any questions, with particular emphasis on the more technical aspects with which the FOCCAS field agents may be less conversant. They then provide access, on the spot, to any of the contraceptive methods that the women may have decided upon (including tubal ligation!). This is still a pilot effort, but it seems to go well, and Marie Stopes has committed to providing this service to any FOCCAS village bank that completes the FOCCAS family planning education module. Marie Stopes was having outreach problems in eastern Uganda, until FOCCAS provided a ready network of women's groups for them to serve. This arrangement does not ensure sustainable access to family planning services, but it does help those women who are ready to take the next step, and it reinforces the messages that FOCCAS staff have been delivering.

Given the high prevalence of HIV/AIDS in Uganda, the need for FOCCAS to address the epidemic is a high priority. Both prevention and mitigation services are necessary, but FOCCAS could not realistically offer healthcare and other mitigation services while aiming to depend solely on revenues from its credit operations. Rather, FOCCAS chose to focus on HIV/AIDS prevention by providing FOCCAS members with the best available information and practical wisdom for reducing their risk of HIV exposure. The field agent also helps members think about HIV/AIDS in the context of the community, to better support those individuals dying of the disease and to encourage others to change their behavior to prevent new infection.

Having access to information does not ensure its use. The field agent must be prepared to address the reasons why women have not adopted or may not adopt beneficial new practices. It is a real challenge to identify and respond to the major obstacles to behavior change in relation to HIV/AIDS. For example, how can a woman act upon her new understanding when she is often not given a choice regarding sex? What should a woman do when she wants to have children but her husband indulges in high-risk behavior or is known to be HIV positive? The field agent facilitates a process of problem-solving, decision-making, and motivation to action that often involves a kind of psychological journey with a number of steps needed before making the decision to change ideas or practices and form new habits. Teaching and maintaining good group facilitation skills among field agents is central to successful behavior-change education. Fortunately, the training for group facilitation serves the microcredit component as well as the education component.

The proper selection of field staff and their training in facilitation skills and HIV/AIDS content is only the beginning. Also required are systems for 1) supervision of education, 2) assessment and feedback on the quality of delivery, 3) monitoring the education impact, and 4) feedback from clients on the education content and quality. Such systems are available and complementary to the systems currently used by most microfinance institutions, but effort is required up-front to adapt the systems, put them in place, and provide the necessary staff skills.

Although FOCCAS restricts its nonfinancial services to education, it recognizes that education alone is insufficient to properly address the HIV/AIDS crisis in eastern Uganda. In the near future, FOCCAS intends to facilitate member access to complementary HIV/AIDS services such as testing and counseling. This will require FOCCAS to identify appropriate local service providers, introduce members to these services, and maintain relationships with these providers.

Challenges of Implementation

Unified vs. Parallel Service Delivery?

The preceding summary of impacts and opportunities of the unified-service delivery model, exemplified by Credit with Education, seems to show that society is better served when microcredit and health/nutrition education are delivered together to the same very poor people, especially women. Moreover, *unified service delivery is operationally feasible. It can produce qualitatively similar, yet more diverse and potentially synergistic, impacts than either microcredit or education alone. And it can do so at considerably less total cost than if both microcredit and education are delivered in parallel by different delivery systems. But how difficult is it actually to run a unified service compared to a parallel service?*

Smith and Jain[25] point out that evidence of complementary microcredit and education outcomes says little about the merits of unifying their delivery within one organization. What is good for society is not necessarily good for a service-delivery business, and vice versa. An organization trying to operate simultaneously in two very different sectors of development activity may compromise its effectiveness and efficiency in one or both sectors. The logic is that specialization in one or the other heightens effectiveness and efficiency; a generalist, multi-sectoral approach decreases effectiveness and efficiency. On the other hand, the impact evidence collected so far does not support this idea that quality of either microcredit or health education *must* be compromised for the sake of unification.

Nonetheless, intersectoral compromise may be very real for some organizations. As the examples in Boxes 2.2 and 2.3 illustrate, what can work well for one organization may not work for another. If managers and field staff are too preoccupied with the credit operations, the education will suffer from neglect (see Box 2.2).

Even if the education component is highly valued by the service clients, they will abandon the unified service when the microcredit service fails to meet their needs or imposes "client-unfriendly" conditions on borrowers (see Box 2.3).

In both cases, it is likely that *fixation on short-term achievement of financial sustainability in the credit operations worked against success in the education service, and against the best interests of the clients.* It can, and often has, worked the other way. *A unified-service delivery system obsessed*

Box 2.2
Quality of the Education Matters:
Supervision and Feedback

The positive changes in mothers' health/nutrition knowledge and practice measured in Bolivia were not nearly as dramatic as those seen in Ghana. In the Ghana site, over the course of the multi-year research, the nutritional status of participants' children showed improvement relative to non-clients' children but this was not seen in Bolivia. An important difference between the Ghana and Bolivia programs was the quality and quantity of education that women received at their regular village bank meetings. Prior to and during the study period in Bolivia, program management showed weak commitment to the education component due to preoccupation with other implementation challenges primarily related to program expansion and internal credit controls. Supervision of field agents was less consistent than in Ghana and field agent turnover was higher. The majority of village banks included in the impact study had a series of field agents working with them, which resulted in inconsistent quality for delivery of health/nutrition education. These findings from the study led Bolivia program management, and other Credit with Education providers, to give better attention and resources to recruitment, training, supervision, and support for field agents, including monetary incentives for complete, good-quality delivery of the education.

Box 2.3
Quality of the Credit Matters:
Client Satisfaction and Retention

In Tanzania, an organization conducted a trial addition of better business and family planning education to its existing village banking services. Several months into the trial, virtually all of the women in village banks getting the education said, when asked, they would pay an additional fee for the education. This is particularly notable since there was widespread sentiment among clients that the interest charged by the program was already too high. But "liking" the education is not enough. This trial was ultimately abandoned when external economic shocks, exacerbated by a variety of lending program policies unfriendly to clients, led to extremely high dropout rates. Of the 506 clients surveyed just before the trial began, only 76 women (15 percent) were still with the same village bank 16 months later. Twenty-one (42 percent) of the 51 village banks included in the trial were no longer operating. While field staff and clients alike agreed that the education was beneficial, it was not enough to keep women in a program whose credit terms and policies (interest rate, mandatory group size, repayment terms, and so forth) imposed costs or risks that outweighed clients' perceived benefits of participation.

with meeting the educational and other needs of clients could easily work against the long-term sustainability of the credit operations, and against the best interests of the clients.

It is a significant challenge to find a working balance between concern for the microcredit service (and the institution it supports) and concern for the education (and the client needs it serves). This duality is not nearly as troublesome when field staff and managers can specialize in one service or the other, such as when two specialized programs or organizations are delivering microcredit and education in parallel.

A microfinance institution considering delivery of additional services in nonfinancial service sectors should ask itself the following questions:

- What additional services are required by the institution's own development objectives?
- What additional services are required to satisfy the needs and wants of the intended clientele?

- What are the feasible options for providing additional services that meet both institutional objectives and client objectives? Links to other, nonfinancial service providers? Creation of a separate institution to provide nonfinancial services? Creation of a separate nonfinancial service unit within the institution itself? Unification of the nonfinancial services with the existing financial service delivery system?

The answers cannot be given here. They depend on the specific situation: the microfinance institution, the clientele, and the other institutions currently or potentially serving this clientele. The unification option is the most demanding, but it also may be the only option or the one most likely to be sustainable in the long term. Even then, *unification is advisable only when the institution wants to add one or more forms of education to microfinance services for relatively large borrower groups that meet regularly with field agents of the institution.*

The education should adhere to principles of effective adult learning, but the content can be varied or singular and drawn from structured curricula or facilitated exchanges of knowledge among the clients themselves. A mix of approaches, as in Credit with Education, can be used. But the education program, whatever it is, must be manageable by the same people, clients and staff, who are involved in the management of the financial services.

As an organization considers the unified option, it should understand why this option is more demanding and be realistic in assessing its commitment to unification.

Analysis of Specific Cases: FUCEC-Togo, BRAC, and Pro Mujer

The three cases detailed in Appendix A illustrate the diversity of real-world responses to the implementation challenges of the unified delivery model. All three organizations share a commitment to offer both group-based lending and various types of education and other services to very poor women. And all three are attempting to do this for the long term, addressing the difficult issues of institutional and financial sustainability in the provision of financial and social services.

FUCEC-Togo is offering Credit with Education as one among several financial products offered by its member credit unions. The unified microfinance-education product reaches rural women who would not have been reached otherwise by the credit unions. There are specialized Credit with Education field agents, but each one is responsible for all the services—microfinance, health and nutrition education, and better business education—provided to the Credit with Education women's groups assigned to that field agent. FUCEC-Togo reports a high level of satisfaction with the performance of the Credit with Education product, both because this line of business approaches profitability for the federation and because the impact on rural women appears to satisfy both the women's and the credit unions' social objectives. Commitment to the fully unified delivery model remains strong.

BRAC provides multiple services to a huge clientele throughout Bangladesh. Microfinance, education, health, and social services are offered to the same clients—97 percent of them women—through functionally independent, sector-specific service programs, each with its own administration and staff and revenue stream. In the past, the same BRAC staff were responsible for all services to their assigned groups. However, "the rigors of running an efficient credit program meant that other sectors and tasks tended to be neglected. Moreover, BRAC realized that a [field agent] who is good at managing credit may not necessarily be suitable for carrying out social awareness-raising programs and vice versa."

BRAC acknowledges that coordination between different programs is sometimes difficult and that the total cost for separate management and staff for each program is higher than if there were a single set of managers and staff for all services. The microfinance program is financially self-sufficient. There is some current and potential cross-subsidy of the education and training programs from BRAC's microfinance and sub-sector development programs such as poultry, silk culture, social forestry, and others. But education and training programs are funded predominantly by external grants, and partial dependence on external funding is expected for the foreseeable future. Evidence of the importance of a holistic approach to development and of specific positive impacts on clients of the combined services maintains BRAC's commitment to providing a broad package of services.

Pro Mujer serves poor women in peri-urban areas of Bolivia with a package of village banking loans and savings and also business development and health services. Both of the latter two provide education at the village bank meetings held at a local Pro Mujer office called a Focus Center and through individualized counseling, including clinical services for reproductive health.

Services are delivered by operating teams, each led by a Credit Officer/ Educator, who supervises all staff assistants providing services at a Focus Center. Credit Assistants advise the client groups on the evaluation, granting, and tracking of loans. Business Assistants provide training and technical assistance for business development. Health Assistants provide preventive health training and primary healthcare services. In addition, there is a business technician and a physician who give technical help to the personnel of these services and coordinate with the Credit Officer/Educators, whose supervision is operational, not technical. Thus, management of the three services is unified from the Focus Center manager on up to the Executive Director. In contrast, the staffing and technical support for delivery of services at the Focus Centers is provided by specialized staff working in parallel.

Nonfinancial services represent 30 percent of costs during fiscal year 2000. Only 20 percent of costs for nonfinancial services were covered by income directly generated by these services. In the future it is planned that financial income and income from nonfinancial services will cover the costs of nonfinancial services. But, until this is achieved, Pro Mujer has sustainability plans based on contributions from the community, its own funds, and new financing. The sustainability of nonfinancial services is an institutional priority because it fully favors clients and because it qualitatively strengthens and improves the performance of the credit service.

In each case, the organization is committed to full financial self-sufficiency of the microfinance operations, but satisfying the broader needs of the clients is as important, it seems, as financial self-sufficiency of the overall institution. Where they differ is in their deployment of managers and field staff. Only FUCEC-Togo is using the same managers and field agents to deliver both microfinance and nonfinancial services, and only FUCEC-Togo is close to full recovery, from the clients, of all costs for the full range of services. But BRAC and Pro Mujer, being willing to go after external funding, offer a broader range of services.

Conclusion

In writing this chapter, I have tried to be objective, although I currently lead an organization heavily committed to integration, and more particularly, unification. It has been a humbling learning experience. There is a wealth of experience in the development community that is barely revealed here—or anywhere else. And much of it seems contradictory. The more I investigate the issues of integrating microcredit with other services, the more I understand the difficulty of the task and the more I realize how little I know how to predict what will work and why.

Design of the delivery system certainly matters, as do competencies of system managers and staff, their policies, procedures, and information for management decisions, and the routines of recruitment, training, and supervision of the delivery agents who make direct contact with the clients/beneficiaries of the system. All of the things we talk about in the microcredit community matter, because microcredit is the controlling—that is, financing—partner in most integrated models. But it seems to me there is a very important factor that we talk about very little—human will.

I am continually impressed by the will of the people for whom we design and implement microcredit and other development services. It is a tribute to the power of their will to survive and succeed that the poor turn the paltry resources and opportunities we offer into something useful and meaningful in their lives. When successful, what we *will* to offer resonates with the *will* of the poor. There seems to be a mysterious concordance of wills. As the old expression in English says, "Where there's a will, there's a way." But it has to be on both sides of the exchange. Of course, will on both sides is insufficient by itself, but it is a *necessary* condition for success. Clearly, microcredit has created, or stumbled into, this mysterious concordance of wills many times, perhaps more often recently than we've seen in other sectors of development. But it is a common mistake to assume that even a microcredit service adhering to the best of practices, yet disembodied from the will of the people who provide them and the will of the people who use them, is guaranteed to be successful.

So it seems to be with integration of microcredit with other development services. Where there's a will, on both sides, there's a way. Conversely, if there is not the will on the part of microcredit managers to achieve financial and institutional sustainability, they will not. If there is not the will to force their way through the obstacles to reaching the poor, they will not. If there is not the will to meet the needs and even consumer demand of the poor for nonfinancial services, they will not. If there is not the will to link microcredit with others who have the will to provide nonfinancial services, they will not. If there is not the will to find the grant funding to support separate but parallel systems of delivering both microcredit and nonfinancial services to the poor, they will not. And if there is not the will to unify different-sector services in one delivery system, unification will fail. There is nothing wrong with lacking a certain will, but we must understand how this will or lack of will actually shapes our perception of the feasibility of a particular proposal and, should we decide to give it a try, the chances for its success.

There are many things that can support or sap the will of programmers considering the unified model of service delivery. Freedom from Hunger has perceived that parallel delivery of microcredit and health/nutrition education is unsustainable, due to grant dependence, and that sustainability of individual programs is crucial for creating enough of them to eventually reach the many tens of millions of people who need both types of service. Hence our commitment to the less expensive but more difficult unified model. When our implementing collaborators in Credit with Education have shared this commitment to unify microcredit with education for better food and nutrition security, such as CRECER, FOCCAS, FUCEC-Togo, and many others, they have maintained the unified model even without our assistance. Without a lasting commitment to public health or other social impacts, some have dropped the education component altogether when the external funding was gone and the inevitable problems arose.

However, it is clear that the pure unified model is not the only way to pursue important social objectives. BRAC tried a unified delivery model in the past and found it too difficult to maintain, especially when it could support a more straightforward parallel model with grants available to such a visibly successful organization in a country that attracts massive international aid flows. Perhaps Pro Mujer has found a good, medium-cost compromise—unified at the level of supervision, parallel at the level of field staff in contact with clients. The will of Pro Mujer to find grant support for this hybrid model is bolstered by the will to self-finance, eventually, with their own program-generated revenues.

Here is my advice to the reader who asks, "What to do?" Do what you *will*.

Notes

1. For more information go to: www.paris21.org/betterworld/setting.
2. Barbara MkNelly and Christopher Dunford, *Are Credit and Savings Services Effective Against Hunger and Malnutrition? A Literature Review and Analysis*, Freedom from Hunger Research Paper No. 1 (Davis, Calif.: Freedom from Hunger, 1996). All Freedom from Hunger publications are available from: info@freefromhunger.org.
3. CGAP, *Linking Microfinance and Safety Net Programs to Include the Poorest: The Case of IGVGD in Bangladesh*, CGAP Focus Note, no. 21 (May 2001).
4. Credit with Education is a unified microcredit-education strategy first developed by Freedom from Hunger in 1989–90 for the purpose of improving household food security and child nutrition. It comprises elements of the Grameen Bank, FINCA village banking, USAID-sponsored child survival programming, and principles of informal adult education. A more complete description of the model was published in the adult education journal *Convergence* 28 (3): 26–35, 1995 (free copies of the article are available from info@freefromhunger.org). As of December 31, 2000, NGOs and community-based financial institutions in fourteen countries were implementing Credit with Education, with past or current assistance from Freedom from Hunger.

   In aggregate, these implementing organizations were reaching 166,642 women, of whom 142,929 were taking current loans averaging $67 each. The total amount of outstanding loans was US$9.59 million, and the total amount of savings was US$1.97 million. The weighted average for operating self-sufficiency, of the implementing organizations reporting complete revenue and expenditure data for the previous six months, was 92 percent. Overall portfolio at risk was 4.21 percent. Other versions of Credit with Education have been developed by other organizations in the past decade without Freedom from Hunger assistance, notably by World Relief Corporation and Project HOPE.

5. Professor Muhammad Yunus, founder of the Grameen Bank, has related to the author that the "Sixteen Decisions" were formulated and promulgated in response to early demand from the women clients of the Bank. In fact, client representatives soon requested more than sixteen "decisions," but Professor Yunus saw that the social change agenda of the Bank could not be allowed to expand further without eventually interfering with the primary work of staff to provide microcredit loans and recover them.

6. Jan Kingsbury, comp., "Directory 2000: Integrated Service Delivery Programs of Member Organizations," Credit with Education Learning Exchange, 2000.

7. Candace Nelson, Barbara MkNelly, Kathleen Stack, and Lawrence Yanovitch (with assistance from the Poverty Lending Working Group of SEEP and participants at the International Conference of Village Bank Practitioners), *Village Banking: The State of the Practice*, Small Enterprise Education and Promotion (SEEP) Network and the United Nations Development Fund for Women (Washington, D.C.: Pact Publishing, 1996).

8. See endnote 4 above.

9. Michael Kevane, *Qualitative Impact Study of Credit with Education in Burkina Faso*, Freedom from Hunger Research Paper No. 3 (Davis,Calif.: Freedom from Hunger, 1996).

   Barbara MkNelly and Christopher Dunford, *Impact of Credit with Education on Mothers and Their Young Children's Nutrition: Lower Pra Rural Bank Credit with Education Program in Ghana*, Freedom from Hunger Research Paper No. 4 (Davis, Calif.: Freedom from Hunger, 1998).

   Barbara MkNelly and Christopher Dunford, *Impact of Credit with Education on Mothers and Their Young Children's Nutrition: CRECER Credit with Education Program in Bolivia*, Freedom from Hunger Research Paper No. 5 (Davis, Calif.: Freedom from Hunger, 1999).

   Barbara MkNelly and Ayele Foly, "Preliminary Evidence from the Freedom from Hunger from Hunger/World Relief Collaborative Evaluation in Burkina Faso," presented at the Credit with Education Learning Exchange, Millwood, Va., August 1997.

   Barbara MkNelly and Karen Lippold. "Practitioner-led Impact Assessment: A Test in Mali." Paper submitted to USAID by AIMS (Washington, D.C.: Management Systems International, 1998). Also available from: aims@msi-inc.com.

   Barbara MkNelly, Chatree Watetip, Cheryl A. Lassen, and Christopher Dunford, *Preliminary Evidence that Integrated Financial and Educational Services Can Be Effective against Hunger and Malnutrition*, Freedom from Hunger Research Paper No. 2 (Davis, Calif.: Freedom from Hunger, 1996).

   Stephen C. Smith and Sanjay Jain, "Village Banking and Maternal and Child Health: Theory and Evidence from Ecuador and Honduras," Working Paper, George Washington University Department of Economics, Washington, D.C., 1999. (Also to be found on the Microfinance Gateway at www.ids.ac.uk/cgap/static/1821.)

10. In both studies (MkNelly and Dunford, 1998, 1999—cited above in endnote 9), two major survey and anthropometric (heights and weights) data collection rounds were carried out—with different mother/child pairs participating in the two time periods. A quasi-experimental design was applied at the community level to minimize possible bias. Following baseline data collection, nineteen study communities were matched and then randomly assigned to either a "program" or "control" group, with the latter not to receive Credit with Education until after completion of the evaluation research. Baseline respondents were later classified as future "participants" or "nonparticipants" depending on whether they joined the program, when and if it was offered in their community. Three sample groups of women with children under three years of age were included in the follow-up research: 1) Credit with Education program participants of at least one year; 2) nonparticipants in program communities; and 3) residents in control communities selected *not* to receive the program for the period of the study. Women for the two nonparticipant groups were randomly selected from comprehensive lists of all women with children less than three years of age. Program impact is evaluated by comparing the magnitude and direction of change in the responses and measurements between the two data collection rounds—program participants versus nonparticipants and residents in control communities.

11. Jennefer Sebstad and Gregory Chen. 1996. "Overview of Studies on the Impact of Microenterprise Credit." AIMS Paper (Washington, D.C.: Management Sciences International, 1996). Available under AIMS Project Publications at: www.mip.org. Barbara MkNelly and Christopher Dunford. *Are Credit and Savings Services Effective Against Hunger and Malnutrition? A Literature Review and Analysis.* Freedom from Hunger Research Paper No. 1 (Davis, Calif.: Freedom from Hunger, 1996). Manoha Sharma and Gertrud Schrieder, "Impact of Finance on Food Security and Poverty Alleviation—A Review and Synthesis of Empirical Evidence." Presentation paper for "Innovations in Micro-Finance for the Rural Poor: Exchange of Knowledge and Implications for Policy" Workshop organized by DSE (Berlin, Germany), IFPRI (Washington, D.C.) and IFAD (Rome, Italy) in Ghana, November 8–13, 1998. Available from: M.Sharma@cgiar.org. Manfred Zeller and Manohar Sharma, "Rural Finance and Poverty Alleviation." *Food Policy Report* (Washington, D.C.: International Food Policy Research Institute, 1998). Available from: ifpri@cgnet.com.

12. Maria Teresa Cerqueira and Christine M. Olson, "Nutrition Education in Developing Countries: An Examination of Recent Successful Projects." Chap. 4 in *Child Growth and Nutrition in Developing Countries*, edited by P. Pinstrup-Andersen, D. Pelletier, and H. Alderman (Ithaca, N.Y.: Cornell University Press, 1995). I. Contento, G. I. Balch, Y. L. Bronner, L. A. Lytle, S. K. Maloney, C. M. Olson, and S. S. Swadener, "The Effectiveness of Nutrition Education and Implications for Nutrition Education Policy, Programs and Research: A Review of Research." *J. Nutrition Education* 27, no. 6 (1995): Special Issue.

13. Stephen C. Smith and Sanjay Jain, "Village Banking and Maternal and Child Health: Theory and Evidence from Ecuador and Honduras," Working Paper, George Washington University Department of Economics, Washington, D.C., 1999. Also to be found on the Microfinance Gateway at: www.ids.ac.uk/cgap/static/1821.

14. Sidney R. Schuler and Syed M. Hashemi, "Credit Programs, Women's Empowerment, and Contraceptive Use in Bangladesh," *Studies in Family Planning* 25, no. 2 (1994): 65–79.

15. To corroborate Freedom from Hunger's longitudinal research study in Ghana (MkNelly and Dunford, 1998), an independent study (unpublished research by Dr. Margaret Armar-Klemesu of the Noguchi Memorial Institute for Medical Research, University of Ghana, Legon) investigated dietary intake of children nine to twenty months old who were in the Ghana follow-up round of data collection. Dietary intake was assessed by the mother's twenty-four-hour recall of all breastfeeding episodes and all meals and snacks consumed by the child on two non-consecutive days. Mothers identified measures used to offer food to the children, how much was offered, and proportions consumed in reference to local measures and fist size. Samples of all foods reported were taken to the lab for calorie and nutrient content analysis using appropriate food composition tables.

16. Barbara MkNelly and Kathleen E. Stack, "Loan Size Growth and Sustainability in Village Banking Programmes," *Small Enterprise Development* 9, no. 2 (1998): 4–16.
    Carolyn Barnes, Gayle Morris, and Gary Gaile, "An Assessment of the Impact of Microfinance Services in Uganda: Baseline Findings," AIMS Paper. (Washington, D.C.: Management Systems International, 1998).

17. See endnote 10.

18. Barbara MkNelly and Karen Lippold, "Practitioner-led Impact Assessment: A Test in Mali," Paper submitted to USAID by AIMS (Washington, D.C.: Management Systems International, 1998). Available from: aims@msi-inc.com.

19. Anastase Nteziyaremye, Kathleen E. Stack, and Barbara MkNelly, *Impact of Credit with Education on Recruitment of New Members to the Credit Unions of the Kafo Jiginew and Nyèsigiso Federations in Mali*, Freedom from Hunger Research Paper in draft, (Davis, Calif.: Freedom from Hunger, April 2001).

20. David S. Gibbons and Jennifer W. Meehan, "The Microcredit Summit Challenge: Working Towards Institutional Financial Self-Sufficiency while Maintaining a Commitment to Serving the Poorest Families," (Washington, D.C.: Microcredit Summit Campaign, 2000). Available online at: www.microcreditsummit.org/papers/papers.htm.

21. Ellen Vor der Bruegge, Joan E. Dickey, and Christopher Dunford. 1999, *Cost of Education in the Freedom from Hunger Version of Credit with Education Implementation*, Freedom from Hunger Research Paper No. 6 (Davis, Calif.: Freedom from Hunger, 1999).

22. The four Credit with Education programs studied were implemented by CRECER (Crédito con Educación Rural) in Bolivia, RCPB (Réseau des Caisses Populaires du

Burkina) in Burkina Faso, Nyèsigiso in Mali, and FUCEC-Togo (Fédération des Unions de Coopératives d'Epargne et de Crédit du Togo) for the three calendar years 1995–97.

23. See endnote 13.

24. Gary Woller, "Reassessing the Financial Viability of Village Banking: Past Performance and Future Prospects," *Microbanking Bulletin,* 5 (September 2000): 3–8.

25. See endnote 13. Also, Stephen C. Smith, 2001, "Microcredit and Health Programs: To Integrate or Not to Integrate?" pp. 41–50 in R. Rodriguez-Garcia, J. A. Macinko, and W. F. Waters, eds. *Microenterprise Development for Better Health Outcomes,* in series *Contributions in Economics and Economic History* (Westport, Conn.: Greenwood Press, 2001): 41–50.

APPENDIX A:
THREE CASE STUDIES

Three organizations with different experiences in integrating delivery of different-sector services were invited to describe their integrated-services delivery systems. The three case studies are presented more or less in the words of the three organizations, with editing—approved by each organization—to fit a common format.

A Case of Unified Delivery by Credit Unions:
Fédération des Unions de Coopératives d'Epargne et de Crédit du Togo (FUCEC-Togo)

FUCEC-Togo[a] is the Togolese credit union league governed by a board of directors elected by the member credit unions, called COOPECs (Coopératives d'Epargne et de Crédit). The first COOPECs were founded in the 1970s. Each COOPEC is a financial cooperative governed by a board of directors elected by the cooperative members (one member, one vote).

The COOPECs provide the typical savings and credit services of a credit union. In addition, since 1996, an increasing number of COOPECs are providing a service to very poor Togolese women through a FUCEC-sponsored program called Crédit-Epargne avec Education (Service CE/E). The service is provided through groups of eighteen to thirty (average twenty-four) women, which are called Groupements d'Interêt Economique et Social (GIES). Within each GIES, members organize themselves as solidarity groups of four to five individuals and elect a management committee to lead the whole GIES.

The GIES service delivery model is a variant of Credit with Education. A GIES meets in its own community with a FUCEC *promotrice* (field agent) for one to two hours each meeting—weekly for the first few loan cycles (sixteen weeks each), then biweekly as the group demonstrates its reliability. One promotrice meets with the group for the joint purposes of providing savings, credit, and educational services at the same meeting. The GIES are generally located in rural areas served by public transportation once a week. Therefore, the promotrices travel to their meetings on motorcycles provided by the Service CE/E.

The promotrice helps the GIES register itself to receive the Service CE/E and provides orientation training in five two-hour weekly sessions. During the first few loan cycles, the promotrice tends to lead the meetings while encouraging members to participate. This leadership role becomes progressively a facilitating role for the more mature groups (with advanced loan cycles), allowing the GIES management committee to take on their group leadership responsibilities. A successful field agent must ensure this transfer of responsibilities within three to six loan cycles.

FUCEC hires, trains, and supervises the promotrices. They are assigned to form and manage the GIESs of the participating COOPECs, which are too small in staff and service area to employ and supervise a full-time promotrice. Before assignment to a program area, the promotrice is provided two weeks of professional orientation to be well equipped to investigate villages to determine potential for the Service CE/E, to promote the program to rural women, and to form groups of women who want to join. The promotrice is trained in adult education and training techniques. The program trainer conducts most of the trainings, but for some specific trainings the FUCEC program benefits from external assistance from Freedom from Hunger or PLAN International Togo.

Microcredit Services

The Service CE/E made its first loans in April 1996. The value of loans outstanding at December 31, 2000, was US$1,470,000 to 13,540 active borrowers (average loan size was US$109) in 550 GIES-served by twenty-one promotrices. Loan funds are provided by FUCEC as investments from its central liquidity fund. This fund is composed of deposits of all member COOPECs and serves the liquidity management needs of all member COOPECs. The ultimate sources of these funds are the savings deposits of COOPEC members, the great majority of whom do not participate in a GIES.

GIES members are not required to borrow but 98 percent had loans at the end of 2000. A borrower must:

- be a member of a GIES (including payment of member fees);
- have a minimum amount of savings on deposit in the group account with the COOPEC;
- have completed the pre-membership training;
- regularly attend GIES meetings;
- have no repayment problems; and
- do an economic activity deemed profitable enough by her solidarity group to allow weekly repayment of the loan.

Educational Services

To receive education from the Service CE/E, women must be GIES members, attend the weekly or biweekly meetings, and be a current saver. Topics covered deal with health and nutrition (diarrhea prevention and management, breastfeeding, infant and child feeding, immunization and family planning), better business development ("Increasing your sales" and "Knowing your real profit"), and GIES management.

Almost every GIES meeting, except when loans are disbursed by the promotrice or repaid in full by the group, includes a learning session. Each learning session takes about half an hour. Each topic, like family planning, requires several learning sessions spread over several meetings, generally concentrated in one "loan cycle" of sixteen weeks duration. Learning sessions are led by the promotrice with assistance of the women in the groups. She uses short "dramas" and sometimes visual images to introduce the subject and various discussion facilitation methods to encourage everyone's contribution to develop and convey the key message. The sources of education materials and technical information, including updates and upgrades, have been Freedom from Hunger and the Togolese Ministry of Health.

One of the more recently introduced education topics of the Service CE/E is family planning. This topic is the favorite among all CE/E members; women are very engaged by the family planning learning sessions. The topic is taught through drama, such as the one about Mouzou and his wife Sena; this couple has seven children. They all become sick at the same time while Mouzou is away. Sena takes them to a health center, where she is given a prescription for medicine, but she holds the prescription for Mouzou to get filled. Days later, Mouzou comes home and finds Sena very sad. He asks what is her problem. She shows him the prescription, but as she expected, Mouzou prefers to go for traditional medicine. While struggling to get proper treatment for her children, Sena is visited by Afi, a former classmate. Afi hardly recognizes Sena, because she has changed so much since her marriage. To help her friend, Afi pays Sena's debts and also shares family planning information with Sena. Then Sena shares this information with Mouzou. The drama closes with the promotrice coming in and explaining a variety of methods of family planning, not only to Mouzou and Sena, but also to their whole community.

This story stimulates very animated discussion, because the women see themselves so clearly in the person of Sena. The methods of family planning introduced are hormonal pills, Norplant implants, quarterly DMPA injections, condoms, the IUD, and others. Women are referred to the nearest health center for more information and access to these methods. As a result of the family planning learning sessions, most GIES members are proud to show off the Norplant implants in their arms!

Evidence of Impacts on Clients and the Program

FUCEC selects communities to receive the Service CE/E because of their reasonable proximity to member COOPECs and their relative remoteness from transportation corridors and cities, reaching out to communities where no financial institution or NGO is active. People in these communities are very poor farmers living on their crops. As further evidence of their relative poverty, GIES members in some of these communities are still borrowing no more than US$40 after ten sixteen-week loans from the program.

Positive impact for GIES members has been documented by an external impact study conducted in February 2001 by two Togolese consultants. The main change in the lives of GIES members is financial. Families are not only sending children to school more easily but they can take them to the hospital while sick. The program has also affected the social life in families. Women receive more respect in their communities, especially from their husbands. They are more recognized as financial contributors to their households.

The program accounts for costs of delivering financial and educational services together because the two services are so unified in the work of program staff and their supervisors and trainers. As of September 30, 2000, income from credit operations covered 94 percent of the unified costs of the Service CE/E. Grant funding for start-ups in new areas has been provided by both PLAN International and Freedom from Hunger. Technical assistance that is funded externally, such as training by Freedom from Hunger, is not included as revenue or expense in the tracking of program costs.

Its experience with the Service CE/E has convinced FUCEC that education added to small loans and savings is essential for changing the lives of poor people in rural communities. Despite difficult economic conditions that limit the potential of their microenterprises, poor women have stayed with the program, according to FUCEC, because they enjoy fellowship with others and the information they receive during learning sessions. This has helped the financial self-sufficiency of the program as well as the women. In addition, FUCEC has become convinced that the financial and educational services can be efficiently and effectively delivered together by the same promotrices, who were serving an astounding average of twenty-six GIESs each!

A Case of Parallel Service Delivery: BRAC (Bangladesh Rural Advancement Committee)

BRAC[b] is a private, nonprofit, nongovernmental organization, founded in 1972 by the current Executive Director, Mr. Fazle Hasan Abed. Initially responding to the devastation caused by the Independence War in 1971,

BRAC soon focused on sustainable development and empowerment of the poor in rural areas of Bangladesh through microcredit, health, education, and training programs.

The BRAC Development Programme (BDP)

In total, BRAC had 3.64 million Village Organization (VO) members in all sixty-four districts of Bangladesh at the end of 2000, 97 percent of whom were women. Within a village, a VO is composed of seven to eight BRAC groups of five, which are formed by individuals to provide each other social collateral as a joint-liability group. Members are recruited by BRAC staff, with the requirement that member households meet three criteria: ownership of less than fifty decimals of land; sale of manual labor to make a living; and total assets amounting to less than the value of fifty decimals of land.

BRAC arranges weekly and monthly meetings with the VO members. Weekly meetings generally focus on credit operations: to collect savings, to decide who should get loans and for what purpose, and to make loan repayments. The monthly meetings are issue-based meetings called *Gram Sobha*. They provide functional education on various issues that women members deem important. All these meetings are held within the community. Other forms of education, whether legal, social, or health-related, are provided at additional meetings that are also held within the community. In addition, more specialized training may be provided at the local BRAC area office or, in some cases, in one of BRAC's training and resource centers (TARCs).

BRAC's members are mostly illiterate women. BRAC education aims to serve the needs of its members and be appropriate to the context of rural Bangladesh. BRAC provides many, mostly nonformal, learning opportunities to VO members who regularly attend credit meetings, deposit savings, and take loans from BRAC. Education meetings are held separately from credit meetings and are led by specialized staff. Field work is carried out by Program Organizers (POs), and there are separate credit POs, social development POs (responsible for Human Rights and Legal Education classes (HRLE) and Gram Sobhas), and Health POs. The POs travel by bike to meet with the VOs and to see individual members.

Microcredit Services

Savings. Collected weekly by BRAC (a minimum of five takas [US$0.09] per week) and earn interest at 6 percent per annum. Savings can normally be withdrawn only when a member leaves the VO. When a member needs access to extra funds (in case of serious illness or natural disaster), she can withdraw her savings by submitting a special application.

Loans. BRAC offers four basic types of loans: *general loans* for use as borrowers decide; *program loans* targeted to certain sectors that BRAC wishes to promote and feels that there is ample scope for poor people's involvement, such as poultry, silk culture, and social forestry; *housing loans* offered to help VO members build homes; and *rural enterprise loans* to set up nonfarm businesses in rural areas, such as small restaurants, grocery stores, laundry, and tailoring shops.

New VO members must wait six to eight weeks before applying for a loan. During this period, the member must regularly attend VO meetings, demonstrate knowledge and adherence to the rules and regulations of the VO, and maintain regular savings. The first loan varies from US$28 to $56. The amount finally approved depends on various factors, such as the amount of savings the member has accumulated (for the first loan, at least 2.5 percent of the loan; for the second and subsequent loans, at least 5 percent), whether she seems competent to use a loan profitably, and whether she has the resources needed to make good use of the loan. The size of the loans gradually increase as a member shows that she is capable of regular and timely repayment of her loans. From the second loan, the amount increases to between US$74 and $93 and will subsequently increase up to $186 after several years of membership in the VO.

Loans are repaid in weekly installments beginning the first week after the loan is taken—forty-six installments, at forty-six meetings, over a maximum of fifty-two weeks at a flat interest rate of 15 percent. While there is generally one credit meeting each week, some may be cancelled due to national holidays or other reasons.

Insurance. When a woman joins a VO, she must pay US$0.19 every year for a life insurance policy. The member must have a nominee who will receive US$93 in event of the VO member's death.

Educational Services

Gram Sobha (village meeting). This provides a forum where women can learn and gain information informally through discussion and consultation with other members and BRAC workers. Various socioeconomic, legal, health, and political issues are discussed, such as the need to prevent early marriages; how to stop domestic violence; how to prevent illegal divorces or bigamy; and where to access various types of services, such as immunization days.

Human Rights and Legal Education (HRLE). This is offered to new VO members within one year of joining BRAC. Twenty-eight topics are covered, broadly divided into land laws, Muslim family law, Hindu family law, constitutional laws, basic human and constitutional rights, and criminal law. The course lasts for thirty days and is conducted by a volunteer called the *Shebika*, a longstanding VO member given special legal training at one of the BRAC TARCs and receiving US$0.37 per learner—half from the group member, the other half from BRAC.

Essential Health Care Program (EHC). BRAC decided to provide health education and basic forms of healthcare when research and experience in the field indicated that illness of a borrower or someone in her family was a primary reason for difficulty in making profitable use of loans. EHC educates both VO and other community members at a monthly education forum in the community, covering various health issues such as local food sources of vitamin A, good nutrition during pregnancy and lactation, protection against six killer diseases through immunization, use of slab-ring latrines, and use of delivery kits for safe childbirth. Each meeting covers a new topic, has roughly twenty to twenty-five participants, and lasts for an average of forty-five minutes to an hour. The health Program Organizer (PO) facilitates the meetings—encouraging learner discussion and participation—with the help of community health volunteers (*Shasthya Shebikas*).

The EHC has decided to replicate a successful pilot project to make men and women in the communities aware of certain reproductive health issues. The project trained *Shasthya Shebikas*, traditional birth attendants, and traditional healers to provide, and discuss at people's doorsteps, information related to sexually transmitted diseases, including HIV/AIDS, reproductive tract infection, sexual hygiene, and domestic violence. BRAC provided all these health workers with flip-charts and picture stories that would explain the main issues and generate further discussion with an audience that is often illiterate. The project also trained the health workers to provide initial assistance and, as needed, to refer people to the appropriate care providers or government health facilities.

The visual aids were developed with great sensitivity to the fact that quite personal and sensitive issues were being addressed in a Muslim social environment. Prior advocacy work was done in the communities to explain the need and relevance of such discussion in the community, and the materials were shown to community leaders to ensure they did not object to any of the content.

The EHC has also started a new component dealing with pregnancy-related care. BRAC realized that although pregnant women are amongst the most vulnerable in its target population, not enough was being done to provide healthcare during that critical period. Through the *Shasthya Shebikas* and the health POs, the EHC is providing prenatal and postnatal care at the community level and has established referral linkages with the basic and comprehensive Emergency Obstetric Care unit of the government.

Vocational Training. BRAC quickly realized that members needed not only capital, but also training and skills to take up various forms of income-generating activities. Thus, BRAC has been training women on poultry and livestock rearing, silk culture, fish culture, and how to run nonfarm-related businesses. Only active VO members qualify. Courses vary in length from three to fifteen days and are mostly held in the BRAC area office, in Union Parishad offices, or at the activity location, in the case of fisheries or tree planting. BRAC employs specialized, highly qualified trainers to conduct all of the vocational courses.

Nonformal Primary Education. BRAC has a separate education program called BRAC Education Programme (BEP) to provide nonformal primary education in communities where there are few schools or for children who cannot attend regular, government-run primary schools. Many of the students in schools run or supported by BEP are members of families with members of VOs.

Evidence of Impact on Clients and on BRAC

Husain[c] found that 27 percent of VO-member households fall within the category of "extreme poverty," 25.1 percent within "moderate poverty," and 47.9 percent above the poverty line. Measuring poverty in terms of economic well-being, Hussain found that "BRAC programs have been able not only to reduce the intensity and depth of poverty, but have also been able to reduce its incidence among its participants, though the reduction in incidence is apparently modest" (p.102).

Long-term, control-comparison impact research has been conducted by BRAC since 1992 in partnership with the International Centre for Diarrhoeal Disease Research, Bangladesh. The analysis[d] shows the following results and impact of BRAC's work:

Nutritional status of children. It was found that the prevalence of severe protein-energy malnutrition has significantly declined among the children of BRAC member households, but not among comparable households of nonmembers.

Food and Family Expenditure. The pattern of intra-household food distribution was examined through observation of a small sample of twenty-five households consisting of both girls and boys. This exercise revealed that among BRAC-member households, girls more commonly receive equal treatment in terms of food distribution. BRAC households also spend significantly more on consumption of food items compared to poor nonmembers.

Family Planning. The current use of family planning methods was greater among currently married BRAC members (57 percent) than among the poor nonmembers (49.6 percent).

Education. The changes in level of education from 1992 to 1993 were measured. While it was found that basic education had increased among all households, the increase was much greater in the case of BRAC-member households and a greater number of girls had obtained basic education.

Child Survival. It was found that the survival rate of children belonging to BRAC households was better than that for children from poor nonmember households, and in fact rather similar to the survival rate of children from non-poor households. The survival advantage associated with BRAC membership among the poor was largely the result of mortality differences in the first few months of life.

The cost of BRAC's credit program is calculated separately from the educational programs. The total cost of delivering financial services includes all financial costs of capital lent to clients as well as all costs of external technical assistance. Based on financial performance in 2000, BRAC's credit program is projected to become completely financially self-sustainable in 2001 and beyond. During year 2000, the credit program was actively expanding from 3.2 million to 3.64 million members.

From the surpluses generated through the credit program and some of BRAC's sector programs such as poultry, silk culture, and social forestry, BRAC is able to fund some of its educational programs. Still, at present, all the educational components of BDP are funded predominantly by external grants. To the extent possible, BRAC has started collecting service charges from its members for certain forms of training or education; however, all of the educational and training components are expected to rely partially for the foreseeable future on external funding.

Field POs are now selected and assigned to specific tasks and programs rather than being expected to master all aspects of BRAC's development programs. A few years ago, there was not such a clear division of responsibilities. When the same staff were responsible for all tasks, the rigors of running an efficient credit program meant that other sectors and tasks tended to be neglected. Moreover, BRAC realized that a PO who is good at managing credit may not necessarily be suitable for carrying out social awareness-raising programs and vice versa.

The management of staff also is specialized, so that credit POs and other POs report to different staff at the BRAC area offices, as well as at the head office. Within BDP, there are separate management sections for Microcredit, Health, and Social Development. Nonformal primary education works as a completely independent program at the head office level, though it targets many children of BDP program members. Initially, all BRAC staff undergo a common training program for introduction to BRAC and its various programs, core values, and method of work. Subsequently, staff receive more specialized training which is directly relevant to their specific program work. Staff periodically get new training for new skills or to keep up with new developments within their field or within the organization.

The most obvious benefits of specialization within BRAC are that staff become very skilled at their particular task; no tasks or programs are neglected; staff can be assigned to particular programs according to their abilities and interests; and there is clarity in terms of tasks to be performed by each person. The disadvantages of having separate staff looking after the different components of BDP are that it is sometimes difficult to ensure coordination between the different programs and the total cost for separate staff and training for each program are obviously higher than if there were a single set of staff serving all BDP components.

There is strong support throughout the organization for taking a holistic approach to development. BRAC field staff definitely see a correlation between participation in education programs and successful use of credit and involvement in the Village Organizations. BRAC, even if starting over again, would still commit to providing a broad package to promote the overall social, economic, and political empowerment of poor people, especially women. When BRAC has prioritized one area, such as economic activities or social mobilization work, more than another, members have shown that they needed and demanded a more integrated package which would address several of their problems, not simply one area of their lives. This stems from the fact that all areas of poor people's lives are interconnected and that a general improvement in their position is not possible without fighting on all fronts—health issues, education issues, legal issues, political issues, and economic issues.

A Hybrid Model of Unified Management and Parallel Delivery: Pro Mujer—Bolivia

Pro Mujer[e] is a nongovernmental organization founded on March 11, 1990. Its mission is, "To support women who live in socioeconomic exclusion with integrated participatory services so that they may achieve personal, family and community sustainability." The institution provides integrated services in the areas of credit, business development, and health. An important element in all services is ongoing training, which is established as a basic pillar in the process of personal and group development. All of these services are provided to Pro Mujer clients who are grouped into Communal Associations—a model adapted from the village banking methodology—and participate in the organization as active clients.

Communal Associations (CAs) have an average of twenty-three members, with a range of fifteen to forty members. Ninety-eight percent of the clients of Pro Mujer are women. Meetings are held every seven, fourteen, or twenty-eight days, depending on the seniority of the group and the credit terms under which they operate. Each meeting lasts two hours, during which, according to the established agenda, there is an organizational stage, a payment session, and a training session (administration, business development, or health), in addition to a session for addressing various matters related to the activities of the group.

Members of a CA organize themselves into Solidarity Groups and elect a Management Committee and a Credit Committee to facilitate administration, implementation and control of resources and services provided by the Communal Association. Business and Health Managers are appointed to maintain the connections between the CA and services offered by Pro Mujer.

CA Meetings are held in Pro Mujer Focus Centers; each CA has an assigned room. The Health Consultant and the office of Business Development are located in the same Focus Center, and clients have direct access to these services on their CA meeting days. More than 80 percent of the clients live less than one-half-hour travel time from the CA meeting places and Pro Mujer institutional offices. The remaining 20 percent live farther away, mainly due to a change in residence. Pro Mujer policy is to organize groups in zones of influence around each Focus Center so that clients do not travel great distances to access the services.

Services are delivered by operating teams, each led by a Credit Officer/ Educator, who supervises all staff assistants providing services at a Focus Center. Credit Assistants advise CAs on the evaluation, granting, and tracking of loans. Business Assistants provide training and technical assistance for business development. Health Assistants provide preventive health training and primary health-care services. In addition, there is a business technician and a physician who give technical help to the personnel of these services and coordinate with the Credit Officer/Educators, whose supervision is operational, not technical.

Financial Services

The Communal Association model is an adaptation of village banking to allow for educational development, growth, and permanent and collective learning, both in the economic and social components. The credit component of Pro Mujer is directed exclusively toward investments in profitable economic activities. Pro Mujer does not grant consumer loans. The loans to individual members vary in amount from a minimum of US$50 to a maximum of US$1,000. A member can access a new loan for a greater amount if she repays the previous loan in a satisfactory manner.

Pro Mujer makes a group loan to the CA, which makes individual loans to its members. The first CA loan is for twelve weeks, the second for sixteen weeks, the third and fourth for twenty weeks, the fifth and sixth for twenty-four weeks, and from the seventh loan onward, the term is twenty-eight weeks. For the first two loans, individual members repay their CA in equal, weekly installments. For the third and later loans, members can repay twice per month, but only if the CA indicators regarding organization, cohesion, administration, and number of members are at acceptable levels.

Loans may be in bolivianos, in which case the annual rate of interest is 48 percent, charged on unpaid balances, with no commission. Alternatively, loans may be in U.S. dollars, with an interest rate of 30 percent per annum on unpaid balances plus a commission of 2 percent.

Before receiving the first loan, the CA members participate in a ten-hour training program to organize the CA and impart information on credit terms and rules of the institution. Once this training is concluded, the CA receives its first loan. The repayment meetings allow for ongoing training, with the objective of strengthening the organization and management of the CA. The management training sessions last thirty minutes per meeting, and depending on the needs of each CA, can total between four and eight hours during the term of each loan.

All CA members who receive loans are required to save. For the first three CA loans, the required savings rate is 20 percent of the loan value; for the next three loans, 15 percent of the loan is required; then for the next three loans, 10 percent is required. However, the CA, by agreement of all the members, can save at a rate higher than required by Pro Mujer in order to strengthen its savings fund. In addition to savings required by Pro Mujer and the CA, members have the option to deposit voluntary savings, which have no minimum or maximum and can be deposited or withdrawn on demand at any payment meeting of the CA. A member's voluntary savings earn a fixed 13 percent annual interest, calculated annually and distributed with the dividend payments.

Each member is a "shareholder" of the CA and receives dividends from CA earnings in the same proportion as her share of the total of required savings on deposit. Earnings of the CA include interest paid to its account in a commercial bank and interest paid by members who take "internal loans" from their CA's (required) savings fund. Dividends are calculated and distributed at the successful close of each CA loan.

Nonfinancial Services: Business Development and Health Service

Business Development has two components. First, there is training given at the CA meetings, totaling three to six hours per loan term. These are motivational and informative sessions on business improvement and the development of business skills among participants. Second, there is technical assistance, consisting of individualized client consultations, beginning with a diagnostic of the business and establishment of a program of improvements to be gradually implemented. Finally, there are follow-up visits to adjust the recommended program.

The *Health Service* also has two components, both of which inform and guide clients regarding contraceptive methods, pregnancy and childbirth, and sexually transmitted diseases (STDs), including HIV/AIDS. First, there is both group training and individual counseling. The participatory group training sessions last for thirty minutes with one topic per session. During each loan term, there are three to six hours of preventive health training per CA. Individual counseling is provided by health service staff to women clients or couples.

The institution has a training unit that periodically develops, evaluates, and adjusts curriculum content and training materials and keeps the training program in line with the needs of the CA members. The material produced is specifically for the target population and for training delivery using participatory methods. This methodology obtains knowledge from the clients, analyzes it, introduces new information and contrasts the information with the experience of the group, generating new knowledge and attitudes. All this is done through various activities that facilitate multi-channel perceptions and participatory integration.

The second component is primary healthcare services, for which the health service provides consulting rooms and trained medical personnel. The health service organizes frequent screening campaigns for early detection of breast and cervical cancer and STDs, so the patients can receive the appropriate treatment and follow-up. The health service coordinates its activities with other community health service organizations. Demand for information and services relating to HIV/AIDS is increasing. For contraceptive methods, the health service offers couples the opportunity to decide on a method and receive it in the same consultation. Couples deciding on a natural method receive orientation in its use and individualized follow-up to ensure correct use of the method.

Impacts on Clients and Program Performance

The target population for Pro Mujer services corresponds to the threshold and moderate levels of poverty reported by the Bolivian National Statistical Institute. New CA members are almost solely socioeconomically marginalized women with no business or only a microbusiness, who have limited access to credit, low family income, few economic resources, and little, if any, education. Fifty-one percent of the population from which CA members are recruited have had a family food crisis in the past year.

After several years of providing financial and nonfinancial services, Pro Mujer conducted impact evaluations[f] that showed that the volume of sales, earnings, and family income is significantly higher among CA members than in a control group. CA members also had more operating capital and investment in inventory and were more likely to have stores, stands, or other fixed points of sale.

CA members have greater access to information on family and reproductive health and are more likely to take their children to a doctor for both preventive and curative care. Homeownership and access to sewer and telephone services is higher. CA members are more likely to expand or diversify their businesses and differentiate business from home activities. They are more likely to participate in community activities and organizations in comparison with the control group, even more likely to hold executive offices.

The benefits identified seem to be the result of the integrated delivery of services. Client satisfaction assessments indicate demand for and acceptance of this type of integrated offer and in both financial and nonfinancial services are highly valued. There is no evidence that quality of either service has suffered from integration with the other.

Pro Mujer had not separately accounted for financial and nonfinancial services, until a new information system allowed for separate financial tracking for each Focus Center, for institutional personnel, and for financial and nonfinancial services as cost centers. Income sources are used separately for financial and nonfinancial services, and the program keeps accounting information separated by funding source. The costs for financial services include all financial expenses, but not those for external technical assistance.

Fiscal years 1999 and 2000 were a period of rapid program service expansion—in 2000 alone, a net increase of 7,152 clients, in both old and new service areas. Operational self-sufficiency, calculated only for the financial services cost center, correspondingly fell from 121 percent in 1998 to 95 percent in 1999 and 94 percent in 2000.

Nonfinancial services represent 30 percent of costs during fiscal year 2000. Only 20 percent of costs for nonfinancial services were covered by income directly generated by these services. In the future it is planned that financial income and income from nonfinancial services will cover the costs of nonfinancial services. But, until this is achieved, Pro Mujer has sustainability plans based on contributions from the community, its own funds, and new financing. The sustainability of nonfinancial services is an institutional priority because it fully favors clients and because it qualitatively strengthens and improves the performance of the credit service.

As indicated above, staff assistants who work directly with clients are specialized in the service they deliver. Technical support is also specialized. On the other hand, the work of supervisory and middle-management personnel unifies all services at the Focus Center level and higher. With this model, each Credit Officer/Educator can supervise ninety CAs (about 2,250 members) with three credit assistants and two nonfinancial service assistants (health and business development).

A monitoring and tracking system by operating team and by service has been developed and is implemented in team and area meetings, during which the fulfillment of goals is analyzed and strategies are proposed for improving service delivery and team performance and maintaining coordination ties. This information and analysis is consolidated monthly in a regional meeting in which reports are presented by team and by service and the difficulties and limitations are analyzed. Finally, strategies are defined for improving the work during the next month and resolving the detected problems.

The executive director and management, as well as personnel and their teams, identify with the institutional mission to deliver integrated services. The teamwork provides strong support for this type of approach. The principal motive for this approach is that there is evidence that the population with which Pro Mujer works has various needs that go beyond a response to economic problems. Their condition of social marginalization is overarching, and therefore the intervention with this population should be integrated in order to give real results. Results of the different evaluations performed have demonstrated to management and staff the value of this type of intervention and the positive impact it has on the lives of clients, on the program itself and on the institution. If Pro Mujer were to start all over again, it would provide integrated services as it does now.

Notes

a. FUCEC-Togo may be contacted for additional information at B.P. 3541, Lomé-Togo (Tel: 228 21-06-32 / 22-25-74; E-mail: fucec@cafe.tg).

b. BRAC may be contacted for additional information at 75 Mohakhali Commercial Road, Dhaka–1212, Bangladesh (Tel: 880 2 882-4180; Fax: 880 2 882-3542; E-mail: rdp@bracbd.net).

c. A. M. Muazzam Husain. 1998. "Poverty Alleviation and Empowerment: The Second Impact Assessment Study of BRAC's Rural Development Programme." BRAC Printers: Dhaka.

d. Sabina Rashid, Mushtaque Chowdhury and Abbas Bhuiya. 1995. "An Inside Look at Two BRAC Schools in Matlab," BRAC-ICDDR,B Working Paper No.8.

Nasreen, Hashima et al., "An assessment of Client's knowledge of family planning in Matlab." BRAC-ICDDR,B Working Paper No. 13 (Dhaka: BRAC-ICDDR,B, 1996).

Rita Das Roy, et al. 1998. "Does Involvement Of Women in BRAC Influence Sex Bias in Intra-Household Food Distribution?" BRAC - ICDDR,B Working Paper No. 25. Dhaka.

Syed Masud Ahmed, et al. 1998. "Two Studies On Health Care Seeking Behaviour and Sanitation Practices of BRAC Member and Non-Member Households in Matlab, Bangladesh." BRAC- ICDDR,B Working Paper no 22. Dhaka.

e. Pro Mujer may be contacted for additional information at Calle 9 No. 455. Edif. "El Zodiaco" Of. 10 Planta Baja., Zona Obrajes, La Paz, Bolivia (Telephone: 591 2 784711; Fax: 591 2 784942; e-mail: lapaz@pro-mujer.org or Executive Director: cvelasco@pro-mujer.org.

f. P. Claure, "Evaluación del Impacto del Programa Integrado de Capacitación y Crédito de Pro Mujer, El Alto," (La Paz: Pro Mujer, 2000).

P. Claure, M. Mollinedo, and S. Paredes, "Evaluación de Resultados del Programa de Capacitación y Crédito de Pro Mujer en Cochabamba," *Informe a Entidades Financieros* (2000).

APPENDIX B:
CLIENT DEMAND AND CHOICE IN
CREDIT WITH EDUCATION

The original designers and proponents of Credit with Education, coming from the public health perspective, started with a reasonable assumption that clients, especially the poorer ones, should not be expected to pay for education they don't yet know they need. And when it is feasible to provide public health education, clients should not be deprived of what they need in order to get many things they clearly want, such as able bodies and live, healthy children. Credit with Education designers assumed that women would pay for financial services but not education, because the benefits of preventive education for better health are not experienced immediately—or even directly, in the case of child health—by the women being educated.

The value of preventive public health interventions is perceived mainly in their absence, when it may be too late for the affected individuals to be helped. The "need" precedes the "want." The consumer demand to which normal business responds is geared to wants rather than needs. "Externalities" (delayed or indirect effects) are the concern of society and government rather than consumers and private business, which is why public health interventions are usually publicly funded. In the case of Credit with Education, which is usually initiated with public or philanthropic funding, the ongoing public health intervention is cross-subsidized by the private revenue from on-going credit services in high demand.

Given that credit for the poor is a low-margin line of business, the education component was designed to be integral to the village banking experience and to impose as little extra cost as possible on either the provider or the client—not just free of extra charge but also making sure learning sessions do not make the village bank meetings too long. Succeeding in this design objective, there has not been an apparent need to charge more than what people are willing to pay for credit services. The evidence in chapter 2 ("Evidence of Impacts on Clients and Institutions") that women, after experiencing the education, place such a high relative value on the education they receive—and might even pay extra for it—and that the education component might convey a competitive advantage to Credit with Education providers has come as a welcome surprise to the original designers and proponents.

The unified design is considered by some to be paternalistic, even unethical, because it "forces" public health education on the microcredit client whether she wants it or not. It would be difficult to debate this point without a philosophical exploration of the moral imperative to intervene on behalf of the disadvantaged—especially of children, whose life or death can hinge on the mundane knowledge and practices of their mothers and other female relatives. Given the public health objectives of the provider institutions, allowing their clients to choose *not* to participate in the health-related education could be considered unethical.

At a practical level, client choice is presumed to apply pressure on the education provider to offer the highest quality, most efficient service. This seems a valid criticism of the original design of Credit with Education. Yet the author knows of no experiments or innovative designs to offer such choice, at least not for relatively new clients. In large part, lack of choice reflects the dominant practice throughout the microcredit movement to offer new clients, and even long-term clients, a single package of services that allows little if any customization to accommodate individual or group choice. The rationale for this inflexibility is that customization imposes extra costs and introduces new risks that threaten the opportunity for financial sustainability of the service. Nonetheless, there is unexplored opportunity for choice and customization in the offer of education.

Even in the original design, it must be understood that there is up-front, full disclosure to potential clients of what is involved in Credit with Education. People make the decision to join or not, knowing that more than microfinance is involved. Many who want access to credit and savings do not join, but almost always for reasons related to the terms and conditions of village banking, not the education add-on. The little anecdotal evidence in chapter 2 indicates that where competition from microfinance-only providers exists and is growing, people are still choosing to join and stay with unified programs. This competition already is heightening awareness among Credit with Education providers of the need to assure quality and efficiency in their unified services.

3

Innovations from the Field:
A Daringly Brief Summary of a Huge Phenomenon

John K. Hatch
with Sara R. Levine and Amanda Penn

Behold what is rapidly becoming the largest self-help undertaking in human history—bringing hope, dignity, and empowerment to tens of millions of the world's poor and poorest families. Behold a movement with global outreach, which has penetrated beyond city slums and market towns to even the most isolated villages. Behold an industry that embraces thousands of NGOs, credit unions, public and private banks, and an infrastructure of hundreds of thousands of community-based peer lending groups that are enabling many of the planet's most disadvantaged households to generate the additional income and savings they need to keep their children alive, nourished, healthy, and able to attend school. Behold a profession that in theory offers a compellingly simple strategy for breaking the vicious cycle of poverty, but which in practice is extremely difficult to implement—first because it involves myriad adjustments to highly different cultural settings, methodologies, and institutional structures while simultaneously facing complex technical challenges involving client services, scale-up, financing, evaluation, governance, training, technical assistance, government regulation, economic instability, civil disturbances, and natural disasters.

When the Microcredit Summit Campaign was launched in 1997—with a nine-year goal of providing credit for self-employment and other financial services to 100 million of the world's poorest families—there were 1,700 members of the Campaign worldwide, of which 800 were members of the Campaign's Council of Practitioners. Five years later the total number of institutions that have joined the Campaign is more than 5,225, of which more than 3,165 (and still continuing to grow briskly) have joined the Campaign's Council of Practitioners (data taken from the Microcredit Summit Campaign database, May 20, 2002). These remarkable numbers represent a diverse spectrum of organizations—public and private, indigenous and international, nonprofit and for-profit, independent and networked, urban and rural, regulated and unregulated. Collectively they display many differences with regard to client focus, mission, strategy, products and services, funding, oversight, managerial expertise, technical sophistication, and governance structures. To an increasing degree the rapidly swelling numbers of microfinance institutions (MFIs) are *not* merely the result of tiny new nonprofit start-ups created to serve the poor. Rather, many of the newest or at least largest entrants are *existing* institutions (mainly banks) that are restructuring themselves to seek new clients among low-income segments of the financial services markets which, until now, were previously seen as unbankable and credit-ineligible.

The very quantity and variety of these microfinance practitioners is already producing intensified competition, including market saturation in a growing number of locales. It is also stimulating widespread innovation and, in a few cases, exciting breakthroughs in scale and depth of outreach. Such competition and innovation is good news for the poor and poorest clients because their range of choice is growing steadily wider. As these clients begin to shop for the microfinance products and services that best fit their needs, such behavior will stimulate even more competition and innovation. Several different *kinds* of innovation are occurring as well. First and foremost, steady improvements are being made in traditional loan and savings products as well as such complementary products such as insurance. In turn, these changes have in some cases led to major shifts in MFI business strategy—like the grafting of the infrastructures of commercial branch banking with the infrastructure of community-based peer lending groups largely created by NGOs serving the poor. Many innovations are also occurring *outside* the financial services area as MFIs create "strategic alliances" with NGOs or companies offering to channel complementary client services such as business skills, healthcare, nutrition, water and sanitation, housing, schooling, human rights, literacy, and many others. At the same time, equally important innovations are occurring in the administration, financing, governance, evaluation, and legal status of the practitioner institutions themselves. Even the traditional profile of clients served is changing, as some MFIs no longer merely seek to serve the poor or the poorest families (as defined by an income or asset criterion) but the most vulnerable or marginal groups within this broad population—such as street children, young adults, families with chronic disease, seniors, refugees, victims of natural disaster or terrorism, pastoral populations, landless rural laborers, outcasts, and tribal groups.

Faced with such a wealth of innovation on the one hand, and a space limitation on the other, the authors have consciously chosen breadth over depth. Rather than covering a few key innovations in detail, we have reported more superficially on nearly four dozen innovations. To counteract a tendency to place disproportionate emphasis on client products and services, we created four additional categories of innovation—financing, administration and governance, program evaluation, and response to emergencies. In late January 2002 the authors sent out an e-mail request to a Microcredit Summit Campaign mailing list. We received about sixty responses, of which we selected twenty of the best-documented or most interesting innovations. A second source (about ten cases) came from among MFIs that were awarded innovation grants under CGAP's Pro-Poor Innovation Challenge Program. A third source (five cases) was case studies gathered in direct contacts with MFI representatives attending the Fifth Annual Microenterprise Conference held at Brigham Young University March 14–16, 2002. A fourth source was SEEP's draft manual entitled *New Directions in Poverty Finance*, which mainly reviews innovation in Village Banking programs. And finally, several innovations were "discovered" while doing web research on microfinance programs in certain regions and countries. Unfortunately, given these diverse sources of reporting, we were unsuccessful in structuring the responses to answer a uniform set of questions about the context of innovations received—such as 1) background and outreach of the innovating program, 2) problem addressed, 3) cost, 4) proof of effectiveness, 5) risks or trade-offs encountered, and so forth. Such deepening of content will need to be incorporated into future efforts to document innovations in our far-flung industry.

We recognize we may have assigned ourselves a "mission impossible." No doubt many readers will be disappointed that most of our descriptions of individual innovations have by necessity been limited to a single paragraph. Other readers who are personally familiar with the cases we have chosen will inevitably find fault with the veracity of the descriptions, that are not based on our own first-hand observations but on brief reports submitted by MFI staff in the field (or cited on their Web sites) and are therefore not as objective or complete as some would like. No doubt there will still be other readers who know of more successful examples of the types of innovations we have reported, or innovations we missed entirely. To these individuals we can only say we mostly reported on innovations from MFIs that took the trouble to answer our e-mails. Those who didn't, or reported late, were simply not well represented in this study. To compensate for some of these defects, however, each innovation description references the name of the sponsoring microcredit institution and its contact information. In this way we hope readers seeking additional detail about a particular innovation will contact the sponsoring institution directly.

INNOVATIONS IN PRODUCTS AND CLIENT SERVICES

Going to Scale

NABARD/India

Of all the innovations reported in this chapter, the one that has achieved the largest scale of outreach to the world's poorest families is clearly the savings-led, self-help group program of the National Bank for Agriculture and Rural Development (NABARD). Building on an infrastructure of 17,000 rural and semi-urban branch banks that it controls or has partnered with, NABARD has also enrolled the participation of 750 NGOs as facilitators of 462,000 client-managed self-help groups (SHGs), averaging seventeen members each, to serve 7.8 million rural saver-borrowers of whom 85 percent are women. These SHGs mobilize their own savings, transforming them into loans to members (average loan size less than $22), and plow their earnings from interest income back into equity. After a year or so the experienced SHG is allowed to supplement their member loan portfolio by borrowing from their nearest NABARD-supported bank branch office. In 2001–02 this bank linkage strategy resulted in loans of $94 million. The program's on-time repayment rate is 95 percent. NABARD is currently negotiating with international donors for loan funding in excess of $1 billion to further expand its hybrid public-private-SHG methodology to tens of millions of additional rural clients both within India and throughout the Asian region. On a cautionary note it bears mentioning that the term "self-help group" is rather elastic, and how well they function for the long term has been inconclusively studied.

Palli Karma Sahayak Foundation /Bangladesh

Palli Karma-Sahayak Foundation (PKSF) was set up in 1990 as an autonomous microcredit fund to facilitate the channeling of funds to microcredit institutions from both government and nongovernment sources. PKSF partners with more than 200 microfinance institutions in Bangladesh. PKSF performs two major functions: financial intermediation and development of sustainable microcredit institutions. The institution has been successful largely due to its unique organizational structure. Although PKSF was established and is funded by the government, it has been kept as an independent organization outside the government bureaucracy. As such, PKSF has been able to channel funds to microcredit institutions cost-effectively and PKSF funds have been lent to more than two million clients. A major advantage of PKSF has been its ability to screen and monitor a large number of microcredit programs according to standard criteria, compared to often inconsistent "ad hoc" evaluations of individual microfinance institutions by donor and government agencies.

WEP/Nepal—Women's Empowerment Program (WEP)

The WEP provides another example of a savings-led approach to financial institution-building. Launched in 1998, WEP was able to train more than 240 local NGOs to organize some 6,265 self-help savings and credit groups serving more than 130,000 women. These clients have been organized in savings and credit groups (average twenty members apiece) similar to village banks but without access to an external loan fund. The program is sponsored by PACT, a nonprofit agency serving as a time-limited catalyst of group development, which uses literacy classes as its primary organizing and training vehicle. In its first four years the program has mobilized more than $2 million in savings and retained earnings, it has self-financed loans for $1.5 million to more than 45,000 group members (average loan $33), and 74,000 women have learned to read and write. WEP's village bankers meet weekly, and every meeting is used for literacy, management skill-training, or other topics of interest to members. Custody of cash is handled with suitcase-size metallic lockboxes, secured with three separate padlocks, each opened by a different key in the possession of the group's president, secretary, and treasurer. Loans are made for a wide variety of uses: business, personal emergency, schooling, and so forth. Each village bank is entirely responsible for collecting, managing, and lending its own savings. WEP did not target the very poor, but survey research has shown that about 45 percent of members were poor, 35 percent the vulnerable non-poor, and 25 percent better off. Research findings also indicate that 82 percent of group leaders were able to maintain their group's books without outside assistance. However, as with NABARD, the long-term sustainability of WEP's groups has yet to be proven.

LPWF/China—Poverty Alleviation Chain

Thanks to the restructuring of its rural economic system and a series of poverty alleviation campaigns, since 1978 the Government of China has reportedly reduced its population living in poverty from 250 million in 1978 to 65 million in 1995. China's remaining poverty is primarily rural, mainly scattered among remote, mountainous, and minority nationality areas in the northwest and southwest. To address this challenge China is shifting from regional development projects to household-based initiatives that are increasingly directed at women. One especially successful example has been the poverty alleviation program sponsored by the Luliang Prefecture Women's Federation (LPWF) in Shansi province. The LPWF began experimenting with non-collateralized credit and technical training in 1989 when it launched its "Poverty Alleviation Chain" with seed capital funding of $16,000 from the provincial government and a training grant from UNICEF for $70,000. This initiative identified "demonstration" households that would be provided subsidized one-year loans mainly for pig farming with the proviso that each household chosen would provide training and supervision to two severely poor neighboring families. By 1996 the initiative had reached 35,400 families, demonstrating in the process that poor families were credit-worthy. The LPWF has now evolved its methodology into a group-lending approach based on the Grameen model, which is currently supported by an annual provincial government loan of $625,000 per year plus a $1 million grant from the World Bank. The program's outreach has now soared to 165,900 participating families.

Reaching the Destitute

Centre Béninois Pour le Développment des Initiatives à la Base (CBDIBA)/ Benin—"Weaning" the Hardcore Poor

CBDIBA serves more than 15,000 clients through a village banking program. Realizing that destitute women were not joining its conventional village banks, CBDIBA created a special "weaning" program where the destitute are placed in small groups of less than ten members. Here each member receives special motivation to establish a savings habit based on very small weekly deposits of about ten cents. Those members who meet their savings plan are rewarded with small loans (average $17) to be invested in income-generating activities, which in turn enhance their savings capacity. These small loans are made and repaid for three consecutive loan cycles of four months each. After a year of successful savings and loan repayment behavior, members are then "graduated" into CBDIBA's normal village banking operations. The program is a recipient of CGAP's Pro-Poor Innovation Challenge award.

CFTS/India—Poultry Raising for Women Agricultural Laborers

CASHPOR Financial & Technical Services (CFTS), working in Uttar Pradesh, India, encountered a similar case of destitute women who worked full-time as farm laborers and had insufficient time to create a self-employment business. CFTS designed a loan product based on the raising of semi-scavenging poultry, that can be locked in a pen when the woman is at work, released when she is home, thus allowing income-generation to occur in the absence of the owner. The program is also a recipient of CGAP's Pro-Poor Innovation Challenge award.

Mata Masu Dubara/Niger—Women's Savings and Credit Group Formation

With a GNP per capita of $190, and an average daily per capita income of less than $0.40 per day, Niger is one of the five poorest countries in the world, a region that is afflicted by chronic drought and famine. Within this terribly difficult environment CARE International has implemented a savings-led credit project that has facilitated the organization of more than 150,000 destitute mothers in 6,000 self-help groups. Mata Masu Dubara (MMD) is a Hausa term for "women on the move." With each member setting aside as little as US 8 cents/week, the movement is generating some $900,000 per year in savings and nearly $3 million in aggregate lending. Given the high rate of illiteracy, record keeping is mainly oral, with all members paying the same savings fee each week and the number of payments measured by rocks deposited into the group's three-lock steel box. Loans are made entirely from group savings, and the average loan is usually for a one-month period. What is especially noteworthy is that CARE has created a technical assistance model that enables the individual MMD group to become self-managing within eight months. During the first three months a CARE field agent gets a group organized, then identifies and trains a Village Agent who will supervise the group—but whose services are financed not by CARE but by MMD service fees. During the second three-month period the field agent's visits diminish to biweekly and then monthly. During the final two months each group works autonomously, receives a final visit from the CARE field agent, and is certified as "graduated." CARE research indicates that more than 85 percent of all groups are able to function autonomously, most increase their savings contributions, and some of the first groups are still operating after ten years.

Changes in Savings and Credit Products

FINCA/Peru—Putting Savings First

Organized in 1993, FINCA/Peru currently serves more than 6,400 clients through 256 village banks. Total loans outstanding amount to $856,000 (average loan $169), but client savings exceed $1,320,000. One of the smallest programs among FINCA International's network of twenty-one affiliates, the average FINCA/Peru client has accumulated four times more savings ($206 per member) than the average for the network as a whole. It has $2 in savings for every $1 of loan capital borrowed from external sources. This result emerged less from conscious design than by necessity, because throughout its history FINCA/Peru has had less access to external sources of loan capital than most other affiliates, so the program learned to depend primarily on the lending of its own savings, much like a credit union. In turn, this strategy has allowed its members to recycle most of their interest income back into group equity.

Pro Mujer/Bolivia—Loan Flexibility

The first village banking programs of the early 1990s were designed with fairly inflexible loan product features—four-month loan cycles, initial loans with fixed amounts for all clients, weekly loan repayments, and so forth. But only a decade later, most village banking practitioners are designing much more flexible loan products. Pro Mujer in Bolivia is a case in point. Organized in 1990, Pro Mujer today serves more than 30,000 clients through a nationwide network of twenty-four branch offices and nearly 1,600 "community associations" of twenty-five to thirty members apiece, 95 percent of whom are women. The program now allows new clients to choose between first loans of $50 to $130 (the average is about $100). After two cycles of weekly payments, clients are allowed to organize sub-groups that can choose between weekly and monthly payments as well as loan terms ranging from four months to eight months. Whereas previous policies limited the maximum loan amount to about $300, Pro Mujer is now able to "grow with its clients" up to a loan ceiling of $1,000. These innovations have helped to lower the program's administrative costs and have enhanced greatly its self-sufficiency.

ASA/Bangladesh—Going Beyond the Group Guarantee

The Association for Social Advancement (ASA) entered the microfinance industry in 1991 and in the space of a decade has become one of the largest and fastest-growing MFIs in the world. The program currently serves more than 1.7 million clients through a network of 1,087 branch offices, has 70,300 village-based client groups, has mobilized $29.7 million in savings, and has an outstanding loan portfolio of $112 million distributed via one-year loans with weekly repayments. With this kind of critical mass in its favor, in 1998 ASA took the radical step of going beyond the group guarantee requirement, such that its clients no longer have to pay for each other's delinquency or default. In its place, ASA enforces a policy of zero tolerance for arrears and currently enjoys an overall repayment rate of 99 percent. ASA also allows its clients fairly unfettered access to their savings (particularly to confront emergencies or seasonal cash needs) without leaving the program and without having to start all over again with entry-level loans.

FINCA/Samara, Russian Federation—Holiday and Transitional Loans

Organized in 1999, FINCA/Samara currently serves 1,539 clients through 266 village bank groups and manages an outstanding loan portfolio of $1.2

million (average loan: $880). Here the loan cycle has been reduced from four months to five weeks. Once clients have completed their third four-month loan cycle, and provided their repayment performance has been excellent, they are allowed to borrow additional five-week "holiday" loans repayable with a single "bullet payment" of capital and interest at the end of the loan term. The maximum amount on holiday loans is $290, and they can be borrowed in addition to the normal loan. FINCA/Samara is also experimenting with a "transitional" loan product that is offered to smaller groups (three to four members apiece) of clients with greater business experience. In order to offset the risk associated with smaller group size, the credit officer is required to do more due diligence and, if appropriate, require collateral from the borrower. Despite these potentially risky innovations, loan repayment stands at 98.2 percent. A very similar seasonal loan product has been developed by FINCA's much larger program (20,000 clients) in Kyrgyzstan.

CARE/Bangladesh—Family Savings Pilot Project

CARE has started a pilot project to provide flexible microfinance products to the "ultra poor." In this initiative, savings collectors visit clients five times per week to collect savings and credit installments. The amount saved by a client on any given day is entirely flexible. Clients are allowed to withdraw any amount of their savings at any time, even at the time of the collector's visit. Clients are also eligible to receive collateral-free loans from the project. Although the loan must be repaid by the end of the designated loan period— usually six months—the amount paid on any given day is also entirely flexible so as to adjust to fluctuations in the daily income of the poor. In certain circumstances of emergency or severe deprivation, the loan period can be extended.

Microfinance Services for Special Purposes and Clienteles

YOSEFO/Tanzania—Education Fund for Children

This program provides more than 1000 destitute families in Dar es Salaam with microcredit and training services. After discovering that loan repayment problems mostly coincided with the beginning of school terms, YOSEFO created a weekly savings product to help clients accumulate resources for school fees. It also allows its clients to borrow for school fees. YOSEFO has received a CGAP Pro-Poor Innovation Challenge award.

WEEC/Kenya—Credit for Pastoral Communities

Since August 1999, the Women Economic Empowerment Consortium

(WEEC) has been providing financial services to Maasai women, who are nomadic herders. Loans are usually made in the form of cattle to help borrowers restock their herds following drought periods. WEEC negotiates bulk purchases of cattle and passes the savings on to its clients. The program links with a public agency that provides training in management practices for cattle breeds that are better adapted to pasture scarcity and yield more milk. The loans are repaid by the borrowers mostly from the sale of milk or excess animals. WEEC has grown to serve more than 2,100 families and has a zero delinquency record. The program is a recipient of CGAP's Pro-Poor Innovation Challenge award.

AlSol Chiapas/Mexico—Life Insurance for Indigenous Populations

Since 1998 Alternative Solidaria (AlSol) has been offering savings and credit services for destitute indigenous families who reside in villages surrounding San Cristobal de las Casas, a region devastated by the Zapatista uprising and subsequent military repression. Currently the program serves more than 1,200 clients. When several AlSol clients had to liquidate assets and go into debt because of the funeral expenses resulting from the death of a relative, AlSol made an arrangement with Zurich Insurance in which a minimum group of 125 of its clients can qualify for $1,000 of life insurance coverage for an annual premium payment of $10. To finance this premium, AlSol collects weekly payments of 20 cents. AlSol soon hopes to extend the coverage to other family members as well. The AlSol program is a recipient of CGAP's Pro-Poor Challenge Award.

UNRWA/Gaza—Solidarity Lending for Female Refugees

The United Nations Relief and Works Agency for Palestine Refugees in the Near East provides education, health, relief, and income-generation services to 3.8 million registered Palestinian refugees in Jordan, Lebanon, the Syrian Arab Republic, the West Bank, and the Gaza Strip. In 1994 UNRWA launched its first microenterprise program based on group-guaranteed loans. Known as the Solidarity Group Lending (SGL) program, by 1998 UNRWA had made 9,075 loans to women (average $150) organized in groups of four to ten members, with a current outstanding loan portfolio of $1.04 million. These clients range in age from eighteen to sixty-eight years of age, 40 percent are illiterate, and they collectively support an average of six dependents apiece. Their UNRWA loans enable most of them to work as street vendors, open small shops in their tent homes, work in camp agriculture, raise small livestock, sew piece-work clothing, pickle vegetables, or make cheese. The program continues to make 250 to 300 loans each month. It is one of the first microfinance projects in the Middle East to achieve operational and financial self-sufficiency. In 1999 the project received UNDP's AgFund Prize for Poverty Alleviation through Microcredit.

Grameen Bank/Bangladesh—Housing Loans

As the flagship program of the world microfinance movement, the Grameen Bank's accomplishments are well known—its outreach to more than 2.4 million borrowers (95 percent women) from 40,000 villages. Yet what is less well known, and much less replicated by other MFIs, is the fact that Grameen offers a housing loan program that has benefited more than 546,000 families since its inception. Grameen housing loans target the most destitute clients whose dilapidated shelters barely distinguish them from the homeless. The average loan is for about $350, at 8 percent interest per year, which finances the necessary building materials—four concrete columns, a prefabricated sanitary slab, and twenty-six corrugated roofing sheets—to erect a standard module one-room dwelling that is flood and water-resistant. The pre-cast materials are mass-produced off-site at very reasonable prices. The dwelling itself is constructed by self-help labor. Other building materials are available as needed. Clients (mostly women) who qualify for these housing loans must hold title to the land on which the house stands. The cumulative amount disbursed by Grameen in housing loans is $188 million. Loan repayment on these loans is reported to be 98 percent.

PMUK/Bangladesh—Financial Services for Street Children

Established as an NGO in 1986, Padakhep Manabik Unnayan Kendra (PMUK) initiated its microfinance program in 1993 to assist street children, of which there are more than 200,000 in Dhaka alone. The program organizes children between the ages of eleven and eighteen years of age into groups of fifteen to twenty, that meet weekly for discussions about personal hygiene, health awareness, AIDS, security issues, and savings lessons. Credit is only disbursed to groups that have completed forty weekly meetings and have accumulated savings. Out of 2,000 participating children and about 40 groups, there are currently 329 children who have received loans (average $10) for selling tea, flowers, shoe-shining, and so forth. Loans are usually made for six months with an interest rate of about 1.5 percent per month.

Beselidhja-Zavet/Kosovo—Peace and Reconciliation Initiative

The Kosovo Credit Information Service (KCIS) is a credit bureau that was established in 2000 by Kosovo's MFI community and now includes nearly all major lending agencies in the province. A founding member of the bureau, Beselidhja-Zavet (BZ) is an MFI sponsored by World Relief. BZ has found that by working with both Albanian and Serbian clients, while carefully cultivating the trust and cooperation of each group, it is possible for microfinance-related activity to become an agent of inter-ethnic business dialogue. According to World Relief's Richard Schroeder, "Commerce has a profound ability to make people put aside their differences and interact with each other." Jointly sponsored by BZ and the United Methodist Committee on Relief (UMCOR), a business center has been set up—complete with internet café, photocopy and fax services, business training seminars, and an ATM machine—where Albanian and Serbian businesspeople have a place to share common interests and relate to each other on neutral territory. Furthermore, with the installation of the ATM machine residents of the enclaves have gained their only access to Kosovo's formal banking system.

The center's motto is "business is business," a great slogan for inter-ethnic reconciliation.

Complementary Client Services and Strategic Partnerships

FONKOZE/Haiti—Managing Remittances

Fondasyon Kole Zepol (FONKOZE) describes itself as "Haiti's alternative bank for the organized poor" and an "economic alliance of peasant organizations, women's collectives, cooperatives, credit unions, women street vendor groups, and religious communities." Through eighteen branch offices nationwide FONKOZE serves more than 25,000 savers and 10,000 borrowers organized into approximately 2,000 solidarity groups, with a loan portfolio outstanding of approximately $1 million. FONKOZE estimates that Haitians living abroad ("the Diaspora"), mostly in the United States and Canada, send back to relatives in Haiti more than $720 million a year, equivalent to 17 percent of the nation's gross national product. But the cost of the typical remittance is high. On a transfer of $100 the sender will pay a commission of $8 to 12, plus an additional $10 to 15 will be lost when the remittance is converted from dollars into Haitian gourds. To provide a cheaper remittance service, FONKOZE negotiated an agreement with the City National Bank of New Jersey (CNB), whose president and CEO is Haitian-born. It then hired a U.S. Customer Service Representative who works out of her home with a computer, an AOL account, and an 800 number. For all remittances to Haiti, whether $100 or $5,000, FONKOZE charges a fixed fee of $10. To qualify, the remittance recipient must open a FONKOZE savings account in Haiti, which is free. The remitter calls the 800 number or sends an e-mail and the amount is transferred to FONKOZE's account with CNB. Once the funds reach CNB, they are immediately available in Haiti. To gain the trust of the Diaspora Haitians residing in the U.S., FONKOZE has organized a series of free "financial literacy" classes for potential remitters.

Meanwhile, the biggest remittance clients are NGOs who wish to transfer funds to finance program operations in Haiti. FONKOZE, which is currently a non-profit foundation, is in the process of spinning off its financial services to form a commercial bank, Bank FONKOZE.

FINCA/Uganda—Health Insurance and Health Services

Organized in 1992, FINCA/Uganda is now the largest country program in the FINCA network with an outreach to more than 30,500 low-income clients (100 percent of them women) through 1,175 village banks. It currently manages an outstanding loan portfolio of $2 million (average loan is $169), has mobilized $1.5 million in member savings, and boasts an on-time loan repayment rate of 98.4 percent. When survey research findings revealed that 1) 80 percent of FINCA's clients were raising one or more AIDS orphans, 2) 75 percent of client income was being spent on health, and 3) that virtually none of its clients had any health or life insurance, FINCA/Uganda began to develop services to meet these challenges. Beginning in 1997 FINCA began to offer life insurance through a partnership with American International Group (AIG), and today more than 123,000 FINCA clients and their dependents are now covered. In the event of a client's death (including accidental death from AIDS), this policy spares the client's family from repaying the outstanding loan balance and pays for burial expenses and twice what the deceased village banker had accumulated in savings. Then in late 1999 FINCA/Uganda introduced a health insurance product for clients, their spouses, and dependents that included coverage for AIDS treatment but not medication. Through a partnership with Nsambaya Hospital, the plan pays for up to three weeks of hospital care in any one three-month period and covers up to $206 in medical costs. There are about 300 families presently covered by this pilot project. The original monthly premium payment of $12 proved inadequate and has now been raised to $14. At $15 per month it is estimated that this health insurance can be extended to 12,500 families while fully covering all fixed operating costs as well as medical treatment.

WOCCU/FFH/Philippines—Credit and Savings with Education and "Grafting"

Since the early 1990's, Freedom from Hunger (FFH) has broken from the prevailing paradigm of village banking with two important innovations. First, FFH has been a strong advocate of a village banking methodology that incorporates a strong client training component that emphasizes health, nutrition, family planning, and business skills. Their argument is that poverty is the product of scarcity—not just of economic resources but scarcity of skills and information. Integrating access to money with access to information is a powerful poverty-alleviation tool. Furthermore, FFH research demonstrates such training is highly valued by the clients, enhances group performance, and promotes client continuity in village banking programs even when faced with a variety of choices for improved loan and savings products. Such results go far in establishing what one scholar has called a "culture of service" versus a "culture of collection." FFH's second innovation was the idea of "grafting" village banking methodology onto existing financial institutions—most notably credit unions—to make them more responsive to the needs of the poorest families. Both innovations were well honed when in 1994 FFH, in partnership with the World Council of Credit Unions (WOCCU), introduced its Credit with Education methodology into the credit union movement of the Philippines. The first loans were made in 1998, and within two years the FFH village banks (functioning as pre-cooperatives) grew from 2,000 clients to 13,000 clients to constitute one-third of the credit unions' total clientele. Those credit unions that adopted the village banking add-on saw a sharp decline in loan delinquency versus those that did not. This result helped to convince WOCCU's affiliates that by partnering with village banking practitioners they could access a new, very large, and very safe market for their financial services.

MEDA/Haiti—Literacy Program

Launched in 1994, the Mennonite Economic Development Association (MEDA) operates three village banking programs in four rural districts of Haiti with a current outreach of 1,500 clients. MEDA/Haiti offers both conventional micro-business loans as well as loans for agriculture. However, when only 8 percent of its clients were able to read and write, MEDA/Haiti decided it would have to offer literacy training if its groups were ever going to be able to demonstrate adequate management and leadership skills. The institution designed a two-stage literacy training model. In stage 1 (alfa), participants learn basic words and numbers by participating in a game. After passing a test, graduates of the alfa stage move on to the post-alfa stage where they learn advanced reading/writing and business skills. Through this literacy program MEDA/Haiti expects that 75 percent of its clients will become functionally literate. The MEDA/Haiti program is also a recipient of CGAP's Pro-Poor Challenge award.

Grameen Bank/Bangladesh—Village Cell Phone Program

With Grameen's village phone program, a micro-entrepreneur can use her loan to buy a mobile phone and operate it as a business. She then sells the use of it on a per minute basis to others in her community. Village phone entrepreneurs in Bangladesh are earning an average net income of more than

US$70 a month (in a country where the average annual per capita income is less than $400), and her entire village benefits. Uses of the phone include being able to communicate with distant relatives, check the market price of goods, search for other important information, or to contact elected officials. By knowing the market price of goods, a person is able to negotiate with middlemen for a better price on her products and thus increase her income. With a phone call one is able to avoid the need to travel some distance in person, and therefore save the costs associated with transportation and the loss of productivity. When the village phone program began in 1997, there were twenty-eight village phones. As of spring 2002 there are more than 11,700. Grameen Telecom continues to expand the village phone program in Bangladesh, and projects that there will be 50,000 mobile phones operating in rural villages by the end of 2004. GrameenPhone Ltd, the telecommunications service provider in which Grameen Telecom is an investor, has a total of more than 500,000 subscribers, including urban clients. GrameenPhone is not only the largest mobile phone service provider in Bangladesh, but in all of South Asia. The Grameen Technology Center is working in partnership with Grameen Telecom to recreate the success that has been achieved in Bangladesh with the village phone program by replicating the model in other developing countries.

INNOVATIONS IN PROGRAM FINANCING

FINCA International—Village Bank Capital Fund

In 1996, with an equity loan of $1 million from the US Agency for International Development (USAID), FINCA International set up its Village Bank Capital Fund (VBCF). The fund's mission is to provide all necessary financial products and services to FINCA affiliates, especially credit enhancements (its original primary service) and direct loans to meet short-term liquidity needs. Additionally, the VBCF functions as a central liquidity fund—transferring capital from capital-surplus to capital-scarce affiliates. It also seeks to protect network assets from currency devaluations by storing excess liquidity in dollar-denominated accounts. As each affiliate reaches break-even and beyond, its growing self-sufficiency makes it eligible to borrow from commercial banks in the host country. The VBCF provides these commercial banks with letters of credit (in dollars) to guarantee their local-currency loans (or credit lines) extended to FINCA affiliates. Direct loans normally average about $250,000 and are repaid in two to four months. Between enhancements and direct loans, by the end of fiscal year 2001, an estimated $10.7 million in total lending occurred thanks to credit enhancement and direct lending originating with the VBCF. Other NGOs have instituted their own loan guarantee programs including Katalysis, CARE, and ACCION.

PRIDE AFRICA—Sunlink Program

PRIDE AFRICA (PA) is a US nonprofit with regional offices in Nairobi, Kenya, that currently serves more than 100,000 clients through a fifty-four-branch network in Kenya, Tanzania, Uganda, Malawi, and Zambia. *Sunlink*, a model created by PA in 1995, seeks to provide financial services to the microenterprise sector while incorporating a direct link with commercial banks to streamline delivery and information services, reduce costs, and enhance client services. The Sunlink model has been designed to be replicated anywhere—a sort of franchising to facilitate rapid growth. Clients are organized in "Enterprise Groups" (EGs) with every ten EGs forming a "Market Enterprise Committee." These structures allow for two levels of loan guarantees, plus, by bundling savings and credit transactions, they provide clients with more favorable interest rates and preferred client status. In turn, the partner bank's transaction costs and loan risks are lowered, providing a growing incentive to move down-market to serve ever poorer clients. Sunlink distinguishes itself through its IT focus on modern equipment and software solutions, which is accompanied by a serious investment in training. Sunlink is now starting to incorporate magnetic-stripe "smartcards." PRIDE Africa hopes that its Sunlink methodology will 1) help liberate MFIs from donor-dependency by facilitating their interface with the commercial banking industry, while 2) creating better incentives for the banks (via NGO partnership) to extend their services to the heretofore under-served market of low-income clients.

URWEGO/Rwanda—Consulting Services

URWEGO, which means "ladder," was organized by World Relief in 1997 and has since become the largest MFI in Rwanda with a current outreach of almost 10,000 clients. Exploring alternatives to traditional sources of program financing, in June 2001 URWEGO introduced an initiative called "URWEGO Consulting Services" (UCS). Essentially, UCS takes advantage of the expertise of its program staff by offering basic microfinance training as well as evaluation services to other NGOs. All revenue earned from UCS goes directly into URWEGO income and helps the organization towards its target of 100 percent self-sufficiency. In addition to the financial return, UCS is able to promote sound practices among other MFIs. In its first nine months UCS completed contracts with ten client organizations based in Rwanda and the Democratic Republic of Congo, generating $9,500 in revenues, equivalent to more than 8 percent of URWEGO's operating budget.

Shared Interest/South Africa—Loan Guarantees for MFIs

Shared Interest (SI) is a not-for-profit social investment fund designed to enhance the access of low-income South Africans to loans from commercial banks. In 1996, together with its Swiss associate RAFAD, Shared Interest established its Thembani International Guarantee Fund (TIGF) for the purpose of providing guarantees for loans for microcredit, small business development, low-cost housing, and rural enterprises in South Africa. SI does its principal fundraising for TIGF in the United States, where it solicits minimum $10,000 investments from individuals and institutions for periods ranging from three to ten years. These funds are invested in the United States, then used as security for South African bank loans to community development financial intermediaries (CDFIs). With an enlarged loan pool, the CDFIs are able to assist many more low-income clients while simultaneously achieving higher self-sufficiency from increased interest earnings. Such resources, coupled with TIGF technical assistance, also help the CDFIs to develop the skills needed to plan, negotiate, utilize, and monitor bank loans on their own. Shared Interest reports that during its first six years of operation it has—through its CDFI partnerships—managed to impact the lives of some 250,000 low-income South Africans, equivalent to about 42,000 families.

CRWRC/Honduras—Recuperated Housing Funds for Microfinance

The Christian Reformed World Relief Committee (CRWRC) has been financing the construction of hundreds of new and repaired homes in Honduras following Hurricane Mitch in 1998. The recipients are expected to pay a portion of the material costs of their new house (from $200 to $1,000) with the loan term and monthly payment adjusted to their ability to repay. As these recuperated funds are repaid, they are used to capitalize microfinance loan funds managed by self-help groups modeled on credit unions, all entirely managed by community members. Member savings in the group are also used as collateral on their housing loans.

INNOVATIONS IN PROGRAM ADMINISTRATION AND GOVERNANCE

WOTR/India—Village Federations of Self-Help Groups

The Watershed Organization Trust (WOTR) is an NGO working to organize self-help groups of women in rural villages of Maharashtra State in India. As reported earlier (see NABARD, at the beginning of this chapter), rural women are first organized in self-help groups (SHGs) of twelve to twenty members. Each group is supported by a local NGO (in this case

WOTR) in charge of training and regular monitoring. The SHGs are likely to differ with regard to savings rates, repayment schedule, and interest rate, but what is uniform is the practice of saving regularly and lending internally. In any given village there may be anywhere from three to fifteen SHGs. All SHGs in one village then form an apex body called "Samyukt Mahila Samiti" (SMS), which is a joint women's committee formed by one to two representatives from each SHG. This SMS federation is encouraged to become legally chartered, to formally interface with the Watershed Organization Trust, and to establish credit relationships with external sources (NABARD and its branch offices). Thus, when an SHG's members are ready for external credit, they compile the individual loan requests of their twelve to twenty members and submit a single, collective loan request. The SMS village federation reviews the requests of its member groups, assesses each SHG's eligibility, and also makes a single collective loan application to the WOTR, which after reviewing the application submits it to the nearest state branch for disbursement of loan funds requested. The system has many advantages. Most of the work is done at the village level, saving time and greatly reducing bank fees. Furthermore, women who are chosen to serve in the village federation (SMS) gain considerable prestige and are often subsequently elected to the local village governing bodies (*gram panchayat*). Finally, the system is simple and easily replicated.

TIF/Slovakia—Traveling Road Show

The Integra Foundation (TIF) operates a microenterprise program for women-at-risk in rural Slovakia. It specifically targets single mothers, divorcees with young children, victims of domestic violence, wives of alcoholics or unemployed husbands, women who are unable to re-enter the workforce following maternity leave, women with disabilities, and ethnic minorities. To serve this vulnerable and dispersed population, Integra has developed an innovative response to the delivery of microfinance services in areas where client density is insufficient to sustain a full and continuing program presence. Integra does a "traveling road show" which selects a new municipality each month. Advertising six weeks in advance, TIF screens and selects about twenty applicants, provides about forty-eight hours of part-time business development services training that results in a business plan, receives and approves loan applications, and finally disburses the loans. Child care services are provided for children of the women who participate in training. Clients also get a CD ROM "Small Business ToolKit" which loan officers use to provide distance mentoring. Six months later Integra staff return to repeat the cycle. Thus program momentum is sustained while avoiding saturation in small, semi-rural marketplaces. Clients keep in touch via trust groups, internet, and phone. They make their monthly loan payments through the local bank or post office. The project reached 178 clients in eight municipalities in 2001 and plans to reach twelve more municipalities in 2002.

SKS/India—Reducing Costs with Smart Cards

Swayam Krishi Sangam (SKS) is a microfinance program that works in the Medak district of Andhra Pradesh, one of the poorest regions of India, plagued with frequent droughts, soil erosion, and severe deforestation. SKS specifically targets the poorest women, mostly the Dalits (untouchables) and others from the lowest castes. Since their inception in 1998, SKS savings, credit, and training services have benefited more than 3,000 women from ninety-one villages. Confronted by the twin challenges of high service delivery costs (inherent to working in remote rural areas) and low interest income resulting from small loan size, SKS chose to reduce costs by using smart cards provided to each client. SKS asserts that this technology allows their loan officers to attend three village-level meetings a day instead of two, allowing them to increase their client load and thus economizing about $2000 per year per branch office, after covering the cost of the cards and the terminals. Computerization of transactions has also helped to minimize errors, provided management with more up-to-date information, and enhanced transparency. Time spent in meetings and on keeping manual collection sheets and passbooks (now eliminated) has been slashed. Each client is provided a smart card. SKS staff come to meetings with a palm pilot-sized hand-held computer (HHC). At the meeting each client's card is inserted in the terminal and her savings and loan transactions automatically recorded and updated. At day's end the loan officer simply uploads the data from the HHC to the branch office computer. Meanwhile, a read-only HHC is left in the village so that members can check their account information. The SKS was awarded a CGAP Pro-Poor Innovation Challenge award for this innovation.

UMU/Uganda—Bank Draft Facility for the Poor

Self-described as the fastest growing MFI in Uganda, the Uganda Microfinance Union was started in 1997 with the mission of providing quality financial services to the poor via client-driven and client-focused services. UMU is now operational in seven districts, has reached 13,000 clients, and is operationally self-sufficient. In 2000 UMU discovered that the inability to transfer money between rural areas and urban trading centers was forcing clients to carry lesser amounts in cash because of the prevailing risk of theft, which in turn was causing higher prices on purchases, lower prices on sales, and higher costs due to more frequent trips. In response UMU designed its

"Micro Draft Facility." A client now deposits funds in her account at the UMU branch in return for which the branch issues a UMU bank check or a pre-bought draft from a commercial bank for the amount desired—either of which will be drawn on UMU's account in a major trading center. To move cash in the opposite direction the procedure is reversed. This innovation has enabled its clients to greatly reduce their risks and losses due to theft dangers and won UMU a Pro-Poor Innovation award from CGAP.

Opportunity International—Accreditation Program

Organized in 1971, Opportunity International has created a network of forty-two autonomous yet affiliated implementing partners in twenty-four countries. In 2001 the network made 243,654 loans (85 percent to women) for a total amount of $62.9 million and with a repayment rate of 98 percent. Since 1999 all OI Network partners with more than 3,000 clients or a portfolio exceeding US$500,000 must pass a two-stage accreditation process every three years. The aims of this process are to promote institutional learning and reinforce partner commitment to common goals. The first stage is highly participatory in that members of a partner's board, management staff, and an OI staff member form a self-assessment team. The team performs a two-day performance review that examines seven areas: 1) vision and values, 2) governance, 3) people and internal relationships, 4) funding and external relationships, 5) administration and control, 6) operational performance, and 7) transformational impact. Using standards set by OI, the team then rates the performance of each area, followed by a plan for improvement. During the second phase, a peer review team composed of experts from OI and other partners reviews and verifies the seven ratings. After resolving any discrepancies between the two sets of performance rankings, the review team creates a new plan for improvement, and the partner is accordingly assigned either full or partial accreditation. OI may issue a warning and eventual non-accreditation if recommended improvements are not implemented. The costs of each accreditation review are shared by OI with the affiliate. It bears mentioning that Catholic Relief Services and other NGOs offer similar accreditation programs.

INNOVATIONS IN PROGRAM EVALUATION

AIMS/SEEP—Evaluation Manual

Perhaps the earliest and most comprehensive contribution to advancing the state of the art of MFI program evaluation is the AIMS/SEEP evaluation manual entitled *Learning From Clients: Assessment Tools for Microfinance*

Practitioners (2001), available free online from the AIMS Web site (www.mip.org). For anyone contemplating an evaluation project, this document is a goldmine of practical technical information. The core of this manual—chapters 4 to 8—consists of five evaluation tools: 1) Impact Survey, 2) Client Exit Survey, 3) Loan Use Strategies Over Time, 4) Client Empowerment, and 5) Client Satisfaction. Each tool includes a sample questionnaire or interview format, hypotheses to be tested and their rationales, guidance for interviewing, and guidelines for data coding, analysis, and statistical treatment. But this manual goes much further. In chapters 1 to 3 it provides a conceptual framework for the impact assessment process, its different levels (individual, household, enterprise, and community), and suggests exercises for MFI staff to identify their own "program impact pathways" and "markers of change." It provides checklists of do's and don'ts in questionnaire design, translation, field testing, interviewing, and post interviewing. It provides a step-by-step program for training field interviewers and supervisors. In chapter 9 it provides detailed guidance on scheduling and budgeting an impact assessment and even provides a suggested generic outline for a final evaluation report. In the Appendix there are many pages of guidance for the statistical analysis of most of the hypotheses and questions found in the tools presented in the text. Last but not least, the manual is linked to an on-line "help desk" to assist readers with any questions they might have. And still, with all this, the manual describes itself as a continuing "work in progress," encouraging readers to pick and choose only those evaluation elements that make sense for their programs, and to provide feedback on their experiences that might further enrich the manual's content in the future.

CGAP—Poverty Assessment Tool

One of the unifying characteristics of microfinance institutions is that they profess to serve "the poor." However, it is a well-known fact that most MFIs do not employ a targeting tool sufficiently rigorous to identify with reasonable certainty which among their new clients is severely poor, moderately poor, or non-poor. Targeting tools such as "Participatory Wealth Ranking," "the housing index," and "means testing" have been advanced by MFIs like Grameen Bank and CASHPOR, which specialize in serving the poorest, but theirs are methodologies where client selection is controlled by the MFI. In contrast, village banking and most self-help group methodologies have generally preferred less rigorous targeting methods (if any at all) by allowing loan size, geography, and client self-selection to be the determinants of which clients are reached; indeed, these MFIs often prefer mixed clienteles (poor and non-poor) to ensure minimum local capacity for bookkeeping and other management tasks.

Given the often contentious debate between targeting and non-targeting MFIs, CGAP has stepped into the breech with its Poverty Assessment Tool. While this tool is "primarily for donors" rather than MFIs, it provides donors as well as practitioners with a relatively inexpensive and scientific way to certify (whether or not they use targeting tools) the extent to which they are in compliance with their mission to reach the poorest. Because it employs inexpensive host-country professionals, the cost of the CGAP poverty assessment tool ranges from $4,000 to $16,000 (with an average cost of $10,000)—which is well within the capacity of many MFIs to afford. CGAP's methodology is based on a survey of 200 MFI clients and 300 comparison households. It collects information on demographics, economic activities, footwear and clothing expenditures, food security and vulnerability, housing indicators, land ownership, and ownership of other assets. For each MFI program evaluated the study establishes a Poverty Index score that categorizes all non-client respondents into three equal poverty categories (each with their own cut-off)—the bottom third, the middle third, and the top third. Using these same cutoffs, the study then compares the distribution of the entering client households.

FINCA—Poverty Targeting Tool

With access to the CGAP poverty assessment tool, it will now become much easier for MFIs to design wildly different poverty-targeting tools, based on their unique methodologies, because the effectiveness of any new tool can now be "certified" by means of a CGAP "poverty assessment survey." Such is the case with John Hatch, founder of FINCA International, who has designed a methodology for targeting not the poorest but the *most vulnerable*. Using this methodology, FINCA field staff—in the very first borrowers organizing meeting—will clearly describe the purpose of the village bank as serving the "most vulnerable." The field staff will then review different kinds of vulnerability and engage participating women in a discussion of who in their community meets any of the following descriptions: 1) single mother who is sole source of support for at least three children; 2) family that has recently suffered a severe loss (such as a natural disaster, fire, robbery, or death); 3) family with school-age children who are not in school; 4) family with children who are under-nourished; 5) family with a member who is chronically ill; 6) self-employed seniors who are raising grandchildren; 7) other vulnerability (determined by participants). This approach is designed to create a Vulnerability Index, which in turn can be correlated with 10 poverty-surrogate indicators collected in a FINCA loan application interview applied to new borrowers. Financed by a CGAP grant, FINCA's poverty assessment tool is currently being field tested with results expected by late 2002.

The Small Enterprise Foundation/South Africa—
Participatory Wealth Ranking

The Small Enterprise Foundation (SEF) has developed Participatory Wealth Ranking (PWR) as a tool to assist the institution in poverty targeting. SEF management argues that unless active poverty targeting is used an institution cannot build microfinance services for the poorest. Their experience suggests that when better-off people are included, this may well discourage the poorest from joining. Hence, even if an institution's aim is not to *exclusively* reach the poorest, unless active targeting is used it is possible the MFIs may inadvertently miss the poorest altogether. PWR is a cost-effective process in which, with the help of a facilitator, members of a village map out the houses in their village. Then, in three or four separate meetings, villagers sort each house into groups according to its poverty level. The results from each meeting are compared to the results from the others. If all groups give consistent answers, their ranking is considered accurate, and programs that wish to serve the poorest clients begin to motivate the villagers from the bottom income groups. The PWR methodology appears best adapted for microfinance programs where staff selects the clients who will participate, but less useful for other programs (village banking) where the organization of peer-lending groups is based on community self-selection and a mix of poor and non-poor is considered desirable.

The CASHPOR Network/Malaysia—The CASHPOR House Index

The CASHPOR House Index (CHI) is a poverty targeting tool developed by the CASHPOR Network headquartered in Malaysia. If housing is a good indicator of the poverty level of families, then by simply examining the houses of potential clients, practitioners can determine with a high degree of accuracy whether those families are among the poorest or not. They do this by inspecting the walls and roof of each house and assigning a numerical score to the condition of each. An assets test is administered to families whose houses had the lowest scores for further verification of poverty levels. Ownership of large farm animals or irrigated land are disqualifiers in such a test. CHI is most widely used in rural Asia, but its use is being expanded and adapted to other areas as appropriate. Grameen Foundation USA has been active in spreading this innovation to its partner programs in Latin America.

Opportunity International—
Performance Measurement and Benchmarking

Faced with the problem of limited ability to compare financial and program performance information among its more than forty partner organizations worldwide, in 1999 OI introduced its Partner Reporting System (PRS) and *Opportunity Quarterly* in order to promote greater accountability, transparency, and performance. The PRS captures information on more than 100 financial and program variables on a quarterly basis. Using ratio and trend analysis, the system tracks twenty quantitative indicators to measure outreach, loan portfolio quality, efficiency, profitability, and sustainability. In addition to measuring total borrowers and average loan size, the PRS also separates portfolio, clients, and arrears by product type—namely, individual, trust bank, and solidarity group loans. Furthermore, partners are classified by small, medium, and large scale of operations and performance outcomes are grouped by region—Africa, Asia, Eastern Europe, and Latin America.

INNOVATIONS IN RESPONSE TO EMERGENCIES

Katalysis—Disaster Response Action Plan

In January 2001 a set of severe earthquakes hit El Salvador. Katalysis's local partner MFIs—PROCOMES and ASEI—had no systematic response to the emergency. This void inspired the development of a thirty-five-page document entitled *When Disaster Strikes: An Action Plan for Preparation and Response for the Unexpected in Central America*. The manual is divided into three sections: one for the local MFI, one for the regional field office, and one for Katalysis headquarters. Mary Morgan, Katalysis program director, describes the document as follows: "Each section lays out how to prepare for a disaster, how to provide moral and emotional support when a disaster strikes, and then how to assess the damage. There are charts for the loan officers to assess the impact of the disaster on clients and their businesses, calculate the amount of portfolio affected, and how to assess which loans should be refinanced or restructured." Copies of the document are available in Spanish and English.

USAID/MBP—Survey of MFI Disaster Responses

The most definitive summary of MFI disaster responses remains that of Geetha Nagarajan's *Microfinance in the Wake of Natural Disasters: Challenges and Opportunities* (March 1998) and financed by USAID's Microenterprise Best Practices (MBP) Project. This study begins with a review of the stages of natural disaster mitigation including 1) pre-disaster, 2) relief, 3) rehabilitation, 4) reconstruction, 5) development. The author then explains which MFI products are applicable at each stage, but with a cautionary analysis of how the structure of each product—fund management, staffing, methodology, objectives, sustainability, outreach, client selection, enforcement, coordination, and so forth—has to be altered between normal periods versus natural disaster periods. Another cautionary chapter is devoted to the tradeoffs between client protection and portfolio protection. The text is saturated with multiple examples of actual MFI disaster response case studies, the most comprehensive being BRAC/Bangladesh's five-stage response. This forty-six-page document ends with recommendations for disaster response actions for donors, policymakers, and MFIs.

CONCLUDING COMMENTS

A Few Disclaimers

In this chapter we have thrown a broad net and captured a heavy load of fish of many different types and sizes. It is important to emphasize that many of the innovations reported are not necessarily the best or the most important of their respective category. Most of them are neither the first nor the only example of the innovation they were selected to represent. A good innovation may best be judged *not* by the claims of success of its creators but by the degree to which it has been imitated by others. As the so-called "father of village banking" I like to make the point that within FINCA programs alone there are over 1,000 field staff that can organize, support, and monitor a village bank far better than I can. Similarly, there may be merit in being the first to innovate, but history clearly shows that the most successful examples of a given innovation will most likely be demonstrated by its replicators, not its creators.

The Location and Pace of Innovation

Where is it occurring? The answer is *anywhere* there are one or more MFIs. This chapter reports on innovations from five continents and from many different countries. One gets the sense there is hardly a country left on the planet where not just one but several MFIs (in some cases dozens) have taken root. Similarly, the competition among MFIs is helping to accelerate the pace of innovation. It has become a fact of life, virtually an imperative, for any MFI to innovate constantly. Indeed, innovation should be considered the rule and business-as-usual the exception.

Government Involvement

Governments are beginning to get more involved, deploying their financial service infrastructures in a way increasingly intended to meet the demand of *most* (if not all) their citizens, not just the political and economic elites. Some of this involvement may have been sincerely motivated by explicit development and poverty-alleviation agendas. But more likely it reflects the need of the state to re-assert its role as regulator of the financial services sector. In some cases it may represent a belated attempt to become once again the primary channel through which external capital will be channeled to the poor. Given these considerations, non-regulated MFIs can expect increasing pressure from local governments to transform into regulated financial intermediaries or get out of the lending business altogether. So as competition, innovation, and government regulation increasingly shake up the current MFI environment, I think it can be safely predicted that many nonprofit NGOs will be forced either to become regulated MFIs themselves or the partners of regulated MFIs. In the next few years we can expect to see significant innovation in how these partnerships can be structured so as to produce win-win-win results for clients, NGOs, and regulated MFIs.

Competitive Advantages

The largest commercial financial service providers are now fully cognizant of the fact that they have a huge advantage with regard to capital, management capacity, and range of financial products, but they are still particularly inexperienced in knowing how to reach and organize the poor. This latter expertise is largely the province of NGOs. But the trends are perfectly clear: the largest and smallest practitioners have a vested interest in partnering with each other, they are now demonstrating how this can be done, and they will increasingly innovate to move in this direction in the future.

Information Technology

It is also clear that innovation information technology is not only revolutionizing the microfinance movement but will continue to intensify that revolution. No matter how large an MFI's outreach (even when it serves millions of clients), thanks to computers it is now possible to track *every single client*, to store and evaluate her accumulated transactions, to monitor the seasonal complexities of her cash flow, to track her asset growth, to measure her family's gains in well-being, and to increasingly customize financial or training products to meet her evolving needs—all at lower cost than the obsolete manual bookkeeping that such innovation is rapidly replacing. Happily, this transformation is also making the process of microfinance management far more transparent.

Recommendations for Going Forward

This work amounts to a small first step in attempting to organize the breadth and diversity of innovation within the microfinance movement. Judging from the feedback received while preparing and circulating early drafts of this document, there is enormous and growing interest within the microfinance movement for the reporting on innovation. I recommend that the function this work attempted to serve be institutionalized. There ought to be an annual innovation report. Gathering information on innovation should be somebody's full-time job, or even that of a well-staffed research unit. Contributions to innovation reports need to be standardized. In addition to a flexible description of the innovation itself, contributing MFIs should be asked to include 1) background on the sponsoring MFI, 2) the problem which the innovation addressed, 3) measurable benefits or results achieved by the innovation, 4) cost of implementing the innovation, and 5) evidence of replication of the innovation by others. Such an annual innovation report could be divided two-thirds into reporting on new innovations and one-third into updating the status of innovations already reported and or being replicated.

In sum, the present work—a one-time, abbreviated chapter, prepared as a voluntary, unfunded contribution for the benefit of the microfinance movement—is hardly a suitable prototype for the innovation reports of the future. Somebody needs to "hold the energy" for this function so it can be accomplished comprehensively, accurately, and systematically. This chapter was a necessary first start, comparable to man's first, clumsy attempt to fly. It is now time to start building many more and far superior prototypes for reporting on innovation. It is now time to start innovating with innovation..

Chapter 3 References

AIMS/SEEP
Further information available at: www.mip.org

AlSol Chiapas/Mexico
AlSol Chiapas, AC, Francisco Leon No.12, San Cristobal de las Casas, Chiapas, C.P. 29250, Mexico
Further information available at: www.gfusa.org/gbrp/latinamerica.html

ASA/Bangladesh
ASA, 23/3 Block-pB, Khilji Road, Shyamoli, Mohamadpur, Dhaka-1207, Bangladesh.
Further information available at: www.asabd.org and in *New Directions*, op. cit., Chapter 6, p .6.
Contact ASA via e-mail at: asa@bd.drik.net

Beselidhja-Zavet/Kosovo
Contact Richard Schroeder at World Relief via e-mail at: RSchroeder@wr.org

CARE/Bangladesh
CARE/Bangladesh, Harun-Or-Rashid, PC-Income II
Contact CARE/Bangladesh via e-mail at: harun@carebangladesh.org

The CASHPOR Network/Malaysia
Anton Simanowitz and Ben Nkuna, "Overcoming the Obstacles of Identifying the Poorest Families: Using Participatory Wealth Ranking (PWR), The CASHPOR House Index and Other Measurements to Identify and Encourage the Participation of the Poorest Families, Especially the Women of those Families."
Available at: www.microcreditsummit.org/papers/povertypaper.htm

Centre Béninois Pour le Développment des Initiatives à la Base (CBDIBA)/Benin
Further information available at: http://afrdh.org/cbdiba/
Contact CBDIBA via e-mail: cbdiba@bow.internet.bj

CFTS/India
CASHPOR Financial & Technical Services Ltd (CFTS), Pili Kothi (Opp. Roadways Bus Station), Mirzapur 231001, Uttar Pradesh, India.
Further information available at: www.cgap.org/assets/images/focusonpoverty-latest.pdf.
Contact CFTS via e-mail at: ahasan@lw1.vsnl.net.in

CGAP

Further information available at: http://nt1.ids.ac.uk/cgap/poverty/

Contact CGAP via e-mail at: cgap@worldbank.org

CRWRC/Honduras

CRWRC, 2850 Kalamazoo SE, Grand Rapids, MI 49560 USA

FINCA International

Further information available at: www.villagebanking.org

Contact FINCA's VBCF via e-mail at: epozo@villagebanking.org.

Contact John Hatch at FINCA via e-mail at: Jhatch@villagebanking.org.

FINCA/Peru

FINCA-Peru: Domingo Casanova 151, Lince, Lima, Peru

Contact FINCA-Peru via e-mail at: finca.peru@infotex.com.pe

FINCA/Samara, Russian Federation

FINCA/Samara, Ulitsa Michurina 52 Room 224, Samara Russian Federation, Samara

Further information available from: FINCA/ Kyrgyzstan, Gogol Str., 127 "a", Bishkek, Kyrgyzstan, tel. 996-312-681-810 (e-mail: jmeikle@finca.org.kg) and in *New Directions*, op. cit., Chapter 6, p. 7.

Contact FINCA/Samara via e-mail at: jferry@finca.ru

FINCA/Uganda

FINCA Uganda, PO Box 24450, 63 Buranda Road, Kampala, tel./fax. 256-41-231-134

Contact Guy Winship at FINCA/Uganda via e-mail at: gwinship@villagebanking.org

FONKOZE/Haiti

FONKOZE, Ave. Jean Paul II, #7 (à l'interieur), Port-au-Prince, Haiti

Further information available at: www.fonkoze.org

Contact FONKOZE via e-mail at: Fonkoze@aol.com

Grameen Bank/Bangladesh

"Housing Microfinance Initiatives: Synthesis and Regional Summary: Asia, Latin America and Sub-Saharan Africa, with Selected Case Studies," Microenterprise Best Practices, p. 55 to 66.

Available at: www.mip.org

Further information available at: www.tech.gfusa.org/projects.shtml

Katalysis
Katalysis, *When Disaster Strikes*, 2001
Available at: www.katalysis.org
Contact Katalysis via e-mail at: mmorgan@katalysis.org

LPWF/China
Susan H. Holcombe and Xu Xianman, "Microfinance and Poverty Alleviation: United Nations Collaboration with Chinese Experiments, 1997.
Available at: www.gdrc.org/icm/country/china-mf1.html

Mata Masu Dubara/Niger
CARE International UK, 10-13 Rushworth Street, London SEI ORB
Further information available at: www.careinternational.org.uk/projects/women/nigerwomenonthemove.html
Contact CARE International via e-mail at: info@uk.care.org

MEDA/Haiti
MEDA, 226 Route de Delmas, BP 2160, Port-au-Prince, Haiti
Further information available at: www.meda.org
Contact MEDA/Haiti via e-mail at: meda@aen2.net

NABARD/India
Hans Dieter Seibel, "SHG Banking: A Financial Technology for Reaching Marginal Areas and the Very Poor," AEF Development Research Center, Working Paper 2001–3.
Available at: www.uni-koeln.de/ew-fak/aef/Working%20Papers.htm

Opportunity International
Further information available at: www.opportunity.org
Contact Opportunity International via e-mail at: reporting@opportunity.net

Palli Karma Sahayak Foundation/Bangladesh
Dr. Salehuddin Ahmed, "Creating Autonomous National and Sub-Regional Microcredit Funds."
Available at: www.microcreditsummit.org/papers/fundspaper.htm
Contact PKSF via e-mail at: pksf@citechco.net

PMUK/Bangladesh
Contact PMUK via e-mail at: padakhep@bdonline

PRIDE AFRICA

Further information available at: www.prideafrica.com

Contact PRIDE/Africa via e-mail at: jfc@africaonline.co.ke

Pro Mujer/Bolivia

Further information available at: www.promujer.org,

Contact Pro-Mujer/Bolivia via e-mail at: lapaz@promujer.org

Shared Interest/South Africa

Further information available at: www.sharedinterest.org

Contact Donna Katzin at Shared Interest via e-mail at: donna@sharedinterest.org

SKS/India

SKS, 3-2-851 Chitrakoot Building, Kachiguda Station Road, Hyderabad, A.P. 500-027, India.

Further information available at: www. Sksindia.com

Contact SKS via e-mail at: info@sksindia.com

The Small Enterprise Foundation/South Africa

Anton Simanowitz and Ben Nkuna, "Overcoming the Obstacles of Identifying the Poorest Families: Using Participatory Wealth Ranking (PWR), The CASHPOR House Index and Other Measurements to Identify and Encourage the Participation of the Poorest Families, Especially the Women of those Families."

Available at: www.microcreditsummit.org/papers/povertypaper.htm

TIF/Slovakia

The Integra Venture, Partizanska 6, 81103 Bratislava 1, Slovakia.

Further information available at: www.integra.sk

Contact Allan Bussard at Integra via e-mail at: allan.bussard@integra.sk

UMU/Uganda

Further information available at: www.lifeinafrica.com/UgandaMicrofinance.htm

Contact UMU via e-mail at: ugandamu@infocom.com.ug

UNRWA/Gaza

UNRWA, PO Box 140157, Amman 11814, Jordan, Tel: (972) 8 677 7333

Further information available at: www.un.org/unrwa/progs/ig/p3.html

URWEGO/Rwanda
Primary contact: Patrick Kelley, BP 6052, Kigali, Rwanda, tel. 250-0848-36-66
Contact URWEGO via e-mail at: Pkelley@wr.org or pgreer@nims.wre.org

USAID/MBP
Geetha Nagarajan, *Microfinance in the Wake of Natural Disasters*, March 1998, USAID
Available through the MBP project at: www.mip.org/pubs/mbp-def.htm

WEEC/Kenya
Women Economic Empowerment Consortium, Off Magadi Road, PO Box, Kiserian, Ngong, Kenya, Tel. (254) 0303 25192
Contact WEEC/Kenya via e-mail at: weec@swiftkenya.com

WEP/Nepal
Jeffrey Ashe, "PACT's Women's Empowerment Program in Nepal: A Savings and Literacy-Led Alternative to Financial Institution Building."
Available at: www.mip.org/pdfs/aims/wep-paper-ashe-parrot.pdf
Contact Jeffrey Ashe via e-mail at: JAAshe@aol.com

WOCCU/FFH/Philippines
See *New Directions*, op. cit. ch. 2, p. 11.
Further information available at: www.freefromhunger.org

WOTR/India
Further information available at: www.wotr.org
Contact WOTR via e-mail at: wotr@vsnl.com

YOSEFO/Tanzania
Youth Self Employment Program (YOSEFO), PO Box 10272, Dar es Salaam, Tanzania
Contact YOSEFO via e-mail at: mill@ud.co.tz

4

Empowering Women through Microfinance

Susy Cheston and Lisa Kuhn

According to the *State of the Microcredit Summit Campaign 2001 Report*, 14.2 million of the world's poorest[1] women now have access to financial services through specialized microfinance institutions (MFIs), banks, NGOs, and other nonbank financial institutions. These women account for nearly 74 percent of the 19.3 million of the world's poorest people now being served by microfinance institutions. Most of these women have access to credit to invest in businesses that they own and operate themselves. The vast majority of them have excellent repayment records, in spite of the daily hardships they face. Contrary to conventional wisdom, they have shown that it is a very good idea to lend to the poor and to women.

So, given these impressive statistics, can we pat ourselves on the back for our service to poor women and assume that women's empowerment and other gender issues will take care of themselves?

Although women's access to financial services has increased substantially in the past ten years, their ability to benefit from this access is often still limited by the disadvantages they experience because of their gender. Some MFIs are providing a decreasing percentage of loans to women, even as these institutions grow and offer new loan products. Others have found that on average women's loan sizes are smaller than those of men, even when they are in the same credit program, the same community, and the same lending group. Some differences in loan sizes may be a result of women's greater poverty or the limited capacity of women's businesses to absorb capital. But they can also indicate broader social discrimination against women which limits the opportunities open to them, raising the question of whether microenterprise development programs should do more to address these issues. And looking at the leadership of many MFIs, we see very few women. Their contributions—whether setting the vision on a board of directors, designing products and services, or implementing programs—are missing. Thus, as the industry becomes more sophisticated in developing targeted products and services, it makes sense to look at both targeting women and empowering women.

Microfinance programs have the potential to transform power relations and empower the poor—both men and women. In well-run microfinance programs, there is a relationship of respect between the provider and the client that is inherently empowering. This is true regardless of the methodology or approach—whether the institution takes a minimalist approach of delivering financial services only or a more holistic or integrated approach. As a consequence, microfinance has become a central component of many donor agencies' and national governments' gender, poverty alleviation, and community development strategies. Several studies and the experiences of a number of MFIs have shown, however, that simply putting financial resources in the hands of poor women is not enough to bring about empowerment and improved welfare.

In this chapter we demonstrate that although microfinance does not address all the barriers to women's empowerment, microfinance programs, when properly designed, can make an important contribution to women's empowerment. We begin by examining some of the theories and assumptions behind the targeting of women for microfinance and the resulting implications for empowerment. Drawing on the studies and experiences of microfinance institutions in Africa, Asia, and Latin America, the paper looks at what evidence is known about impact on women, in terms of both welfare and empowerment. While acknowledging that there is no set of indicators of empowerment that can be applied universally across cultures and regions, we present evidence of several types of changes that are relevant and important for empowerment across a range of cultures. The heart of the chapter is an in-depth case study of the impact on women achieved by Sinapi Aba Trust (SAT), Opportunity International's partner in Ghana. Based on that study and the experiences of other MFIs, we identify several programmatic factors and strategies that can make a positive contribution to women's empowerment and holistic transformation, including business training, discussion of social issues, support and advice for balancing family and business responsibilities, experience in decision-making and leadership, and ownership and control of the credit institution. We also look at the role that women's economic contribution to the household and community plays in empowering them. We then look at some strategies used by MFIs for reaching and empowering women and their results, identifying some of the most promising.

Our reading, research, and experience have turned up rich examples of empowerment, but have also raised many questions that suggest some important areas for future work. We therefore conclude by issuing a call to action for practitioners and donors, so that the tremendous potential of microfinance to empower women can be fulfilled.

This chapter is not meant to be a comprehensive and exhaustive presentation of all that is known about the subject of microfinance and empowerment. We seek to build on the growing body of research on the topic, blend academic and practitioner perspectives and experiences, and encourage further exploration and dialogue on the subject. Throughout the chapter, we provide references so that those interested in exploring specific aspects of empowerment can find more in-depth information. At the outset of our research, we had hoped to find more data that would allow us to differentiate between the types of impacts that can be expected from different types of microfinance delivery mechanisms and methodologies, but we found very little. Although this paper focuses primarily on group-lending methodologies, we want to acknowledge that empowerment can take place through individual lending as well and encourage further research in that area. A number of other areas related to empowerment merit further research but could not be addressed in the scope of this paper; these include empowerment indicators and measurement techniques, the contribution of microinsurance and savings to empowerment, technology transfer through MFIs, the relationship between participation in microfinance programs, empowerment, and family planning, and the effects of cultural norms and particularly religion on the ability of microfinance programs to empower women.

Targeting Women

International aid donors, governments, scholars, and other development experts have paid much attention to microfinance as a strategy capable of reaching women and involving them in the development process. The microfinance industry has made great strides toward identifying barriers to women's access to financial services and developing ways to overcome those barriers. A 2001 survey by the Special Unit on Microfinance of the United Nations Capital Development Fund (SUM/UNCDF) of twenty-nine microfinance institutions revealed that approximately 60 percent of these institutions' clients were women. Six of the twenty-nine focused entirely on women. Among the remaining twenty-three mixed-sex programs, 52 percent of clients were women.[2] The study also showed, however, that those programs offering only individual loans or relatively high minimum loan amounts tended to have lower percentages of women clients. These findings affirm the importance of designing appropriate products for women.

According to USAID's annual *Microenterprise Results Report* for 2000, approximately 70 percent of USAID-supported MFIs' clients were women. Considerable variation among the regions was seen, however, with percentages of women clients ranging from 27 percent in the Near East to 87 percent in Asia. In Eastern Europe, where USAID has traditionally supported individual-lending programs, the percentage of women clients dropped as low as 48 percent in 1999[3] before rising to 54 percent in 2000, when USAID began to support more group-lending programs offering smaller loans.[4] Although the UNCDF study found that larger programs tended to have lower percentages of women clients, data collected by the Microcredit Summit Campaign found no statistically significant correlation between the number of very poor clients[5] served by each institution and the percentage of those clients who were women.

Microfinance institutions around the world have been quite creative in developing products and services that avoid barriers that have traditionally kept women from accessing formal financial services such as collateral requirements, male or salaried guarantor requirements, documentation requirements, cultural barriers, limited mobility, and literacy. Nevertheless, in a number of countries and areas few or no institutions offer financial services under terms and conditions that are favorable to women. Together, these findings confirm that the type of products offered, their conditions of access, and the distribution of an institution's portfolio among different products and services affect women's access to financial services. They also suggest that much more can be done to serve poor women in certain cultural and economic contexts.

Why Target Women? Theories, Assumptions, and Reality

Many different rationales can be offered for placing a priority on increasing women's access to microfinance services.

Gender and Development   Research done by UNDP, UNIFEM, and the World Bank, among others, indicates that gender inequalities in developing societies inhibit economic growth and development. For example, a recent World Bank report confirms that societies that discriminate on the basis of gender pay the cost of greater poverty, slower economic growth, weaker governance, and a lower living standard of their people.[6] The UNDP found a very strong correlation between its gender empowerment measure and gender-related development indices and its Human Development Index. Overall, evidence is mounting that improved gender equality is a critical component of any development strategy.

Microfinance has come to play a major role in many of these donors' gender and development strategies because of its direct relationship to both poverty alleviation and women. As CIDA recognizes in its gender policy, "Attention to gender equality is essential to sound development practice and at the heart of economic and social progress. Development results cannot be maximized and sustained without explicit attention to the different needs and interests of women and men."[7] As part of its poverty reduction priority, CIDA supports programs that provide "increased access to productive assets (especially land, capital, and credit), processing, and marketing for women."[8] By giving women access to working capital and training, microfinance helps mobilize women's productive capacity to alleviate poverty and maximize economic output. In this case, women's entitlement to financial services, development aid, and equal rights rests primarily on their potential contribution to society rather than on their intrinsic rights as human beings and members of that society.[9]

Women Are the Poorest of the Poor   It is generally accepted that women are disproportionately represented among the world's poorest people. In its 1995 Human Development Report, the UNDP reported that 70 percent of the 1.3 billion people living on less than $1 per day are women.[10] According to the World Bank's gender statistics database, women have a higher unemployment rate than men in virtually every country.[11] In general, women also make up the majority of the lower paid, unorganized informal sector of most economies. These statistics are used to justify giving priority to increasing women's access to financial services on the grounds that women are relatively more disadvantaged than men.

Although many scholars and development agencies have noted an apparent trend toward the "feminization of poverty," measuring the extent to which this is occurring presents many challenges. Because most methods of measuring poverty assess the level of poverty of the household as a whole, it is likely that poverty experienced by women as a result of discrimination against them *within* their households is underreported to a great extent. In addition, Baden and Milward note that, "Although women are not *always* poorer than men, because of the weaker basis of their entitlements, they are generally more *vulnerable* and, once poor, may have less options in terms of escape."[12] By providing access to financing for income-generating activities, microfinance institutions can significantly reduce women's vulnerability to poverty. A reduction in women's vulnerability can sometimes also translate into empowerment if greater financial security allows the women to become more assertive in household and community affairs.

Women Spend More of Their Income on Their Families   Women have been shown to spend more of their income on their households; therefore, when women are helped to increase their incomes, the welfare of the whole family is improved. In its report on its survey findings the Special Unit on Microfinance of the UNCDF explains, "Women's success benefits more than one person. Several institutions confirmed the well-documented fact that women are more likely than men to spend their profits on household and family needs. Assisting women therefore generates a multiplier effect that enlarges the impact of the institutions' activities."[13] Women's Entrepreneurship Development Trust Fund (WEDTF) in Zanzibar, Tanzania, also reports that "women's increased income benefits their children, particularly in education, diet, healthcare, and clothing." According to a WEDTF report, 55 percent of women's increased income is used to purchase household items, 18 percent goes for school, and 15 percent is spent on clothing. In her research on the poverty level of female-headed households, Sylvia Chant, a researcher at the London School of Economics, cites a number of studies on Latin America that lend credibility to the commonly held belief that women spend a greater percentage of their income on their households than do men. She writes, "In Guadalajara, Mexico, for example, Gonzalez de la Rocha notes that men usually only contribute 50 percent of their salaries to the collective household fund. In Honduras, this averages 68 percent, and from my own survey data in the Mexican cities of Puerto Vallarta, Leon and Queretaro in 1986, the equivalent allocation is 67.5 percent. Women, on the other hand, tend to keep nothing back for themselves, with the result that more money is usually available in women-headed households for collective household expenditure."[14] And Naila Kabeer writes, "There are sound reasons why women's interests are likely to be better served by investing effort and resources in the collective welfare of the household rather than in their own personal welfare." But Kabeer also cautions that it is important to recognize that those incentives may change when women become empowered and have new options.[15] Women who are empowered will have the power to make the life choices that are best for them, and although many empowered women will choose to invest in their families, development organizations must be prepared for the possibility that some will not.

Efficiency and Sustainability   Arguments have been made for and against targeting women on the grounds of efficiency and sustainability. Proponents of targeting women on the grounds of sustainability cite women's repayment records and cooperativeness. A collective wisdom has emerged that women's repayment rates are typically far superior to those of men. Lower arrears and loan loss rates have an important effect on the efficiency and sustainability of the institution. Many programs have also found women to be more cooperative and prefer to work with them for that reason as well.

Box 4.1
Experience with All-Male Lending Groups
Sinapi Aba Trust, Ghana

After running a successful women's Trust Bank program, Sinapi Aba Trust began forming men's Trust Banks in mid-1998. By the second loan cycle, the all-male Trust Banks were already performing worse than the all-female Trust Banks in terms of arrears. By mid-2000, arrears in the men's Trust Banks constituted 20 percent of the total arrears of the Trust Bank program, in spite of the fact that men represented less than 8 percent of total Trust Bank clients; the arrears rate in all-male Trust Banks was 2.5 times that of all-female Trust Banks. Among the reasons for the higher arrears cited by Sinapi Aba staff were the fact that male clients were often in direct competition with each other and were more apt to take risks like selling their goods on credit. Staff also reported that men's groups were more difficult to control and did not have a positive attitude toward meeting attendance. They also noted that the men were not committed to the mutual guarantee of the group even though its importance was stressed to them. As a result, Sinapi Aba discontinued all-male Trust Banks and now serves men primarily through its individual-lending program and as a minority in mixed Trust Bank groups.

The experience of Sinapi Aba Trust, Opportunity International's partner in Ghana, demonstrates a clear difference in men and women's repayment records in its Trust Bank program, a group-lending methodology similar to village banking.[16]

In spite of the large number of institutions serving exclusively or predominantly women while maintaining high levels of financial sustainability, some people argue that institutions that place a priority on serving women also have a tendency to place social goals ahead of efficiency, leading to poorer financial performance. Based on his experience at MicroRate, Damian von Stauffenberg offers one hypothesis along these lines: "In our experience, on average 60–70% of borrowers of MFIs are female. We sometimes see higher percentages of women borrowers but in those cases portfolio quality tends to suffer. Why this is so is not entirely clear, but one hypothesis is that MFIs which concentrate exclusively on women may place ideological goals ahead of technical competence. Whether this is true remains to be proven."[17] Although it is true that some socially driven institutions may choose to offer additional social services to their clients that may make them less profitable than those institutions focusing solely on profitable financial service delivery, there appears to be no reason that portfolio quality should have to suffer or that social objectives and technical competence cannot go hand in hand. In fact, a deeper understanding of the social context and forces in which microfinance operates can allow for more effective risk management and more appropriate product and process design that may improve portfolio quality in the long run. In its survey, however, SUM/UNCDF did not find any clear correlation between outreach to women and financial self-sufficiency. The report states, "If anything, in this very limited pool, the institutions with higher levels of self-sufficiency served proportionally more women than institutions less self-sufficient."[18]

A related belief is that group-lending programs that reach women and poorer clients are less sustainable than institutions reaching higher-level clients with individual loans, yet this concern has been thoroughly addressed by Gary Woller in his comparative analysis of village banking institutions and individual lending institutions for the *Microbanking Bulletin*. His conclusion is that the answer to the question "'Can village banking institutions become self-sufficient?' is 'Yes!' Not only that, VBIs [village banking institutions] can reach levels of self-sufficiency achieved by solidarity group and individual lenders."[19]

Programs that serve a significant number of men are more likely to use methodologies that require collateral and more extensive monitoring procedures to help reduce the risk of default, while programs designed to serve primarily women tend to replace formal monitoring procedures with social guarantees. Generally, MFIs are able to balance more costly procedures with larger loans, while many institutions targeting women have relied on client capacity for self-monitoring and cooperation to reach out to women who otherwise might have been excluded because of the small amount of capital they require.

Women's Rights Perspective   Women's equal access to financial resources is a human rights issue. Because access to credit is an important mechanism for reducing women's poverty it has been an explicit focus of a variety of human rights instruments. Both the Convention on the Elimination of Discrimination Against Women (CEDAW) and the Beijing Platform for Action (BPFA) address women's access to financial resources. For example, the BPFA includes thirty-five references to enabling poor women to gain access to credit. International and national instruments that establish women's rights to credit promote government responsibility and accountability in meeting commitments to women's rights.[20]

Box 4.2
Snapshots of Empowerment

- Nury, an illiterate Trust Bank client at AGAPE in Colombia, formerly too shy to speak to strangers, became the treasurer for her Trust Bank.

- A group of widows in Bali received loans from WKP to start simple projects raising pigs. Over time, they grew in confidence and solidarity and expanded to form a pig-feed cooperative that became the major supplier for their village.

- Hanufa, a member of CODEC in Bangladesh, defends her rights against an illegal divorce but ultimately decides that she is better off on her own. "I can walk on my own shoes now."

Empowering Women   Last, but not least, one of the often articulated rationales for supporting microfinance and the targeting of women by microfinance programs is that microfinance is an effective means or entry point for empowering women. By putting financial resources in the hands of women, microfinance institutions help level the playing field and promote gender equality.

What Do We Mean When We Talk about Empowerment?

Most of us, when asked, have a great deal of difficulty defining *empowerment*. The word does not even translate literally into many languages. Yet most of us know empowerment when we see it.

One loan officer at Sinapi Aba Trust in Ghana defined *empowerment* as "enabling each person to reach his or her God-given potential." Some clients have used the terms *self-reliance* and *self-respect* to define it. According to UNIFEM, "gaining the ability to generate choices and exercise bargaining power," "developing a sense of self-worth, a belief in one's ability to secure desired changes, and the right to control one's life" are important elements of women's empowerment.[21] Empowerment is an implicit, if not explicit, goal of a great number of microfinance institutions around the world. Empowerment is about *change, choice,* and *power.* It is a process of change by which individuals or groups with little or no power gain the power and ability to make choices that affect their lives. The structures of power—who has it, what its sources are, and how it is exercised—directly affect the choices that women are able to make in their lives.[22] Microfinance programs can have tremendous impact on the empowerment process if their products and services take these structures into account.

In order for a woman to be empowered, she needs access to the material, human, and social resources necessary to make strategic choices in her life. Not only have women been historically disadvantaged in access to material resources like credit, property, and money, but they have also been excluded from social resources like education or insider knowledge of some businesses.

Access to resources alone does not automatically translate into empowerment or equality, however, because women must also have the ability to use the resources to meet their goals. In order for resources to empower women, they must be able to use them for a purpose that they choose. Naila Kabeer uses the term *agency* to describe the processes of decision-making, negotiation, and manipulation required for women to use resources effectively. Women who have been excluded from decision-making for most of their lives often lack this sense of agency that allows them to define goals and act effectively to achieve them. However, these goals also can be heavily influenced by the values of the society in which women live and so may sometimes replicate rather than challenge the structures of injustice. The weight of socialization is eloquently expressed by one woman activist from Prishtina, Kosovo: "There is education in the family: first you shouldn't speak because you are a girl, then later you shouldn't speak because no one will marry you, then later you shouldn't speak because you are a new bride. Finally, you might have the chance to speak but you don't speak because you have forgotten how to."[23]

The influence of society over the range and exercise of choice also means that if we seek to promote empowerment, we must also consider factors affecting women's status and rights as a group. Although many microfinance programs promote social solidarity at some level, most microfinance organizations tend to focus their attention on promoting changes at an individual level—a woman who, for instance, is now able to send her children to school, negotiate lower prices for her raw materials, or even dream bigger dreams for herself, her family, and her business. The achievements of individual women can have a powerful impact on the way women are perceived and treated within their communities, but the levels of empowerment individual women may achieve are usually limited if women as a group are generally disempowered. For that reason many organizations also include elements designed to uplift women and communities as a collective rather than just as individuals. Some examples:

- A women's Trust Bank in Colombia organizing to bring electricity to their barrio,
- Women fighting against domestic violence after learning about their rights in their lending centers in Nepal, and
- Working Women's Forum in India organizing women weavers to break the monopoly access to raw materials that the all-male government-sponsored weavers' cooperatives enjoyed.

At Opportunity International empowerment is a critical part of our vision for holistic transformation. Seeking to enable the poor to become agents of change in their communities, our approach encompasses social, economic, political, and spiritual empowerment within the individual, household, business, and community. In most cases, we have found that these processes are mutually reinforcing. The empowerment of women at the individual level helps build a base for social change. Movements to empower women as a group increase opportunities available to individual women, and economic empowerment can increase women's status in their families and societies. Practically speaking, the interrelatedness of different aspects of empowerment and between empowerment and development makes it very difficult to move far ahead in any one area without corresponding changes in other areas. Sooner or later, lack of empowerment will slow down economic and political development, just as a lack of progress in meeting people's basic needs will limit empowerment because poverty itself is disempowering.

Why Should MFIs Care about Women's Empowerment?

"Empowerment of women and gender equality are prerequisites for achieving political, social, economic, cultural, and environmental security among all peoples."[24]

As this statement from the Fourth United Nations World Conference on Women and much of the evidence presented thus far in this paper have shown, women's empowerment is a critical part of sustainable development. Yet microfinance's great potential to empower poor women to a large extent often goes unrealized. Although studies show that microfinance *can* and *does* empower women, it has the potential to empower many more, even more greatly.

Objections to a Focus on Empowering Women

Given the enthusiasm that many donors and practitioners have shown for the empowering potential of microfinance, why are many MFIs reluctant to focus on women's empowerment when designing their systems and programs? Their rationales range from the belief that empowerment will happen naturally as a result of a good microfinance program to the concern that paying attention to empowerment will distract MFIs and their managers from running their institutions sustainably. In this section we explore a few of these concerns.

Does Access to Credit Automatically Lead to Empowerment?   The basic theory is that microfinance empowers women by putting capital in their hands and allowing them to earn an independent income and contribute financially to their households and communities. This economic empowerment is expected to generate increased self-esteem, respect, and other forms of empowerment for women beneficiaries. Involvement in successful income-generating activities should translate into greater control and empowerment. Closer examination shows us, however, that this equation may not always hold true and that complacency in these assumptions can lead MFIs to overlook both opportunities to empower women more profoundly and failures in empowerment.

The ability of a woman to transform her life through access to financial services depends on many factors—some of them linked to her individual situation and abilities, and others dependent upon her environment and the status of women as a group. Control of capital is only one dimension of the complex and ever-changing process by which the cycles of poverty and powerlessness replicate themselves. Women also face disadvantages in accessing information, social networks, and other resources they need to succeed in business and in life. Only by evaluating the needs of women will an MFI be able to maximize its empowerment potential.

Programs Seeking to Become Financially Sustainable Cannot Afford to Focus on Women's Empowerment   Some practitioners are reluctant to adopt women's empowerment as a central focus of their programs because they fear that it will interfere with the efficiency and professionalism of their financial operations. They fear that an intentional focus on women's empowerment may lead them to additional activities that could draw resources and energy away from the core business of providing financial services to the poor in a sustainable way. We do find, however, that there are "empowering approaches" to delivery of traditional microfinance services that are often compatible with and no more costly than other ways of achieving organizational efficiencies. An empowering approach is often found among organizations that are committed to excellence and particularly excellent customer service. For instance, FORA in Russia places a high priority on short turnaround times between loan approval and disbursement, as a means of respecting the client's time and business, and a 1997 study of Sinapi Aba Trust in Ghana found that the most empowering aspect of its various programs was the respect with which clients were treated by people at all levels of the organization. These practices are empowering without being costly.

Knowing and understanding your clients and potential clients is an important part of ensuring that products and services are empowering for them. Maria Otero, President and CEO of ACCION International, reminds us of the basics of designing products for women that were groundbreaking just twenty to thirty years ago. She writes: "a sustainable institution that empowers women can do so by first paying attention to the following: 1) understand the characteristics of women's economic activity (for example, smaller businesses than men, smaller cash flow, more likely reaches a smaller market); 2) know the skill and time constraints of women (less literacy, fewer marketable skills, domestic and child care responsibilities)."[25] This kind of client awareness helps MFIs offer loans and other products that are appropriate and empowering. Sofol-Compartamos, an ACCION affiliate in Mexico, has successfully created this client feedback loop by bringing together the general manager, loan officers, and some clients to discuss the characteristics of current products as well as products that clients would like to access in the future. It does not have to be expensive to incorporate client input into program design. Sofol-Compartamos—a fully financially sustainable, regulated finance company—has grown to serve more than 100,000 clients while continuing to be responsive to clients' needs. CETZAM, an Opportunity partner in Zambia, estimates that just a 1 percent drop in arrears resulting from program improvements would pay for the cost of its impact and client satisfaction monitoring.

"Soft" services like health education, literacy training, business training, or discussion and support groups on issues like domestic violence or divorce rights are often assumed to be costly and to lack clear, easily measurable outputs and outcomes.[26] Yet, as Christopher Dunford so eloquently argues in chapter 2, "Building Better Lives," there can be powerful synergies between the provision of financial services and some nonfinancial services like education. Programs with development objectives can achieve "economies of scope" by "packaging two or more services together to minimize delivery and management support costs and to maximize the variety of benefits for people's multiple needs and wants" (p. 80). And, in an innovative example of incorporating nonfinancial services in a cost-effective way, village banking programs invest in client leadership development in return for cost savings as clients take on some of the responsibilities for managing loan repayments and other transactions of their lending groups.

Another reason for the lack of attention to women's empowerment in mainstream microfinance is that MFIs fear that building empowering elements into their programs will threaten their financial sustainability ratios and limit their access to funds from major bilateral and multilateral donor agencies. Many donors agencies' funding criteria focus primarily on outreach and institutional sustainability criteria and do not "reward" programs that are able to demonstrate greater and more sustainable impact on their clients. The incentive structures lead many MFIs to consider including program elements intentionally empowering for women as "extras" or "luxuries" rather than as an integral part of their program design and goals.

But many MFIs with a strong focus on empowerment maintain very high levels of operational and financial sustainability, suggesting that a great deal can be done to enhance women's empowerment even within the constraints of financial sustainability. Working Women's Forum (WWF) in India, for example, is fully financially sustainable and offers a range of nonfinancial services, including organizing women in the informal sector to achieve better wages and working conditions. WWF also empowers poor women through its institutional structure by training them to act as health promoters and credit officers in their neighborhoods.

Several Women's World Banking affiliates also manage to maintain a balance between strong financial performance standards and empowerment. For example, ADOPEM, in the Dominican Republic, has more than 28,000 borrowers and a financial sustainability ratio of 127 percent and is in the process of becoming a regulated financial institution. Yet ADOPEM, whose mission is to incorporate women and their families into the economic and financial system through the provision of credit and training, and to strengthen the position of women entrepreneurs with micro-, small-, and medium-sized businesses, provides more than just loans to its clients. ADOPEM not only provides business training for its clients but offers training in a range of areas including democratic processes and civil society participation designed to encourage women's empowerment and leadership. In addition, ADOPEM supports the Association of Women in Small and Microenterprise (ANAMUMPE), which provides access to information on training events and legislative issues and has given women an opportunity to participate in working groups organized by the government on issues affecting microenterprise.[27]

Women's Empowerment Is a "Western" Concept   The question has been raised, not only in microfinance but also in the broader field of international development, whether it is ethical and appropriate for development institutions to promote women's empowerment. The empowerment or disempowerment of women and other groups in each society is closely linked to the culture of that society. The promotion of women's empowerment implies advocacy for cultural and social change, which some fear is an inappropriate imposition of "Western" values on non-Western societies.

Yet, even if we set aside culturally relative values for a moment and look objectively at human welfare, we can see that gender inequalities and discrimination against women contribute directly to the perpetuation of poverty in many nations. Many independent, indigenous women's organizations around the world have contributed to their countries' development by leading long and successful struggles for women's empowerment. Organizations like SEWA and Working Women's Forum in India have organized and mobilized hundreds of thousands of Indian women to work for women's empowerment and rights with little or no "outside" assistance or influence. For example, in areas where women beedi-rollers' poverty[28] was exploited by contractors, and often led to permanent indebtedness and child mortgage or bondage, WWF successfully organized women to demand higher wages and the release of children from bondage.[29] Moreover, in some cases poor countries have surpassed developed countries in terms of women's representation, existence of women's machineries and ratification of instruments and conventions. This illustrates government awareness of the need to address women's empowerment. Although desired outcomes and goals of empowerment are culturally relative, empowerment itself is *not* a Western concept.

Evidence of Empowerment

Although the process of empowerment varies from culture to culture, several types of changes are considered to be relevant in a wide range of cultures. Some of these changes include increased participation in decision-making, more equitable status of women in the family and community, increased political power and rights, and increased self-esteem. Although most microfinance institutions can share anecdotal evidence of empowerment, very few have studied the effects of their programs on empowerment. The information and evidence that are available give us a mixed picture, showing successes as well as some limitations.

Impact on Decision-Making

Women's ability to influence or make decisions that affect their lives and their futures is considered to be one of the principal components of empowerment by most scholars. It is much less clear, however, what types of decisions and what degree of influence should be classified as empowerment in different contexts.

In spite of the difficulties, some microfinance institutions are finding ways to evaluate their impact on women's decision-making. The Women's Empowerment Program in Nepal, for example, conducted a study that showed an average of 89,000 out of 130,000 or 68 percent of women in its program experienced an increase in their decision-making roles in the areas of family planning, children's marriage, buying and selling property, and sending their daughters to school—all areas of decision-making traditionally dominated by men.[30] The Centre for Self-Help Development (CSD) also reported that women were able to make small purchases of necessary items like groceries independently. But larger purchases and personal purchases, like jewelry, always required the consent of the husband, representing incomplete progress toward empowerment in this area.[31] World Education, which provides literacy and other education to existing savings and credit groups, found that the combination of education and credit put women in a stronger position to ensure more equal access for female children to food, schooling, and medical care.[32] TSPI, an Opportunity partner in the Philippines, found that the percentage of women who reported being the primary household fund manager increased dramatically from 33 percent to 51 percent after participation in the program. In the comparison group only 31 percent of women were the primary managers of household funds. Similarly, the percentage of women managing their enterprise funds nearly doubled from 44 to 87 percent. Only 1 percent of clients relinquished control of enterprise fund management after joining the program, and only 5 percent relinquished control of household fund management during that period.[33]

Through in-depth interviews with thirteen clients, URWEGO, a World Relief partner in Rwanda, found that 54 percent of the clients experienced an increase in their ability to control or influence business decisions, 38 percent experienced an increase in decision-making in their families, 38 percent in their communities, and 54 percent in their churches.[34] URWEGO's impact on decision-making, while far from universal, is significant in that the program was only about eighteen months old at the time of the evaluation.[35]

Many microfinance institutions focus their attention on women's use of the loan and ability to make decisions about her business as the most direct impact of their program. Nirdhan Utthan Bank, Ltd. in Nepal found that most of their women clients were making decisions about business investments jointly with their husbands, which represents a step forward because previously these women's husbands would have made such decisions alone.[36]

CSD found that most women do have a say in the utilization and management of their loans although occasionally men pressure CSD to give their wives loans so that the husband can use it. They also found that a fair number of loans are ultimately invested in "male" activities like rickshaws, for which it is difficult to ascertain the level of control and influence the women may have.[37] In her study of the Small Enterprise Development Program (SEDP) in Bangladesh, Naila Kabeer found that although empowerment and well-being benefits substantially increased when women controlled their loans and used them for their own income-generating activities, just the act of bringing financial resources to the household in the form of credit was enough to secure at least some benefits for the majority of women in her study.[38]

Impact on Self-Confidence

Self-confidence is one of the most crucial areas of change for empowerment, yet it is also one of the most difficult to measure or assess. Self-confidence is a complex concept relating to both women's perception of their capabilities and their actual level of skills and capabilities. It is related to Kabeer's concept of *agency* that allows women to define and achieve goals as well as the sense of power women have within themselves. Jeffrey Ashe and Lisa Parrott's study of the Women's Empowerment Project in Nepal showed that an increase in self-confidence and enlarged spheres of influence were the top two changes reported by 200 sampled groups.[39] URWEGO in Rwanda found that the greatest impact of its program on empowerment had been on self-esteem, with 69 percent of clients reporting increased self-esteem. Self-esteem and self-confidence are closely linked with knowledge as well. Fifty-four percent of URWEGO clients reported an increase in their level of knowledge about issues that affect themselves and their families, and 38 percent of clients reported an increase in business knowledge.[40]

Impact on Women's Status and Gender Relations in the Home

Access to credit and participation in income-generating activities is assumed to strengthen women's bargaining position within the household, thereby allowing her to influence a greater number of strategic decisions. Particularly in poor communities, men's domination of women is strongest within the household. As Naila Kabeer points out, "Many feminists recognize that poor men are almost as powerless as poor women in access to material resources in the public domain, but remain privileged within the patriarchal structure of the family."[41] In some societies, being seen by neighbors as in control of his family and wife is a key element of men's social prestige—particularly in impoverished communities where men may be able to boast of few other status symbols. In Costa Rica, for example, none of

ADAPTE's women clients who were surveyed reported feeling that their gender limited their occupational choices. One woman even commented that she thought that she could do better at business *because* she was a woman. Such responses seem to indicate that these Costa Rican women enjoyed a great deal of freedom of choice in their occupations. Yet many of the responses of the husbands of ADAPTE clients reflected a deep ambivalence and struggle with their wives' new economic independence. One husband commented that he appreciated his wife's ability to earn her own income so that she could pay for things she wanted without asking him for money. He liked his wife's independence because "although she doesn't give me anything, neither does she ask for anything from me." He considers the growth of her business to be generally positive but then adds that it has not been easy for him to become accustomed to it. When asked how he felt about his wife's increasing independence and growing tendency to make decisions alone, he explained, "Because of my *machismo* I see [the changes] as negative, but deep down, I know that they are positive for her."[42]

In spite of the difficulty that some men have in accustoming themselves to their wives' new role, most women report improved relationships with their husbands and families. Evidence of changes in gender roles within the household, however, is limited. World Education reported that although husbands, in-laws, and children help out at home while the women attend program meetings, women's workload increases as they start utilizing their loans more. Also working in Nepal, CSD found that the economic role of women remained restricted to managing the loans and supplementing household income to meet household expenses but did not lead to a substantial change in gender relations in the home in the majority of households.

Impact on Family Relationships and Domestic Violence

Although there have been a few studies[43] that have asserted that women's participation in microfinance leads to an increase in domestic violence, most practitioners have reported the opposite experience. The concerns arise over a "backlash effect" that may occur as a result of women challenging gender norms and asserting their rights. Microfinance programs can strengthen women's economic autonomy and give them the means to pursue nontraditional activities. In some cases, women who begin to assert themselves and their opinions in their households incur the wrath of angry husbands who feel their authority and sometimes their reputations are being threatened by their wives' behavior.

Although there are many good reasons for MFIs to be watchful for potential rises in domestic violence, the bulk of the evidence and experience thus far seems to point to the conclusion that participation in microfinance strengthens and improves family relationships rather than destroying them. Poverty, scarcity, and feelings of helplessness take an undeniable toll on personal relationships. Many practitioners have found that family relationships can be strengthened when the home becomes a more comfortable place to be, and when each member of the family feels secure in his or her ability to contribute productively to the family. Women at Sinapi Aba Trust in Ghana, for example, clearly attributed the increase in respect from their husbands and the reduction in arguments to their economic contribution and a reduction in scarcity. Naila Kabeer's study of SEDP shows women making a direct causal link between their contribution to the household and a reduction in abuse. For example, one client of SEDP quoted by Kabeer states:

He gives me more value since the loan. I know, because now he hands all his earnings to me. If I had not gone to the meeting, not taken a loan, not learnt the work, I would not get the value I have, I would have to continue to ask my husband for every taka I needed. . . . Before, my husband used to beat me when I asked him for money, now, even if he doesn't earn enough every day, I can work, we don't have to suffer.[44]

Balbina, a client of ASPIRE, Opportunity's partner in the Dominican Republic, described the frustration that she and her husband felt about their poverty and their inability to work productively to change their situation. That changed when she used her first loan to invest in a business making and selling *chicharrones* (pork rind snacks) together with her husband. She talked about the difference within their home as a result of having productive work and greater assets: "We were fighting tooth and nail because my husband was unemployed and we had nothing to do. Now we work together, and each of us has something productive to do and a way to direct our energies."[45]

Hashemi et al. found fewer incidences of violence against women among women who were members of credit organizations than they found among the general population. Although fear of public exposure clearly played a role in the reduction of violence, there is considerable anecdotal evidence of women attributing the reduction of abuse directly to their access to credit and their economic contribution to the household. Another study by Schuler et al. suggests that the level of women's economic contribution to the family may also be significant.[46]

Evidence suggests that participation in microfinance programs may give women the means to escape from abusive relationships or limit abuse in their relationships. Working Women's Forum found that 40.9 percent of its members who had experienced domestic violence stopped it because of their personal empowerment, while 28.7 percent were able to stop it through group action.[47] CSD in Nepal also noticed a greater resistance to wife beatings and alcoholism among its clients.[48] And in Bangladesh, where social pressure to remain married is high, Kabeer found that several women in abusive relationships were able to establish spheres of autonomy for themselves within their marriage so that they would have to depend on their husbands as little as possible.[49]

There is anecdotal evidence of reducing domestic violence against children as well. For example, Sabina Cutiba, a client of ADEMCOL, Opportunity's partner in Bogotá, Colombia, had experienced a lifetime of abusive relationships but learned a new way to interact with her children as a result of her Trust Bank program. "I used to fight, complain a lot, be negative. I would complain to friends of mine and cry out with my frustrations. . . . This lady who has been giving these conferences and talking with me has really strengthened me. I've had a total change. . . . Before I used to beat my children. I hit them a lot. But not anymore—now I'm a different person."

In spite of fears by some that giving loans to women could disrupt social order and destroy families,[50] there is little evidence of this occurring. In her study of both male and female clients of SEDP, Naila Kabeer found that women were much more likely to seek the strengthening of their relative position within an interdependent relationship with their husbands than they were to seek independence and autonomy.[51]

Impact on Women's Involvement and Status in the Community

Several microfinance and microenterprise support programs have observed improvements in women's status in their communities. Contributing financial resources to the family or community confers greater legitimacy and value to women's views and gives them more entitlements than they would otherwise have. Studies of microfinance clients from various institutions around the world show that the women themselves very often perceive that they receive more respect from their families and their communities— particularly from the male members—than they did before joining a microfinance program. Where women have the freedom to move about publicly, their success in business is often highly visible in the community. Their success can pave the way for them to become respected and valued members of society. For example, in Zanzibar, Tanzania, women from one of WEDTF's credit groups enjoyed considerable prestige and empowerment as a result of their successful joint business selling kerosene:

Before the credit support we never even went to the market. We were solely dependent on our husbands. Now group activities and the intensive training from the scheme have opened our eyes. We now know that we are better in business than men. We were the only women selling kerosene in the village. The whole community admired our determination. We have urged our fellow women to put their veils down. Some have started their own income generating activities.—Halima Juma Hamadi[52]

Most studies have been based on women's perceptions of how others treat and perceive them, so it is possible that their responses were affected by their own increasing self-esteem and self-confidence as much as by actual changes in the way they were perceived in the community. Some women, however, do cite specific examples of how their interactions in the community have changed and how the improvement in their status is manifested. One woman in Ghana commented that men no longer spoke to her disrespectfully but spoke to her rather more as an equal. Other women noted that they have been invited to participate in and speak at community meetings, whereas before they would have been ignored or excluded. Similarly, a study done by Freedom from Hunger on its program in Ghana noted that significantly more participants than nonparticipants were giving advice in their communities—particularly on topics they had studied in their credit groups. Eighty-seven percent of Credit With Education clients had given business advice in the last six months at the time of the study, compared with 35 percent of nonparticipants and 50 percent of members of control communities. The Freedom from Hunger study also showed that substantially fewer (44 percent) of these women had given business advice in the six months before joining the program three years earlier.[53]

In the CSD program, women members own their center houses that provide them with a social space for gatherings. These houses are a symbol of their unity, strength, and positive contribution to the community and are a source of pride for the women.[54] In CSD communities, the perception of women's economic role is slowly changing. Women are gaining respect for their work, which has traditionally been undervalued. Women's increased economic role is improving their position in society by allowing them to prove their economic capabilities. The awareness of the importance of their economic roles has given some women the confidence to detach themselves from the conservative practices of *purdah* that used to confine their activities to their homes.

As we have shown in this section, women *are* gaining respect. CSD, however, found no noticeable change in traditional gender relations and socially prescribed roles and norms—particularly at the level of the household. Women's mobility has increased, but only as related to income-generating activities. Although CSD's centers have succeeded in creating a space for women to gain experience in making decisions and acting upon them, a social stigma is still attached to women's mobility that has not changed significantly since CSD began its operations.[55] CSD concluded that these limitations were due in part to the program's central focus on creating income-generating opportunities for women who had never had them before and that "women's empowerment takes much more than access options. The program needs to consider some strategic or structural changes and incorporate gender mainstreaming actions in order to inch toward the overall empowerment of women."[56]

Many programs, however, do encourage women from village banks, self-help groups, lending centers, and Trust Banks to organize to bring about social change or solve community problems as a group. Trust Bank members from Opportunity's partner AGAPE in Barranquilla, Colombia, organized to bring electricity to their community. Trust Banks from ADEMCOL, Opportunity's partner in Bogotà, often organize health fairs for their families and communities, bringing the services of doctors, dentists, and psychologists within easy access of poor communities that lack their own health services. They also organize day care and community social events. Organizing such events has proven to be an important learning experience in and of itself, because for many women it is their first contact with local authorities. In order to gain permission and support to hold the events, women must learn to navigate through the bureaucracies that affect their daily lives.

Impact on Political Empowerment of Women and Women's Rights

Widespread political empowerment is a fairly rare outcome of most microfinance programs. Although microfinance programs offer services and products that can enhance individual women's abilities to participate effectively in politics, few microfinance organizations explicitly seek political mobilization or structure their programs in such a way as to deliberately nurture collective action. Nevertheless, many examples testify that women's participation in lending centers and groups increases their knowledge of political parties, processes, and channels of influence. Women clients of Opportunity Microfinance Bank in the Philippines have gained leadership experience and confidence as leaders of their Trust Banks and have gone on to be elected as leaders within their *barangays*.[57] Women clients of what is now FORA in Russia organized to campaign for democracy during recent Russian elections. Esmeralda Castaños, a former Trust Bank leader from Opportunity partner IDH in Honduras, recently ran for mayor of her small town of San Mateus. And a number of Trust Banks of AGAPE in Barranquilla, Colombia, helped organize a protest march to bring better sewage systems to their community.

Some programs, such as BRAC, offer training programs with the specific aim of creating political and social awareness. In a study comparing the empowerment effects of participation in Grameen Bank and BRAC microfinance programs, Hashemi, Schuler, and Riley found that participation in BRAC had a stronger effect on participation in political campaigns and public protests than did Grameen. They believe that this "may be because BRAC provides more opportunities for its members to participate in training programs, which give them an opportunity to travel outside their villages, and because of its greater emphasis on creating awareness of social and political issues."[58]

Other programs such as Working Women's Forum (WWF) in India are very active politically. WWF has a union and advocacy branch as well as a lending program and has been successful in mobilizing very large numbers of women for political and legal changes that support women's rights and opportunities. According to WWF, over 89 percent of its members had taken up civic action for pressing problems in their neighborhoods, showing that microfinance and political empowerment can be complementary processes.[59] And Human Development Initiatives Nigeria (HDI) has successfully combined education of widows about inheritance, legal, and property rights with training in business skills and microfinance. The education has allowed some widows to reclaim their husbands' property and to gain access to their bank accounts. HDI's counseling and mediation services have also helped them resolve conflicts with their husbands' families.

Even programs that are not explicitly addressing women's rights and political participation have had some impact on political and legal empowerment. By contributing to women's knowledge and self-confidence and by widening their social networks, many microfinance programs give women the tools and skills they need to participate more effectively and successfully in formal politics and to informally influence decisions and policies that affect their lives.

For example, World Education, which focuses on literacy rather than political rights training, has found that women who have been through their literacy program are more likely to stand for elected positions such as ward representative or health committee member. A study of Freedom from Hunger's Credit With Education clients in Bolivia found that clients were significantly more likely to have been a candidate for public office or to have been a member of the community's *sindicato* than nonclients.[60] Candidacy for public office can be a good indicator of women's self-confidence and efficacy and the community's respect for women as well as political empowerment; however, it is important to know the broader political conditions affecting their candidacy and role in office. For example, in Nepal, ninety-six women from CSD's program were elected to village and district develop-

Box 4.3
Helen Todd, Editor, CASHPOR

Helen Todd studied Grameen Bank's impact on long-term borrowers in Tangail, Bangladesh. She found that "the most successful families in our small sample were those husbands and wives working in partnership, where both were major economic actors. . . ." She also found that out of the forty borrowers she interviewed, ten had no control over their loans. "They were just taking the money and pipelining it to a husband, a son, a father-in-law, or some other male within the household—sometimes a male outside the household, which was an even more exploitative situation." Goetz and Sen Gupta's study found that the percentages of women who had little or no control over loans ranged from 10 percent in the Grameen Bank to 63 percent in RD-12, a government credit program. The overall average of the four programs studied was 39 percent (*World Development*, January 1996).

In an interview with the Microcredit Summit Campaign, Todd comments, "People are using this study . . . to argue that there is less benefit to opening microcredit opportunities to women than the "evangelists" say. . . . That is not the way I interpret this study. Thirty-nine percent having little or no control means that 61 percent have partial or full control. That is a lot better than the kind of powerlessness with which these women begin.

"There is another more useful way to look at these figures. If there is, in one country—Bangladesh—within one culture, this huge variation between 10 percent and 63 percent in terms of empowerment, . . . then we have got to look at how those programs are designed and try to figure out what are the processes [and] what are the mechanisms in that program which are encouraging or discouraging women's own loan use."

Excerpt from *Countdown 2005 Newsletter*, Microcredit Summit Campaign, September 1998. CASHPOR, a network of Grameen Bank replications, provides training, technical assistance, and information to its members and promotes new replications.

ment committees, but the study also showed that women tended not to have any significant influence over decisions after being elected.[61]

Negative Impacts on Women and Limitations to Empowerment

Both men and women assume risks when taking out a loan—which becomes debt with all of its accompanying stresses and responsibilities. In addition, some studies of the impact of microfinance programs have raised legitimate concerns about the potentially negative impact that programs can have on women, particularly in highly restrictive environments. One often-reported concern is that clients' husbands or other household members take control of the women's loans, yet the client herself retains responsibility for paying off the loans, thus increasing her level of stress and dependency.[62]

Other studies question the success of microfinance programs in effecting lasting change in women's economic welfare or empowerment.[63] Some scholars, such as Linda Mayoux, argue that microfinance institutions cannot have more than a limited impact on women's empowerment unless there are changes in wider gender inequalities in the broader social and economic contexts in which they operate.[64] In light of these limitations, Mayoux recommends that MFIs intentionally address women's empowerment as part of their goals, objectives, operations, and product design. In addition to the issue of domestic violence previously discussed, other common concerns raised include the increased burden that microenterprise activities place on women's time, MFIs' reinforcing rather than challenging gender inequalities, and the possibility that children will be kept out of school to help in their mother's business. The studies raise some important questions which we examine below.

How Does Women's Participation in Microfinance Programs and Microenterprises Affect the Use of Their Time?   Microfinance programs can affect women's use of their time through two main channels: meeting time and expanded enterprise activity. Most methodologies that target women rely on women being able to spend time together to learn about effective financial management and to repay and disburse loans. Although time is precious and scarce for many poor women, it is one resource that most women can utilize to gain access to financial services. It is a key factor in facilitating cost-efficient delivery of services. There are concerns, however, that MFIs are increasing women's work burden by involving them in time-consuming meetings and income-generating activities without taking any action to reduce their traditional responsibilities.

Many women report an increased workload and responsibilities as a result of their loans. Several cases of women suffering ill health and exhaustion as a result of overwork have been reported. In other cases, though, women report that they are more than happy to assume the extra burden because of the respect, personal satisfaction, and improved standard of living they experienced as a result of their income-generating activities. In her study of the Small Enterprise Development Program in Bangladesh, Naila Kabeer found that the majority of women who experienced an increased workload were happy and felt that the benefits outweighed the costs of participation. In the words of one Bangladeshi woman interviewed,

My labour has increased, my husband can also see that. . . . I have less time to do the usual things so he is more tolerant. My labour has increased, but it means we are better off. You need to work. Now we have bought a loan and put it to work, if we have to work harder, that makes no difference to me, we do it with pleasure. The pleasure is that I do the work and I will make an extra bit of money. This was not the case before. The problem before was that I would think I need 500 takas for something, but where would I get the money from? We would have to borrow it. Now we are in position to lend.[65]

Several women interviewed in Ghana also affirmed that in spite of their increased workload and responsibilities, they felt a great deal of pride and personal satisfaction in being able to make a substantial economic contribution to their household.[66]

In some cases, studies have revealed that other family members substantially increase their participation both in the business and with the household chores. A study by Opportunity partner TSPI in the Philippines revealed that the percentage of women whose daughters participated in their businesses increased by 88 percent. Surprisingly, more sons started helping with housework after their mothers joined the program.[67] These findings suggest that it may be important to evaluate the impact of microenterprise not only on the women clients themselves but also on their adult and young children.

While the implications of microfinance for the demands on women's time vary considerably according to each individual's situation, MFIs need to be aware that their programs do affect women's time, not always in positive ways, and should be prepared to assist them in negotiating a reasonable and sustainable balance between life and work.

Do Good Repayment Rates Depend, in Part, on Women's Disempowered Condition?   Supporters of microfinance claim that solidarity groups, self-help groups, and village banks help build the social capital of their communities. Other scholars and development experts, however, worry that by using existing social capital in communities to ensure repayment, MFIs are introducing new stresses and pressures on community life and may damage important support relationships. They observe that MFIs may owe much of their high recovery rates to the lack of alternatives and powerlessness of their client base. It has been well documented that microfinance figures into poor women's risk-management strategies and that continued access to credit is a major incentive for repayment.[68] But, in this sense, incentives for repayment are little different from those for the formal financial markets. No one wants a bad credit record that could keep him or her from accessing financing in the future. The difference is that poor women have even fewer options and alternatives, so the incentive is even stronger. Because most microfinance approaches were developed to work with women in their disempowered condition, however, institutions need to be prepared to change and develop as the women and communities they serve change, become empowered, and have more options.

Do MFIs Reinforce Women's Traditional Roles Instead of Promoting Gender Equality?   Some critics have argued that the majority of microfinance programs are structured in such a way as to have their greatest impact in helping women perform traditional roles better. They argue that by emphasizing the benefits that women's families receive from their access to credit and helping them earn income in such a way that it does not interfere significantly with their traditional duties, microfinance institutions may reinforce traditional gender roles and relations rather than alter them. The reality that many of women's practical needs are closely linked to traditional gender roles, responsibilities, and social structures contributes to a tension between meeting women's practical needs in the short term and promoting long-term strategic change.

Yet by helping women meet their practical needs and increase their efficacy in their traditional roles, microfinance programs can help women gain respect and achieve more in their traditional roles, which in turn can lead to increased esteem. Although improving women's ability to perform traditional roles is not sufficient to ensure empowerment, it may well be a necessary precondition. Enhancing women's sense of efficacy and financial security may contribute decisively to women's ability and willingness to challenge the social injustices and discriminatory systems that they face. In the experience of ENDA Inter-Arabe in Tunisia, it is often an economic crisis such as divorce or the loss or illness of a wage earner that threatens a woman's ability to care for her family, draws her out of her submissive and dependent role, and leads her to take actions that surpass the expectations that others have of her. ENDA Inter-Arabe finds that generating and controlling income is the starting point for other forms of empowerment.[69] "Financial autonomy brings with it *dignity*. Their newly-gained knowledge and capacity to take and influence decisions provides them with *self-confidence*."[70] Armed with the increased access to knowledge that the program provides, combined with their new sense of self-confidence and dignity, many of ENDA Inter-Arabe's women clients are willing and able to take the next step by participating in public meetings, joining political parties, and assuming leadership roles in the community.

As we have shown in this section, although microfinance has helped empower many women in many different ways, empowerment is not an automatic outcome for all women. A closer look at the role that microfinance programs play in women's empowerment and success in business will allow us to begin to understand the causes of both positive and negative outcomes and to develop programs that can enhance the positive and minimize the risk and rate of negative outcomes.

What Role Does Microfinance Play in Empowering Women? A Case Study of Sinapi Aba Trust, Ghana

In November 2001, Opportunity International carried out qualitative research with its partner Sinapi Aba Trust in Ghana in order to learn how and under what circumstances participation in SAT's program led to significant transformation and empowerment. In this section we use the findings from this and other impact studies conducted with Sinapi Aba Trust to take a more in-depth look at how and through what processes microfinance programs can empower women.

First, focus-group discussions were held with loan officers from SAT to identify indicators of transformation and empowerment and to learn from their observations about how SAT's program affected the process of transformation of women clients. In-depth interviews were then conducted with ten women clients and eleven husbands of clients. The women clients were selected on the basis of both their longevity in the program and the significant degree of change that they were observed to have experienced. The women, who have participated in the program between two and six years, were asked about changes in their lives at the business, household, personal, and community level. Particular efforts were made to gather information about changes in relationships, economic condition or well-being, gender roles and equality, skills and capabilities, and spiritual lives, community service, and ethics. The eleven spouses were interviewed about their opinions of the program and their wives' participation. They were also asked to discuss changes in their homes, communities, wives' businesses and character, and personal beliefs that have occurred since their wives joined the program. The men selected for the study came from the same communities as the women being interviewed, but only three husband-wife pairs were interviewed.

The first round of research, while involving only a few clients and not generalizable to the clients at large, gave great insights into the processes of transformation and SAT's particular role in enabling poor women to transform their lives. These qualitative findings were used to inform further more extensive qualitative and quantitative studies using specially adapted versions of all five AIMS client assessment tools.[71] The follow-up studies focused on the areas of empowerment (41 clients), loan and savings use (56 clients), general impact (320 clients, 270 nonclients), reasons for exit (178 ex-clients), and client satisfaction (19 groups of 8 to 10). In all, more than 1,200 people were interviewed in the second round of research.

The Trust Bank Program of Sinapi Aba Trust

SAT operates a total of sixteen branches in all ten regions of Ghana. As of March 31, 2002, Sinapi Aba Trust was reaching 22,765 clients, 93 percent of which were women, with an operational self-sufficiency of 199 percent and financial self-sufficiency of 140 percent. Its primary lending methodology is Trust Banks. Trust Banks at SAT are composed, on average, of twenty to thirty poor and very poor women[72] living or working in the same community and often working in the same sector. Loan officers are usually assisted in the recruitment of new members by local community leaders such as market "queens" and the leaders and members of existing Trust Banks operating in the area. All members have at least some business experience before they join. In Ghana, women are heavily involved in trading commodities such as plantains, cassava, tomatoes, and oranges. Most women have done at least some small trading or had a service business to help make up for shortfalls in their husbands' income or household contribution.

Women joining Trust Banks participate in an extensive orientation before receiving their first loan. Group leaders are elected and play an important role in the management of loan disbursement and repayment as well as in arranging the program at the weekly meetings. Loans to individuals are guaranteed by the other group members, and repayments are made weekly. In addition to loan-management activities, a program is held at each meeting. Topics are chosen by the women themselves in cooperation with their loan officer. Women receive training in business skills such as customer care, pricing, marketing, and selling on credit, and they have the opportunity to exchange business tips among themselves. They also discuss social and community issues. Particular attention is given to topics that will help women manage the expectations, responsibilities, and challenges they face as income-earners, mothers, and wives. Outside resource persons are occasionally brought in to address specialized topics, particularly those related to health.

Sinapi Aba Trust, like other Opportunity International partners, is interested in promoting the holistic transformation of its clients' lives. For that reason, its Trust Bank program is designed to go beyond the promotion of business growth to share skills, ideas, and strategies that can empower its clients to play an important and beneficial role in their families and communities.

Box 4.4
Empowerment through Increased Capital
Nana Addai

"Before joining SAT, I did not have much money, so I had to collect the goods from somebody, sell them, and give her the profit before she would give me some. . . . Every week I would have to render accounts to the supplier—what had been bought, what is left, etc., before she would give me other goods to sell. . . . Because I now have my own money, I am able to negotiate well for good prices and . . . if what my suppliers are selling is not nice, I can go to a different store to purchase what I think people will buy. . . . The time that I spend with my business has reduced because I now have my own money, unlike the past where I was working for somebody so I had to be able to sell all day long before she would give me my share. So always I was tired and in a rush to make sure that I spend more time at the business to ensure that people buy it. But now I have my own business and money, and I can organize myself better to get time to rest."

Business Impact

Since the most direct anticipated benefits of microcredit concern clients' businesses, we begin with a discussion of the effects of SAT's program in that area.[73] Running a successful business not only contributes to women's improved welfare, it contributes both directly and indirectly to their empowerment. The studies showed that through SAT's program, women's businesses became more successful in the following ways: an increase in working capital, improved relationships with suppliers and customers, more strategic planning and pricing, and diversification and expansion into more profitable product lines.

The increase in working capital is particularly important for women's empowerment. Although most major markets in Ghana have highly developed systems of in-kind credit, accounts usually must be settled daily, and the availability of cash credit is still rare. As a result, when women have their own capital or have access to cash credit, they have considerably more power and prestige in the marketplace. All ten of the women from the November study and 76 percent of the women from the follow-up studies indicated that their working capital had increased as a result of their loans from SAT. For half of them, their loans and earnings have been enough to break their dependency on supplier credit, and the rest were able to purchase more stock using a combination of cash and credit. A quantitative study revealed that 42.9 percent of mature clients are now able to buy directly from wholesalers and producers, compared with only 31 percent of nonclients. And 33 percent of mature clients now employ other people, compared with only 24 percent of new clients. In almost all cases, the increase in capital has given women more options and greater control over their businesses—and their lives. Nana Addai, a SAT Trust Bank client since 1999, shared her experience of empowerment as she transitioned from selling used school uniforms that she obtained on credit to managing her own used-clothing business.[74]

Women who participated in SAT also gained a reputation for trustworthiness and responsibility that enhanced their relationships with their suppliers and customers and improved their businesses. As women used the loans, business training, and advice they received from SAT to expand into more profitable lines of business and build their customer bases, they reported feeling that both men and women respected them more. Ninety-three percent of the women interviewed for the empowerment study reported feeling that they are now accorded much respect and are more accepted in their communities. In many ways, the women interviewed have been able to capitalize on the increased respect they have received as successful businesswomen and breadwinners to increase their influence in community and household affairs.

Impact on the Household and Family Relations

All of the men interviewed said they were supportive of their wives' joining the program from the beginning. Those who said that they had reservations about their wives' participation primarily feared that their wives would not be able to pay the money back and they would be saddled with debt, prosecuted by the courts, or otherwise dishonored as a family because of their inability to honor their obligations. Most believe that women should earn income if they can and expressed appreciation for their wives' financial contributions to the household. As a consequence, they were grateful for any program, such as SAT's, that could help them become more successful and earn more income.

In Ghana, the complete appropriation of women's loans by men is fairly rare, and women typically control their own income from their business. Even though several men reported assisting their wives with their accounts, planning, or other aspects of business, in only one case did the husband interviewed seem to be the dominant manager of the business. The follow-up study of loan use confirmed an almost complete absence of husbands' interference in decision-making about loan use. Only one woman reported that her husband had decided how her first loan should be used but that she was involved in subsequent decisions.

But women's increased economic independence can lead to other problems. Focus-group discussions with loan officers revealed that in a number of cases the man's contribution to the household decreased once his wife began to earn more income and became able to cover more of the household's expenses. Occasionally the husband withdrew his support to the extent that the woman was forced to spend her loan primarily to meet consumption needs instead of investing it in her business, leading to repayment difficulties later. Loan officers reported that some women hid their loans and sometimes even their businesses from their husbands in order to protect their income and investments from them. Although the extent to which loan hiding is a problem among SAT clients is difficult to gauge, the follow-up research revealed that half of SAT's clients were hiding savings for fear that their husbands would withdraw their financial support.

Although most women in Ghana have a say in how a certain portion of household income is spent, many are still in a dependent position and have little influence over how much they are given to spend or how the rest of the money their husbands earn is spent. Women are typically given housekeeping money by their husbands to be used for the family's daily needs. However, often the money is not enough, so women are forced either to ask for more money from their husbands or to find a way to generate some income themselves to make up the shortfall.

Because women are traditionally responsible for providing food, clothing, children's allowances (pocket money), and cooking and cleaning supplies, a woman's earning a little money to cover household expenses will not necessarily earn her more respect in the eyes of her husband. If, however, she earns enough to help cover typically male expenditures like school fees, rent, furniture, and transport, her decision-making power often increases greatly.

The women interviewed were particularly proud of their financial contribution to their children's education not only because it helped them earn the respect of their husbands but also because it gave them the opportunity to ensure the best possible education for both their daughters and their sons. Their husbands, in turn, appreciated this support and said they valued their wives' opinions on school and other major decisions. SAT loan officers emphasize the importance of girls' education in Trust Bank meetings and lead discussions geared to convincing the women that their jobs and activities should not be limited by their gender. Women are putting what they have learned into practice by educating both their daughters and their sons, treating them as equals, and not discriminating between boys' work and girls' work. Some women are even sending their girls to college and trade school, and others have taught their boys to cook and do housework. They are thus expanding their daughters' opportunities and transforming gender norms in future generations.

Most men expressed the belief that cooking, child care, cleaning, and washing are women's responsibilities in spite of their increased respect for them as wage earners and businesswomen. Nevertheless, several of them shared domestic responsibilities with their wives. Washing seemed to be the most common and generally acceptable male contribution to housekeeping, but some also reported that they care for the children when their wives are away and help her with meal preparation. Although a few husbands occasionally helped out before, most commented that they felt it was their duty to help their wives because their wives were now helping meet the financial obligations of the family. One man even commented that he had just been doing the family laundry before he came for his interview. He explained that because his wife is in the market, she does not have time to do it, so he helps. In a separate interview, his wife confirmed this, saying, "My husband knows I am very busy, so he can wash our things and cook for us, and I think it's because I am helping him financially."[75]

All the men and women interviewed said that their relationships with their spouses (where applicable) had either improved or remained good since the woman joined SAT. Women placed a high priority on being able to provide adequately for their children. They reported that their children accorded them more respect, now that they are able to provide for their needs and for their participation in social functions, even if they are now able to spend less time with them. Several women also commented that being able to provide for their children gave them more confidence to get involved in their lives. The women believed that their financial contribution had helped them earn greater respect from both their husbands and their children. Both men and women cited women's having to ask for money as the major cause of quarrels in their homes. In all cases, these had subsided or disappeared entirely once women began to earn a substantial income of their own. Ninety-eight percent of the women in the follow-up empowerment study believed themselves now to be financially independent and able to satisfy their personal needs from their own income.

A number of women commented that their husbands sometimes borrowed money from them or that they paid for expenses that their husbands normally would have. The men, too, talked about borrowing money from their wives and were relieved that their wives could help cover the household expenses when their incomes were not sufficient. Among the interviewees, this arrangement seemed to be one of partnership and shared responsibility. Many of the women were not only happy to have reduced their dependency on their husbands but were also pleased to be able to help them. Both women and men mentioned that they planned together, especially toward the goal of buying a plot of land and building a house. The men saw the women's help with household expenses as allowing them to save more, but they also respected the woman's needs for business capital. Although the women were happy to help their husbands financially, the husbands said they made a point of repaying the money they borrowed from their wives whenever possible.

SAT makes a deliberate effort to provide women with skills and advice that will allow them to cope with the competing pressures of their domestic responsibilities and their businesses as well as working with them on communication and relationship skills. Most of the women interviewed indicated that they had learned to communicate their feelings, thoughts, and opinions more effectively. A few of the women commented that they had been extremely shy and scarcely able to speak to anybody when they joined the Trust Bank group. They now speak freely and contribute to group discussion and decision-making. They engage more actively in the decision-making in their households and extended family meetings as well.

Because in Ghana it is seen as socially undesirable for a woman to openly complain, argue, or object, learning effective communication techniques that allow women to express their opinions in such a way as to be heard, yet not be categorized as quarrelsome, is an important part of empowerment. The strategies taught in the Trust Banks—both by SAT loan officers and the women themselves—seem to be effective in minimizing resistance and backlash against the women at both household and community levels. Several of the men commented that, contrary to the conventional wisdom that women become proud and disdainful when they become more financially independent, their wives' attitudes and behavior continued to be cooperative and considerate.

Both married women and widows reported having better relationships with their extended family and in-laws and gaining increased respect from them. Extended families are very important social support networks in Ghana, and the widows, in particular, had had to call on their support in times of need, straining their relationship. But through SAT, they had been able to save a little to take care of emergencies so that they no longer have to borrow or do without. A few of the women recalled specific incidents that they believe raised their status in their family. In most cases, the woman gained respect by resolving a family crisis because she had financial resources and the confidence to act, often while brothers and uncles stood by, unsure of what to do. Margaret Asare, the client quoted at the beginning of this paper, described her family's new-found respect for her very clearly: "At first my family members did not count me worthy to be called when there was a problem or decision-making, but now through SAT I am numbered among human beings." The widows as well as the married women all felt that the lessons they learned from SAT about caring for their children and balancing their domestic and business responsibilities had helped them look after their children better and have a better relationship with them.

Impact on the Community and Women's Role and Status in It

Although leadership skills, self-confidence, and solidarity play an important role in changing women's role and status in the community, women's economic success plays a role in shaping the community's perception of them as well. In a number of communities, SAT members have become quite well known for their business successes and hard work. Several of the women, particularly the widows, noticed that men generally respected them more because they saw that they were serious in their business, and in the case of the widows, capable of supporting their families alone. Five of the spouses interviewed commented that their wives were now well respected in the community because of their businesses and their leadership roles with SAT. One man, whose wife is a Trust Bank leader and a "queen" in her market area, proudly claimed, "She has respect, and it has brought glory to the family."[76] One woman stated that all her neighbors respect her because they have seen what she has been able to do, and they now believe her family to be "well-to-do." Several of the women have been invited to participate in community meetings because they are now in a position to contribute and are also now able to make contributions at funerals, a major symbol of social status among the Asante.

Women are beginning to advise neighbors in business, family, health, and community matters. The quantitative impact survey revealed that nearly half of SAT's clients are advising others—this in comparison with the 29 percent of women who reported that they were too shy to associate with others in the market or community prior to joining SAT. One woman interviewed had even become an agent for the Planned Parenthood Association of Ghana in her community and regularly gave talks about health and reproductive issues.

Women's giving advice is another positive sign of empowerment for several reasons. First, women are learning and putting into practice what they learn. Furthermore, they are sharing their knowledge and helping others, which means that the knowledge benefits of the program are having an impact beyond its members. Second, women have enough self-confidence to offer advice and assistance to others. Giving advice also generates community respect for the women involved so that a positive cycle of self-esteem and respect in the community begins. Ninety-eight percent of the women interviewed for the follow-up empowerment study claimed that they now feel adequate to do everything others do.

This increase in self-confidence seems to spill over into women's community involvement as well. All the women interviewed in the November study play active roles in their communities. Although no statistically significant difference was found between clients and nonclients in terms of participation in voluntary activities, almost half of all women reporting that they now hold leadership positions claim to have learned those skills through SAT. They say that they have learned how to be patient and how to handle and motivate people; they have also gained organizational skills from their experience in Trust Banks. These skills have helped them take on leadership positions outside the Trust Bank, with some women becoming officers in their churches or members of community assemblies and political parties. One woman, who has helped more than 100 women join SAT Trust Banks, sees helping to advise and organize Trust Banks as her main contribution to the community. She points out that she is helping more people work and expand their businesses. Some of those she has helped are now employing others in the community to help them. Other women are using the leadership skills they have learned in the Trust Banks to organize women's groups in their churches, community clean-ups, and other projects. Virtually all women now contribute either financial resources or labor to community development projects and urge others to do the same. Their activity and contributions have brought SAT members recognition as a group for being hardworking, trustworthy, responsible, and generally of good character—all highly valued traits in Ghanaian society.

Clients are clearly positive about their changing role and status in the community:

"Before, people didn't know me, but now everywhere I go, people are calling my name. Auntie Maggie!"

—*Margaret Asare*

"A lot of people know me, and everywhere that I reach and I need help I receive help, so I feel very happy about it and to be part of SAT."

—*Mary Forkuo*

"Some people even marvel at what SAT has done for us. If you are with SAT Trust Bank, there is no way you have to look down upon yourself."

—*Victoria Owusu Ansah*

Contributions to and Limitations of Empowerment

On the basis of the experiences shared by the men and women interviewed, the Trust Bank program of Sinapi Aba Trust has clearly contributed to the empowerment of women in a number of ways. Access to credit and business training have helped women expand and improve their businesses, leading to increased respect and decision-making power in the home and community. Advice and peer support have helped women manage their triple roles as mothers, wives, and businesswomen. Education and experience in leadership have helped women become more confident and capable leaders. It is important to note that these substantial evidences of empowerment have been displayed in the context of a highly sustainable institution that is experiencing rapid growth and is on the path to becoming a regulated savings and loan institution.

The study, however, also revealed some mixed outcomes. Although SAT's message that women should continue to perform their traditional duties and be "respectful and submissive" to their husbands limits backlash and promotes family unity, it may also limit the scope of empowerment for women. In many ways, gender stereotypes and expectations remain unaltered. For example, although women have substantially increased their decision-making power—especially regarding the purchase of household assets—and are consulted more often in the decision-making process, men still tend to have the final word on major decisions. Very few men showed any signs of change in beliefs about gender roles, and all were quite satisfied with their wives' "character" and performance of their traditional duties as a wife and mother. One man even commented that people were now using his wife as an "example" of what wives should do. She is contributing to the household finances, but she has not become arrogant or shown any signs of "bad character."[77] All these were regarded as positive outcomes by the men, but they also show that women are still expected to conform to gender norms even if they are also pursuing nontraditional roles for themselves.

The interviewees' responses also show a consensus among men and women that women have an important role to play in organizing other *women*, but none of the men considered the possibility that the women could organize and lead *men*, and a couple of the women even said that they would step away from their church or community leadership posts if a man were to become involved. Yet women are gaining experience in leading men in many of SAT's mixed-gender Trust Banks, and this experience may ultimately empower them to lead men in other public spaces.

Lessons from Experience: Key Programmatic Factors That Can Contribute to Empowerment

Developing a program that strikes a balance to maximize empowerment, well-being, economic development, and sustainability can be very challenging. No single program fits all environments and populations, and no program strategy will have identical results for all potential clients. Naila Kabeer sums up the challenge well, explaining, "Different aspects of women's disempowerment, and hence empowerment, are closely related so that initiatives in relation to one aspect are likely to set off changes in other aspects, although not in easily predictable ways."[78] The most effective program strategies will be devised when staff at microfinance institutions listen to clients and carefully evaluate their resource bases, strengths, and vulnerabilities so that they develop products and services that build on strengths and existing resources. As Noni S. Ayo, managing director of ARDCI, in the Philippines, expresses it: "All efforts at improving an MFI's impact on women boil down to really understanding a woman's needs, her predicament and what she dreams of. Even before all the questions can be answered, the basic question that must first be answered is who she is."[79]

At the outset of our research, we hoped to find evidence of the impacts of different program strategies that were intentionally designed to empower women. We hoped to be able to determine not only which program elements made the greatest difference in empowering women but also which were the most cost-effective. However, we found objective data hard to come by.

Nevertheless, drawing on our own experience within Opportunity and the experiences of many other MFIs, in this section we present some promising program practices that have achieved good results in their particular context or across a range of countries—many of which have a low incremental cost, and many of which are equally applicable to minimalist and holistic programs.

Business Training

Business training can benefit poor women entrepreneurs when the training is carefully designed to complement their existing skills and address their most pressing needs. With the help of market research and other tools to ensure relevance for clients, business training can be a valuable component of microlending programs. At Sinapi Aba Trust, most of the women interviewed commented that their ability to plan, calculate, and project profit, and manage money had improved considerably as a result of the training they received from their orientation and Trust Bank meetings. Several of these women especially appreciated the training in "customer care" they had received from their Trust Banks because they believe that it has helped them sell their goods faster, retain customers, and work less. In Costa Rica, the majority of the spouses of ADAPTE's clients indicated that the training their wives received from ADAPTE was the most important aspect of the program. Interviews with ADAPTE clients revealed that they value both the training and the credit they received, and in a recent round of focus-group discussions on client satisfaction SAT clients indicated that they would be willing to pay even more for more extensive training.

Opportunity's experience in integrating business training into its Trust Bank lending groups is discussed in the paper "Bundling Microfinance and Business Development Services: A Case Study from ADEMCOL in Colombia."[80] The paper notes that "ADEMCOL's loan officers also have found that those clients who have received business training services and have remained with ADEMCOL are often the best-performing clients." Seamstress Diana Rojas, an ADEMCOL Trust Bank member in her fifth loan cycle, attributes her increased ability to retain and satisfy her clients to her participation in business training offered by ADEMCOL. Ana Moreno Ruiz, a saleswoman who has been a client of ADEMCOL for three years, has participated in several training modules, including those on human relations, costs, marketing, and bookkeeping, and says that "With the training I have received, I have learned to work better with people, and this has permitted me to increase my sales. I have retained my clients." Since the introduction of more advanced business training, ADEMCOL's client retention rate has increased substantially, meaning that more women are staying in the program longer—and presumably enjoying benefits from their participation.

At SAT, too, 66.5 percent of existing clients liked training on business topics best. Eighty-five percent of current clients interviewed with the empowerment tool said that they now have a better relationship with their customers and suppliers as a result of the training on customer care and retention, planning and good pricing, and up-front payment of suppliers. Several of the women interviewed even mentioned that they now have the confidence to share business skills and ideas with their friends and other competitors because they are not afraid of competition. This is in comparison with 24 percent of the clients who said that before they joined SAT they felt too shy to associate with other traders and competitors in the market because they thought their businesses were unimpressive and would be mocked by what they called the well-to-do in the market.

ACCION International's Diálogo de Gestiones (loosely translated as "A Dialogue about Work") is a program of training with over forty modules on topics including assertiveness training, negotiating skills, confidence-building, leadership skills, business training, and learning new trades—as well as a gender module designed specifically to address women's needs. After a three-year development process, the program is being carried out in eleven countries with thirty-one institutions and has trained 158,000 clients. ACCION has found the program to be so essential that it is also offered independently of its credit programs: a recent study found that 51 percent of the trainees also receive credit, but 49 percent have no credit at the time of training.[81]

Women's General Education and Literacy

"As it is often said, knowledge to the poor is power to the poor. It is this that empowers the rural poor in VAWA projects."[82]

Women's general education and literacy are important if they are to reach their full potential and become empowered. Illiteracy creates a situation of dependency on others that can limit an individual's prospects for empowerment. Many MFIs have found illiteracy to be a major stumbling block for their clients. Some, like WEDTF, try to adapt by making sure that there is at least one literate member in every group or that at least one member has a literate child who can assist the group. Many MFIs use participatory training techniques that do not require literacy to educate clients, but very few are able to offer literacy training since most methods for providing it are relatively expensive and time-intensive for both staff and clients. Although many illiterate entrepreneurs are able to keep accounts in their heads, their ability to interact with the formal sector will always be limited. Some NGOs such as World Education and Women's Empowerment Project in Nepal have come up with innovative and low-cost methods of training women in literacy that have significantly enhanced the empowerment benefits of the savings and credit groups to which the women belong. By using existing lending groups and providing materials for women to train themselves, the literacy programs have grown rapidly for a relatively low cost in contrast to many literacy initiatives. These programs have shown that literacy and education contribute powerfully to empowerment and complement the financial independence that microfinance provides. In the case of WEP, the literacy rate among its members rose from 21 percent to 85 percent during the first thirty months of the program.

Helen Sherpa of World Education writes, "In new groups these women start as 'nobodies' leading groups that have no money and no respect. These groups' funds grow and they become increasingly self-reliant breaking the hold of male money lenders and male family members over economic decisions. This suddenly elevates the status of the groups as well as the individual members and leaders. Leaders in the groups become role models because these are 'women like them'—poorer women, women who have become literate later in life."[83] In addition, educating women has additional benefits for their children. World Education has documented that women who attend education programs dramatically increase their commitment to educating their children and to educating their daughters in particular.[84] Because lack of money for school fees is the major cause of school dropouts in Nepal as well as in many other countries, the income generated from microenterprises plays an important role in helping women realize their dreams for their children. Kashf in Pakistan found a similar linkage. An independent study found that 35 percent of Kashf members see their educated loan officers as role models for their daughters. More than 50 percent of the women wanted to educate their daughters, and more than 40 percent wanted to pursue a different future for them.[85]

Balancing Family and Work Responsibilities

In addition to educational disadvantages, one of the most difficult challenges that many women face as they start or expand businesses is the balancing of their increasing business responsibilities with their household responsibilities. Although the ultimate goal may be for household responsibilities to be shared between the men and women in the household, this sharing never happens overnight. In many cases, women's businesses remain small and concentrated in less profitable sectors in large part because of the time constraints that women's domestic responsibilities create. Not only do women have limited time to spend on their business activities, but often they also must be able to abandon them altogether for periods to deal with family crises or children's illnesses. As a result, many women's employment opportunities are limited to those that can be done on a part-time and often irregular basis. The experiences of Opportunity International's partners have demonstrated that women often need help to develop strategies for managing and meeting the expectations of family and community members while still having the time and energy to run their businesses well. Women also need support in negotiating the complex changes in gender roles that must ultimately take place in order for them to succeed as microentrepreneurs. Many of Sinapi Aba Trust's clients as well as clients of Opportunity International's other partners in Africa have highly valued the advice on time management and "managing your husband" that they have received.

Some Opportunity partners and other MFIs are also recognizing that more outreach efforts are necessary to secure husbands' cooperation and support. It comes as no surprise that the most successful clients of many MFIs are the ones who have the most supportive husbands and that those with more problems often have problems with their husbands as well. Because most MFIs deal primarily with women, however, husbands are often not directly included. Some MFIs are experimenting with ways to influence husbands through including them in selected orientation sessions, having special events for spouses, and inviting them to group meetings occasionally.

Dialogue on Social and Political Issues

Discussion of social issues affecting women's lives and communities can lead to greater awareness of the causes of the problems they face and allow them to take more effective action to address the problems that are holding them back. Discussion of women's rights, community problems, politics, and common family problems can foster a sense of solidarity that can empower women both as individuals and as a group to address their problems. With some support, groups of economically empowered women can take steps to address the cultural and legal barriers that limit their social and political empowerment. CSD, for example, found that as a result of the discussions of social and legal issues held in lending centers, women have greater knowledge of their civil and legal rights and are more aware of their position and the choices they can make. They have increased knowledge of how relevant institutions can help them when they need legal assistance, and this knowledge has allowed more women to resist domestic violence and alcoholism and demand fair minimum wages.[86]

Several studies point to the importance of social and cultural structures in determining an individual's level of empowerment or social value. For example, a study by Drèze and Sen shows us that "structural variables making up gender relations in different parts of India are far more important in determining the extent to which the girl child is valued within the family than the individual characteristics of their parents."[87] Other studies show that structural characteristics are more important in determining the social value or empowerment of an individual than any of the individual's actions or circumstances are—including participation in microenterprise programs.

These findings underscore the importance of at least *attempting* to address some of the wider social structures that are contributing to the disempowerment of women as well as helping women tackle some of the personal problems that are limiting their potential. More formal training programs on topics such as women's rights, domestic violence prevention, and family planning could substantially improve women's ability to face these challenges. Such education efforts, however, will likely be most successful when they are developed in cooperation with the clients themselves. At SAT, Trust Banks develop their own education and training programs in each loan cycle in cooperation with their loan officers. This ensures that the training provided and the topics discussed are those most relevant and useful to the clients. In many Grameen replications, the women control their own program through their centers. Such training and discussion does not have to be expensive to provide, and the potential benefits of empowerment far outweigh the costs. Involving the women themselves in planning and even preparing training can help keep costs low while at the same time giving women the power to control their program.

Experience in Decision-Making and Leadership

One of the positive contributions that group-based lending methodologies make to women's empowerment is the opportunity for women to gain experience in making decisions and leading and influencing others. As Essma Ben Hamida of ENDA Inter-arabe in Tunisia puts it, "Participation in the micro-credit programme constitutes an apprenticeship of democracy through the self-managed solidarity groups which elect their president and treasurer: in many mixed groups, a woman has been elected as president, an astounding development in a still male-dominated society."[88]

When they join microfinance programs, many women have had little opportunity to voice their opinions or participate in decision-making. Some will have had little experience even formulating an opinion that can be expressed since they have had little opportunity to do so. A synthesis study done by Jennefer Sebstad and Monique Cohen found that "[lending] groups provide a means for women to know and be known by other women; a forum for learning leadership and public speaking skills; and a basis for development of trust, friendship, and financial assistance."[89] Although actual levels of control vary according to methodology, in most cases, women are called upon to develop and use skills in group dynamics and persuasion, to exercise authority, and to command the respect of others—some for the first time in their lives.

Opportunities for leadership are affected not only by the structure of the program but also by the group's internal policy. Groups that set policies to rotate their leadership frequently give more women a chance to develop leadership skills than ones that do not, although groups without a rotation policy can allow a few women to develop even stronger and more lasting leadership skills. In addition, if the rotation of leadership is coupled with specific training on leadership and organizational skills, it can help foster a sense of equality among the women and break down other social barriers such as caste as well as gender. Programs like SAT's deliberately try to break down traditional notions of leaders being chosen from an elite in order to instill the idea that everyone is capable of being a leader. Mixed-sex and mixed-caste lending groups have the potential to empower, but if such groups do not make a deliberate effort to stimulate the meaningful participation of all members, they may end up replicating existing patterns of social inequality. Much depends on the policies established, however, and some trade-offs

Box 4.5
Building a Member-Owned, Member-Managed
Credit and Savings Society
Janashakti Women's Development Federation, Sri Lanka[90]

Janashakti Women's Development Federation of Sri Lanka is a Women's World Banking partner that has carefully built a multitiered network of banking societies owned and managed by their members. Janashakti has evolved from a grassroots organization focused on health and nutrition to a 28,168-member institution offering seven loan products, five savings products, and life insurance in addition to other services such as training in business, health, and nutrition. Poor women themselves built the organization and continue to lead and manage it at all levels. This structure has the advantage of helping achieve Janashakti's main objective of "eradicating poverty by developing and promoting individual and collective strength and self-reliance." Through participation in the leadership and management of the organization, poor women build nontraditional technical and professional skills that can allow them to go beyond their traditional gender roles in society. Although Janashakti is 90 percent financially self-sufficient, it does face a number of challenges, many of which are inherent in its structure. There are some tensions between grassroots ownership and depth of outreach. Janashakti has also identified a need to build stronger technical skills among its membership in order to manage the sophisticated demands of the growing organization so that it can maintain its unique structure of member management.

in empowerment may apply, because allowing groups complete freedom to establish their own policies incurs a greater risk of replicating existing social structures and putting the same people in power inside the lending group as outside. In contrast, setting guidelines for internal policies can help promote healthy leadership experiences but constrains the autonomy of the groups. MFIs can help maximize the empowerment potential of lending groups by providing training and coaching to client leaders, developing cost-effective methods for clients to manage their own loans and savings, ensuring that women have a chance to lead in mixed lending groups, and encouraging the active participation of all group members.

Ownership, Control, and Participatory Governance

One contribution to empowerment that self-help groups and other savings-based community groups offer to members is the pride of ownership and autonomy. Even though some self-help groups are given training and support from NGOs, the majority of even these externally supported groups rely primarily on member savings for their capital instead of on external capital as most village banks or solidarity groups do.

Savings-based approaches that rely on minimal external support have several advantages. Women are proud to own their capital and have savings they can rely on. The capital stays in the community, and the women manage it themselves according to their own needs and interests. Because the external support costs are minimal, women are able to charge a lower rate of interest, and a large percentage of that interest goes back to the women in the form of interest on their savings and community projects.

The empowerment benefits derived from independence and autonomy are often partially offset, however, by weaker economic empowerment benefits. By depending on the savings of very poor community members, capital is more limited than it would be with external support, which in turn limits the growth potential of women's enterprises and income. Although independent savings-based self-help groups are viable alternatives for reaching remote and impoverished rural areas, the very poverty of these areas may make it difficult to amass the savings necessary to extend credit in the amounts necessary to stimulate the development of a vibrant microenterprise sector. Microfinance institutions should continue to experiment with models that combine women's control of programs and resources with access to greater amounts of capital.

Building Institutions Responsive to Women's Needs

Women in Leadership   Does it matter whether men or women are at the helm of microfinance institutions? Women have been important as policy-setters and influential donors—through USAID, CGAP, and DFID, for example. They have also been innovators, as seen at SEWA, Pro Mujer, Women's World Banking, Working Women's Forum, and other organizations. A glance at microfinance trainings and conferences shows plenty of women in attendance. Yet men predominate on boards of directors of MFIs, in senior management, in program design, and sometimes as loan officers. That means that women and men are not equally involved in critical areas of decision-making including setting the vision, defining the client target population, and designing products and services.

Within Opportunity International, 85 percent of clients are women. An August 2000 survey on gender issues reported that "the majority of staff

(57%) are women, but that women tend not to serve in key leadership roles, especially as senior managers and board members. . . . However, the largest area of gender inequity is at the board level." Interestingly, the survey showed that the inequity was just as present among the OI fund-raising partners in North America, Europe, and Australia as it was for OI partner MFIs in developing countries.

Florence Abena Dolphyne, a Ghanaian scholar, feels strongly that women have a key role to play in good governance. She writes, "In the search for ways of promoting women's emancipation in Africa, the importance of competent women in policy-making positions at all levels cannot be overemphasized. Such women can help initiate and ensure the implementation of programmes and activities that would promote the welfare of women, and encourage women's greater participation in national development. They can also provide the necessary insights into women's concerns that would ensure that government policies, projects and programmes have the desired impact and achieve the desired goals precisely because due account has been taken of the concerns and views of the different groups in the society."[91] Recognizing the importance of increasing women's representation in governance, Interaction, the association of U.S.-based PVOs in international relief and development, has launched a Campaign for Gender Equity on Boards for their members.

In Opportunity International the creation of a women-led subsidiary, the Women's Opportunity Fund, transformed the vision and mission of the entire organization, resulting in new products and services for women and dramatically increasing the number and percentage of women clients served.[92]

Women as Field Officers   Even more interesting than the issue of women in governance is the question of whether it is more desirable to have women as loan officers when most of the clients are women. Grameen Bank is noteworthy for championing women's rights to credit in groundbreaking ways, and about 95 percent of its clients are women. It also reaches beyond most MFIs in that the Bank, which is "owned" by borrowers, includes women clients on its board.[93] According to Alex Counts, executive director of Grameen Foundation USA, as of January 2002, "all 9 borrower-elected Directors of Grameen are women. . . . Despite there being about 100,000 male borrowers, there has never been more than one of the nine elected members who have been men."[94] This governance structure includes not only women's perspectives but, more important, client perspectives. Yet, according to Counts, for many years the percentage of female loan officers (called center managers) has remained between 5 percent and 10 percent, with new efforts to recruit female staff balanced by retirements and resignations. "Grameen

Bank is certainly not the only agency in Bangladesh where the nature of the work is rural and field-based that struggles with this issue."[95]

In the Opportunity International Network approximately 50 percent of all loan officers are women. Anecdotal evidence suggests that the experience of having male loan officers treating women clients with respect and dignity is empowering in and of itself.[96] Yet other women clients say that they can relate more easily to a female loan officer and that female loan officers provide a role model of achievement. Our research at Sinapi Aba Trust in Ghana suggests that female loan officers are especially valued by women clients as role models for their daughters, showing an unplanned secondary impact of the program. In our experience, a key factor is gender sensitivity—of both female and male loan officers—in ensuring that women are empowered through microfinance. We have found it helpful to screen for gender sensitivity during the hiring process and to provide gender sensitivity training to all staff to ensure that both male and female loan officers are giving the same message about gender and empowerment.

In addition, organizations can take a number of steps to help loan officers become more empowering in their work. Many loan officers interviewed in our research felt that the time they were able to spend with clients was too limited. By minimizing loan officers' paperwork, MFIs can help loan officers spend more time in the field with clients. Also, loan officers could be given performance incentives based on client empowerment as well as portfolio size and quality to reward them for the extra effort they put in to make sure clients are succeeding. Loan officers also should be an MFI's early warning system against negative impacts. Creating an internal feedback loop so that loan officers' knowledge of client empowerment and struggles is fed into product design and implementation can be one of the most cost-effective means of ensuring that programs are responsive to women's needs.

It is important for MFIs to review policies that discriminate against women, whether intentionally or not. An MFI in Zimbabwe did not hire women as loan officers because it was considered culturally inappropriate for women to ride motorcycles, and this was a requirement for reaching remote clients. CETZAM in Zambia, however, was able to challenge this norm and now has motorcycle-riding women on its staff. An MFI in Colombia found that it was unintentionally paying a higher wage to male program staff for similar work. An MFI in the Philippines with a client base that is 99 percent women included "preferably male" among the qualifications for a post being advertised, explaining that it was not safe for women to travel alone into their target communities. An MFI in El Salvador had a similar informal policy until a male loan officer was shot while on his rounds; it then realized that the issues of security for women were also issues for men, and implemented changes to protect both men and women on its staff. Around the world, microfinance field staff often face physical discomfort and unsafe conditions along with a cultural bias against women. Some MFIs have been able to challenge these cultural biases and accommodate for the discomfort and lack of safety; others have simply let women select themselves out of the running; and others have intentionally expressed a bias for male field workers. Developing organizational policies to promote gender equity and sensitivity at all levels of the organization is one way to guard against discrimination and build an institutional culture that is supportive of women. These choices are part of the message that MFIs send their clients about women's potential and capacity.

Managing the Challenges of Rapid Growth   As the industry grows and matures, women may be adversely affected by institutional changes resulting from rapid expansion, consolidation, and commercialization. Opportunity's experience is that several partners have provided a lower percentage of loans to women as they have grown. This is, of course, not all bad news: in the context of aggressive growth, the absolute number of women receiving services grows, even if the percentage of women clients decreases. Yet there are some trends that should be monitored, such as the tendency to drop group loans in favor of individual loans. Again, this is not all bad—as long as the individual loan product is thoughtfully designed with women's needs in mind, and as long as the poorest and most marginalized women are not left behind.

The consolidation issue likewise has pro's and con's. Opportunity's recent experience with a few consolidations shows that, as with any consolidation, it is a delicate matter to bring together different systems, policies, and products. The blended organizational culture may be stronger in gender sensitivity and gender equity—or it may be weaker. And, as MFIs transform into regulated financial institutions, they must meet the demands of the supervising authority, creditors, and investors. Pressure to select the most financially profitable products and delivery systems may reduce the accessibility and benefits for women. Part of the pressure is to increase loan sizes—and women, who are disproportionately among the poorest, have a greater need for smaller entry level loans. Therefore, in the midst of this growth, it is important to develop client-centered products that acknowledge not only women's economic needs but their potential for empowerment as well.

Designing Products to Meet Women's Needs   Through impact assessments, monitoring, market research, and client feedback, many MFIs have begun to develop and adapt new products to address the shortcomings of their traditional products and keep pace with clients' changing needs. For example, some MFIs in Africa are beginning to explore giving family business loans to encourage cooperation between the husband and wife, in particular, but also to increase the number of income earners in the family and extended family. ADEMCOL in Colombia is piloting a Senior Trust Bank program to meet the needs of women whose businesses are maturing and need larger loans and more advanced business training, yet do not want to leave the group-lending program.

Another example of client research leading to the development of more empowering products is research by the Council for Economic Empowerment for Women of Africa-Uganda (CEEWA-U). Research with several MFIs in Uganda found that very few women are able to acquire assets through group-loan programs. One negative consequence of this for the women and their businesses was that the productivity of women's businesses was not improving dramatically, nor were women able to access larger individual loans, which often require assets as collateral or a guarantor. In some cases, this hindrance was due to policies requiring loans to be used for working capital only, but in others, it was due to loan terms, amounts, and repayment schedules that did not allow for the purchase of a long-term asset. CEEWA-U developed a capital asset loan product called Kikalu to meet this need, combining a longer repayment period, group guarantee, and flexible disbursement schedule.[97]

Conclusions

Microfinance has the potential to have a powerful impact on women's empowerment. Although microfinance is not *always* empowering for all women, most women do experience some degree of empowerment as a result. Empowerment is a complex process of change that is experienced by all individuals somewhat differently. Women need, want, and profit from credit and other financial services. Strengthening women's financial base and economic contribution to their families and communities plays a role in empowering them.

In some cases, access to credit may be the only input needed to start women on the road to empowerment. But power is deeply rooted in our social systems and values. It permeates all aspects of our lives from our family to our communities, from our personal dreams and aspirations to our economic opportunities. It is unlikely that any one intervention such as the provision of credit or the provision of training will completely alter power and gender relations. Women often value the noneconomic benefits of a group-lending program as much as or more than the credit. Some of the most valued benefits include expanded business and social networks, improved self-esteem, increased household decision-making power, and increased respect and prestige from both male and female relatives and community members.

Targeting women continues to be important in the design of products and services, both because women by default have less access to credit and because they face constraints unique to their gender. Product design and program planning should take women's needs and assets into account. By building an awareness of the potential impacts of their programs, MFIs can design products, services, and service delivery mechanisms that mitigate negative impacts and enhance positive ones. Even when products and services target primarily women, women still face considerable disadvantages relative to men because of more limited business networks and opportunities, greater domestic burden, weaker self-confidence, less education, and, in many cases, a restrictive legal environment. These disadvantages can sometimes be perpetuated in microfinance programs, with men dominating mixed lending groups and women receiving smaller loan amounts than men.

As Wariara Mbugua of UNFPA says, "No longer can this strategy be reduced to simple income-generating activities through revolving funds, but rather it entails and includes other elements of empowerment such as leadership, self-management, networking and entrepreneurship."[98] By adopting a holistic approach that takes into account cultural, economic, and political factors affecting women's empowerment, MFIs can ensure that women are more deeply and consistently empowered through their programs.

Call to Action

Although there is much we would still like to know about targeting women and empowering women through microfinance, our research excited us enough about the potential that we would like to issue a few challenges.

We would like to see practitioners:

- gather information on women's needs and design products specifically to meet those needs. This existing strength should not be lost as the microfinance industry grows.

- incorporate programmatic elements such as training or leadership opportunities that contribute to women's empowerment.

- track empowerment benefits along with institutional financial performance and economic impact indicators.

- bring women and women's perspectives into the governance, management, and implementation of microfinance programs.

- collect gender-disaggregated data for use in the design and improvement of programs.
- review organizational policies to ensure gender sensitivity and gender equity.
- design individual loan products and graduation strategies that meet the needs of women.
- create performance incentives for loan officers and other staff based on client empowerment in addition to portfolio quality and quantity.

We would like to see donors:

- support holistic approaches to microfinance as part of an ongoing commitment to innovation, research, and development.
- conduct and support action research on best practices in empowering women.
- conduct and support research on appropriate measures of empowerment that practitioners can use to monitor and improve their empowerment impact.
- promote women in leadership in the MFIs they support.
- consider empowerment impacts when evaluating microfinance program performance and making funding decisions.

APPENDIX:
MORE PROMISING PRACTICES

A number of institutions have invested in developing products and services that help address some of the additional constraints to women's ability to successfully utilize credit and savings for income-generating activities. Other institutions have focused on promoting women's leadership within their organizations as well as among their clients. This section presents some of these ideas and innovations.

Group Loans for Group Businesses When Women Are First Initiating Economic Activities

Women's Empowerment and Development Trust Fund (WEDTF) operates on the island of Zanzibar in Tanzania. Zanzibar is an Islamic society in which men have traditionally practiced polygamy and women have not traditionally been involved in public or commercial activities. As is the case in a number of other countries, however, economic pressures are slowly reducing the practicality of polygamy and increasing the acceptability of women entering the labor force.

WEDTF serves exclusively women using a methodology similar to Grameen's. Money is lent to women in groups of five who mutually guarantee the loan amount. Women participate in center activities with other groups where they receive training and discuss issues of importance to them. A high percentage of WEDTF clients are extremely poor and unable to meet their families' daily needs. Very few women are literate or have any business experience.

One of the unusual aspects of WEDTF's program is that, at first, the five-member solidarity groups often go into business together rather than establish their own separate enterprises. Group enterprises were especially dominant in the beginning, with only a few women wishing to set up their own businesses, but now women are beginning to prefer individual undertakings. Unlike cooperatives or income-generating activities that have been promoted by some development institutions in the past, WEDTF's clients *chose* to form group enterprises based on the existing needs and interests of the group members rather than being asked to join businesses or cooperatives set up by others.

WEDTF suggests that the initial preference for group enterprises may have been significantly linked to the perceived risks of individual undertakings. Most women in the program were new to credit and to business. Because they lacked confidence and experience, they used the group to gain experience and build up confidence in their ability to manage business affairs. Illiterate women, in particular, relied on the groups to gain the skills they need and, in some cases, still use group secretaries to keep their accounts. For these reasons, WEDTF believes that women preferred to spread the risk among the group in the event that the project would fail. A group undertaking also can minimize the work and time burden of each individual woman, allowing her more flexibility and ensuring the continuation of income if she should fall sick or become pregnant and be unable to work for a time. Another possibility suggested by WEDTF is that group activities and investments help protect the business assets and capital from male appropriation.

Giving women the opportunity to work together and build on each other's skills while minimizing risks is a strategy that should be explored in other contexts where women are initiating economic activity for the first time. WEDTF's impact study showed that women gained new skills in business management, trades, and decision-making while working in their groups. They increased their economic contribution to their households and communities and gained self-confidence and the respect and trust of their families and communities.

Combining Credit Unions with "Credit with Education"

In 1998, Freedom from Hunger and the World Council of Credit Unions (WOCCU) launched the Credit Union Empowering and Strengthening (CUES) program on the island of Mindanao in the Philippines. The joint effort seeks to integrate Freedom from Hunger's "Credit With Education" village banking product into the array of financial services already offered by credit unions. Credit unions have several characteristics that make them potentially empowering to the poor and women. Like many self-help groups (SHGs) and rotating savings and credit associations (ROSCAs), credit unions offer their members the empowering benefits of owning and controlling their own capital and having a say in the governance of the institution. Unlike the SHGs and ROSCAs, however, members of credit unions are not constrained in the amount that they can borrow by the amount of savings that their small group of very poor individuals is able to amass. By opening membership to a mixed clientele, credit unions are able to mobilize the larger deposits of some of their wealthier members for making loans to the poor. In this way, credit unions are able to maintain the positive aspects of control and ownership found in very small community-based savings and credit plans while alleviating some of the constraints on the amount of capital available. Yet, despite this potential, many credit unions struggle to attract and serve poorer members of their communities.

Although credit unions offer many benefits to the poor, they lack the solidarity and the learning experiences that come from weekly participation in the financial administration and decision-making of SHGs, ROSCAs, village banks, and solidarity groups. Typically, they also do not offer the educational opportunities provided by many village banking–style programs like Freedom from Hunger's Credit With Education and Opportunity International's Trust Banks. Some of the poorest, most disempowered women could significantly benefit from the education and experience offered through group-lending programs that would later allow them to benefit more fully from the options and control that credit unions offer.

The CUES program provides women with the benefits of credit unions and village banks at once. It offers a "savings and credit with education" product to groups of poor women in rural and urban communities through eighteen credit unions. Women form groups, and each group counts as one member of the credit union. Women receive group loans and training based on Freedom from Hunger's Credit With Education model provided by a credit union (loan officer). Training is provided in the areas of health and nutrition, microenterprise management and development, savings and credit association management, and self-confidence. After the initial sixteen-week cycles are completed and the women have repaid successfully, they have the choice of staying with the group-lending program, becoming an individual member of the credit union, or borrowing as an individual member but remaining in the lending group as well in order to continue the fellowship and learning experience.

As of May 2001, the eleven credit unions that joined the CUES program in 1998 (7 joined later) have a total of 21,909 borrowers and 23,641 savers enrolled in the Savings and Credit With Education program. Operating expenses were 9.9 percent of average assets as of September 30, 2001.

Promoting Change through Women-led Organizations

In 1992, 42 percent of Opportunity International's clients were women. By 1998, that number had increased to 85 percent. In addition, where there had been one woman executive director among all of Opportunity's partners, by 1998 fifteen out of sixty were women. And where many partners' boards of directors had had no women members, by 1998 only two partners lacked women board members, and a few partners had achieved gender equity on their boards. What brought about this dramatic change? One big factor was the Women's Opportunity Fund (WOF), which Opportunity created in order to focus more on outreach to women. With predominantly women on its board (eleven of the twelve founding board members were women), WOF worked with Opportunity's partners to create and refine the Trust Bank group-lending methodology in order to reach extremely poor women with a program promoting holistic transformation. Not only did it bring program innovation to the Opportunity Network, it also brought funding power, as the board took responsibility for donating and raising funds to support its own activities. This independence in fund raising meant both freedom and power to pursue the program activities that best fit its vision of empowering poor women.

By 1996 Opportunity had made the decision to promote WOF's Trust Bank program as its primary program and fund-raising focus. It also adopted a gender policy prioritizing outreach to women. The adoption of more and more of WOF's vision and focus by both the programmatic and fundraising arms of the Opportunity International Network led to a merger in 2001. The fundraising arm of WOF merged with the Opportunity International Network's U.S.-based fundraising partner (OI-US), combining both boards of directors into one large board with 40 percent women, while at the same time retaining funding independence for WOF. WOF program specialists joined OI Network's technical assistance and policy and research teams and continue to be a force for women-focused products and services. For Opportunity, although many factors were involved, the creation of a predominantly women's organization was key to reaching more women clients, designing products to serve them, and increasing the number of women in leadership.

Empowering Women to Lead through Participatory Governance[99]

Agricultural and Rural Development for Catanduanes, Incorporated (ARDCI), was formed by the privatization of the government-sponsored credit program of Catanduanes Agricultural Support Programme (CatAg).[100] Registered in 1998, ARDCI today serves close to 11,000 households, and by 2003, it plans to extend its reach to 23,000 households in all six provinces in the Catanduanes region of the Philippines, where the poverty incidence is 56 percent. Eighty-six percent of ARDCI members are women. Since being privatized, the program's orientation has shifted to become owned, controlled, and managed by the people who participate in it, resulting in an increase from 75 percent to 86 percent in the proportion of women in leadership roles in the guarantee group and Savings and Loan System (SLS) levels.

Women currently participate in all levels of leadership in ARDCI, and at the municipal level in numbers that reflect their proportion of ARDCI's membership. ARDCI members form Grameen-style five-member guarantee groups that hold weekly meetings to gather savings and repayments and recommend loan proposals. Three to six guarantee groups within a village form a Savings and Loan System (SLS), which directs ARDCI loan funds to guarantee groups and remits payments to ARDCI. The SLSs also perform supervisory and advisory functions, assisting members with investment plans and monitoring loan use. Eighty-six percent of guarantee group leaders are women, and 86 percent of SLS chairpersons, who are elected from among the guarantee group leaders, are also women.

The SLS chairpersons within a municipality elect four municipal representatives, who in turn elect a board of trustees that is the policy-making body of ARDCI. ARDCI has 11 trustees, two of whom are women. Two-thirds of the representatives are women (twenty-two of thirty-three). To qualify to serve on the ARDCI board, an individual must have been an active member for one year, have a secondary education, and have knowledge, skills, and values aligned with ARDCI's standards (excellence, integrity, servant leadership, transparency, and stewardship). According to managing director Noni S. Ayo, the women in leadership roles have demonstrated not only their organizational leadership but also a nurturing nature that keeps teams working and highly motivated.

To prepare clients for leadership positions, ARDCI provides training through the SLSs in transformational leadership, team building, conflict management, and performance standards. They also visit other successful microfinance organizations within the Philippines in order to learn from them.

In addition to substantial leadership from women clients, ARDCI's program also benefits from having six highly qualified women executives, including the managing director, the deputy director, and the head of monitoring and evaluation.

According to Ayo, women who participate in ARDCI enjoy higher respect among their family members, especially their children, and within their communities. Women are proud of their achievements and of becoming more equal partners in supporting their families. One woman who used her ARDCI loan to purchase a motorized boat, says, "Before, each day, I would wait for my husband to come home and look at his share of the catch to see whether we'll have a good dinner or not. Today, I would wait for my husband so I could help him sell his catch."

A 1999 impact report based on interviews of 180 randomly selected individuals confirmed the social benefits of participating in the program. Respondents included SLS members, SLS officers, and persons who are not program members. The report showed that program members experienced greater improvement in economic conditions than nonmembers and that women members have greater economic independence and greater involvement in activities beyond their home. The study found that fully 70 percent of women members were involved in income-generating activities, compared to the 67 percent of women nonmembers who said that their days revolve around only household chores. Seventeen percent of male members said that their days revolve around a combination of household chores and income-generating activities, compared with only 6 percent of male nonmembers.

When asked what they consider as the most important influence of the SLS on themselves as head of the family and as member of the community, 83 percent of women answered that it is 1) the acquisition of new skills and knowledge, 2) improved attitude, reinforced values, and a changed way of thinking or a combination of 1) and 2).[101] Eighty-eight percent of officers, both male and female, gave this response, compared with 77 percent of members who are not officers. Only 8 percent of participants cited only monetary gains as the most significant benefit.

Noni Ayo states, "In ARDCI's experience, becoming involved with an organization (whether in a village level or apex level) that recognizes and celebrates a woman's need for other social responsibilities beyond her domestic obligation is already the start of empowerment." One women currently serving on ARDCI's board of trustees who barely dared to speak at her first board meeting now proudly says, "I don't feel embarrassed that I've not gone to college and that I sit among male leaders. My experiences as a mother, as a wife, and as a chairperson of the SLS are all that it takes to contribute to the board meeting." According to Ayo, a remarkable change occurs when female members are given more responsibilities to chair the SLSs or sit in the board of trustees. She notices an increased capacity to put forward ideas and assert their views every time they attend board meetings.

Notes

1. The Microcredit Summit Campaign defines poorest as the bottom half of those living below their nation's poverty line. The Campaignís greatest challenge lies in bridging the gap between its commitment to reaching the poorest and the lack of a sufficient number of effective poverty measurement tools in use. Therefore, every mention of the term poorest in this report should be read within the context of this dilemma. It is expected that, with every successive report, the use of high-quality poverty measurements will increase, and therefore, so too will the quality of the data reported.

2. Rani Deshpanda. Increasing Access and Benefits for Women: Practices and Innovations among Microfinance Institutions—Survey Results (New York: UNCDF, 2001), 3.

3. USAID. Reaching Down and Scaling Up: Focus on USAID's Development Partners: USAID Microenterprise Results Reporting for 1999 (Arlington, Va.: Weidemann Associates, 2000), 22.

4. USAID. Microenterprise Development in a Changing World: US Agency for International Development Microenterprise Results Reporting for 2000 (Arlington, Va.:

Weidemann Associates, 2001), 31.

5. The Microcredit Summit Campaign asks institutions to report the number of their clients who are in the bottom half of those living below their country's poverty line.

6. World Bank, Engendering Development: Through Gender Equality in Rights, Resources, and Voice—Summary (Washington, D.C.: World Bank, 2001); www.worldbank.org/gender/prr/engendersummary.pdf.

7. Canadian International Development Agency (CIDA), "CIDA's Policy on Gender Equality" (Hull, Canada: CIDA, 1999), 5.

8. CIDA, "CIDA's Policy on Gender Equality," 11.

9. See works by Linda Mayoux and Naila Kabeer for more information on the implications of the instrumentalist approach on development policy, practices, and evaluation. See especially Linda Mayoux, Women's Empowerment and Microfinance: A Participatory Learning, Management, and Action Approach. Resource Manual for Practitioners and Trainers, draft (UNIFEM, 2001); Naila Kabeer, 'Money Can't Buy Me Love'? Re-evaluating Gender, Credit and Empowerment in Rural Bangladesh, IDS Discussion Paper 363 (Brighton, England: Institute of Development Studies, University of Sussex, 1998).

10. UNDP, 1995 Human Development Report (New York, UNDP, 1996), 4.

11. See the World Bank's Web site at genderstats.worldbank.org.

12. Sally Baden and K. Milward, "Gender and Poverty," BRIDGE Report, no. 30 (Sussex: IDS, 1995).

13. Deshpanda, 15.

14. Sylvia Chant, "Women-Headed Households: Poorest of the Poor? Perspectives from Mexico, Costa Rica and the Philippines," IDS Bulletin 28, no. 3 (1997): 39.

15. Naila Kabeer, The Conditions and Consequences of Choice: Reflections on the Measurement of Women's Empowerment, UNRISD Discussion Paper No. 108 (1999), 49; www.unrisd.org.

16. Mike Mends, Sinapi Aba Trust, in an e-mail to Suzy Salib, 14 August 2000.

17. Damian von Stauffenberg, MicroRate, in an e-mail to Susy Cheston and Lisa Kuhn, 24 September 2001.

18. Deshpanda, 4.

19. Gary Woller, "Reassessing the Financial Viability of Village Banking: Past Performance and Future Prospects," Microbanking Bulletin 5 (2000): 4.

20. For more information, see the Convention on the Elimination of All Forms of Discrimination Against Women, Beijing Declaration and Platform for Action, and other documents on UNIFEM's Web site: www.undp.org/unifem.

21. UNIFEM, Progress of the World's Women (New York: UNIFEM, 2000).

22. Mayoux, Women's Empowerment and Microfinance, 18.

23. An activist in the Drita Women's Group, Prishtina, Kosovo, as quoted in International Helsinki Federations for Human Rights (IHF), Women 2000: An Investigation into the Status of Women's Rights in Central and South-eastern Europe and the Newly Independent States (Helsinki: IHF, 2000).

24. Beijing Platform for Action, Fourth United Nations World Conference on Women (Beijing, 1995), paragraph 41.

25. E-mail message to authors from Maria Otero, President and CEO of ACCION International, on 6/27/02.

26. See chapter 2 for more information on the costs, benefits, and rationale of integrating nonfinancial services in microenterprise development programs. Some services that can be offered include nutrition education, business training, distribution of contraception, and education about reproductive health and prenatal care.

27. Information gathered from the Web site of Women's World Banking (www.swwb.org) and e-mails from Celina Kawas, of Women's World Banking.

28. Beedi-rollers are usually very poor women and children who are contracted, often under very poor conditions, to roll the thin beedi cigarettes.

29. Working Women's Forum, Social Platform through Social Innovations: A Coalition with Women in the Informal Sector (Chennai, India: Working Women's Forum, 2000), 25, 39.

30. Jeffrey Ashe and Lisa Parrott, Impact Evaluation of PACT's Women's Empowerment Program in Nepal: A Savings and Literacy Led Alternative to Financial Institution Building (Waltham, Mass.: Brandeis University, 2001), 8.

31. Milan Shrestha, Report on Self-help Banking Program and Women's Empowerment (Nepal, 1998), 28.

32. Helen Sherpa, World Education response to e-mail survey, 20 October 2001.

33. Jesila Ledesma, "Empowerment Impact Report on TSPI's Kabuhayan program," draft, April 2002.

34. URWEGO staff defined empowerment in the Rwandan context as "an increase in self-esteem, an increase in decision-making, and an increase in knowledge of what to do and how to access resources (to solve problems, achieve objectives, etc.)." World Relief Rwanda, "Impact Assessment of TF UK Clients in the World Relief Rwanda URWEGO Program" (1999), 4.

35. World Relief Rwanda, 7.

36. PLAN International, Mid-term Evaluation of Nirdhan/PLAN Microfinance Program in Nepal (PLAN International, 2001), 37.

37. Shrestha, 24, 28.

38. Kabeer, 'Money Can't Buy Me Love'? 21.

39. Ashe and Parrott, 8.

40. World Relief Rwanda, 7.

41. Kabeer, Conditions and Consequences, 20.

42. From surveys conducted by ADAPTE loan officers in October–December 2001 on behalf of the authors.

43. See, for example, Anne Marie Goetz and Rina Sen Gupta, "Who Takes the Credit? Gender, Power, and Control over Loan Use in Rural Credit Programs in Bangladesh," World Development 24, no. 1 (1996): 45–63.

44. Kabeer, 'Money Can't Buy Me Love'? 44.

45. Personal interview.

46. S. M. Hashemi, R. R. Schuler, and A. P. Riley, "Rural Credit Programs and Women's Empowerment in Bangladesh," World Development 24, no. 4 (1996): 635–53; S. R. Schuler, S. M. Hashemi, A. P. Riley, and A. Akhter, "Credit Programs, Patriarchy and Men's Violence against Women in Rural Bangladesh," Social Science and Medicine 43, no. 12 (1996): 1729–42.

47. Working Women's Forum, 22.

48. Shrestha, 30.

49. Kabeer, 'Money Can't Buy Me Love'? 43–54.

50. In the early days when Opportunity International was developing targeted loan products for women, a few local leaders expressed concern about the potential disruption of the family as a result. The most extreme comments included "Giving loans to women will destroy families" and "Providing loans to women goes against God's natural plan for the universe."

51. Kabeer, 'Money Can't Buy Me Love'? 66–67.

52. Women's Entrepreneurship Development Trust Fund (WEDTF), information on microfinance and empowerment of women, Zanzibar, Tanzania, 52.

53. Barbara MkNelly and Mona McCord, "Credit With Education Impact Review No. 1: Women's Empowerment." (Freedom from Hunger, 2001), 9–10.

54. Shrestha, 18.

55. Shrestha, 29–30.

56. Shrestha, iii.

57. A barangay is a community-level political unit in the Philippines.

58. Syed Hashemi, Sidney Schuler, and Ann Riley, "Rural Credit Programs and Women's Empowerment in Bangladesh," World Development 24, no. 4 (1996): 649.

59. Working Women's Forum, 22.

60. MkNelly and McCord, 11.

61. Shrestha 21, 31–32. Note that because political parties in some countries such as Nepal and India must meet quotas of women, women's election to community posts is not necessarily an indication of empowerment or a reliable indicator of program impact—but it can be construed as a step toward an enabling environment for women's political empowerment.

62. This phenomenon has been most widely studied in Bangladesh. For more information on borrowers' perspectives on lending in Bangladesh, see Goetz and Sen Gupta; Aminur Rahman, "Micro-credit Initiatives for Equitable and Sustainable Development: Who Pays?" World Development 27, no. 1 (1999): 67–82; Helen Todd, Women at the Center: Grameen Bank Borrowers after One Decade (New York: Westview Press, 1996); and Kabeer, 'Money Can't Buy Me Love'?

63. For more discussion on this topic, see Goetz and Sen Gupta. See also Rahman.

64. Mayoux, Women's Empowerment and Microfinance, 111.

65. Kabeer, 'Money Can't Buy Me Love'? 31.

66. Personal interviews, November 2001.

67. Ledesma.

68. For more information on risk-management strategies, see Jennefer Sebstad and Monique Cohen, Microfinance, Risk Management, and Poverty (Washington, D.C.: CGAP, 2001); Graham A. N. Wright et al., "Vulnerability, Risks, Assets and Empowerment—The Impact of Microfinance on Poverty Alleviation," paper contributed to World Development Report 2001; and Ronald Chua et al., "Risk, Vulnerability, Assets and the Role of Financial Services in Reducing Vulnerability: A Study of the Women Clients of CARD Bay Laguna, Philippines," paper submitted to CGAP, October 1999.

69. Essma Ben Hamida, "Empowering Women Through Micro-Credit: A Case Study From Tunisia," paper presented at the Civil Society Workshop Rehearsal, Cairo, Egypt, March 2000, 7.

70. Ben Hamida, 9.

71. The AIMS tools for client impact assessment were developed by USAID's Assessing the Impact of Microenterprise Services project and the Small Enterprise Education and Promotion (SEEP) Network. They include a quantitative impact survey, a quantitative exit survey, and three qualitative tools looking at client empowerment, satisfaction, and loan use. These tools can be downloaded from USAID's Microenterprise Innovation Project's Web site: www.mip.org.

72. Only those ranked as poor and very poor on a means test are eligible to join the Trust Bank program, and the majority of the clients are in the very poor category.

73. This kind of economic empowerment is not unique to women, and it is an empowerment effect of microenterprise programs generally rather than an effect that comes about specifically when empowerment is a focus of microenterprise programs, although these effects can be enhanced by carefully designing services and products with empowerment in mind.

74. Personal interview with Nana Addai, an SAT client.

75. From interviews with SAT client Afia Konadu and her husband, John Kwaku Donkor.

76. Interview with John Gyimah, the husband of an SAT client.

77. Interview with Kwaku Agyei, husband of an SAT client.

78. Kabeer, 'Money Can't Buy Me Love'? 21.

79. Noni Ayo, "Empowering Women Through Microfinance: ARDCI's Experience" (Catanduanes, Philippines: ARDCI, 2001), 2.

80. Suzy Salib et al., "Bundling Microfinance and Business Development Services: A Case Study from ADEMCOL in Colombia," USAID Microenterprise Best Practice Business Development Services Case Study No. 10 (Washington, D.C.: Development Alternatives International, 2001).

81. E-mail to authors from Maria Otero on 6/27/02.

82. ARMTI, 4. VAWA members receive training in the areas of business management, local credit management, group formation and dynamics, skills development (food processing, bee keeping, and so forth), leadership, extension services, rural health, family planning, environmental and personal hygiene, and dietary and harmful traditional practices—especially for the girl child.

83. Helen Sherpa, in a survey completed 20 October 2001.

84. Sherpa.

85. Roshaneh Zafar, "Microfinance and the Empowerment of Women: The Experience of Kashf Foundation, Pakistan, " paper presented at the Microcredit Summit Meeting of Councils, New Delhi, India, 1–5 February 2001, 7.

86. Shrestha, 31–32.

87. Cited in Kabeer, Conditions and Consequences, 43.

88. Ben Hamida, 9.

89. Sebstad and Cohen, 86.

90. For more information about Janashakti Women's Development Federation, see Alessandra Del Conte, Participatory Governance and Management Structures in Microfinance: The Case of Janashakti (New York: International Coalition on Women and Credit, 2000); available on Web site of Women's World Banking: www.swwb.org.

91. Florence Abena Dolphyne, The Emancipation of Women: An African Perspective (Accra: Ghana Universities Press, 1991), 48–49.

92. See the Appendix for more information.

93. Nevertheless, Aminur Rahman, in "Micro-credit Initiatives for Equitable and Sustainable Development," finds that most borrowers in the study were not aware of purchasing shares in Grameen Bank or of owning the Bank.

94. Alex Counts, executive director of the Grameen Foundation USA, in an e-mail to Susy Cheston, 30 January 2002.

95. Alex Counts in an e-mail to Susy Cheston, 21 February 2002.

96. In 1997, Opportunity carried out in-depth case studies of holistic transformation within its programs. One of the unexpected findings was that one of the most transforming and empowering aspects of its work was the simple fact of an MFI staff member treating a client with respect.

97. For more information, see Yawe Agnes, "Engendering Microfinance Services: Beyond Access," presented at the Women's Empowerment or Feminisation of Debt? workshop in London, March 2002 (available at www.oneworldaction.org).

98. Wariara Mbugua, e-mail to Microcredit Summit, 30 April 2002.

99. The information for this case study was provided by Noni S. Ayo, managing director of ARDCI, and an impact study based on interviews conducted February 26 through March 12, 1999, of clients and nonclients of the ARDCI/CatAg credit programs. Another impact study is planned for 2002.

100. ARDCI owns the first microfinance rural bank in the Philippines, which was approved by the Central Bank on 3 April 2002 and is expected to open in September 2002.

101. Female responses: 1) acquired new skills, knowledge—12 percent; 2) improved attitude, reinforced values, changed way of thinking—48 percent; 3) combination of 1 and 2—23 percent. Male responses: 1) 12 percent; 2) 62 percent; 3) combination 8 percent.

5

Financing Microfinance for Poverty Reduction

David S. Gibbons and Jennifer W. Meehan

There is no doubt that strong demand exists for microfinance services, among the poor. More than nineteen million of the poorest households around the world now have access. That is encouraging because the number has increased substantially since 1997 when the Microcredit Summit Campaign (MSC) was launched. But it is daunting that there are still 81 million poorest families to be reached before the Campaign target of 100 million is achieved.

There is no dearth of microfinance institutions (MFIs), but most of them are small. If only 10 percent of the 1,580 MFIs that have reported to the MSC and are serving the poorest could be scaled up to serve an average of 500,000 very poor households each, then the shortfall of 81 million could be overcome.

A lot of effort is being put into institutional capacity building for MFIs that have the vision and willingness to provide microfinance services to large numbers of poor households. New effective management tools are being created and disseminated to microfinance institutions. Training is being provided from the Consultative Group to Assist the Poorest (CGAP) training hubs around the world, and by networks of MFIs.

Much less thought and effort has been put into sourcing the amounts and the right kinds of capital which will be required to scale up the next generation of microfinance leaders. The issue is not a lack of onlending funds, but the equity with which to leverage them—and financing to meet the inevitable operating deficits that arise with rapid scaling-up.

To overcome this major hurdle, a new financing paradigm is needed. First, alternatives to traditional equity must be identified. Equity-like financial instruments, or quasi-equity, such as subordinated debt, convertible debt, preferred stock, and Special Drawing Rights (SDRs), likely more acceptable alternatives to traditional equity financing for many funders, may be a large part of the answer.

Second, MFIs must adjust their balance sheets to present a truer and fairer picture of their financial health. Marking below-market rate borrowings, or soft loans, to market to capture the implicit subsidy inherent in its lower interest rates, and capitalizing that subsidy as a "grant" on the balance sheet as equity, is an important part of this solution. Finally, the prevailing microfinance standards on capital adequacy, that inflate the amount of equity (already in limited supply) MFIs should hold on their balance sheets, must be challenged.

Readers should understand that this is not a call for the kind of "creative" accounting that is getting big business into difficulty these days. Rather it is a proposal for analysis of already audited financial statements, so as to present a truer and fairer picture of the financial health and capital adequacy of MFIs.

The combined effect of these three initiatives is to: 1) increase the availability of funds to meet operating deficits through quasi-equity, 2) minimize the amount of equity and equity-like financing MFIs must raise, and 3) maximize their ability to leverage onlending funds from banks and other commercial and semi-commercial sources. The bottom line: the equity hurdle can be overcome, allowing for more rapid scaling-up of outreach to the poor.

CASHPOR Financial & Technical Services Limited (CFTS) has been working among the poor and poorest rural households in Mirzapur District eastern UP India, for the past five years. Institutional financial break-even has been reached by providing financial services to 25,000 of the poor and the poorest rural women. Loan portfolio quality is good, with less than 2 percent at risk. Most importantly, the deficits of CFTS prior to break-even were financed almost entirely by quasi-equity, which CFTS was able to leverage significantly in order to achieve its targets. The impact of marking soft loans to market to present a fairer picture of financial health moved CFTS's capital adequacy from negative territory to 10 percent, well in line with international standards. While CFTS may be an extreme case, financing its deficits exclusively with quasi-equity, it shows that the three steps outlined above are a feasible approach to financing scaling-up.

CGAP, as the leader in organizing support services for the microfinance industry, is asked to take the lead in mobilizing quasi-equity from its member-donors, perhaps channeled through national and regional quasi-equity funds, for MFIs with the vision and will to build the necessary institutional capacity, including the necessary transparency, to reach large numbers of the poorest.

The Need for a New Financing Paradigm

Demand for Microfinance Services

There is no doubt that strong demand exists for microfinance services, among the poor around the world. Recent statistics on the global outreach of MFIs report that as of December 31, 2000, over 30 million families had access to microfinance services, *of which more than 19 million qualified as poorest.* This is both encouraging and daunting. Encouraging because the number has increased substantially since 1997, when the Microcredit Summit Campaign was launched. Daunting because that still leaves 81 million poorest families to be reached by 2005 if the Campaign target of 100 million of the poorest is to be achieved. On a regional basis, coverage remains extremely low. In Asia, where almost 15 million poorest families have access to microfinance services, still only 9.3 percent of all poorest families are being reached. And in Africa and Latin America, only 6 percent of all poorest families have access to financial services.[1] It is not surprising, therefore, that NGO-MFIs wanting to increase their outreach to the poorest, having the necessary institutional capacity and access to the necessary funding, have no difficulty in attracting new clients.[2]

Figure 5.1   Regional Breakdown of Access to Microfinance

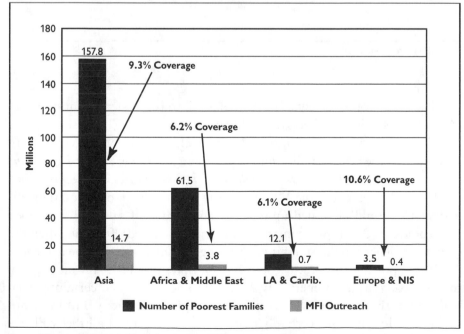

Source: Microcredit Summit Campaign, January 2002

Figure 5.2a   Outreach to All Clients by Size of MFI

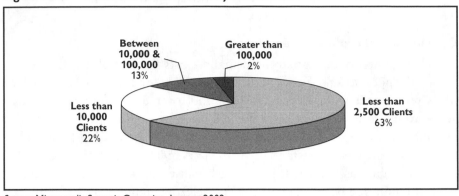

Source: Microcredit Summit Campaign, January 2002

Figure 5.2b   Outreach to Poorest Clients by Size of MFI

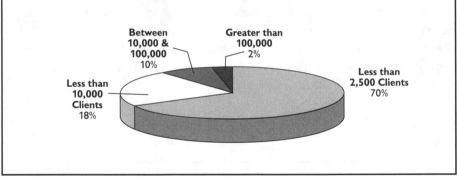

Source: Microcredit Summit Campaign, January 2002

The failure of MFIs outside of Bangladesh to reach significant numbers of poor households in their own countries is not because of a shortage of MFIs. As of December 2000, over 1,600 MFIs (mostly NGO-MFIs) were reporting to the Microcredit Summit Campaign. *However, the significant majority of these MFIs are very small, serving less than 2,500 clients each.*[3]

If only 10 percent of the MFIs currently serving the poorest, or approximately 158 could be scaled up to serve an average of 500,000 very poor households, or 316 (approximately 20 percent) to 250,000 clients, then the goal of the Microcredit Summit of reaching 100 million could be achieved.

It is important to acknowledge up front that not all MFIs want to grow to reach truly large numbers (say 250,000 to 500,000) and certainly some will not be able to build the necessary institutional capacity. But there are many that do and can—certainly more than 10 percent of all the MFIs reporting to the Microcredit Summit Campaign.

Capacity Building as an On-going Task

The MFIs around the world that are interested in scaling up their outreach to large numbers of poor households are already seeking the institutional capacity to do so. This is easier today than ever before because of the pioneering work of service providers in the industry, like CGAP World Bank, SEEP, the Microfinance Network, Women's World Banking, ACCION, FINCA, the Grameen Trust, and CASHPOR, among others. Much of the training materials needed can be downloaded from the Web sites of these organizations. New, more cost-effective management tools are being developed and disseminated continually and MFIs are being required to build the capacity to utilize them. Capacity for scaling-up is being built, and more will be built. There is little, if any, human resource constraint.[4]

Donors and other funders are also requiring more and better information from the MFIs, whether NGOs or formal financial intermediaries that they finance. They are asking for greater financial transparency. USAID, for example, requires not only externally audited financial statements, but also that they be converted into the CGAP standard international format to make possible accurate financial analysis. So MFIs are having to build the institutional capacity to do this.

Recognizing Capital[5] as a Critical Constraint

While we recognize the on-going importance of capacity building, we do not see it as the only constraint. Even when capacity is built, lack of capital blocks rapid expansion.

CGAP recently published an interesting and provocative *Viewpoint* titled *Water, Water Everywhere but Not a Drop to Drink*, which undertook an assessment of the funding environment for MFIs. It recognized that funding to the microfinance sector is on the rise, with donors and governments participating, often through apex and wholesale facilities as well as private investors. But then it asked the critical question; "With all the funds pouring into the sector, why do MFIs find it difficult to access needed financing?" Why do "managers of many high-potential MFIs face serious funding constraints"? The answer CGAP provided: "Much of the supply of funds to microfinance is ineffective—narrowly targeted and poorly structured."

The first problem is that while donors played a critical role in building the microfinance industry by providing early support to pioneers, they seem reluctant to graduate a new generation of industry leaders. Everyone wants to fund the established "winners," rather than take the risk of funding and helping to build new winners from among the hundreds of smaller MFIs looking for funding. This means that profitable MFIs get subsidized funding, crowding out the commercial investors who do have the vast resources to allow for rapid scaling-up. The venture capital role of the grant funding donors should instead be directed at potential winners, those with the vision to reach large numbers of the poorest, strong management teams, a commitment to transparency and professionalism and a drive towards efficiency and sustainability. As the CGAP Viewpoint states ". . . the principal task of donors should be to identify and bet on promising MFIs and leave the known winners to commercial investors."

A second problem is that donors have a hard time moving money—funding is not designed to meet the needs of the MFIs, but rather the priorities of donors or governments. These can include country or regional priorities and/or an unhelpful insistence that the funds be used only for onlending. Limitations can be compounded by internal organizational concerns—country-level versus global programming—and a lack of local knowledge.

CGAP's current peer review exercise among its member donors, aimed at disseminating best-practice financing for microfinance, should result in a significant reduction of the current funding mismatch. However, it is not directed specifically at the main funding problem of MFIs, *the dearth of equity and equity-like financing for microfinance institutions at any stage of maturity. In fact, this is the major funding problem in the industry and will remain so for the foreseeable future—an issue that has yet to be accepted broadly by its non-practitioner actors.*

The Primary Obstacle Is Equity

In the lively discussion that followed the posting of the CGAP Viewpoint on the Internet, it became clear that it is not just a lack of supply in general, which is hindering growth in outreach, but rather the type of financing being made available. Practitioners in particular focused on this point. Nejira Nalic, Executive Director of MI-BOSPO in Bosnia and Herzegovina, noted that "our decision-making processes are lead by our environment and we are in a way suppressed by lack of capital base. . ." Roshaneh Zafar, Managing Director of Kashf Foundation in Lahore, Pakistan, also expressed the need for "socially motivated equity funds." Our experience in Asia, through CASHPOR, reaffirms these views. A recent workshop in the Philippines, *Financing Microfinance for Poverty Reduction,*[6] attended by leading MFIs from across the region, indicated that 72 percent of those attending were constrained in their growth specifically by a lack of funds to cover operating losses, prior to break-even of the expansion.

As we are targeting 81 million new clients, and if we assume an average loan outstanding of US$100, then around $8.1 billion would be needed in onlending funds. Assuming a capital adequacy requirement of 8 percent, about US$650 million would be needed as capital for leverage.

International financier George Soros, in his book *George Soros on Globalization*, observes that:

> . . . The difficulty [of microlending] is in scaling it up. Successful microlending operations, although largely self-sustaining, cannot grow out of retained earnings, nor can they raise capital in financial markets. To turn microlending into a big factor in economic and political progress, it must be scaled-up significantly. This would require general support for the industry as well as capital for individual ventures.[7]

We agree—even when MFIs become profitable, accumulated profits will not support the kind of large-scale growth required to reach large numbers. Until now, many MFIs have utilized grants from donors to support their operations both in the early years and as they scale up. Yet such grants, already limited in size and availability, are becoming harder to come by as the pool of global MFIs grows. Unfortunately, beyond donors, there really are no private sources of equity financing available to MFIs around the world, particularly those working with the poorest.

We must start thinking more innovatively—as most commercial businesses do—about our financing strategies. This will require the microfinance industry to embrace the concept of quasi-equity, to adjust their financial statements to reflect a truer and fairer picture of their financial strength, to challenge prevailing standards for calculating capital adequacy and to set levels appropriate for different MFIs, according to their risk profiles.

Covering Operating Deficits

Two decades ago pioneers such as Muhammad Yunus of the Grameen Bank showed the world that poor, rural women without collateral were bankable. It is time that we recognize that microfinance institutions working with the poor, but lacking conventional capital adequacy, are also bankable. The reason is the same: most poor women, supplied with capital on reasonable terms, will invest it profitably and repay the loans, plus interest, faithfully in full on time. Just as this makes poor women bankable so too does it make MFIs servicing them bankable.

The problem is not onlending funds. Local commercial banks are being persuaded that MFIs are worthy, if somewhat unconventional, customers; experience in Asia and Latin America proves this true. Apex institutions have been established in some countries, particularly in Asia, with the support of the World Bank (PKSF in Bangladesh) and the Asian Development Bank (PCFC in the Philippines and RMDC in Nepal), offering financing to

MFIs on semi- or near-commercial terms. And social investors and large international NGOs still play an important role in financing loans for onlending. Savings, where MFIs are able to use this as a source of funds, can also play a critical role.

Operating deficits to break-even are typically covered by grants, and where possible, private investment. After that, gradual expansion can be covered by retained profits. But few MFIs working with the poor have been able to attract much investment. And few donors are keen to sink funds into what they see as the bottomless pit of operational losses. Some donors insist that their grants be used *only* to finance onlending, ignoring the reality that onlending costs money. Even were this to change, none of these traditional sources—grants, investment (for non-NGO MFIs), and profits—are available in anywhere near enough supply to propel MFIs to meet the massive demand for microfinance that exists. *Given the potential of microfinance to reduce poverty, we must look for prudent alternatives to traditional equity that would allow for faster growth of its outreach to the poor.*

A Solution: Quasi-Equity

The most important element of the new financing paradigm is to identify alternatives to traditional sources of equity financing to cover the deficits prior to break-even.

Equity-like instruments, or quasi-equity, are attractive for a number of reasons. First, they are able to absorb losses. Second, since they are legally subordinated to other borrowings of the institutions, they can be included in total equity for purposes of assessing the capital adequacy of MFIs. Finally, we believe that such instruments, particularly subordinated loans which have defined repayment terms and interest rates, would be more attractive to social investors and microcredit funds who prefer to lend, but who are able to be flexible on the terms and conditions of that lending.

Such quasi-equity must be structured to meet the needs of microfinance institutions; blindly adopting the instruments available generally in the market will not be appropriate. Key criteria that quasi-equity must include, in the form of subordinated loans, are shown in Table 5.1.

As will be seen below, such quasi-equity, subject to certain limitations, can be considered as Tier II capital for purposes of calculating capital adequacy.

Some funders recognize the critical importance of such finance. The Grameen Trust and the Grameen Foundation USA currently offer such financing. At least one national microcredit fund, the People's Credit Financing Corporation (PCFC) in the Philippines, extends parallel financing of 10 percent of the onlending funds to MFIs for financing capacity building. The

Table 5.1   Key Criteria for Quasi-Equity

Key Criteria	Explanation
Ability to Absorb Losses	Without the ability to cover operating deficits, quasi-equity will not address the critical hurdle to growth among MFIs. These funds cannot be restricted for onlending. An adequate proportion must be available for financing deficits prior to break-even.
Legal Subordination to Other Obligations	In order to be treated as quasi-equity, it must be structured so that it is legally subordinated to any senior loans that the MFI may have from commercial or other sources. Think of it this way: if your MFI is no longer a going concern, there would be a line of people outside your door trying to collect on loans and investments they made in your MFI. Where people stand in that line—in order of priority—depends on the type of financing they offered. First would be senior lenders. And last would be those that have invested in your organization—the owners. Somewhere in the middle are the quasi-equity providers who have agreed to "subordinate" their rights and take a position behind senior lenders, but who at the same time have greater certainty of repayment than equity holders.
Long Term with Grace Period on Repayments	This financing must be made available on a long-term basis with a grace period so that repayments can be made from profits after break-even; interest payments can be made from the start. We recommend a loan term of between 7 to 8 years, with a grace period of 3 to 5 years, depending on the MFI' s projections for break-even.
Minimal Interest Rate	As far as possible, interest rates on quasi-equity, particularly that used to finance operating deficits in the first year or two of scaling up, should be minimized. Generally speaking, the minimum rate should be equal to inflation in the country where your MFI operates; this allows funders to keep the value of their investment whole. However, as requirements for quasi-equity rise, so too might the interest rates. This must be taken into consideration in the business planning process. The ability to pay higher rates will depend on the MFI and its clients.

Table 5.2   MFI Funding Requirements at Different Stages of Development

Type of Expenditure	Start-up Years 1–2	Years 3–5	Operational Self-Sufficiency	Full Self-Sufficiency
Operating	• Grants • Equity	• Quasi-Equity	• Interest Income • Social Investment • Quasi-Equity	• Interest Income • Social & Commercial Investment • Quasi-Equity
Onlending	• Grants • Quasi-Equity	• Quasi-Equity • Savings • Near-Market Rate Loans	• Savings • Near-Market Rate Loans • Guarantee Funds • Market-Rate Loans	• Savings • Market-Rate Loans

Small Industries Development Bank in India (SIDBI), makes grants for capacity building to its partner MFIs. But none of this has been anywhere near enough to overcome the shortage of capital.

MFI Funding Requirements and Stage of Development

Funders need to understand that MFIs have different funding requirements at different stages of development. Table 5.2 suggests the types and possible sources of funding at each stage.

Quasi-equity is critical in the years prior to break-even, to cover deficits not financed by grants and to provide early on-lending funds that cannot yet be borrowed from banks. Savings only become large enough to be an important source of onlending funds, from about Year 3 onwards.

While this table may appear intuitive and simple, it has been largely ignored in financing MFIs in the past, as the CGAP Viewpoint highlights. It is essential that funders play their part in ensuring the efficient use of financing for microfinance, particularly operating deficit financing which is in such short supply. In order to get the most "bang for their buck," funders need to make sure these resources are leveraged as much as possible with onlending funds from banks, savings, apex institutions, social investors, and other sources. This has not always been the case, particularly with MFIs that have enjoyed grant financing to cover both operating deficits and onlending needs.

An excellent example of efficient financing is SHARE, a Hyderabad, India-based MFI working with the poorest, which in 1997 received a US$2 million grant from CGAP. SHARE used this to increase outreach in its NGO and to establish a community-owned non-banking finance company, SHARE Microfin Limited (SML), which has rapidly scaled up outreach to over 100,000 clients (from approximately 3,000) through more than fifty branches. With an equity base of US$1.1 million, SML has been able to leverage approximately US$6 million in loans from various domestic and international lenders.

The Inherent Strain between Growth and Profitability

Funders also need to recognize the implications of rapid scaling-up on profitability. Rapid growth inevitably generates significant up front losses that place downward pressure, sometimes severe, on profitability. The result is that, all else being equal, a rapidly growing MFI will show lower profitability than one that is not. This can be seen in Asia with Activists for Social Alternatives (ASA), based in Thiruchirapalli, India. They were close to achieving break-even, but recently added twelve new branches with the goal of scaling-up, pushing OSS (Operational Self-Sufficiency) down to less than half of its previous level.

In order to address this issue, more work needs to be done on scaling-up microfinance in sustainable modules, perhaps as separate legal entities, that are designed to maximize outreach, efficiency, and profitability; each would have its own financing strategy. One possible solution is for MFIs to form holding companies, and then operate separate sustainable modules (perhaps at the district or regional level) underneath the holding company. Alternatively, most NGO-MFIs that have established regulated financial intermediaries maintain some of their microfinance operations in the NGO. The NGOs could form new branches and scale up until break-even, at which time branches could be transferred to the regulated entity.

We do not believe traditional equity, especially in the form of private investment, will be available in the huge amounts required to finance the deficits of providing microfinance to another 80 million poor households around the world. To the extent that such investment is available, it should be utilized. Quasi-equity offers an alternative that meets both the needs of the MFIs and the needs of funders and stakeholders in microfinance.

But quasi-equity does not provide a complete solution. There are other considerations that must be taken into account, including the stringent capital adequacy requirements widely applied in the microfinance community and the need to adjust MFI financial statements to present a truer and fairer picture of financial health of MFIs. These two issues are addressed in the next section.

Presenting a Truer and Fairer Picture of Capital[8] Adequacy

Internationally recognized standards for microfinance have developed dramatically over the last few years, with a particular emphasis on profitability, efficiency and portfolio quality. One issue that has been somewhat overlooked, however, has been capital adequacy. Capital adequacy is a ratio used globally to assess the financial strength of financial institutions. In very general terms, it compares an institution's capital to its total assets. If the ratio falls below a certain limit, which based on current international standards developed for banks in 1988 by the Basel Committee[9] is 8 percent, then the bank is said to be under-capitalized. In other words, the bank does not have the level of capital deemed necessary to protect or insure against future, unexpected losses, based on the riskiness of its asset base.[10]

As MFI reliance on commercial and development banks (who possess the vast resources that will allow for scaling-up of onlending to the poor and poorest) and savings (where appropriate) increases, there is no denying that capital adequacy will take on increasingly more significance. It already has for many of the NGO-MFIs in Latin America and Asia that have transformed into regulated financial entities. From a financing perspective, the greater the capital adequacy ratio of an MFI, the less risky it is deemed and therefore the greater will be its ability to collect savings and to borrow. Another way of putting it is that an MFI's potential for borrowing—and thus its ability to grow—is limited by the amount of equity it has.

Stringent Requirements for Microfinance

In microfinance, there is as yet no formally agreed-upon standard for MFI capital adequacy, but donors and social investors often seek capital adequacy ratios—measured simply as equity to average assets[11]—in the 20 percent range, as compared to the international standard for banks of 8 percent. This is primarily due to the perceived riskiness of an MFI's business as compared to that of a conventional bank. The logic appears to be that because they are often group-based, MFIs can experience sudden steep increases in their non-performing loans. This is true. It is difficult for the poor to repay faithfully. When they see a group member not paying and, apparently, nothing happening to her, there is great temptation not to pay also. In this way repayment problems can become crises quickly, especially in solidarity group programs. What is not so well known, however, is the good record of MFIs in overcoming such repayment problems.[12] That is how many of them have been able to maintain enviable overall repayment rates.

There are a number of ways in which the definition of capital adequacy does not reflect realities in microfinance. First, it does not recognize the nature of, and thus disallows the inclusion of, quasi-equity in the numerator of the capital adequacy ratio. The result is that MFIs are not able to use their quasi-equity to leverage additional financing, even if they are able to raise it to cover operating deficits. Second, despite historical long-term trends of better portfolio quality among MFIs than conventional banks, a much higher equity cushion is required for MFIs. And finally, the current practice does not recognize the different risk levels of individual assets MFIs hold on their balance sheets.

Since the capital adequacy ratio is meant to ensure that a financial institution has enough capital to cover its underlying risk, current requirements for MFIs reflect neither real access to capital to cover losses, nor the real risks of microlending. A new, more appropriate standard should be adopted for MFIs—to allow for more efficient management and growth of their businesses based on capital requirements that reflect more accurately the risks of doing microfinance with the poor.

The International Capital Adequacy Standards

In July 1988, the Basel Committee issued a paper entitled *The Interna-*

tional Convergence of Capital Measurement and Capital Standards, or the "Basel Accord," which outlined new standards for international capital adequacy for the banking sector. The primary focus of the paper was determining minimum capital adequacy requirements through calculation of the capital adequacy ratio, which compares total capital to risk-adjusted assets. That was fourteen years ago. These standards are in general use within the banking world, but microfinance has not yet caught up with them! In fact, these standards address each of the three weaknesses in the current thinking in the microfinance industry about capital adequacy.

Recognizing Quasi-Equity as Capital   First, international standards recognize a broader definition of "capital," the numerator of the ratio. Capital is divided into two components: Tier 1 and Tier 2. Tier 1 capital is referred to as core or basic equity and is comprised of paid up capital, capitalized grants, and accumulated, reported retained earnings (for example, profits) of a banking institution. Tier 2 capital, or supplementary capital, includes subordinated debt, hybrid debt/equity capital instruments, general provisions, loan loss reserves, asset revaluation reserves, and undisclosed reserves. So Tier 2 capital can include quasi-equity—the financing we propose for covering operating deficits going forward! These two elements of capital are combined to meet the minimum capital requirement of a bank. The one catch is that Tier 2 capital is limited to a maximum of 100 percent of the total of Tier 1 capital. So of the minimum 8 percent capital required, Tier 2 capital can meet up to 4 percent.

There is nothing tricky nor imprudent about including quasi-equity in this calculation, as the Basel Committee recognizes. It states that "there are a number of other important and legitimate constituents of a bank's capital base which may be included within the system of measurement"[13] that meet both the needs of the banking institutions themselves and their funders. The same reasoning should hold for MFIs.

Not More Risk, Less!   The basic intent of capital adequacy is to cover the major risk that all financial institutions face, whether MFIs or conventional banks: credit risk, or the risk that a borrower will not repay a loan according to the original terms of a loan agreement and may eventually default, exposing the financial institution to losses. Put another way, it is to offset a potential decline in loan portfolio quality.

It should be increasingly difficult to ignore the overwhelming evidence—track records of well over ten years in many institutions—that microfinance is *less* risky than conventional finance. Statistics from the *Microbanking Bulletin*,[14] a leading industry newsletter on professional standards, in No-

Table 5.3   Microfinance Is Less Risky Than Conventional Finance

	Average Portfolio-at-Risk > 90 Days	Standard Deviation
All MFIs (148)	2.1	1.9
Financially Self-Sufficient MFIs (57)	2.1	2.1

vember 2001, offers the evidence, as shown in Table 5.3.

That on average, MFIs have portfolio-at-risk of only 2.1 percent, with the majority of those reporting falling within the range of .2 percent and 4.0 percent, is compelling. Regional averages, as well as cross-sections of data based on age of institution, size, and legal structure, all reaffirm the above results. Such portfolio quality is enviable. This evidence suggests that perhaps MFIs are less risky than even commercial banks in developed countries, particularly in retail financing services offered to the general public. In developing countries, there is no comparison.

According to an April 2002 report from the Asian Development Bank, non-performing loans as a percent of total loans (including those not disposed of by asset management companies set up to sell bad loans) were 50 percent in Indonesia, 25 percent in Thailand, 18 percent in the Philippines, and 12 percent in Malaysia.[15] Similar statistics for China and India have been cited at 50 percent and 25 percent, respectively.[16] In Japan, one of the most significant areas of banking sector concern in Asia, the Financial Services Agency (FSA) estimates that as of September 2001, banks had ¥36.8 trillion (over US$294.4 billion) in bad debt on their books. Some private estimates of bad debts reach ¥100 trillion (or US$800 billion) and the FSA "has admitted that the total potential problem loan pile, including 'watchlist loans,' could be as much as ¥150 trillion" (approximately US$1.2 trillion).[17]

That MFIs should then be required to have higher capital adequacy ratios than conventional banks does not logically follow. At the very least, MFIs should be subject to the same international standards as traditional commercial banks—currently 8 percent.

Risk Adjusting Assets   Finally, overcoming the third weakness of the microfinance industry thinking on capital adequacy for MFIs, is risk adjustment of an MFI's assets. Recognizing the varying levels of risks of different types of assets, the Basel Committee has provided a schedule for weighting assets, the denominator of the capital adequacy ratio, according to broad categories of relative riskiness.

Table 5.4   Risk Weights for On-Balance Sheet Assets

Risk Weight	Asset Account for Which Risk Weight Applies
0%	• Cash • Balances due from Central Government and Central Banks (e.g., Federal Reserve or U.S. Government in the U.S.)
20%	• Demand Deposits • Checks in Process of Collection
50%	• Loans Fully Secured by Mortgage on Residential Property
100%	• Unsecured Loans and All Other Assets

For purposes of calculating the denominator of the capital adequacy measure, to meet current standards, each MFI's asset accounts would be multiplied by a certain risk weight to determine the asset base against which the level of capital necessary to meet the 8 percent requirement is determined. In all cases, the risk adjusted weight will be lower than that pure asset balance reported on the balance sheet. The impact then is to increase the ratio.

Do the International Standards Go Far Enough?   More properly assessing the risk of MFIs and calculating the ratio according to international standards would have the combined effect of reducing the amount of new core equity—extremely difficult to raise in the existing funding environment—an MFI must raise in order to grow and would allow for more leverage of MFI's existing capital bases.

But the international standards, designed for large international banks rather than microfinance institutions working with the poor, have one major weakness that must be overcome to arrive at an appropriate standard of capital adequacy for microfinance. That is that the use of Tier 2 capital (quasi-equity) is limited to 100 percent of Tier 1 capital. If we seek to use quasi-equity as a financing method for rapid scale-up in microfinance, this limitation will have to be overcome. A significant part of the solution of this problem is marking an MFI's below market-rate debt to market, thereby recognizing the true nature of an MFI's financial strength.

Marking Debt to Market

There is a subsidy element in soft loans. It is the difference between the interest rate of the soft loan and the rate that MFIs would have to pay to borrow the funds commercially from the money markets. For example, if the interest rate payable on a soft loan is 2 percent per annum, and the commercial rate for the same amount of funds is 15 percent per annum (not uncommon in poor countries), then the element of subsidy in the soft loan would be 13 percent per annum. Since the funder explicitly intended this "subsidy" element, it must be quantified and capitalized on the adjusted balance sheet as equity (Tier 1 capital) like any other grant, for purposes of calculating capital adequacy.

This is not an attempt to rival Enron's creative accounting. Such a "re-classification" of soft loans on the balance sheet is for analytical purposes only, in order to get a better picture of the financial strength of the institution. Thus, marking to market is not something that an MFI must get approval for from its external auditors. Rather, audited statements serve as the basis of this analysis. The logic of this post-audit accounts analysis is very similar to those adjustments made to financial statements, for subsidies and inflation, universally accepted within the microfinance industry today.

How does marking to market work? The market value of a soft loan is determined by discounting the two primary cash flows that take place during the life of a loan, both principal and actual interest payments, by the commercial rate of interest. So conceptually, if an MFI has two identical loans, except one is at the commercial rate of 15 percent and the other is at a subsidized rate of 2 percent, the only difference between these cash flows that take place during the life of the loan is the difference in interest rates of 13 percent. If the loan size is 100,000, then the interest payment on the commercial loan is 15,000 each year and the interest payment on the soft loan is 2,000 each year, for a difference of 13,000. But we cannot simply say today that 13,000 is the value of the subsidy inherent in a soft loan. Why? Because these interest payments are made in the future—say at the end of each year—so the difference of 13,000 is the *future* value of the difference. Since we want to know the value of the subsidy *today*, we must discount, or divide, the different interest rate payments by the commercial interest rate.[18] The difference between the discounted value of the interest rate payments on the commercial loan and the soft loan is equal to the subsidy element inherent in the soft loan.[19]

Let's take a very simple numerical example to illustrate this point and to take the analysis one step further. As above, assume that an MFI received two loans of US$100,000 on January 1, 2002, both repayable in one-time, bullet payments in five years time. All other conditions are the same, except Loan A bears a commercial interest rate of 15 percent, while Loan B is a soft loan with a rate of 2 percent. Interest is paid annually. As of January 1, 2002, the subsidy element of the soft loan and today's market value of the

Table 5.5   Subsidy Value of Soft Loan and Today's Market Value

	Jan-02	Dec-02	Dec-03	Dec-04	Dec-05	Dec-06
Loan A						
Interest Payments (a)		15,000	15,000	15,000	15,000	15,000
Principal Repayments (b)		0	0	0	0	100,000
Total Cash Flows (c)		15,000	15,000	15,000	15,000	15,000
Discount Factor (d)		1.15	1.32	1.52	1.75	2.01
Sample Calculation (As of Jan.1, 2002)						
Interest Discounted by Year (a/d)	50,282	13,043	11,342	9,863	8,576	7,458
Principal Discounted by Year (b/d)	49,718	0	0	0	0	49,718
Present Value of Cash Flow	100,000	13,043	11,342	9,863	8,576	57,175
Book Value of Debt per period	100,000	100,000	100,000	100,000	100,000	100,000
Market Value of Debt per period	100,000	100,000	100,000	100,000	100,000	100,000
Grant Component per period	0	0	0	0	0	0

* Discount Factor in each year in equal to 15% commercial rate adjusted for the number of years since the loan was issued.

	Jan-02	Dec-02	Dec-03	Dec-04	Dec-05	Dec-06
Loan B						
Interest Payments (a)		2,000	2,000	2,000	2,000	2,000
Principal Repayments (b)		0	0	0	0	100,000
Total Cash Flows (c)		2,000	2,000	2,000	2,000	102,000
Discount Factor (d)		1.15	1.32	1.52	1.75	2.01
Sample Calculation (As of Jan.1, 2002)						
Interest Discounted by Year (a/d)	6,704	1,739	1,512	1,315	1,144	994
Principal Discounted by Year (b/d)	49,718	0	0	0	0	49,718
Present Value of Cash Flow	56,422	1,739	1,512	1,315	1,144	50,712
Book Value of Debt per period	100,000	100,000	100,000	100,000	100,000	100,000
Market Value of Debt per period	56,422	62,885	70,318	78,866	88,696	100,000
Grant Component per period	43,578	37,115	29,682	21,134	11,304	0

* Discount Factor in each year in equal to 15% commercial rate adjusted for the number of years since the loan was issued.

Comparison of Discounted January 2002 Interest Rates	
Loan A Discounted Interest (a)	50,282
Loan B Discounted Interest (b)	6,704
Difference (a–b)	43,578

debt are calculated as shown in Table 5.5.

In the case of Loan A, since the commercial interest rate and the actual rate charged were equal to 15 percent, there is no difference between the book value and market value of the loan, either at January 1, 2002, or in the future—so there is never a subsidy element that can be capitalized as a grant on the balance sheet. In the case of Loan B, however, there is a difference between the market value and book value, representing the difference between the market rate of 15 percent and the soft rate of 2 percent. Today's value of the subsidy element is equal to $43,578, which is equal to the difference between the discounted interest payments of $50,282 of Loan A and $6,704 of Loan B. As you can see in Table 5.6, the discounted value of principal is identical in both examples, at $49,718.

Now that we have made these calculations, we can reclassify the soft loan to more accurately reflect its true nature. Instead of recording $100,000 on the books as a loan, the MFI would record the subsidy element of $43,578 as a grant, thereby increasing Tier 1 equity as of January 1, 2002. In order to keep the balance sheet in balance, the value of loan is decreased by the amount of the subsidy, $43,578, with the resulting market value of $56,422.

This is not a static analysis. The market value of soft loans and their subsidy element must be recalculated regularly in order to reflect payments (both interest and principal) that have been made on the loan. As the loan moves closer to maturity, the amount of the debt obligation will rise while the grant component declines, until finally, on the date of maturity, they are equal. This makes logical sense. If the only difference between Loan A and B in the example above is the interest payments, as there are fewer and fewer interest payments left as you move closer to maturity, the value of the subsidy declines. This dynamic is reflected in Table 5.6, where the subsidy element of Loan B declines, while the market value of debt rises, as it moves towards maturity.

Once the adjustments for marking debt to market and for inflation and subsidies are completed and reflected in the audited financial statements, capital adequacy can be recalculated using international standards, where Tier 1 now includes the grant component of the soft loan. *By increasing the amount of Tier 1 equity, we can increase the amount of Tier 2 equity that can be used in the numerator, thus increasing the capital adequacy ratio to reflect a truer and fairer picture of the MFI's financial position.*

Is Capital Adequacy a Major Constraint?

It is not yet widely accepted in the microfinance industry, particularly by donors, that capital adequacy is a constraint to growth—to leveraging of funds from commercial institutions. Yet, it is frequently cited as an obstacle by those institutions seeking to reach large numbers, particularly larger, regulated, specialized MFIs.

CFTS Ltd.: Crucible of the New Paradigm

CASHPOR Financial & Technical Services Limited (CFTS), a Grameen Bank (GB) adaptor, has been working among the poor and poorest rural households in Mirzapur District eastern UP India, for the past four and a half years and has developed and implemented an approach to scaling up an MFI working with the poorest that is effective in that difficult part of India.[20] Institutional financial break-even and best practice levels of efficiency will be reached within five years (that is, by September 2002), as opposed to the historical average of eight to nine years for GB-type MFIs, by providing

Table 5.6   CFTS's Actual Performance against Target

Key Indicators[a]	Targets	Actual Performance	% Achieved
1. Outreach to the Poor			
a) Scope: Savers	22,283	18,035	81%
Borrowers	19,246	15,048	78%
b) Depth: Total Savings (US$)	$130,445	$110,203	84%
Total Loans Outstanding (INR)	$1,528,051	$1,124,752	74%
c) Dropouts	18%	15%	120%
2. Quality of Loan Portfolio			
a) Portfolio-At-Risk > 30 days	2.0%	1.9%	106%
b) Loan Write-Off Ratio	1.0%	0.7%	147%
c) Loan Restructuring Ratio[b]	0.0%	0.0%	100%
3. Institutional Efficiency			
a) Administrative Cost Ratio	14%	27%	52%
b) Active Loan Client per CSR	258	190	74%
c) Loan Portfolio per CSR	$18,181	$14,237	78%
d) Centers per CSR	9	9	97%
e) Savers per Center	30	26	86%
f) Operating Cost Ratio	20%	39%	51%
g) Yield on Portfolio	33%	32%	97%
4. Financial Performance			
a) Cost of Funds (US$)	$131,134	$102,608	78%
b) Administrative Cost (US$)	$227,775	$240,153	105%
c) Operational Self-Sufficiency (OSS)	104%	80%	77%
d) Full Financial Self-Sufficiency (FFS)	79%	64%	81%
5. Impact of Poverty			
a) Significant Reduction of Poverty	75%	75%	
b) No Longer Poor	25%	0%	

a.   The exchange rate used is 48.7 rupees per US$.
b.   Only one loan has been restructured since the start of CFTS's operations.

financial services to 23,000 of the poor and the poorest rural women. Loan portfolio quality is good, with less than 2 percent at risk. *Most importantly: the deficits of CFTS prior to break-even were financed almost entirely by quasi-equity. And CFTS is using marking-to-market to show its true capital adequacy.*

As of fiscal year end March 31, 2002, CFTS's actual performance against target in a number of key areas was as shown in Table 5.6.

While CFTS may be an extreme case in the sense that most MFIs may not have to rely so heavily on quasi-equity, it shows that it is a feasible approach. Small MFIs with the vision to reach large numbers of the poorest households, regardless of their approach, can be scaled up, with the part of their deficits prior to break-even that cannot be financed conventionally being financed by quasi-equity.

How CFTS Was Financed

Essential to the idea of rapid scaling-up, or fast-track, is the need to secure up front the funds to cover operating deficits to break-even. CFTS was started with about US$35,000 in investment from CASHPOR Technical Services Ltd (Malaysia), which is an associated company of CASHPOR Inc., the regional Network of GB-type MFIs in Asia. The Grameen Trust of Bangladesh committed to provide US$682,000 over four years to finance the operating deficits and a portion of the onlending fund requirements for the six-branch model that was to break-even within four years, by providing financial services to about 20,000 poor, rural households. The funds for deficit financing were provided as zero interest, eight-year term loans, with a grace period of five years. The onlending funds carried an interest of 2 percent per annum, and were also for eight years, with a grace period of six. Both loans were designed to be repaid out of profits, after institutional financial break-even.

In reality, the Trust was able to provide only half ($344,000) of the committed amount. As a result, and in light of the need at the time to establish more than the planned six branches, it allowed CFTS to use the entire amount for deficit financing. Grameen Trust also agreed to reschedule the loans to a term of twelve years, with a nine-year grace period, and to legally subordinate them to any other loans that CFTS would raise in India. *This turned out to be an important breakthrough in funding for CFTS.*

It enabled CFTS to attract onlending funds (about US$970,000) from: 1) the Small Industries Development Bank of India (SIDBI), at a near market rate of 11 percent per annum; 2) later from Friends of Women's World Banking India (FWWB), approximately US$350,000 at a market rate of 14 percent per annum; 3) from the National Bank for Agriculture and Rural Development (NABARD), approximately US$225,000, at 9 percent per annum; and 4) finally, from an Indian Commercial Bank, ICICI Bank, approximately US$250,000 at 14 percent per annum, with a 50 percent guarantee from Deutsche Bank Micro Credit Development Fund of New York. In total, about US$1.8 million in onlending funds were borrowed by CFTS at near market and market rates, from Indian development banks, an Indian wholesaler to MFIs, and an Indian commercial bank.

This funding from Indian banks and a wholesaler was possible because the funders accepted that operating deficits were being funded with quasi-equity from the Grameen Trust and the Calvert Social Development Foundation. None of the funders insisted on conventional collateral from CFTS. They accepted 10 percent security deposits, or hypothecation of its book debt and moveable assets as sufficient collateral.[21]

Inevitably, CFTS ran up against a capital adequacy barrier, however. This happened as a result of an independent rating commissioned by SIDBI, its lead funder, in early 2001. The rating agency gave CFTS alpha for overall management and alpha for its systems, but it gave only beta for capital adequacy. Furthermore, it stated explicitly that SIDBI, or any other funders, should not lend any more to CFTS until it had increased its equity accordingly. This was the moment of truth for CFTS. It needed to borrow about another Rs.3 crore (about US$1.5 million) to attain the volume of loans outstanding that were needed for institutional financial break-even. As CFTS was still loss-making, there was no hope of attracting private investments. Even donors were wary of putting grants into a possibly bottomless pit. CFTS could not raise enough additional conventional equity to meet the likely requirements of the rating agency.

The rating agency refused to include quasi-equity into its calculation of capital adequacy. CFTS appealed to SIDBI, and it eventually applied its own formula, which gave enough weight to the quasi-equity so that it could continue lending to CFTS.

Only a total of US$325,000 was borrowed from abroad: $50,000 from the Calvert Social Development Foundation (for working capital) and $275,000 from the Grameen Foundation USA (for onlending).

The practical difficulties notwithstanding, CFTS was able to finance its deficits prior to break-even largely from quasi-equity, and it was able to obtain most of its onlending funds from Indian development banks at near commercial rates (9 to 11 percent per annum). So the suggested new financing strategy has been tested. If it was done in India, it can probably be done anywhere.

The funding of CFTS's institutionalization and its outreach to 23,000 poor, rural women in Mirzapur District eastern UP India *shows the value of quasi-equity in covering operational deficits prior to institutional financial break-even, and in attracting near-commercial and commercial funding from financial institutions for onlending.* That the financial institutions were willing to lend to CFTS for onlending to the poor, despite the lack of conventional capital adequacy on the part of CFTS, provides the empirical basis for suggesting some revisions in the computation of capital adequacy for MFIs working with the poor.

Taking the Strategy One Step Further

As has been seen above, there were potentially serious consequences for CFTS in its almost exclusive reliance upon quasi-equity as a source of financing. Looking at CFTS's audited balance sheet, one is immediately struck by the fact that liabilities are greater than assets. The result: a negative equity and negative capital adequacy. In conventional accounting terms, this would imply technical insolvency. Such a conclusion, however, would be very misleading, as it would ignore the nature of CFTS's liabilities as well as its strong underlying operations and high quality asset base.

CFTS has been very strategic in the type of borrowings it has undertaken. Quasi-equity financing has been designed so that terms are long, and the interest rate low, so that CFTS can repay out of profits after break-even. Such a commitment by funders is much more equity-like than debt-like. Moreover, CFTS was able to borrow at below-market rates, which in India would be almost 15 percent, by accessing funds from SIBDI and NABARD, as highlighted above. As we have seen in the previous section ("Presenting a Truer and Fairer Picture of Capital Adequacy"), there is an implicit grant element in such below-market rate funds.

To better analyze its financial strength, on a six-month basis, CFTS marks its debt to market, adjusts its financial statements for the effect of inflation and subsidies and then recalculates capital adequacy according to international norms. This complete analysis and the adjusted statements for September 30, 2002, appear in Tables 5.7, 5.8, and 5.9.

These calculations allows for a clearer and fairer representation of CFTS's financial health, resulting in a capital adequacy of 10 percent.

Financing Scaling-up

CFTS intends to expand its outreach to the poor district-wise in modules of ten branches, possibly with different legal identities, and to finance its deficits, when necessary, by quasi-equity marked to market.

Table 5.7   Marking Debt to Market: CFTS Case Study (as of September 30, 2001)

Step 1: Discounting Cash Flows

SUMMARY MARKET VALUE DEBT ANALYSIS				
Market Rate Used in Discounting		15%		
	Actual Interest Rate	Book Value of Debt	Market Value of Debt	Subsidy Element (New Equity)
Grameen Bank				
Tranche 1	2.0%	8,536,280	3,866,645	4,669,635
Tranche 2	0.0%	5,690,853	2,585,919	3,104,934
GF USA				
Tranche 1	2.0%	10,456,615	6,243,598	4,213,017
SIDBI				
Tranche 1	11.0%	4,166,668	4,088,341	78,327
Tranche 2	11.0%	9,343,750	8,796,035	547,715
Tranche 3	11.0%	5,930,000	5,514,471	415,529
Tranche 4	6.0%	1,950,000	240,224	1,709,776
TOTAL		46,074,166	31,335,233	14,738,933

Step 2: Making Adjustments for Inflation & Subsidized Expenses
(6 months from April 1 to Sept 30, 2001)

1) **Cost of Equity - Inflation Adjustment**
    Since fixed assets are greater than adjusted equity, no inflation adjustment has been made.

2) **Subsidized Cost of Funds**

Average Debt Outstanding	61,902,933
Market Rate Cost of Funds	4,642,720
Actual Interest Expense Paid	2,236,212
Adjustment for Subsidy	2,406,508

3) **In Kind Subsidies**
    The Executive Trustee is not currently drawing a salary, so an adjustment of 50,000 rupees per month has been added.

The combined impact of the above adjustments to the adjusted Balance Sheet are:
1) Step 1: To reduce the value of debt reported on the balance sheet to the market value and to increase equity by the same amount. The balance sheet remains in balance.
2) Step 2: To increase expenses by the amount of the cost of funds adjustment, thereby reducing equity and reducing cash on hand. The balance sheet remains in balance.

THE RESULTING ADJUSTED BALANCE SHEET IS USED TO CALCULATE CAPITAL ADEQUACY.

Step 3: Calculating a More Meaningful Capital Adequacy

Before Adjustment		After Adjustment	
Tier 1 Capital	(9,510,723)	Tier 1 Capital	2,521,702
Tier 2 Capital*	0	Tier 2 Capital	2,521,702
Total Equity	(9,510,723)	Total Equity	5,043,403
Risk Adjusted Assets	51,039,384	Risk Adjusted Assets	50,498,082
CFTS Capital Adequacy Ratio	–18.6%	**CFTS Capital Adequacy Ratio**	10.0%

*   Tier 2 Capital is limited to 50% of Tier 1 Capital. In the before adjustment scenario, since equity is negative, no Tier 2 Capital is reported. In the after adjustment scenario, Tier 2 capital is limited by the amount of Tier 1 Capital.

Table 5.8 CASHPOR Financial & Technical Services Ltd: Adjusted Financial Statements

BALANCE SHEET			As On September 30, 2001
	AUDITED Financial Performance	Adjustments	ADJUSTED Financial Performance
ASSETS			
Current Assets			
Cash & Non-Interest Bearing Accounts	11,808	0	11,808
Deposits at Bank	1,865,480	0	1,865,480
Fixed Deposits	4,800,000	(2,706,508)	2,093,492
Total Loan Outstanding	39,019,032	0	39,019,032
(Loan Loss Reserve)	(556,500)	0	(556,500)
Net Loan Outstanding	38,462,532	0	38,462,532
Other Advances	2,054,095	0	2,054,095
Grants Receivable	0	0	0
Workshop Fee Recoverable	0	0	0
Total Current Assets	**47,193,915**	**0**	**47,487,407**
Long-Term Assets			
Deferred Revenue Expenditure	7,873,882	0	7,873,882
Fixed Assets	3,369,874	0	3,369,874
(Accumulated Depreciation)	0	0	0
Net Fixed Assets	3,369,874	0	3,369,874
Total Long-Term Assets	**11,243,756**	**0**	**11,243,756**
TOTAL ASSETS	**58,437,671**	**0**	**55,731,163**
LIABILITIES			
Current Liabilities			
Accounts Payable	415,932	0	415,932
Collective Responsibility Fund	0	0	0
Provisions	0	0	0
Other Current Liabilities	1,232,136	0	1,232,136
Total Current Liabilities	**1,648,068**	**0**	**1,648,068**
Long-Term Liabilities			
Savings	0	0	
Sr. Secured Loans	37,211,578	–2,751,347	34,460,231
Sr. Unsecured Loans	14,861,615	–4,213,017	10,648,598
Subordinated Loans	14,227,133	–7,774,569	6,452,564
Total Long-Term Liabilities	**66,300,326**	**–14,738,933**	**51,561,393**
TOTAL LIABILITIES	**67,948,394**	**0**	**53,209,461**
EQUITY			
Paid-Up Capital	1,530,000	0	1,530,000
Grant Component of Debt Financing	0	14,738,933	14,738,933
Current Year Donations	0	0	0
Accumulated Donations	0	0	0
Inflation Adjustment	0	0	0
Operating Profit/Loss - Current Year	(1,912,181)	–2,706,508	(4,618,689)
Accumulated Consolidated Profit/(Loss)	(9,128,542)	0	(9,128,542)
TOTAL EQUITY	**(9,510,723)**	**0**	**2,521,702**
TOTAL LIABILITIES + EQUITY	**58,437,671**		**55,731,163**

Table 5.9   CASHPOR Financial & Technical Services Ltd:
Adjusted Financial Statements

INCOME STATEMENT		As On September 30, 2001	
	AUDITED Financial Performance	Adjustments	ADJUSTED Financial Performance
Financial Income			
Income on Loans to Poor Women	5,299,380	0	5,299,380
Other Income	393,892	0	393,892
Participants/Workshop Fee	0	0	0
Total Operating Income	5,693,272	0	5,693,272
Financial Costs			
Interest on Borrowing	2,236,212	2,406,508	4,642,720
Other Interest	0	0	0
Bank Charges	69,443	0	69,443
Total Financial Costs	2,305,655	0	4,712,163
Loan Loss Provision	183,765	0	183,765
Administrative Expenses			
Personnel	3,510,865	300,000	3,810,865
Travel	949,049	0	949,049
Rent	196,480	0	196,480
Supplies	305,633	0	305,633
Communication	50,300	0	50,300
Professional Charges (including audits)	209,014	0	209,014
Training/Workshop	174,890	0	174,890
Miscellaneous	185,984	0	185,984
Depreciation	129,361	0	129,361
Other Provisions	(593,544)	0	(593,544)
Total Administrative Expense	5,118,032	300,000	5,418,032
OPERATING PROFIT/(LOSS)	(1,914,180)	2,706,508	(4,620,688)
Non-Operating Income (Grants & Donations)	1,999	0	1,999
Non-Operating Expenses	0	0	0
NON-OPERATING PROFIT/(LOSS)	1,999	0	1,999
TOTAL PROFIT/(LOSS)	(1,912,181)	2,706,508	(4,618,689)

Instituting the New Financing Paradigm

Sources of Quasi-Equity

From where would the quasi-equity come? One thinks immediately of bilateral and multilateral donors interested in financing poverty reduction. However, bilateral donors are not used to extending loans; they prefer to give grants, as it is simpler. While grants, if carefully structured like those of CGAP to selected MFIs, can increase capital adequacy and improve an MFI's ability to leverage funds from commercial financial markets, there are not enough of them available to meet a significant proportion of the demand. Moreover, quasi-equity marked to market would give donor funds more impact, as they would increase Tier 2 capital as well as Tier 1.

As the amount of soft loans (quasi-equity) required to finance MFIs to reach the remaining 81 million poorest women in the world would be huge, however, it would be best to have microcredit funds at the national or regional level[22] as well, especially in the poorer countries and regions, which could be financed by grants from bilateral donors and/or by very soft loans from multilateral lenders. At least three national-level microcredit funds are performing well in Asia: PKSF in Bangladesh, PCFC in the Philippines, and RMDC in Nepal. Perhaps significantly, each has a multilateral development bank behind it, the World Bank in the case of PKSF and the Asian Development Bank in the case of PCFC and RMDC.

A Leadership Role for CGAP   CGAP, if it agrees with this analysis and on the potential importance of quasi-equity, could play a critical role in building the institutional capacity of additional national and regional-level microcredit funds, in encouraging its member donors to finance them with grants, and in monitoring and evaluating the performance of the funds. CGAP has experience itself in identifying and scaling up promising MFIs. It could transfer these skills and the lessons of its experience to national and regional microfinance funds.

Multilateral Banks   Multilateral agencies like the World Bank, IFAD, and the Asian Development Bank are used to dealing with loans. In addition to proving funds for national-level microcredit funds, they could be a major source of quasi-equity for large MFIs that want to rapidly expand.

Social Investors and Development Foundations   Development oriented foundations like the Grameen Foundation USA, the Calvert Social Development Foundation,[23] HIVOS, Ford Foundation, CRS, and the Grameen Trust (as it did in the case of CFTS), could also adopt quasi-equity as one of their main instruments for financing microfinance for the poor. National-level development banks could also play a role in the provision of quasi-equity to MFIs.

Development and Commercial Banks   It is from domestic development and commercial banks that most of the onlending funds will have to come. MFIs that want to reach large numbers of poor households will have to build the capacity to pay market rates, of 12 to 18 percent, for these funds. They will also have to establish a track record with these banks, starting with relatively small loans. Although the banks will not be very interested initially, several years of repayment in full, on time, adequate quasi-equity to cover losses prior to break-even, and steady progress toward it should build the confidence of the banks to offer larger amounts and more leverage over time.

Guarantee Funds   Guarantee funds can play a critical and timely role in enabling well-managed MFIs, with little or no conventional equity, to secure their first loans from commercial banks. Although this would mean relatively high interest rates, because the cost of the guarantee funds are added to the market rate for the loan funds, it would be worthwhile for MFIs to pay them, in order to have the chance of establishing a track record with the banks (the cost of getting the proverbial foot in the door).

Other Forms of Financing to Overcome the Equity Hurdle

In reply to the circulation of an earlier version of this chapter, the authors received several creative suggestions for other forms of funding that could help to narrow the operating deficit financing gap. One interesting suggestion was that if investment by private individuals and entities in MFIs working with the poorest were 100 percent tax deductible, and the dividends were tax free up to a return of say 10 percent per annum, compounded from the date of the original investment, huge amounts of private investment would be made available to microfinance.[24] These may be ways of getting the private sector involved in providing capital for microfinance.[25] It was pointed out that many actors in microfinance are non-stock, nonprofit NGOs. A financing instrument that would be suitable for them is the equity equivalent (or EQ2). This is a community development debenture that legally permits "equity-like" investments in not-for-profits. Like a near equity investment but different from a simple subordinated debt, EQ2 is a general obligation of the issuer that is not covered by any of its assets. It is fully subordinated to all other debts, is designed to raise cash for the issuer, has a rolling term and therefore an indeterminate term, but does not confer voting rights.[26] And of course, the creative use of SDRs for financing the expansion of microfinance for the poor, as is being suggested by George Soros, should be given further serious consideration. It is clear, therefore, that there are plenty of good "blue sky" ideas on financing of microfinance for poverty reduction.

Putting the Pieces Together

Of course not all funders are going to agree with nor play the roles identified for them above. CGAP, however, could maximize the number that do, by working with its member donors to include funding for quasi-equity, either directly or indirectly, as an important part of their assistance to MFIs working with the poor.

CGAP and others leading the drive for microfinance standards, such as the *Microbanking Bulletin* and international and regional networks, should also carefully consider and move forward with some of the "out-of-the-box" thinking that this chapter has generated—in particular marking soft loans to market and rethinking capital adequacy so that they are more appropriate for the microfinance industry.

Taken together, as CFTS illustrates, efforts to "massify" microfinance could become a reality.

Endnotes

1. Microcredit Summit Campaign, "State of the Microcredit Campaign Report 2001," (Washington, D.C.: Microcredit Summit Campaign, 2001), 11.

2. Good examples are SHARE in India, CARD in the Philippines, FINCA in Uganda and CRECER in Bolivia.

3. Efforts of CGAP World Bank (CGAP) to "massify" microfinance, through such intermediaries as rural post offices and even public telephone kiosks, are welcome. But these efforts are new and it would be unwise to neglect the institutions that to date have provided most of the microfinance for the poor—that is, MFIs.

4. In most poor countries, certainly in the bigger ones like India and Indonesia, there are huge pools of underemployed, educated youth. Experience tells us that within three months most of them can be trained to identify and motivate poor women to see microfinance as a good opportunity for themselves, and to manage the provision of microfinance services to them. We also know that educated young people in the rural areas, who have never touched a computer, can, using user-friendly software, learn to perform data entry at the branch-level. The manpower is waiting for microfinance, at least in the poorer countries.

5. The term "capital" as used in this first section of the chapter refers to all sources of financing available to microfinance institutions. Please see Glossary, definition a.

6. CASHPOR-PHILNET workshop June 5–7, Manila, the Philippines.

7. George Soros, George Soros on Globalization (New York: Public Affairs, 2002), 83–84.

8. Use of the term capital in this section of the chapter is more limited to that used in the first section ("The Need for a New Financing Paradigm"). It refers to the financial strength of the organization, and includes equity and quasi-equity only. Please see the Glossary, definition b.

9. The Basel Committee is a group of central banks, bank supervisors, and regulators from the major industrialized countries that meets every three months at the Bank of International Settlements in Basel. Through papers and reports, they provide broad policy guidelines that the supervisors of each country can use to determine supervisory policies in their own countries.

10. Those being protected include both depositors and lenders.

11. It should be noted that the Microbanking Bulletin, a leading industry newsletter of standards, does allow for the inclusion of quasi-equity in the numerator of its capital adequacy calculation. Total adjusted equity is defined as total equity, including quasi-equity and adjusted net income.

12. The Grameen Bank (GB) itself has a history of overcoming repayment problems: first in Tangail District in 1984 and then in Rangpur District in 1991–92. Currently it has re-engineered itself to bring back nearly all of the large number of defaulters that left it after 1995. See *Credit for the Poor* 34, available from cashpor@yahoo.com. Other well-known GB-type MFIs that have overcome serious repayment problems are Ahon Sa-Hirap and Dungganon in the Philippines.

13. Basel Committee on Banking Supervision, "International Convergence of Capital Measurement & Capital Standards," *Basel Committee Publications no. 4* (July 1988): 4.

14. CGAP, "Focus on Transparency," *Microbanking Bulletin* 7 (November 2001): 52.

15. Regional Economic Monitoring Unit of Asian Development Bank, *Asia Economic Monitor*, April 2002, 17–19.

16. Thomas Au Yeung, "NPLs of Taiwan banks estimated to reach 18%," *The China Post* (25 April 2002).

17. Hiroshi Inoue, "Interview: Ex-BOJ Tamura: Japan FSA, Banks Lag in Reform," *The Wall Street Journal Online* (18 June 2002).

18. If the payment is one year in the future, the payments would be discounted by the commercial rate of interest, which is 15 percent; for purposes of the calculation, (1+15 percent) or 1.15 is used. If the interest payment is two or more periods in the future, the commercial rate would have to be adjusted to reflect the compounding effect of more than one period. For example, if the payment was in two years, and you wanted to know today's value, you would have to divide the payment by 1.15 and then again by 1.15; more simply, you would divide by 1.15 squared (raised to the power of 2). If the payment was in three years and you wanted to know today's value, you would have to divide by 1.15, again by 1.15 and then again by 1.15; more simply, you would divide by 1.15 raised to the third.

19. The marking to market analysis cannot be used on loans that are callable, since request for early payment of those loans rests with the lender.

20. Although CASHPOR Financial & Technical Services Ltd (CFTS) in Mirzapur, eastern UP India, is only four and a half years old, institutional financial break-even is projected before the end of its fifth year of operation (30 September 2002), at which time it will be providing financial services to about 23,000 poor rural women who will have about 78 million rupees (around US$1.6 million) loans outstanding in their hands, with less than 2 percent of it at risk.

21. Even though CFTS had negotiated from banks the funding they needed to break even, actually getting the funds in a timely manner was another major hurdle. Few banks in India will follow an agreed-upon disbursement schedule with MFIs. Late arrival of onlending funds caused serious problems for CFTS on the ground. New clients got tired of waiting and dropped out, wasting the resources that were spent on their group formation. The pace of new group formation had to be slowed so that there would not be too many frustrated new clients. Rumors spread that CFTS had run out of money and might not be able to offer subsequent loans to clients who repaid their existing loans on time. Some clients protected their liquidity by stop-

ping repayment. Portfolio at risk began to rise again. Payment schedules should be contingent upon reasonable achievement of business plan targets (at least 80 percent), but they should be implemented in a timely manner once the conditions have been met. Additionally, new conditions should not be imposed except in connection with new loans.

22. CASHPOR, the Asia regional network of GB-type microfinance institutions for the poor, has played the role, on a limited scale, of a regional provider of operating funds for scaling-up, on behalf of UNDP and the Government of Finland. It has just signed a contract with AusAID to provide "package" funding against achievement of business plan targets for selected MFIs in Indonesia. It is prepared to do more in this regard, including the wholesaling of quasi-equity on behalf of donors. The Philippine national network of GBRs, PHILNET, could be further strengthened to do the same in the Philippines, as could INDNET in India. These networks are in a good position to know which of their member institutions need what kind of funding, and to monitor and report on the use of such funds. The achievements of PKSF in this regard in Bangladesh, of PCFC in the Philippines, and RMDC in Nepal are evidence of the significant role that national networks can play in scaling up the outreach of microfinance, if adequately funded themselves.

23. Shari Berenbach, executive director of Calvert, suggested one way to make quasi-equity financing attractive to social investors might be to include a layer of credit enhancements in an investment vehicle so that investors are confident of remaining whole.

24. We are grateful to Ramesh Bellamkonda, project director of Bharta Swamukthi Samsthe (BSS) of Bangalore, India, for this suggestion that certainly merits further consideration. He can be reached at swamukti@blr.vsnl.net.in.

25. Horacio Navarette of Monsanto Corp. has suggested that we consider addressing the issue of a possible role for the private sector as a source of quasi-equity.

26. Benjie Montemayor of Opportunity International contributed this interesting idea. He can be reached at BMontemayor@opportunity.org.

APPENDIX
GLOSSARY

Callable Loan

A loan where the lender retains the right to request or "call" the money back before maturity. This is normally subject to certain conditions. With respect to MFIs, this right is often retained in international lending given the foreign exchange exposure, and therefore added credit risk, of such loans. Soft loans that are callable cannot be marked to market.

Capital

This term is used very widely in the world of finance and means different things to different people. Two primary definitions are provided below.

a) In the microfinance community, the term capital is often used to refer generally to all sources of financing available to microfinance institutions, including liabilities (savings and borrowings), quasi-equity, and equity. This is how it is used in the capacity vs. capital debate.

b) In the banking industry, capital is used more specifically to refer to the financial strength of the organization, which is the sum of Tier 1 and Tier 2 capital.

Capital Adequacy

A ratio that measures the minimum amount of total capital (see definition b) to risk-adjusted assets an MFI must have. International standards require a minimum of 8 percent, where total capital is equal to the sum of Tier 1 and Tier 2 capital. Risk adjustment of each asset class is also undertaken.

Convertible Debt

A loan that can be converted to equity based upon pre-negotiated conditions between the Borrower (the MFI) and the Lender. This is classified as quasi-equity, or Tier 2 capital.

Loan (Borrowings)

Funds provided to an MFI that it promises to repay on terms and conditions agreed to between the MFI and the lender.

Operating Deficits

Occurs in the early years of start-up or during rapid expansion when costs incurred to operate an MFI's business, including administrative expenses, interest expense, are greater than operating income, leading to losses or deficits. Onlending requirements are not considered in this calculation.

Paid-Up or Paid-In Capital

Generally speaking, this refers to ownership positions held in an MFI; since NGOs cannot have ownership, paid-up capital or investment is only available as a source of financing to companies, financial institutions, and other profit-making entities with an appropriate legal status. These "owners" in the MFI own a share in the success or failure of the business. This is classified as core equity, or Tier 1 capital.

Preferred Stock

Stock that pays a fixed dividend and has a claim to assets of a corporation ahead of common (paid up) stockholders in the event of liquidation. This is classified as quasi-equity, or Tier 2 capital.

Quasi-Equity

An investment that combines the characteristics of equity and loans. This includes subordinated debt, convertible debt, and preferred stock, among other financial instruments.

Retained Earnings

Profits (or losses), after any distributions such as dividends, that are plowed back into and used in the MFI's business. These profits/losses are accumulated on the balance sheet as part of total equity. This is classified as core equity, or Tier 1 capital.

Senior Loans

Debt that has priority of claim ahead of all other obligations of an MFI. Senior debt securities have claim to assets of an organization before subordinated date in the event of a liquidation. This is not included in capital (see definition b above), as it is a liability.

Special Drawing Rights (SDRs)

Created in 1969 and issued by the International Monetary Fund (IMF), these are monetary reserve assets that serve as a unit of account and as a means of payment among IMF members, itself, and others. SDRs constitute a part of a country's official foreign exchange reserves. The value is determined by a basket of four major currencies—US$, euro, yen, and pound sterling.

Stock

Interest in a corporation, representing a claim of ownership.

Subordinated Loans

Loans having a claim against the borrower's assets that is lower ranking, or junior to, senior loans and is therefore paid after claims to senior lenders are satisfied. This is classified as quasi-equity, or Tier 2 capital.

Tier 1 Capital

Also referred to as core capital, and includes paid-up capital (common stock) and retained earnings. In the case of MFIs, this would also include cumulative grants.

Tier 2 Capital

Secondary source of equity-like financing that can be included in total equity for purposes of calculating quasi-equity. This includes subordinated debt, convertible securities, and a portion of loan loss reserves.

Traditional Equity

In this paper, used to describe the way most MFIs have historically covered operating deficits; this includes grants, investment, and where relevant, profits after break-even. This is classified as core equity, or Tier 1 capital.

Uncallable Loan

A loan where the Lender is unable to request the money back prior to maturity, unless the Borrower does not meet pre-agreed terms and conditions and/or defaults. Uncallable soft loans can be marked to market.

6

Policies, Regulations, and Systems That Promote Sustainable Financial Services to the Poor and Poorest

Women's World Banking

This chapter is intended for policymakers, microfinance leaders, and other stakeholders that are working to build financial systems that work for the poor majority. It is intended to reflect experience and lessons from around the world on how policies, regulations, and systems can be shaped to promote the development of a sound and responsive microfinance industry. It is based on work by Women's World Banking (WWB) leaders and many others to build consensus among major actors that has resulted in important policy changes in many developing countries. Each section features concrete examples of good practice.

The chapter highlights key developments in the microfinance industry. It summarizes research to understand what poor women want in microfinance services, since this should be the foundation for building pro-poor, pro-microfinance policies. It begins from the global consensus that microfinance should both work for the poor and be financially sustainable.

Microfinance needs to be treated as a vital part of the financial system, with the special needs and features of microfinance operations and institutions recognized in financial sector policies and regulations. We highlight the important role that a broad range of regulated and unregulated financial institutions can and do play in the provision of microfinance services, and the importance of building policies and support systems that encourages a range of institutional types to enter and expand microfinance services. The key roles that government policymakers can play in microfinance are outlined.

Recognizing that the majority of microlending institutions are likely to remain unregulated, the chapter emphasizes the importance of microfinance networks, wholesalers, rating agencies, and others in building systems to monitor performance using common indicators and definitions. This is not a substitute for prudential regulation, which is vital for those institutions that mobilize savings from the public. Performance monitoring systems are important in building transparency and a common commitment to excellence among the range of microfinance retailers.

The chapter highlights the key features of policy and regulatory change that will be needed to help ensure sound, responsive microfinance operations—whether these are by regulated microfinance institutions or form a small part of a commercial bank's loan portfolio—as well as key features in the available legal structures for those microfinance institutions that seek to become for profit, regulated legal entities.

Evolution of the Microfinance Industry

Microfinance involves financial services to poor people, provided in an efficient, responsive, and financially sustainable manner. While institutions need to build toward financial sustainability over time, experience now demonstrates that, in most settings, microloans can be provided to the poor and poorest, in ways that cover operating and financial costs, once institutions reach moderate numbers of microborrowers—10,000 clients in most settings. While the focus over the last ten to twenty years has been on expanding microloans to support the economic activities of the poor, it is clear that microfinance needs to encompass a range of financial services—lending, savings, and insurance—that help poor people build their income and assets, lubricate their household economies, and mitigate the risks that poor families face.

Microfinance has a number of roots. For hundreds of years, poor people in Africa and Asia have formed savings and lending groups. Moneylenders and the informal curb market have provided quick services, at very high costs, to poor households who had no access to mainstream financial institutions. In the last century, cooperatives and credit unions in developing countries have focused on savings mobilization and lending with rural households, many of which are poor. Over the years, governments have created lending programs for poor entrepreneurs and producers; most of these programs have suffered from subsidized interest rates, political patronage, and low repayments.

In the last twenty years, the "microfinance industry" has emerged. During the 1980s and 1990s, particularly in Asia, Africa, and Latin America, thousands of microfinance NGOs were established to provide microloans, using individual and group lending methodologies. In the 1990s, while many of these NGOs failed to reach scale or financial sustainability, others led the way in demonstrating that:

- Poor people, particularly poor women, are excellent borrowers, when provided with efficient, responsive loan services at commercial rates.
- Microfinance institutions can provide microloans to poor people in an efficient and financially sustainable way, once the number of clients reaches reasonable scale—10,000 to 20,000 borrowers in most settings.
- Microfinance—lending, savings, and other financial services to poor people—is an effective way to help poor people help themselves build income and assets, manage risk, and work their way out of poverty.

Most of the growth in the microfinance industry over the last ten years has taken place in the absence of specific financial sector policies for microfinance. In Bangladesh, where about one third of the world's estimated 30 million active microborrowers reside, the growth has come from specialized microfinance NGOs and Grameen Bank. Grameen Bank has its own special legal structure, and does not fall under regulatory oversight of the central bank. In Bolivia, which has been a leader in building microfinance policies and regulations, most of the growth in outreach came before the regulations. Since the regulations have been put in place, growth has been more rapid among unregulated MFIs, with the rapid growth in portfolios of regulated MFIs coming mainly from growth in average loan size. In Indonesia, Bank Rakyat Indonesia, a state-owned commercial bank, succeeded in building the world's largest commercial microfinance savings and lending services for millions of poor people in an otherwise ineffective bank, using existing banking regulations.

Beginning in the mid-1990s, leading microfinance institutions have worked together to build performance indicators and standards for the microfinance industry. These initiatives have been motivated by recognition among practitioners that:

- Microfinance must demonstrate very high performance on portfolio quality, efficiency, and financial sustainability if microfinance institutions are to be recognized as integral members of the financial system, able to mobilize commercial borrowings.
- Effective ways of looking at efficiency, risk, and profitability need to differ for microfinance portfolios relative to traditional banking activities, with microfinance practitioners well placed to determine the

appropriate performance indicators and standards for the industry.

- Microfinance institutions that do not mobilize savings from the public are not likely to warrant regulation by traditional bank supervisors; other means need to be found to build transparency, accountability, and pressure to perform for non-regulated MFIs.

Many global-, regional- and country-level networks have adopted or are adopting similar performance indicators, standards, and institutional evaluation methods which reflect key success factors in microfinance. These performance indicators, standards, and approaches to evaluating MFIs have been adopted by international donors. However, implementation has been uneven. Similar evaluation methods and performance indicators have been adopted by the new set of "rating agencies" that have emerged in the microfinance industry.

Recent Focus on NGO "Transformation"

During the 1990s, a phenomenon emerged in parts of the donor and microfinance community that focused on the felt need to "transform" or convert microfinance NGOs into regulated, for-profit structures, owned and governed by shareholders. The rationale in promoting this "commercialization" model was that:

- Microfinance institutions should rely on savings and commercial borrowings rather than donor grants.
- Institutions that mobilize savings from the public should be subject to prudential regulation.
- Regulated structures would provide more assurances to commercial lenders and investors.
- Microfinance NGOs have no owners, and NGO boards can be dominated by social objectives, resulting in structures that have limited accountability or focus on efficiency and profitability.

To date, this "transformation" model has had limited success and several unintended consequences:

- Only about twenty-five of the thousands of microfinance NGOs around the world have converted to for-profit, regulated structures.
- Most countries do not have the legal structures or regulatory regimes in place that would make such conversions feasible or desirable.

- The pool of domestic commercial investors in for-profit microfinance institutions in most developing countries is extremely limited. In fact, the ownership structure of all converted microfinance NGOs is dominated by various combinations of donors, donor funded funds, international NGOs, and the originating NGO (see Annex 6.1). The benefits of converting from an NGO to a "private" structure with ownership and governance dominated by donors and NGOs is questionable, in terms of accountability, know-how, consistency in target group, and performance focus.

- Few if any converted MFIs have developed broad-based savings mobilization from the public; most rely on a narrow set of institutional depositors, donor-funded equity and debt, and commercial borrowings as their sources of funds (see Annex 6.2). With limited efforts to mobilize savings from the public, the underlying rationale for prudential regulation is not fulfilled.

- Many microfinance NGOs are not yet of the size, efficiency, and/or profitability to make incurring the costs of legal conversion and regulation feasible or desirable.

- In countries where the performance thresholds for becoming a regulated MFI have been low, weak NGOs have become weak regulated MFIs, with little of the anticipated benefits in performance improvements or mobilization of commercial finance.

Over the last five years, a number of private mainstream commercial banks, finance companies, and insurance firms have entered microfinance, as retailers or wholesalers in microfinance. Many of these institutions see microfinance as a large potential market; most have top managers who are motivated by community concerns as well as profits. These traditional financial institutions have learned from microfinance institutions (MFIs) and pioneer banks how to reduce the high transaction costs in microlending. Some are combining labor-intensive lending methodologies and distribution systems with the use of technology. In addition to private financial institutions, a few government banks have established large, efficient, and profitable microfinance operations—breaking from the tradition of low efficiency, low profitability, low repayment, and subsidy approaches to lending to the poor. Most public and private mainstream financial institutions are not resource constrained; they have established broad-based savings mobilization, they are fully integrated into domestic financial markets, and major coverage in microfinance can be achieved with a small percentage of a bank's assets. While the long-term commitment to microfinance is questionable with some mainstream financial institutions, those that do commit can invest in building microfinance capabilities, products, and management information systems (MIS), while using a small portion of their financial resources, their branch infrastructure, and their internal systems to achieve significant outreach.

Major Differences in Regional and Country Patterns

The broad sweeps of the microfinance industry and movement over the last twenty years are described here. However, patterns differ radically across regions and across countries. Microfinance is at very different stages of development. The present and potential importance of different legal structures, distribution systems, and methodologies differ widely.

Building Financial Systems That Work for the Poor Majority

Listening to the needs of poor clients has provided the basis for developing financial services and delivery systems that work for the poor majority. Research by WWB and others to understand what poor women want in financial services yields common responses across continents. These responses lead us to design responsive financial products and systems, based on the needs of clients.

Microfinance needs to be recognized as a vital part of the financial system, dedicated to meeting the financial needs of poor clients in a responsive and profitable manner. This financial systems approach recognizes the important role that different organizational and legal structures can and do play in meeting the evolving financial service needs of poor households. It recognizes the important roles of both regulated and unregulated institutions in the microfinance system: grassroots savings and credit groups and microfinance NGOs, along with universal commercial banks, finance companies, cooperative banks, regulated MFIs, insurance companies, and wholesale financing institutions. This approach looks to remove policy, regulatory, and legal barriers to the provision of sound financial services to poor people by each class of institution. It also looks to building the institutional infrastructure to: facilitate access to finance by high performing institutions at different stages; build shared performance standards in the microfinance industry; and encourage capacity building and innovation.

The integration of microfinance into the financial sector does not mean that all microfinance institutions should be regulated. It does mean promoting strong regulated and unregulated institutions of all types that work to provide services on a sustainable basis, and creating enabling regulatory frameworks and legal structures for those MFIs that seek to mobilize and

Box 6.1
Creating a Pro-Poor Policy Framework: Listening to Clients

The voices of microfinance clients provide a clear picture of what is required to build systems which work for the poor:

- Microfinance clients want more, faster, and better financial services
- They value speed and convenience
- They want access to larger loans
- They want respect and recognition

Low income women and men define microfinance broadly:

- They want business loans
- They want to be able to deposit voluntary savings
- They want housing and education loans
- They want health and life insurance
- They are willing to pay what it costs for responsive, sustainable services

Poor people prefer individual loans over group loans. As their experience grows, clients of group loans resent the time that group meetings take, and the need to guarantee repayment by other members of the group.

How do we create a policy environment that responds to these needs?

- Create an environment which encourages microfinance institutions to operate efficiently and to innovate such that clients are served rapidly and close to their places of business.
- Remove interest rate ceilings and remove subsidy cultures that inhibit sustained access, competition, and innovation.
- Encourage competition in the industry so that costs go down for all clients and so that a range of products—including housing and education loans as well as voluntary savings and insurance—are provided that meet the needs of clients at different stages.
- Eliminate collateral requirements that most poor clients cannot meet and that effectively denies them access to the financial system.
- Ensure prudential requirements that protect the savings of the poor.
- Facilitate ways in which clients can participate in the ownership of MFIs.

intermediate savings from the public.

Broad consensus now exists that microfinance needs to work for poor people and be financially sustainable. During the 1990s, polarizing debates seethed between advocates of the "commercial" approach and those that saw their mission as serving the "poorest of the poor." Consensus also exists among most major microfinance actors that microfinance must work for the poor and must be financially sustainable. It is also recognized that microfinance is not the answer for all of the world's poorest families; some will need support other than microfinance, if they are to move out of poverty. Experience demonstrates that the financial needs of poor people are best served by encouraging a broad range of institutional types to provide the efficient and responsive lending, savings, insurance, and other financial services that poor people need to build their businesses, increase income and assets, and reduce risks. Poor people need sustained access to an evolving set of financial products and services. These can only be provided by financially sustainable institutions, dealing with diverse segments and products, each in the position to increase outreach and grow with their clients.

While donors and other sources of subsidized funds will continue to have important roles to play in supporting MFIs on the road to financial sustainability, microfinance in the twenty-first century will be dominated by those institutions that are or can get integrated into domestic financial markets, through wholesale financing arrangements, commercial borrowings and/or broad-based savings mobilization. Consensus statements by leading MFIs in Bangladesh and India, by microfinance leaders from the thirteen African microfinance networks that comprise AFMIN, and by policy leaders convened by WWB from around the world demonstrate a convergence around core principles on financial systems that work for the poor majority (see Annex 6.3).

Savings mobilization is key as a highly valued service to poor people, as a source of funds, and as a basis for real local accountability. In WWB surveys conducted in Latin America, Africa, and Asia, the service most desired by poor clients is the capacity to save small amounts with their microfinance institution, as savings help poor people build assets and manage risks. Many grassroots, cooperative, and banking institutions in Africa and Asia have demonstrated the desire and capacity to save among rural and urban poor households. As demonstrated by SEWA Bank in India, Bank Rakyat in Indonesia, and other successful pioneers, when simple, responsive savings products are offered, broad-based savings can become the dominant source of funds for the microloan portfolio. In contrast, most microfinance NGOs that have converted to regulated MFIs have not used their new legal structures to mobilize broad-based savings from the public. Most rely primarily

Box 6.2
The Importance of Savings to Clients and to MFIs
Poor people value the ability to save for a variety of reasons:

- To cope with emergencies such as death or the effects of natural disasters.

- To cope with unexpected investment opportunities such as purchasing items needed for their businesses when prices are low.

- To manage irregular income streams particularly those entrepreneurs engaged in seasonal work.

- For long-term investments such as purchasing land, financing children's education, and business needs such as tools and machinery and vehicles.

- For social and religious obligations such as marriage, religious holidays, and pilgrimages.

- For old age, sickness, and disability.

Savings are important to MFIs for a variety of reasons:

- Mobilizing deposits serves as an additional source of funds for on-lending to clients thereby enabling growth of the portfolio.

- Mobilizing deposits can enable microfinance institutions to reduce their dependence on donors because they can be used to finance the MFI's loan portfolio.

- Mobilizing deposits imposes a strict financial discipline on MFIs that ultimately benefits the institution.

—Marguerite Robinson

Source: Marguerite Robinson, *The Microfinance Revolution: Sustainable Finance for the Poor* (Washington, D.C.: The World Bank, 2001), ch. 7.

on term deposits from a narrow set of institutional investors. It is clear that institutions that have focused on microloans need to develop a distinct set of capacities to successfully mobilize savings from the poor and non-poor. Experience demonstrates that MFIs need to make substantial investments up front to build the capacity to mobilize savings from the public; however, if well-designed, this deposit base can become the major funding source and the basis for long-term institutional sustainability. Prudential regulation is key in broad-based savings mobilization to protect depositors. For poor people, the loss of savings deposits can have a devastating impact on their ability to build and maintain a personal safety net. Specialized microfinance institutions that seek to mobilize savings from the public need to comply with prudential regulations, with these regulations adjusted to reflect prudent governance and management, operating systems and business practices, financial and operating ratios, and portfolio quality in microfinance.

Across countries and regions, policies, regulations, legal structures, and industry infrastructure are needed that encourage a range of institutional types to enter and expand sound, efficient, and financially sustainable microfinance operations—rather than pinning hopes on a single model. Most policy and regulation can be built for microfinance as an activity, applied across the range of regulated legal structures. While most growth in microfinance services is likely to continue to come from traditional financial institutions and microfinance NGOs, a subset of strong microfinance NGOs will seek to become regulated, for-profit financial institutions, as a means to mobilize savings from the public and to facilitate the rapid expansion in commercial financing. Therefore, in addition to building policies and regulations tailored to the needs of microfinance as an activity, in many countries, new legal structures will be needed for deposit taking MFIs, or existing legal structures will need to be modified to fit the nature of microfinance. These policies, regulations, and legal structures need to balance promotion of the microfinance industry with the need to protect savers, investors, and the industry itself.

Government needs to remove itself from direct lending to poor people. Government programs—normally based on a social welfare, subsidy approach—nearly always end in being used as vehicles for political patronage, extremely low repayments, market distortions, and eventual truncation of services. Government banks can play important roles as retailers—if they are given autonomy in selecting clients, if they are required to charge unsubsidized lending rates, and if microfinance operations are either separated from inefficient, normal banking operations or are part of a commercially oriented, efficient state bank.

Government has important roles to play in building a pro-poor, pro-microfinance policy, regulatory framework, and set of legal structures. Recognition by finance ministries, central banks, and bank superintendencies of microfinance as an important, legitimate loan class, with its own characteristics within the financial system, is important. Government needs to help ensure that the mix of wholesale financing, performance monitoring, and capacity building mechanisms are in place to promote the sound growth of microfinance in institutions with different legal structures, at different stages of development. Government needs to recognize the important roles of different legal structures in microfinance—microfinance NGOs, credit unions and cooperatives, finance companies, commercial banks, regulated MFIs, grassroots groups, and insurance companies. Government needs to create general regulations and norms to encourage sound and responsive microfinance operations across the range of regulated legal structures, and government needs to remove the policy, regulatory, and legal barriers in each of these structures that may undermine their use in providing efficient, responsive, sustainable financial services to the poor.

Policymakers and microfinance leaders have built a consensus on the key elements of policy frameworks for microfinance. Some of the best policy environments for microfinance have been created when leaders of finance ministries and central banks engaged deeply and directly with microfinance practitioners in identifying the key features. These mutual learning and consensus-building processes can create deep understanding among policymakers of how rigorous microfinance is done, and can build appreciation among MFIs of banking norms and standards. In addition to building shared visions and principles for microfinance (see Annex 6.3), these processes lead to clarity on the most effective role of different actors in promoting a sound microfinance industry that responds to the evolving needs of poor clients in efficient, financially sustainable ways. Based upon consensus-building processes undertaken globally, and in several countries of Africa, Asia, and Latin America, policymakers, microfinance practitioners, and international funds have built agreement on key features of a policy framework that supports the development of a robust and responsive microfinance industry. These features include:

- A pro-poor economic policy stance, including the recognition of sustainable microfinance services as a key vehicle in tackling poverty.
- Solid macroeconomic policies, avoiding high inflation.
- Liberalized interest rates for microfinance, using competition rather than interest rate ceilings to encourage efficiency and lower interest rates over time.
- Elimination of market-distorting retail subsidies, notably in government programs.
- Modifications in financial sector policies, regulations, and legal struc-

tures to promote the entry and expansion of sound microfinance services by a range of structures, and to encourage the offering of multiple financial products and the explicit recognition of the important roles that unregulated NGOs and grassroots structures have in the delivery of microfinance services.

- Promotion of performance indicators and standards that encourage transparency and sound performance across the range of institutions engaged in microfinance.

- Permission to mobilize deposits from the public for those regulated institutions that meet prudential standards, with more liberal treatment of savings mobilization from MFI borrowers.

- Fair tax treatment, including temporary tax incentives for microfinance institutions undertaking the costs of converting to formal, regulated structures.

- Simple reporting requirements and supervision for microfinance activities and institutions, with a focus on performance.

Building Transparency and Performance Standards in Microfinance

Shared performance standards, transparency, and accountability are key to building solid and responsive financial services for poor households—for both regulated and unregulated microfinance institutions. Since prudential regulation will only cover a small number of those institutions involved in microlending, the role of microfinance networks, wholesale lenders, microfinance rating agencies, auditors, and international funders will all be key in building transparency and performance in the microfinance industry.

The basics for strong performance by regulated and unregulated MFIs are sound governance and management, appropriate microfinance operating systems, strong MIS, and internal controls. The ability of bank regulators to evaluate these capabilities and systems specific to microfinance is key. Regulators will also need to learn the key performance indicators and standards in microfinance, to be able to evaluate performance. Standards of efficiency, profitability, portfolio quality assessment, and capital adequacy need to be based on good practice in microfinance, not on conventional commercial banking norms. Since most microfinancing institutions are not likely to be regulated, it is important to establish industry norms and standards for unregulated microfinancing institutions, and to develop appropriate means to reinforce these performance standards.

Table 6.1   Key Performance Indicators in Microfinance

DIMENSION	INDICATOR[a]	WWB	AFMIN	MBB	MicroRate	ACCION	GIRAFE PlaNet Finance	WOCCU	Philippines Coalition	PKSF
Outreach	Number of Active Borrowers	X	X	X	X[b]	X	X		X	X
	Number of Active Savers	X	X				X	X		X
	Loan Portfolio Outstanding	X	X	X	X	X	X	X		
	Savings Portfolio	X	X			X	X			
	Average Loan Size/Average Loan Balance	X	X	X		X	X			X
Efficiency and Productivity	Operating Expense Ratio	X	X	X	X	X	X	X	X	X
	Caseload	X		X	X	X	X			X
Portfolio Quality	Portfolio at Risk	X	X	X	X	X	X	X	X	
	Loan Loss Reserve Ratio	X			X	X		X		
	Write Off Ratio	X			X					
	Loan Loss Provision Ratio	X		X	X	X	X	X		
Sustainability/ Profitability	Operational Self-Sufficiency	X	X	X		X	X	X	X	X
	Financial Self-Sufficiency	X	X	X		X	X	X	X	X
	Adjusted Return on Assets	X		X	X	X	X	X		
	Adjusted Return on Equity	X		X	X	X	X	X		
Capital Structure	Debt to Equity Ratio	X		X	X	X			X	
	Capital to Asset Ratio					X		X		X
	Leverage - Capital to Equity Ratio						X			
Liquidity	Current Ratio				X	X			X	
	Liquidity Ratio			X				X		X

Key actors in implementing this system of performance monitoring at global and country levels included: wholesale financing institutions, microfinance networks and associations, rating agencies, and international funders.

Notes: a. Definitions may vary from one network or agency to another but the same terminology for the indicator is used.
b. MicroRate has used number of loans, which is equivalent to number of active borrowers.

Sources: WOCCU & ACCION: SEEP FSWG - Performance Monitoring Systems Report; MicroRate: Technical Guide, Actual Report; PlaNet Finance: www.planetfinance.org, Appraisal and Rating Report

Box 6.3
Pali Karma-Sahayak Foundation (PKSF)

PKSF is a semi-autonomous, national-level wholesale financing institution in Bangladesh. It provides loans to about 150 retail-level MFIs in rural Bangladesh, at interest rates slightly below commercial borrowing rates, utilizing donor funds principally from the World Bank. It plays an important role in the areas of capacity building and advocacy.

PKSF has been successful in establishing eligibility criteria that reflect high performance standards and solid institutional evaluations. While most MFIs in Bangladesh use various group-lending methodologies, eligibility for funds is not based on the use of a particular group or individual lending method.

PKSF uses core financial and operating performance indicators and definitions that are similar to those used by leading microfinance networks and rating agencies (Box 6.5). Its institutional assessment tool focuses on:

- The adequacy of systems and methodologies used by the MFI to evaluate borrowers.

- Viability of the MFI, including operating methods and systems, human resource development programs, building of an institutional culture, financial management, and internal controls.

- Financial and operating performance of the institutions, including measures of self-sufficiency, portfolio quality, productivity, and financial ratios.

PKSF is playing a leading role in building a simple system of performance indicators and definitions, for use in building transparency and performance in the microfinance industry in Bangladesh. The managing director of PKSF chairs the technical committee which the central bank governor has asked to build these performance indicators for the microfinance industry as a whole; CDF, the microfinance network in Bangladesh, and leading microfinance practitioners participate in this committee.

It is important to establish key performance indicators and norms for microfinancing institutions, across the spectrum of size, stage, and legal structures. These indicators and norms can be used by regulators in monitoring

Box 6.4
Sa-Dhan in India

Sa-Dhan, the Association of Community Development Finance Institutions, is the leading network of microfinance institutions in India. Established in 1998, during the policy change work led by Indian microfinance practitioners, FWWB and WWB, Sa-Dhan has played a leading role in getting the recommendations of the 1998 policy forum and 1999 task force implemented. Part of the consensus report for the policy forum was consensus on key performance standards in microfinance.

In the last two years, Sa-Dhan has led the work to build common performance indicators and standards among its members. Sa-Dhan has developed consensus and understanding among MFI leaders on which performance indicators are the most important, and why the collection, verification, and dissemination of performance standards by Sa-Dhan is key.

Sa-Dhan's work on developing performance indicators and standards has produced the following consensus among leading MFIs in India:

- All MFIs should commit to incremental performance improvements on all key dimensions, and should commit to eventually achieving high absolute performance levels.

- MFIs should receive support in building the capabilities to meet high performance standards, and to using performance indicators as internal management tools.

- A careful process was adopted to gather information, build capacity, create agreed indicators, establish good and best practice standards over time, and see meeting the standards as a step to meeting full regulatory standards where appropriate.

In the early days, Sa-Dhan saw its work on performance indicators as a precursor to building a body for "self-regulation" of the microfinance industry. Sa-Dhan and its members now see this work on performance indicators and standards as a key measure in itself in building transparency and commitment to performance improvements in the range of microfinance institutions in India. Sa-Dhan works closely with the Micro-Credit Rating and Guarantees International Ltd., formerly M-CRIL. This India-based rating agency for microfinance institutions has played a key role in building transparency and commitment to performance among the MFIs it has rated.

Box 6.5
Microfinance Rating Agencies

At present, three specialized rating agencies operate in the microfinance industry. Each has a different regional focus, and each uses its own standardized approach to evaluating MFIs.

	MicroRate[a]	Micro-Credit Ratings and Guarantees International Limited (formerly M-CRIL)[b]	PlaNet Finance[c]
Geographic Scope	Mostly Latin America	Asia	Sub-Saharan Africa, Middle East/North Africa, Latin America, Eastern Europe, Asia
Number of Institutions Rated	70 (since 1997)	97 (since 1998)	34 (since 1999)
Methodology	This methodology analyzes five core areas of MFI financial and operational performance: Management and Governance, Management Information Systems, Financial Conditions, Credit Operations, and Portfolio Analysis.	The rating instrument uses minimum financial and other performance conditions in addition to scoring on governance aspects (13%), management factors (38%) and financial performance (49%) to arrive at a risk grade.	The 26 indicators are grouped under six areas of risks (GIRAFE): Governance, Information, Risk Analysis, Funding, Efficiency, and Profitability. There are two stages to the rating process: evaluation and formal rating.
Rating Scale	Does not actually rate institutions, but offers opinions of creditworthiness by marking an evaluation with "Recommend", "Watch", or "Caution".	From α+++ (highest safety, excellent systems —most highly recommended) to γ (highest risk, poor systems —not worth considering).	A global rating is given, from G1 to G5, along with a composite rating, scoring the six areas of assessment from "e" to "a".
Approach Bias	Strong on financial track record and benchmarking against peers.	Strong on capacity constraints based on specific issues.	Strong on management, governance, and best practices.

Sources: a. MicroRate Web site; b. Mcrilnews, M-Cril newsletter, vol. 4 no. 4, July 2002; c. PlaNet Finance Web site

the microfinance portfolios and organizational capabilities of regulated banks, finance companies, MFIs, and cooperative banks. For the broader set of unregulated MFIs, these performance indicators and standards can be used to build transparency in the microfinance industry, and to gear the entire industry to similar performance objectives.[1] Table 6.1 provides the key performance indicators in microfinance, used by a range of country, regional, and global networks, international funders, and microrating agencies. While definitions still differ slightly across groups, there is a rapid convergence in definitions that will make it possible to compare performance of institutions around the world.[2]

• Wholesale financing institutions should use rigorous absolute and incremental performance standards in establishing eligibility criteria for microfinancing institutions accessing loan funds on commercial or semi-commercial terms. While some government wholesale or apex institutions have gotten caught in mandates to move large amounts to institutions that do not meet rigorous performance standards, the best private and wholesale institutions have been successful in using rigorous eligibility criteria in providing loan funds to induce transparency, consistency in reporting, and performance improvements in retail microfinance institutions.

• Microfinance networks and associations have major roles to play in building consensus on which performance indicators will be used, building capabilities in MFIs to establish and use performance data, collecting and verifying the performance data, and determining with network members when to make performance data available to other MFIs, funders and the general public, in the aggregate or for individual institutions.

• Specialized microfinance rating agencies play important roles as third party evaluators of microfinance institutions. Most of these agencies do not actually rate MFIs; rather they provide a systematic, external evaluation of operations and performance. For both regulated and unregulated institutions, these rating agencies can help provide reassurances to domestic and international investors on the relative and absolute institutional soundness and performance of microfinance institutions. Also, by using standardized evaluation approaches and performance definitions across MFIs, a rating agency encourages transparency, benchmarking, and performance improvements in the institutions rated.

While microfinance rating agencies provide an important information bridge between MFIs and some commercial investors, other commercial sources still are looking for ratings from traditional, internationally recognized rating agencies such as Standard and Poor's. Microfinance rating agencies have begun forging alliances with the traditional rating agencies to build joint credit risk rating products. It would be an important step if mainstream rating agencies were to get involved in rating MFIs, based on a clear understanding of the special nature of microfinance. There are currently some steps being taken in the right direction:

- Publications by the *Microbanking Bulletin* and others on the performance of a growing number of largely successful microfinancing institutions, enabling benchmarking with institutions of similar sizes from similar contexts.

- Donors that use similar performance indicators and evaluation methods reinforce the performance standards and norms in the industry. A number of donors have done extensive work to develop a coherent set of performance indicators for microfinance. It is important that head office and field-level staff of all donors are familiar with microfinance performance indicators and institutional evaluation methods, to avoid undermining the local microfinance industry.

- Audit firms. Though most accounting firms are not yet skilled at understanding how to evaluate microfinance institutions or portfolios, their use of similar performance indicators would increase the rigor, thoroughness, and credibility of audits of MFIs.

These performance monitoring systems are *not* self-regulation. Much confusion has been created around the loose use of the term self-regulation. The authors believe that the use of the term regulation should be used only when the regulator has the power to disband the institution, withhold a license, or provide other censures. While these performance monitoring systems are important in building transparency and commitment to excellence in the microfinance industry, they should not be seen as a substitute for building the changes in prudential regulations and legal structures needed to encourage sound microfinance by regulated financial institutions and the increased reliance on savings and commercial borrowings by microfinance institutions. Performance monitoring systems are intended to:

- Build transparency in the microfinance industry, by introducing common performance indicators and definitions.
- Create shared commitment and healthy competition among MFIs to improve performance.

- Facilitate the flow of concessional, semi-commercial, and commercial funding to high-performing institutions at different stages of development.

- Help networks and other service providers tailor the mix of technical and financial services, to help MFIs improve performance, outreach, and innovation.

Banking Regulation That Fits the Needs of Microfinance Portfolios

Until recently, most central banks and bank superintendencies have not seen the importance of understanding the nature of microfinance. This is changing. From Uganda to the Dominican Republic to the Philippines, top policymakers from finance ministries and central banks recognize the importance of microfinance, and are ensuring that those officials responsible for drafting laws and regulations and for supervising MFIs understand the business and the special features of providing financial services to large numbers of poor people.

One key measure that central banks and bank supervisors have taken is to modify conventional regulatory requirements to fit the needs of microfinance operations—regardless of whether these operations are conducted by a specialized microfinance institution or form a small part of the overall portfolio of a commercial bank (see Annexes 6.4 and 6.5). These special features of microfinance include:

- The limited size of the microfinance market relative to the assets of the financial sector, due to the need for very small loans by large numbers of poor people, reducing the risks of microfinance to the financial system.

- The practice among most successful microfinancing institutions of mitigating credit risk not by requiring conventional collateral, but rather by making very small, short-term loans with gradual increases in loan sizes and maturities, using simple processes for evaluating business and credit risk, and executing strong systems to ensure excellent on-time repayment.

- The high transaction costs of making very small loans, necessitating high interest rates to cover operating and financial costs.

- The importance of providing rapid and convenient access to financial services to poor people spread across urban slums and dispersed rural areas, necessitating different approaches to branching and distribution systems, use of simple loan documentation systems, and recognition that in many settings cash transactions will need to take place outside branch premises.

- The fact that, in most countries, microfinance services to the poor have been built by non-bank, unregulated institutions, that, while performing well, may not have the scale or sophistication to deal with typical reporting requirements.

Key dimensions in policy, banking regulation, and supervision adapted to the needs of microfinance include the following:

- *Interest rates ceilings need to be removed on microloans.* The single most effective way for the government to promote financial services for the poor is to liberalize interest rates. The single most damaging thing a government can do to destroy access to financial services by poor people is to impose interest rate caps. Microfinance institutions need to be able to cover the high transaction costs of making very small loans. Poor borrowers want sustained access to financial services, not subsidies. While some microfinance operations use high interest rates to cover inefficiencies, experience demonstrates that competition from a range of suppliers is the best way to introduce pressure to improve efficiency. Government policymakers and politicians have a key role to play in getting the general public to understand why interest rates for microloans must be higher than for corporate finance. Building this broad understanding of why relatively high interest rates are needed if financially sustainable financial services are to be built for millions of poor people is key—avoiding and countering attacks that MFIs and banks are charging the poor usurious interest rates.

- *Evaluating portfolio risk.* Most bank regulation bases risk assessment of the portfolio on the strength of the collateral on the loans. In most microfinance methodologies, traditional collateral is not used. In most individual lending methodologies, risk is reduced through: evaluations of the cash-flow of the microbusiness and the household, increasingly complemented by loan scoring; by the provision of very small loans with short maturities, with the amounts and maturities increased based on excellent on-time repayments; and the use of personal guarantees. In group lending, peer pressure and guarantees, mandatory savings amounts, and disciplined delivery and collection on small loans are used to reduce risk. The insistence by bank regulators that institutions use conventional collateral would radically reduce the ability of institutions to serve poor clients with limited assets. In several countries—including the Philippines, Bolivia, the Dominican Republic, and Pakistan—bank regulators no longer base their risk assessments of microfinance portfolios on the underlying collateral. Rather, the regulators now look at the maintenance of excellent aggregate portfolio quality, with rigorous standards on loan loss provisioning and reserves, and at the adequacy of systems to evaluate risk and maintain portfolio quality.

- *Reporting and underlying loan documentation.* It is important that reporting requirements are rigorous, but simple, to reflect the relative small size of many MFIs. While large scale financial institutions are accustomed to and able to deal with elaborate reporting, one incentive to encourage bank involvement in microfinance would be to keep reporting requirements on microfinance portfolios simple. Underlying loan documentation should be available at the institution, but the large numbers of small transactions make it too cumbersome and costly to include individual loan documents as part of the reporting system. Summary reports on clients and loans can be generated from the MFI's management information system.

- *Microfinance capabilities and systems.* Regulations and norms on microfinance activity need to include a review of the rigor and appro-

---

Box 6.6
Creating a Sound Country Regulatory and
Policy Framework: The Case of the Philippines

Over the last five years, microfinance leaders—operating as members of the Philippine Coalition on Standards in Microfinance, and as representatives on the Credit Council—have helped policymakers in the Central Bank, Monetary Board, and key ministries gain a deep understanding of microfinance, and establish a set of pro-poor, pro-microfinance policies and regulations. WWB has supported the initiatives of country leaders at key junctures.

Beginning in 1991, the government took a decidedly pro-microfinance stance and enacted legislation that was favorable to the sector. The National Strategy for Microfinance was adopted in 1996, and had as its principles:

- Creating a greater role for private sector MFIs in providing financial services.

- Building an enabling policy environment.

- Enacting market-oriented financial and credit policies.

- Ensuring the non-participation of government in provision of credit.

Some of the key measures taken by the Central Bank and Government of the Philippines—issued as policy statements, legislative changes, and administrative circulars—include the following:

- Exemption from rules on interest rates for microfinance activities, with a statement that interest rates charged on microloans should not be lower than prevailing market rates, to reflect the higher costs of making small loans, and to ensure the financial sustainability of microfinance activity.

- Government has removed itself from direct involvement in making microloans, eliminating over 100 subsidy-based, failed government microcredit programs.

- The risk on a financial institution's microloan portfolio is no longer evaluated on the basis of collateral, but rather on the aggregate portfolio quality and track record, with no collateral required, but with rigorous portfolio quality, provisioning and loan loss reserve requirements.

- For rural, thrift, and commercial banks that desire to build microlending as part of their core business, requirements include: a vision statement expressing commitment to reach low income clients; managers and staff with experience in microfinance; at least 20 percent of the paid-up capital needs to be by persons or entities with experience in microfinance; and the operations manual needs to be consistent with the core principles of microfinance.

- Rural, development, and commercial banks that have microfinance as their principal activity are exempted from the moratorium on the establishment of new banks, and the moratorium on establishing new branches; rural banks established for microfinance are exempt from gross receipts tax for five years from license date.

Source: Circulars 272,273,282 and Rural Banks Act 1992.

priateness of risk-evaluating methodologies and manuals, the adequacy of loan documentation, well-integrated management information systems that generate the needed reports in a timely and reliable manner, and adequate internal controls. Performance indicators need to reflect good practice in microfinance. It is critically important that the central bank or bank superintendency invests in training its own staff to understand how to evaluate the key systems, capabilities, manuals, and performance of microfinance portfolios, operations, and institutions. In a number of cases, special units in the central bank and bank superintendency have been created to provide the needed specialized know-how in microfinance.

- *Branch operations.* Microlending and microsavings operations can operate out of conventional bank branches; normally these need to be supplemented by smaller, simpler outlets, including collection points, temporary outlets in marketplaces, mobile banking, or the use of village groups as distribution points for disbursements and collections. In many countries, the definition of a branch needs to be modified to accommodate these unconventional structures. Also, institutions engaged in microfinance need to be able to conduct cash transactions outside the branch premises. Finally, where the bank regulators have created limitations on the establishment of new branches, microfinance institutions need to be given exemptions, since they are targeting a set of clients not reached by conventional bank operations.

Legal Structures That Work for Regulated Microfinance Institutions

In addition to building policies and regulations that fit the nature of microfinance as an activity, legal structures need to be built or adapted to enable a subset of strong microfinance NGOs to convert to regulated financial institutions that can mobilize public savings and rapidly expand commercial funding. Specialized legal structures for deposit-taking MFIs may be established or the parameters of existing legal structures can be modified to fit the needs of microfinance.

Sooner rather than later, many of the larger microfinance institutions will need to rely on a combination of equity capital, commercial loans, mobilization of institutional and individual savings, and bond issues to finance their growth. Recent experience indicates the advantages that regulated financial institutions have over NGOs in offering borrowers deposit facilities, mobilizing institutional savings, issuing bonds, and providing assurances to commercial lenders.

Bank regulation is established to protect savers, investors, and the banking industry. It is now agreed in most quarters that:

- MFIs engaged exclusively in microlending—be they NGOs, trusts, or companies—need not be subject to banking regulation.

- Microfinance institutions that mobilize mandatory savings as a collateral substitute for borrowers and do not intermediate this savings should not be subject to prudential banking regulation.

- Except for small cooperative and other community-based institutions, entities that mobilize more than small aggregate amounts of savings from non-borrowers should be subject to regulation, either by the central bank or its designated authority.

There is still debate as to whether unregulated microfinance institutions should be able to mobilize voluntary savings from borrowers. Until recently, the consensus was that most microfinance borrowers will be net borrowers, meaning that if the MFI were to fail, the borrower will owe more to the institution than the institution owes to the borrower. However, while this may be true in the aggregate, it may well not be true for all borrowers. What seems clear is that unregulated MFIs that mobilize savings from borrowers should deposit these savings in a bank, should not be free to use these savings to finance its lending portfolio, and should attempt to ensure that borrowings exceed savings at the individual account level as well as in the aggregate.

For specialized MFIs that seek to become regulated financial institutions, features of the available legal structures are key. In the Philippines, for example, available legal structures—commercial banks, rural banks, thrift banks, and cooperatives—have been adequate vehicles to enable solid microfinance NGOs to convert to regulated financial institutions, without requiring modifications in the legal structures. By contrast, in Colombia, the only private equity structures are commercial banks and commercial finance corporations (CFCs). While local leaders are working with policymakers to make needed changes in the CFC structure, the present CFC structure offers few advantages to a microfinance NGO: CFCs have not been allowed to borrow from the banking system, CFCs cannot mobilize savings from the public, and CFCs have high minimum capital and capital adequacy requirements. Thus, until the needed modifications are made, a microfinance NGO converting to a CFC in Colombia would need to incur the increased costs of compliance, reporting, and taxation, with an actual reduction in powers to

---

Box 6.7
Regulations on Ownership of Regulated MFIs

In the Philippines, the central bank provides for 100 percent local ownership in rural banks, the structure that CARD Bank adopted, and that other microfinance NGOs that seek to convert are likely to adopt. This policy reflects the belief that locally owned structures provide the strongest accountability for relatively small banks that focus on financial services to local communities. CARD Bank's ownership comprises the NGO, board and staff, and clients. This option may have underestimated the value of international investors as sources of funding and expertise.

In contrast, the draft legislation in Uganda for Microfinance Deposit Taking Institutions (MDIs) allows a single entity to own no more than 20 percent shares. In the context of Africa, this runs the risk of having regulated MFIs be 80 percent owned by international donors and donor funded international NGOs, facilities, and banks. This formula introduces the risk of local institutions losing control.

---

mobilize capital or integrate itself into domestic financial markets.

In several countries, including Bolivia, the Philippines, Gambia, Ghana, Uganda, and Pakistan, measures have been taken to create microfinance-friendly legal structures that enable regulated MFIs to mobilize equity, savings, and commercial borrowings, and which reflect the nature of microfinance. Key dimensions include:

- Relatively low minimum capital requirements. Experience demonstrates that minimum capital requirements should be set high enough to discourage a plethora of small, weak, undercapitalized institutions, but low enough to encourage solid MFIs that wish to mobilize deposits from the public to enter the regulated financial system. Depending on country contexts, the minimum capital requirements should probably be set at US$500,000 to US$5 million.

- Appropriate capital adequacy ratios. Views differ on whether capital adequacy ratios should be set at the same levels as for commercial banks (normally 8 percent) or higher. Normally, strong MFIs experience less volatility in portfolio performance than do commercial banks, meaning that 8 percent would be conservative and prudent. However,

Box 6.8
Taxation in Microfinance: Case Study on Russia

The lack of a legal basis and an inadequate tax structure for microfinance activities in Russia for non-banking institutions has been a major obstacle for expansion of their own operations and for the development of the sector in general. In early 1999, The Russia Women's Microfinance Network (RWMN) identified these constraints; subsequently, RWMN built strategies to address these obstacles, with technical and financial support from WWB. The following are results to date:

- Profit Tax on Grants. On May 6, 1999, President Yeltsin signed a new law on non-taxable grants, which extended this tax exemption to NGOs involved in "technical support." Microfinance programs fall under the definition of technical support activities and therefore are now free to receive grant funding without paying 35 percent profit tax on the grant amount. These important changes in the law were incorporated due to the intensive advocacy work of RWMN and other NGOs. RWMN also influenced other key changes in the law that reduced burdensome requirements for foreign institutions that provide grant support to Russian organizations. The law was signed in May 1999.

- Microfinance as a Main Activity for Non-Banking Institutions. Again, due to efforts by RWMN, official letters from President Putin and Speaker of the Duma, G. Selesnev, were received by RWMN formally communicating that non-banking institutions engaged in microlending do not require licensing.

- Value-Added Tax (VAT). Changes proposed by RWMN to the Law on VAT made it possible for non-banking institutions registered as private funds to be engaged in microlending activities and to be exempt them from the value-added tax. The Law was signed by the President in January 2000 and became effective immediately.

- Interest Expense Deduction. Amendments to Part II (Profit Tax), Article 25 of the Tax Code made it possible for non-banking institutions to deduct interest expense on loans from their taxable income. The Law was signed by the President in August 2001 and became effective in January 2002. This measure reduces costs of MFIs working with borrowed funds, and also helps MFI clients who can now deduct interest expenses on loans obtained from MFIs.

as the Bolivian experience demonstrates, if there is deterioration in portfolio quality of MFIs, contagion across institutions can occur. While microfinance institutions tend to have highly diversified portfolios by sector and low concentration of portfolios, grassroots or political moves can create a run on microfinance loans. Thus, while this situation has occurred only rarely, a slightly more conservative capital adequacy ratio such as 10 to 12 percent may be justified. Furthermore, conservative capital adequacy ratios can serve to boost investor confidence in this relatively young industry, as investors learn how to evaluate microfinance institutions.

• Ownership structures. Regulations regarding the equity structures and ownership mix in regulated microfinance institutions will be key to the future of the industry. Regulations should be flexible, enabling a balance in stakeholders, which can include: the originating NGO; board, staff, and clients of the originating and converted structures; and domestic and international commercial and social investors. One worrying trend is the dominance of international donors and donor-funded funds in the ownership of some MFIs. It is important that the originating NGO have a substantial stake in the converted MFI ownership structure, to help ensure that the focus on the poor and high performance are maintained. Choosing domestic or foreign partners with knowledge of and commitment to sustainable finance for the poor is key. Experience demonstrates the value of having the originating microfinance NGO retain major interests and accountability in achieving the mission and performance. It also shows the value of voiding major interests by those donors or donor-funded funds which do not have the depth of knowledge or sustained commitment to microfinance, as well as the importance of cultivating local commercial and social investors to reinforce local accountability.

High Performance Standards

It is essential that licensing requirements include norms that help ensure that only high-performing microfinance NGOs are allowed to become regulated financial institutions. These norms and prerequisites need to fit what works in microfinance; bank supervisors responsible for reviewing the systems and performance of MFIs applying to become regulated institutions need to understand the nature of microfinance.

• MFIs should be fully financially self-sufficient, with positive returns on assets, prior to considering conversion or being allowed to convert.

Box 6.9
Regulation and Supervision of MFIs:
The Case of Uganda

The Micro-Deposit Taking Institutions Bill of 2001 (MDI Bill) provides an example of regulation and supervision that allows those institutions that are ready, willing, and able to mobilize deposits in a prudent manner to do so. By adopting a tiered structure to the regulation of microfinance activities, the MDI Bill creates an enabling environment for the continued development of MFIs in the country. It acknowledges that microfinance NGOs are a legitimate and important part of Uganda's financial system, acknowledges their unique needs, and furthers the capacity building of these organizations.

The MDI Bill creates a tiered system: Tier 1 institutions are commercial banks; Tier 2 institutions are licensed credit institutions; Tier 3 Microfinance Deposit-Taking Institutions (MDIs) may take deposits from the public and on-lend them to the public; Tier 4 institutions may only accept compulsory savings from clients, and Tier 4 cooperatives may take voluntary savings from members and on-lend them only to members. As part of the MDI Bill, an MDI Deposit Protection Fund will be established by the Bank of Uganda to protect depositors.

Of the approximately 500 MFIs currently in operation in Uganda, it is expected that only a very few (three to five) will qualify for MDI status upon passage of the MDI Bill. This means that the vast majority of MFIs in Uganda will not be subject to Bank of Uganda regulation and supervision. As these Tier 4 institutions grow, they may qualify for a Tier 3 MDI license and be subject to the provisions of the MDI Bill. There is currently a variety of Tier 4 organizations, including: approximately ten to fifteen medium sized MFIs (with 5,000 to 25,000 clients); approximately forty smaller MFIs (with 500 to 5,000 clients); and a large number of MFIs with fewer than 500 clients.

To assist with the expansion of these Tier 4 institutions, the Ugandan Microfinance Network (AMFIU), with support from the Bank of Uganda and the Ministry of Finance have begun to develop a set of performance indicators that can be used as benchmarks for the various categories of Tier 4 MFIs.

Source: Micro-Deposit Taking Institutions Bill of 2001

Even in microfinance-friendly policy environments, the conversion, compliance, and tax costs will create an additional burden on MFIs.

- Only those MFIs that have excellent portfolio quality, efficient and well-documented lending procedures, strong internal controls, and a strong track record of operating at a reasonable scale of operations should be allowed to convert.

- MFIs that are converting should have begun work to build their capacity to mobilize savings and manage deposits prudently, if they intend to mobilize savings from the public.

Appropriate Tax Treatment

In some countries, MFIs may face cascading tax burdens, including tax on grants, profits, value added, and/or interest. These cascading tax burdens should be removed (see Box 6.8 on Russia). In many countries, microfinance NGOs are not subject to taxation. Conversion to a regulated structure normally involves high conversion costs in addition to permanent cost increases due to regulatory and reporting requirements. The immediate introduction of high tax burdens can make this transition extremely burdensome. To encourage converting MFIs to maintain their focus on financing for the poor, temporary tax relief may be justified.

Prudential regulation is only as good as the supervision behind it. Until recently, most central banks and bank superintendencies have not seen the importance of understanding the nature and nuances of microfinance. Often, legislation and regulatory measures for microfinance have been drafted without due consideration to the actual burdens of supervising many small, unconventional microfinance institutions. As some wise regulators say, do not regulate what you cannot supervise. It is important both to the regulated MFIs as well as to the regulators that reporting requirements be rigorous but simple. It is also important to anticipate the number of institutions that are likely to be regulated over a period, and to build this capacity in the supervising entity.

Conclusion

Listening to the needs of poor clients and the institutions that serve them needs to shape the policies and regulations for microfinance. Poor clients say that they want:

- Access to loans that are provided quickly and close to their place of business.

- Facilities to deposit their voluntary savings.
- A range of financial products, including business, housing, and education loans, various saving vehicles, and insurance.
- Access to financial services, not subsidies.

A policy environment that responds to the financial services that poor people want:

- Encourages institutions to operate efficiently.
- Enables institutions to build delivery systems that go to the clients.
- Removes interest rate ceilings and subsidy cultures, encouraging competition as the means to reduce costs to poor clients.
- Encourages sustainable microfinance services and institutions, that grow with their clients—eliminating subsidized, short-lived government programs.
- Eliminates traditional collateral requirements that most poor clients cannot meet.
- Ensures prudential regulations that protect the savings of the poor.
- Removes policy barriers to the profitable provision of microlending, savings, insurance, and pension services to the poor, to help poor people build economic activities and assets, and mitigate risks.

Microfinance needs to be recognized as a vital part of the financial system, dedicated to meeting the financial needs of poor clients in a responsive and financially sustainable manner. This financial systems approach recognizes the important roles that a broad range of regulated and unregulated institutions can and do play in providing financial services to poor people.

Shared performance standards, transparency, and accountability are key to building solid and responsive services for poor households—for both regulated and unregulated microfinance institutions. Since prudential regulations will only cover a small number of those institutions involved in microlending, the role of microfinance networks, wholesale lenders, microfinance rating agencies, auditors, and international funders will all be key in building transparency and performance standards in the microfinance industry. A strong consensus is emerging on the key indicators and definitions to measure outreach, efficiency, portfolio, profitability, capital structure, and liquidity. These performance monitoring systems are not self-regulation. Rather, they are important in building transparency and commitment to excellence in the microfinance industry.

Emphasis needs to be given to introducing changes that reflect the needs of microfinance operations—regardless of whether these are conducted by a specialized microfinance institution or form a small part of the overall portfolio of a commercial bank or finance company. The policy and regulatory framework for microfinance is to encourage entry and expansion of microfinance services by a broad range of regulated financial institutions. Increasingly, policymakers and regulators are recognizing microloans as an important and legitimate loan class, with its own features. Key policy and regulatory measures are:

- Removal of interest rate ceilings on microloans.

- Evaluation of risk based not on collateral, but on a rigorous evaluation of the aggregate quality of the microloan portfolio and operational soundness, with strict provisioning policies and reserve requirements.

- Rigorous, but simple, reporting requirements on microlending operations.

- Flexibility in establishing branches and distribution systems, including allowance of cash transactions outside branch premises, particularly in rural areas.

Prudential regulation is needed for those specialized MFIs that seek to mobilize savings from the public. Banking regulation need not apply to MFIs engaged exclusively in microlending: those that mobilize mandatory savings from borrowers as a collateral substitute or small community-based institutions that mobilize small amounts of savings from non-borrowing members. Debate exists on whether unregulated microfinance institutions should be able to mobilize savings from borrowers. If done, these savings should be deposited in a bank and not be used to finance the microloan portfolio, and MFIs should seek to ensure that borrowings exceed savings at the individual account level as well as in the aggregate.

For the small but important subset of specialized MFIs that seek to become regulated financial institutions, new legal structures may be needed, or existing legal structures adapted to incorporate the following key features:

- Relatively low minimum capital requirements, in most contexts between US$500,000 and US$5 million.

Annex 6.1 Ownership Composition by Investor Type: Selected MFIs (Latest available data, 2000–2002)

Name	Country	Foreign			Local			
		ID	PFI	Total	LNGO	LCI	LGSI	Total
CARD	Philippines			0.00%	100.00%			100.00%
PRODEM	Bolivia			0.00%	83.64%	16.36%		100.00%
BancoADEMI	Dominican Republic	17.00%		17.00%	83.00%			83.00%
EcoFuturo	Bolivia	22.02%		22.02%	75.21%	2.77%		77.98%
CERUDEB	Uganda	24.00%		24.00%		4.60%	71.40% (1)	76.00%
FIE	Bolivia	24.11%	1.75%	25.86%	70.14%	4.00%		74.14%
Mibanco	Peru	29.47%		29.47%	61.43%	9.10%		70.53%
Compartamos	Mexico	32.50%		32.50%	62.80%	4.70%		67.50%
BancoSolidario	Ecuador	40.61%		40.61%	36.26%	23.14%		59.39%
FINAMERICA	Colombia	41.31%		41.31%		4.59%	54.10% (2)	58.69%
CALPIA	El Salvador	41.85%		41.85%	40.40%	0.21%	17.54%	58.15%
Caja los Andes	Bolivia	46.70%		46.70%	46.90%	6.40%		53.30%
ACLEDA	Cambodia	49.00%		49.00%	51.00%			51.00%
XacBank	Mongolia	58.59%		58.59%			41.41% (3)	41.41%
K-Rep	Kenya	61.20%		61.20%	38.80%			38.80%
BancoSol	Bolivia	73.45%		73.45%	23.64%	2.91%		26.55%

(1) Mainly religious foundations; (2) Mainly government development bank; (3) Local NGO investors

ID: International Donors and Donor-backed Investors; PFI: Private Foreign Investors; LNGO: Originating NGO, Board, Staff, Clients; LCI: Local Commercial Investors; LGSI: Local Government and Social Investors

Sources: Institutional annual reports, Virtual Microfinance Market Web site, Microfinance Network Web site; MicroRate rating report, institutional Web sites

Annex 6.2 Most Regulated MFIs Rely on Institutional Not Individual Deposits (US$ equivalents, end 2000)

Name of MFI	Country	Gross Portfolio Outstanding	Active Deposits	AD/GPO	Active Deposits	
					Institutional	Individual
Caja los Andes	Bolivia	52,633,750	25,278,962	48%	74%	26%
PRODEM	Bolivia	33,627,864	25,280,800	75%	84%	16%
BancoSolidario	Bolivia	72,221,000	44,590,000	62%	86%	14%
Fincomun	Mexico	3,500,000	8,500,000	243%	89%	11%
BancoADEMI	Dominican Republic	64,875,950	25,265,700	39%	92%	8%
FIE	Bolivia	27,483,000	11,025,000	40%	98%	2%

Institutional deposits normally refer to time deposits mobilized from a narrow set of institutions, often being other financial intermediaries.

Annex 6.3   Statements of Core Principles in Building Financial Systems That Work for the Poor Majority

	India Consensus Report 1998	AFMIN Consensus 2002	Country Scorecard 2000
Microfinance is one of the effective means to reduce poverty.	X	X	X
Poor entrepreneurs want rapid and simple access to financial services, not subsidies.		X	X
Microfinance is about investing in people and institutions, rather than subsidizing clients or relying on permanent subsidies for microfinance institutions.		X	X
Institutions engaged in microfinance should be able to charge the interest rates needed to cover the high costs of making small loans, and to become sustainable.	X	X	X
Laws and regulations should encourage a range of legal structures to provide financial services to poor people, including credit and savings cooperatives, NGOs, regulated microfinance institutions, finance companies, and commercial banks with microfinance portfolios.	X	X	X
Regulation and supervision should fit the various stages and legal structures of organizations engaged in microfinance.	X	X	X
Performance standards, prudential norms and regulations, and reporting requirements should fit the characteristics of the microfinance sector, for example: reliance on overall portfolio performance rather than on traditional collateral on loans.	X	X	X
Microfinance institutions (MFIs) that meet appropriate safety and soundness standards should be given the regulatory structures that allow them to mobilize voluntary savings from borrowers and from the general public.	X	X	X
Appropriate legal structures are needed to enable institutions engaged in microfinance to be financially viable, to meet the needs of target clients, and to mobilize domestic and international resources.	X	X	X
Favorable tax treatment can encourage the development of the needed infrastructure in microfinance institutions, and reflect the high costs of providing financial services to poor people.	X	X	X

Annex 6.4   Examples of Regulation under Banking Law and Special Microfinance Legislation

	Country	Nature of Legislation/Clauses
Under Banking Legislation	Bolivia	BancoSol became a commercial bank under banking legislation.
	Kenya	KREP Bank was established as commercial bank, with only one adjustment to banking law dealing with regulations on branching.
	Philippines	Prior legislation allowed small, medium, and large banks to mobilize savings: commercial banks as well as rural banks, as well as thrift and cooperative banks. In 2001 and 2002, Central Bank Circulars made adjustments to reflect the needs of microfinance.
Special Legislation	Bolivia	Specialized structure—Private Financial Funds—enabled four microfinance NGOs to convert to for-profit, regulated equity structures. They are able to mobilize institutional and limited individual deposits.
	Colombia	Commercial Finance Company (CFC)—draft law would reduce minimum capital and capital adequacy requirements, and allow CFCs to borrow from financial institutions and mobilize savings from the public.
	Uganda	New legislation recognizes four sets of institutions for microfinance: commercial banks, cooperatives, deposit-taking MFIs, and microfinance NGOs. Only those specialized MFIs that mobilize and intermediate voluntary savings will be regulated. Four to six of the 500 microfinance NGOs are expected to convert into deposit-taking MFIs over the next three years.

Annex 6.5   Regulatory Components, Challenges, and Solutions for MFIs

Components of Regulation	Hurdles for MFIs	MFIs' Needs	Solutions
Licensing requirements	Conditions may be too onerous.	Simple procedures and documentation; enough time between granting of license and establishment of new institution.	Simple, straightforward licensing requirements, reasonable timeframe.
Minimum capital requirements	Minimum capital requirements are often barriers to entry.	Entry capital requirements that are reasonable.	Low minimum capital requirements, commensurate with risk profile of MFI.
Capital adequacy	Higher capital adequacy ratios than for traditional banks (under the Basel Committee guidelines).	Fairness across institutions.	Fairness in how assets are held.
Liquidity / Reserves	Requirements may be onerous; costs of maintaining reserves.	Adequate protection in case of downturn.	Fairness in how assets can be held.
Restrictions in the amount of lending without collateral	Rule on secured lending.	Unsecured loans or use of non-traditional collateral, generally without conventional collateral on microloans.	Require outstanding aggregate portfolio performance-based on portfolio at risk, with adequate loan loss provisioning and reserves.
Provisioning	Rules may be too complex.	Adequate provisioning is important in order to protect a loan portfolio not backed by collateral.	Clear rules and reporting requirements; not too many risk categories.
Reporting requirements	Heavy reporting requirements. Ratios institutions are required to report on may have different meanings, loan documentation requirements too heavy.	Simple reporting requirements focusing on overall performance indicators, generally without requiring reporting on individual loans.	Rigorous, but simple reporting requirements with MIS of MFI producing key reports.

Annex 6.5 (continued)

Components of Regulation	Hurdles for MFIs	MFIs' Needs	Solutions
Restrictions on operations	Branching limitations; too much interference into operations.	Decentralized branch/delivery structures, with flexibility on the location of new branches, and convenient hours of operation. Transparent and needs-based hiring and remuneration.	Freedom to operate; regulations based on assuring sound governance and professionalism, but not interventionist in terms of freedom to operate.
Ownership and equity	Limitations to ownership; Central Bank approvals.	NGO may be positioned to be principal shareholder; institution may want to have local ownership dominate with limited partnership of foreign investors.	Regulations which allow more concentration in ownership than for traditional banks; foreign investors may enter with relatively small share of capital.
Management	Requirements may not fit profile of those leading microfinance.	Need governance and management structure with strong skills in banking and microfinance.	Requirements based on needs of microfinance
Systems and Procedures	Expenditures regarding MIS, internal audits may be too high for smaller MFIs; excessive intrusion in operations	Systems designed for MFIs; freedom to operate	Requirements based on what it takes to make an MFI work.
Performance Standards	Performance indicators and standards often geared to commercial banks.	Performance indicators and standards geared to microfinance	Internationally recognized standards and common definitions

- Appropriate capital adequacy ratios, normally between 8 and 10 percent.

- Availability of a range of appropriate legal structures.

- Flexible ownership structures that encourage strong participation by the originating microfinance NGO, dominant local control, and a balance of stakeholders which can include, in addition to the originating NGO: board members, staff, and clients; and local and foreign commercial and social investors. Dominance by donors and donor-funded funds should be avoided.

- High-performance standards for those MFIs seeking to become regulated entities.

- Appropriate tax treatment, including provisions for temporary tax relief for those MFIs that convert.

- Limitations in banking supervision capacity recognized and addressed.

Increasingly, financial sector policymakers are recognizing the importance of microfinance, understanding its special features, and working with local microfinance leaders to ensure that the needed changes are made in financial sector policies, regulations, and support systems to encourage the growth of a sound, responsive financial system that works for the poor majority. While consensus exists on the key features of pro-poor financial systems, policies, regulations, and support services need to be designed to respond to each country context.

Endnotes

1. Performance indicators focus on key outreach, efficiency, and sustainability measures. These are distinct from 1) full institutional evaluations of an MFI and 2) detailed analysis of the poverty of borrowers or of the impact of loans. Each of these instruments is important for different purposes.
2. The recently released "Definitions of Selected Financial Terms, Ratios and Adjustments for Microfinance," available on the CGAP Web site, is the result of roundtable discussions between specialists from three Washington, D.C.-based development agencies (IDB, USAID, and CGAP) and three rating agencies specializing in microfinance (Microrate, M-CRIL, and PlaNet Rating). This document proposes standard definitions and suggests a standard method of calculating certain financial rations.
3. Bangladesh, Benin (West African Monetary Union), Bolivia, Bosnia-Herzegovina, Colombia, Dominican Republic, India, Kenya, Pakistan, Philippines, and Uganda.

Bibliography

ACTION. "ACTION's Women Development Activities." Unpublished paper. India.

ADAPTE. Client and spouse impact surveys collected October–December 2001 in Costa Rica.

ADEMCOL. "Social and Community Work as a Result From the Trust Bank Program." Unpublished report. Bogota, Colombia.

Ahmed, Syed Masud et al. "Two Studies on Health Care Seeking Behaviour and Sanitation Practices of BRAC Member and Non-member Households in Matlab, Bangladesh." BRAC-ICDDR,B Working Paper no. 22. Dhaka, Bangladesh: BRAC-ICDDR,B, 1998.

Amolat, Filipinas R. *Client Impact Assessment: KMBI Program Impact Assessment for Microfinance Implementation for Region 1.* 2001.

Ani, Carlos. *State of Microfinance in Bangladesh.* Presented in Dhaka, Bangladesh, April 2002. www.devjobsmail.org/bangla/page1.html.

Agricultural and Rural Management Training Institute (ARMTI). "Empowering Women Through Microfinance: ARMTI's Contribution." Unpublished paper. Nigeria, 2000.

ARMTI. "Empowering Women Through Microfinance: ARMTI's Contribution."

Ashe, Jeffrey and Lisa Parrott. *Impact Evaluation of PACT's Women's Empowerment Program in Nepal: A Savings and Literacy Led Alternative to Financial Institution Building.* Waltham, Mass.: Brandeis University, 2001.

Asian Development Bank, Regional Economic Monitoring Unit. "Asia Economic Monitor." Manila, Philippines: Asian Development Bank (April 2002): 17–19.

Asociación de Ayuda al Pequeño Trabajador y Empresario (ADAPTE). Client and spouse impact surveys collected October–December 2001 in Costa Rica.

Asociación para el Desarrollo Empresarial Colombiano (ADEMCOL). "Social and Community Work as a Result from the Trust Bank Program." Unpublished report. Bogotá, Colombia.

Ayo, Noni. "Empowerment of Women Through Microfinance: ARDCI's Experience." Catanduanes, Philippines: ARDCI, 2001.

Bagati, Deepali. "Microcredit and Empowerment of Women." Paper based on Ph.D. dissertation research at Bryn Mawr College, Pa., 2001.

Bangladesh Extension Education Services. "Empowering Women through Microfinance." 2001.

Bank for International Settlements: Basel Committee on Banking Supervision. "International Convergence on Capital Measurement & Capital Standards." July 1998.

Bank for International Settlements: Secretariat of the Basel Committee on Banking Supervision. "The New Basel Accord: An Explanatory Note." January 2001.

Barnes, Carolyn, Gayle Morris, and Gary Gaile. "An Assessment of the Impact of Microfinance Services in Uganda: Baseline Findings." AIMS Paper. Washington, D.C.: Management Systems International, 1998.

Bass, J. *Diagnostico del Programa de Microcrédito*. Proyecto de Innovación de la Microempresa (MICROSERVE). Washington, D.C.: USAID, May 1999.

Beijing Platform for Action. Fourth United Nations World Conference on Women, Beijing, China, 1995.

Ben Hamida, Essma. "Empowering Women Through Micro-Credit: A Case Study From Tunisia." Paper presented at the Civil Society Workshop Rehearsal, Cairo, Egypt, March 2000.

Bresnick, S. and Barbara MkNelly. *Poverty Profile of CRECER Credit with Education Client Households*. Davis, Calif.: Freedom from Hunger, 1999.

Canadian International Development Agency (CIDA). "CIDA's Policy on Gender Equality." Hull, Canada: CIDA, 1999.

———. *Guide to Gender-Sensitive Indicators*. Hull, Canada: Minister of Public Works and Government Services, 1997.

———. *The Why and How of Gender-Sensitive Indicators: A Project Level Handbook*. Hull, Canada: Minister of Public Works and Government Services, 1997.

Cerqueira, Maria Teresa and Christine M. Olson. "Nutrition Education in Developing Countries: An Examination of Recent Successful Projects," ch. 4 in P. Pinstrup-Andersen, D. Pelletier, and H. Alderman, eds. *Child Growth and Nutrition in Developing Countries*, Ithaca, N.Y.: Cornell University Press, 1995.

Chalfin, Brenda. "Risky Business: Economic Uncertainty, Market Reforms and Female Livelihoods in Northeast Ghana." *Development and Change* 31 (2000): 987–1008.

Chant, Sylvia. "Women-Headed Households: Poorest of the Poor? Perspectives from Mexico, Costa Rica and the Philippines." *IDS Bulletin* 28, no. 3 (1997): 26–48.

Cheston, Susy and Larry Reed. *Measuring Transformation: Assessing and Improving the Impact of Microcredit*. Washington, D.C.: Microcredit Summit Campaign, 1999. www.microcreditsummit.org/papers/impactpaper.htm.

Cheston, Susy, et al. *Measuring Transformation: Assessing and Improving the Impact of Microcredit, Part II: Implementing Impact Assessments and Monitoring Systems: A Practitioner Perspective from Zambia*. Washington, D.C.: Microcredit Summit Campaign, 2000.

Chua, Ronald T. et al. "Risk, Vulnerability, Assets and the Role of Financial Services in Reducing Vulnerability: A Study of the Women Clients of CARD Bay Laguna, Philippines." Paper submitted to CGAP, October 1999.

Churchill, Craig. "Bulletin Highlights and Tables—Reaching the Poor." *Microbanking Bulletin* 5. (September 2000). www.calmeadow.com/mbb2_index.html.

Clark, Gracia. *Onions Are My Husband: Survival and Accumulation by West African Market Women*. Chicago: University of Chicago Press, 1994.

Claure, P. "Evaluación del Impacto del Programa Integrado de Capacitación y Crédito de Pro Mujer, El Alto." La Paz: Pro Mujer, 2000.

Claure, P., M. Mollinedo, and S. Paredes. "Evaluación de Resultados del Programa de Capacitación y Crédito de Pro Mujer en Cochabamba." *Informe a Entidades Financieros* 2000.

Community Development Centre (CODEC). *Report on Women's Empowerment*. Bangladesh, 2001.

Conroy, John D. and Robyn Cornford. *The Role of Central Banks in Microfinance in Asia and the Pacific: Country Studies*. Manila, Philippines: Asian Development Bank, 2000.

Conroy, John D., Paul B. McGuire, and Ganesh B. Thapa. *Getting the Framework Right: Policy and Regulation for Microfinance in Asia*. Brisbane: Foundation for Development

Cooperation, 1998.

Consultative Group to Assist the Poorest (CGAP). "Linking Microfinance and Safety Net Programs in Include the Poorest: the Case of IGVGD in Bangladesh." *CGAP Focus Note,* no. 21 (May 2001).

———. *Focus on Financial Transparency: Building the Infrastructure of a Microfinance Industry,* CGAP Brochure. Washington, D.C.: CGAP, 2001.

———. "Focusing on Transparency." *Microbanking Bulletin* 7 (November 2001).

———. *The Poverty Audit: Guidelines for Determining the Depth of Outreach and Poverty Impact of Microfinance Institutions.* Draft. Washington, D.C.: CGAP, 2001. www.cgap.org.

———. "Water, Water Everywhere and Not a Drop to Drink." *Viewpoint,* January 2002.

Contento, I., G. I. Balch, Y. L. Bronner, et al. "The Effectiveness of Nutrition Education and Implications for Nutrition Education Policy, Programs and Research: A Review of Research." *J. Nutrition Education* 27, no. 6 (1995): Special Issue.

Creevey, Lucy. *Changing Women's Lives and Work: An Analysis of the Impacts of Eight Microenterprise Projects.* London: Intermediate Technology Publications, 1996.

Deere, Carmen Diana, Helen Safa, Peggy Antrobus et al. "Impact of the Economic Crisis on Poor Women and Their Households" in Visvanathan, Nalini et al., eds. *The Women, Gender and Development Reader.* London: Zed Books Ltd., 1997.

Del Conte, Alessandra. *Participatory Governance and Management Structures in Microfinance: The Case of Janashakti.* New York, N.Y.: International Coalition on Women and Credit, 2000. Available on the Web site of Women's World Banking: www.swwb.org.

Department for International Development (DFID). "Maximising the Outreach of Microfinance in Russia." *Research and Impact Assessment: Terms of Reference for FORA.* London: DFID, 2001.

Deshpanda, Rani. *Increasing Access and Benefits for Women: Practices and Innovations among Microfinance Institutions—Survey Results.* New York: UNCDF, 2001.

Dolphyne, Florence Abena. *The Emancipation of Women: An African Perspective.* Accra, Ghana: Ghana Universities Press, 1991.

Druschel, Kate et al. "State of the Microcredit Summit Campaign Report 2001." Washington, D.C.: Microcredit Summit Campaign Secretariat, 2001.

Dunford, Christopher. *What's Wrong with Loan Size?* Davis, Calif.: Freedom from Hunger, March 2002. www.ffhtechnical.org/publications/summary/loansize0302.html.

———. "Building Better Lives: Sustainable Integration of Microfinance with Education in Health, Family Planning and HIV/AIDS Prevention for the Poorest Entrepreneurs." Washington, D.C.: Microcredit Summit Campaign, 2001.

———. "The Holy Grail of Microfinance: 'Helping the Poor' and 'Sustainable'?" *Small Enterprise Development* 11, no. 1 (2000): 40–44.

Engle, Patrice. "Father's Money, Mother's Money, and Parental Commitment: Guatemala and Nicaragua." In Blumberg, RaeLesser et al., eds. *EnGENDERing Wealth and Well-Being: Empowerment for Global Change* Boulder, Colo.: Westview Press, 1995.

FDEA (Women Enterprise Development in Africa). Untitled report. 2000.

Gallardo, Joselito. *A Framework for Regulating Microfinance Institutions: The Experience in Ghana and the Philippines.* The World Bank, Financial Sector Development Department. Washington, D.C.: The World Bank, October 2001.

Getu, Makonen and Samuel Afrane. "The Transformation Side of Microfinance: An Impact

Study of UGAFODE's Micro-lending Program." Oak Brook, Ill.: Opportunity International–U.S., 2001.

Gibbons, David and Jennifer Meehan. *The Microcredit Summit Challenge: Working Towards Institutional Financial Self-Sufficiency while Maintaining a Commitment to Serving the Poorest Families.* Washington, D.C.: Microcredit Summit Campaign, 2000. www.micro creditsummit.org/papers/challengespaper.htm.

Goetz, Anne Marie and Rina Sen Gupta. "Who Takes the Credit? Gender, Power, and Control over Loan Use in Rural Credit Programs in Bangladesh." *World Development* 24, no. 1 (1996): 45–63.

Gons, Nathalie and Brian Branch. "The Road to Jinotega." Madison, Wisc.: WOCCU, 2001.

Gonzalez-Vega, Claudio. *Profile of the Clients of CRECER and their Households in Bolivia.* Preliminary results, Rural Finance Program, Ohio State University, August 2001.

Gulli, Hege. *Microfinance and Poverty: Questioning the Conventional Wisdom.* Washington, D.C.: Inter-American Development Bank, 1998.

Hannig, Alfred and Edward Katimbo-Mugwanya, eds. *How to Regulate and Supervise Microfinance—Key Issues in an International Perspective.* Proceedings of the High-Level Policy Workshop, Kampala, November 1999. Kampala: Bank of Uganda & German Technical Co-operation Financial System Development (FSD) Project, 2000.

Hashemi, Syed, Sidney Schuler, and Ann Riley. "Rural Credit Programs and Women's Empowerment in Bangladesh." *World Development* 24, no. 4 (1996): 635–53.

Hickson, Robert. "Financial Services for the Very Poor–Thinking Outside the Box." *Small Enterprise Development* 12, no. 2 (June 2001): 55–67.

Hossain, Mahabub and Catalina P. Diaz. "Reaching the Poor with Effective Microcredit: Evaluation of a Grameen Bank Replication in the Philippines." *Journal of Philippine Development* 44, no. 24 (1997): 275–308.

Hulme, David. *Client Exits (Dropouts) from East African Micro-Finance Institutions.* Kampala: MicroSave-Africa, 1999. www.microsave-africa.com.

Human Development Initiatives. *Empowering Women Through Microfinance.* 2001.

Husain, A. M. Muazzam. "Poverty Alleviation and Empowerment: The Second Impact Assessment Study of BRAC's Rural Development Programme." Dhaka: BRAC Printers, 1998.

Inoue, Hiroshi. "Interview: Ex-BOJ Tamura: Japan FSA, Banks Lag in Reform." *The Wall Street Journal Online,* 18 June 2002.

International Network of Alternative Financial Institutions (INAFI). *Charting the Future of Microfinance.* Background paper for the 4th Global Assembly of the International Network of Alternative Financial Institutions, 2001.

Jansson, Tor. *Microfinance: From Village to Wall Street.* Washington, D.C.: Inter-American Development Bank, November 2001.

Jimenez, Miguel. *A Poverty Assessment of Micro-finance CRECER, Bolivia on behalf of the Consultative Group to Assist the Poorest.* CGAP, Draft, 2002.

Johnson, Susan. "Gender Impact Assessment in Microfinance and Microenterprise: Why and How." *Development in Practice* 10, no. 1 (February 2000): 89–93.

Kabeer, Naila. "Agency, Well-being & Inequality: Reflections on the Gender Dimensions of Poverty." *IDS Bulletin* 27, no. 1 (1996): 11–21.

———. *The Conditions and Consequences of Choice: Reflections on the Measurement of Women's Empowerment.* United Nations Research Institute for Social Development (UNRISD) Discussion Paper No. 108. 1999.

———. "Editorial: Tactics and Trade-Offs: Revisiting the Links Between Gender and Poverty." *IDS Bulletin* 28, no. 3 (1997): 1–13.

———. *'Money Can't Buy Me Love'? Re-evaluating Gender, Credit and Empowerment in Rural Bangladesh.* IDS Discussion Paper 363. Brighton, England: Institute of Development Studies, University of Sussex, 1998.

———. *Reversed Realities: Gender Hierarchies in Development Thought.* London: Verso, 1994.

Kelly, Marcy. "The Tahoua Women's Savings Project, Final Evaluation Report." Niger: CARE-Niger, December 1997.

Kevane, Michael. "Qualitative Impact Study of Credit with Education in Burkina Faso." *Freedom from Hunger Research Paper no. 3*, Davis, Calif.: Freedom from Hunger, 1996.

Khan Osmani, Lutfun. "Impact of Credit on the Relative Well-Being of Women: Evidence from the Grameen Bank." *IDS Bulletin* 29, no. 4 (1998): 31–38.

Kingsbury, Jan, comp. "Directory 2000: Integrated Service Delivery Programs of Member Organizations" *Credit with Education* Learning Exchange. Davis, Calif.: Freedom from Hunger, 2000.

Lampietti, Julian and Linda Stalker. "Consumption Expenditure and Female Poverty: A Review of the Evidence." *Policy Research Report on Gender and Development Working Paper Series* no. 11. Washington, D.C.: The World Bank Development Research Group/Poverty Reduction and Economic Management Network, 2000.

Ledesma, Jesila. "Empowerment Impact Report on TSPI's Kabuhayan program." Draft. April 2002.

MacIsaac, Norman. "The Role of Microcredit in Poverty Reduction and Promoting Gender Equity: A Discussion Paper." Hull, Canada: CIDA, 1997.

Manuh, Takyiwaa. "Ghana: Women in the Public and Informal Sectors under the Economic Recovery Programme." In Visvanathan, Nalini et al., eds. *The Women, Gender and Development Reader.* London: Zed Books Ltd., 1997.

Mayoux, Linda. *From Vicious to Virtuous Circles? Gender and Micro-Enterprise Development.* Occasional Paper No. 3. UNIFEM. United Nations Fourth World Conference on Women, 1995.

———. *Micro-Finance for Women's Empowerment: A Participatory Learning, Management and Action Approach.* Milton Keynes, U.K.: UNIFEM, 2001.

———. "Participatory Learning for Women's Empowerment in Micro-Finance Programmes: Negotiating Complexity, Conflict and Change." *IDS Bulletin* 29, no. 4 (1998): 39–51.

———. *Women's Empowerment and Microfinance: A Participatory Learning, Management, and Action Approach. Resource Manual for Practitioners and Trainers.* Draft. UNIFEM, 2001.

Mends, Michael et al. "SAT Impact Assessment Report." Draft. April 2002.

Microcredit Summit Campaign. *State of the Microcredit Summit Campaign Report 2001.* Washington, D.C.: Microcredit Summit Campaign, 2001.

———. "Cutting Extreme Poverty in Half by 2015: Setting the Goal but Missing the Mark." Press release, 2002.

Microenterprise Development Review, "Regulating Microfinance," Washington, D.C.: Inter-American Development Bank, vol. 1, no. 2. December 1998.

Microfinance Gateway. "Discussion on CGAP View: Water, Water Everywhere and Not a Drop to Drink." October 22 to November 6, 2001. www.ids.ac.uk/cgap/water.

MkNelly, Barbara and Christopher Dunford. "Are Credit and Savings Services Effective Against Hunger and Malnutrition? A Literature Review and Analysis." *Freedom from Hunger Research Paper no. 1.* Davis, Calif.: Freedom from Hunger, 1996.

———. "Impact of *Credit with Education* on Mothers and Their Young Children's Nutrition: CRECER *Credit with Education* Program in Bolivia." *Freedom from Hunger Research Paper no. 5.* Davis, Calif.: Freedom from Hunger, 1999.

———. "Impact of *Credit with Education* on Mothers and Their Young Children's Nutrition: Lower Pra Rural Bank Credit with Education Program in Ghana." *Freedom from Hunger Research Paper no. 4.* Davis, Calif.: Freedom from Hunger, 1998.

MkNelly, Barbara and Ayele Foly. "Preliminary Evidence from the Freedom from Hunger/ World Relief Collaborative Evaluation in Burkina Faso." Presented at the *Credit with Education* Learning Exchange, Millwood, Va., August 1997.

MkNelly, Barbara and Karen Lippold. "Practitioner-led Impact Assessment: A Test in Mali." Paper submitted to USAID by AIMS. Washington D.C.: Management Systems International, 1998.

MkNelly, Barbara and Mona McCord. "Credit With Education Impact Review No. 1: Women's Empowerment." Davis, Calif.: Freedom from Hunger, 2001.

MkNelly, Barbara and Kathleen E. Stack. "Loan Size Growth and Sustainability in Village Banking Programmes." *Small Enterprise Development* 9, no. 2 (1998): 4–16.

MkNelly, Barbara, Chatree Watetip, Cheryl A. Lassen, and Christopher Dunford. "Preliminary Evidence that Integrated Financial and Educational Services can be Effective against Hunger and Malnutrition." *Freedom from Hunger Research Paper* no. 2. Davis, Calif.: Freedom from Hunger, 1996. E-mail: info@freefromhunger.org.

Moortele, Jan Vande. *Are the MDGs Feasible?* New York, N.Y.: United Nations Development Program Bureau for Development Policy, June 2002.

Morduch, Jonathan. *Does Microfinance Really Help the Poor? New Evidence from Flagship Programs in Bangladesh.* Department of Economics and HIID, Harvard University and Hoover Institution, Stanford University, 1998. www.wws.princeton.edu/~rpds/macarthur/downloads/avgimp~6.pdf.

Morduch, Jonathan and Barbara Haley. *Analysis of the Effects of Microfinance on Poverty Reduction.* Prepared by RESULTS Canada for the Canadian International Development Agency, November 2001.

Nasreen, Hashima et al. "An assessment of Client's knowledge of family planning in Matlab." BRAC-ICDDR,B Working Paper no. 13. Dhaka, Bangladesh: BRAC-ICDDR,B, 1996.

Navajas, Sergio, Mark Schreiner, Richard L. Meyer, et al. "Microcredit and the Poorest of the Poor: Theory and Evidence From Bolivia." *World Development* 28, no. 2 (2000). www.microfinance.com/English/Papers/Bolivia_Poorest.pdf.

Nelson, Candace, Barbara MkNelly, Kathleen Stack and Lawrence Yanovitch (with assistance from the Poverty Lending Working Group of SEEP and participants at the International Conference of Village Bank Practitioners). *Village Banking: The State of the Practice.* Washington, D.C.: SEEP Network and the United Nations Development Fund for Women, 1996.

Nteziyaremye, Anastase and Barbara Mknelly. "Mali Poverty Outreach Study of Kafo Jiginew and Nyesigiso Credit and Savings with Education Programs." *Freedom from Hunger Research Paper* no. 7. Davis, Calif.: Freedom from Hunger, 2001.

Nteziyaremye, Anastase, Kathleen E. Stack and Barbara MkNelly. "Impact of *Credit with Education* on Recruitment of New Members to the Credit Unions of the Kafo Jiginew and Nyèsigiso Federations in Mali." *Freedom from Hunger Research Paper.* Davis, Calif.: Freedom from Hunger, 2001.

Parker, Joan and Doug Pearce. "Microfinance, Grants and Non-financial Responses to Poverty Reduction: Where Does Microcredit Fit?" *CGAP Focus Note* 20. Washington, D.C.: CGAP, 2001.

Pitt, Mark M. and Sahidur R. Khandker. "Household and Intrahousehold Impact of the Grameen Bank and Similar Targeted Credit Programs in Bangladesh." *World Bank Discussion Paper no. 320*. Washington, D.C.: The World Bank, 1996.

PLAN International. *Mid-term Evaluation of Nirdhan/PLAN Microfinance Program in Nepal*. PLAN International, 2001.

PlaNet Rating. *Rating: Crédito Con Educación Rural* (CRECER). Paris: PlaNet Finance, 2002.

Quisumbing, Agnes and John Maluccio. "Intrahousehold Allocation and Gender Relations: New Empirical Evidence." Policy Research Report on Gender and Development Working Paper Series, no. 2. Washington, D.C.: The World Bank Development Research Group/ Poverty Reduction and Economic Management Network, 1999.

Rahman, Aminur. "Micro-credit Initiatives for Equitable and Sustainable Development: Who Pays?" *World Development* 27, no. 1 (1999): 67–82.

Rashid, Sabina, Mushtaque Chowdhury and Abbas Bhuiya. "An inside look at two BRAC schools in Matlab." BRAC-ICDDR,B Working Paper no. 8. Dhaka, Bangladesh: BRAC-ICDDR,B, 1995.

Razavi, Shahra. "From Rags to Riches: Looking at Poverty from a Gender Perspective." *IDS Bulletin* 28, no. 3 (1997): 49–62.

Reddy, S. and T. Pogge. "How Not to Count the Poor, Version 4.0." 2002 www.socialanalysis.org.

Remenyi, Joe. "Microfinance best practice: ten parameters of success for development NGOs." *Development Bulletin*, no. 57. Development Studies Network, Australian National University, 2002.

Robinson, Marguerite. *The Microfinance Revolution: Sustainable Finance for the Poor*. Washington, D.C.: World Bank, 2001.

Rosenberg, Richard and Robert Peck Christen. *The Rush to Regulate*. CGAP Occasional Paper no. 4. Washington, D.C.: CGAP, April 2000.

Roy, Rita Das et al. "Does Involvement of Women in BRAC Influence Sex Bias in Intra-Household Food Distribution?" BRAC-ICDDR,B Working Paper no. 25. Dhaka, Bangladesh: BRAC-ICDDR,B, 1998.

Rutherford, Stuart. *The Poor and Their Money*. New Delhi: Oxford University Press, 2000.

Saith, Rubi and Barbara Harriss-White. "The Gender Sensitivity of Well-Being Indicators." *Development and Change* 30 (1999): 465–97.

Salib, Suzy. *FORA's Impact among Migrants: Primary Findings*. Oak Brook, Ill.: Opportunity International Network, 2001.

Salib, Suzy et al. "Bundling Microfinance and Business Development Services: A Case Study from ADEMCOL in Colombia." USAID Microenterprise Best Practice Business Development Services Case Study No. 10. Washington, D.C.: Development Alternatives International, 2001.

Schuler, Sidney R. and Syed Hashemi. "Credit Programs, Women's Empowerment, and Contraceptive Use in Bangladesh." *Studies in Family Planning* 25, no. 2 (1994): 65–79.

Schuler, Sidney, Syed Hashemi, and Ann Riley. "The Influence of Women's Changing Roles and Status in Bangladesh's Fertility Transition: Evidence from a Study of Credit Programs and Contraceptive Use." *World Development* 25, no. 4 (1997): 563–75.

Schuler, S. R., S. M. Hashemi, A. P. Riley, and A. Akhter. "Credit Programs, Patriarchy and Men's Violence against Women in Rural Bangladesh." *Social Science and Medicine* 43, no. 12 (1996): 1729–42.

Sebstad, Jennefer and Gregory Chen. "Overview of Studies on the Impact of Microenterprise Credit." AIMS Paper. Washington, D.C.: Management Sciences International, 1996.

Sebstad, Jennefer and Monique Cohen. "Microfinance, Risk Management, and Poverty." AIMS paper. Washington, D.C.: Office of Microenterprise Development, USAID, 2000. www.mip.org.

SEILANITHIH. "Client Satisfaction Survey Report." Cambodia, July 2000.

Sen, A. "Gender and Cooperative Conflicts." In I. Tinker, ed. *Persistent Inequalities: Women and World Development*, New York, N.Y.: Oxford University Press, 1990.

Sen, Gita. "Engendering Poverty Alleviation: Challenges and Opportunities." *Development and Change* 30 (1999): 685–92.

Shakti. "Study on the Trend of Living Condition of Shakti Members." Bangladesh.

Sharma, Manohar and Gertrud Schrieder. 1998. "Impact of finance on food security and poverty alleviation—a review and synthesis of empirical evidence." Paper presented for "Innovations in Micro-Finance for the Rural Poor: Exchange of Knowledge and Implications for Policy" Workshop organized by DSE (Berlin, Germany), IFPRI (Washington, D.C., USA) & IFAD (Rome, Italy) in Ghana, November, 1998.

Sherpa, Helen. World Education response to e-mail survey, 20 October 2001.

Shrestha, Milan. *Report on Self-help Banking Program and Women's Empowerment*. Nepal, 1998.

Simanowitz, Anton. *Appraising the Poverty Outreach of Microfinance: A Review of the CGAP Poverty Assessment Tool (PAT)*. Brighton, UK: Imp-Act, Institute of Development Studies, 2002. www.Imp-Act.org.

———. "Client Exit Surveys: A Tool for Understanding Client 'Drop-Out'." *Journal of Microfinance* 2, no.1 (2000).

———. "From Event to Process: Current Trends in Microfinance Impact Assessment." *Small Enterprise Development* 12, no. 4 (2001a).

———. "Microfinance for the Poorest: A Review of Issues and Ideas for Contribution of Imp-Act." *Learning Note no. 4*. Brighton, UK: Imp-Act, Institute of Development Studies, 2001b. www.Imp-Act.org.

Simanowitz, Anton, Ben Nkuna, and Sukor Kasim. *Overcoming the Obstacles of Identifying the Poorest Families: Using Participatory Wealth Ranking (PWR), the CASHPOR House Index (CHI), and Other Measurements to Identify and Encourage the Participation of the Poorest Families, Especially the Women of Those Families*. Washington, D.C.: Microcredit Summit Campaign, 2000. www.microcreditsummit.org/papers/povertypaper.htm.

Small Enterprise Development, Special Theme Issue: Microfinance Regulation, 11, no. 4, December 2000.

Small Enterprise Education and Promotion Network (SEEP). *Learning from Clients: Assessment Tools for Microfinance Practitioners*. Washington, D.C.: SEEP, 2001.

Small Enterprise Education and Promotion (SEEP) Network and the United Nations Development Fund for Women. *Village Banking: The State of the Practice*. Compiled by Candace Nelson, Barbara MkNelly, Kathleen Stack, and Lawrence Yanovitch. Washington, D.C.: Pact Publishing,1996.

Smith, Stephen C. "Microcredit and Health Programs: To Integrate or Not to Integrate?" In R. Rodriguez-Garcia, J. A. Macinko, and W. F. Waters, eds. *Microenterprise Development for Better Health Outcomes.* In series *Contributions in Economics and Economic History.* Westport, Conn.: Greenwood Press, 2001.

Smith, Stephen C. and Sanjay Jain. "Village Banking and Maternal and Child Health: Theory and Evidence from Ecuador and Honduras." Working Paper, Department of Economics, George Washington University, Washington, D.C., 1999.

Snodgrass, Donald and Jennefer Sebstad. *Clients in Context: The Impacts of Microfinance in Three Countries.* AIMS Synthesis Report. Washington, D.C.: Office of Microenterprise Development, USAID, 2002. www.mip.org.

Soros, George. *George Soros on Globalization.* New York, N.Y.: Public Affairs, 2002.

Staschen, Stefan. *Regulation and Supervision of Microfinance Institutions: State of Knowledge.* Eschborn, Germany: Deutsche Gesellschaft für Technische Zusammen-arbeit, August 1999.

———. *Women at the Center: Grameen Bank Borrowers after One Decade.* New York, N.Y.: Westview Press, 1996.

Todd, Helen. *Women at the Center: Grameen Bank Borrowers after One Decade.* New York: Westview Press, 1996.

United Nations. *United Nations Millennium Declaration.* 2000. www.un.org/millennium/declaration/ares552e.htm.

United Nations Development Programme (UNDP). *1995 Human Development Report.* New York, N.Y.: UNDP, 1996.

———. *World Development Report 2000/01: Attacking Poverty.* New York, N.Y.: UNDP, 2001.

United States Agency for International Development (USAID). *Microenterprise Development in a Changing World: U.S. Agency for International Development Microenterprise Results Reporting for 2000.* Arlington, Va.: Weidemann Associates, 2001.

———. *Reaching Down and Scaling Up: Focus on USAID's Development Partners: USAID Microenterprise Results Reporting for 1999.* Arlington, Va.: Weidemann Associates, 2000.

Valenzuela, Liza and Robin Young. *Consultation on Regulation and Supervision of Microfinance: A Workshop Report.* Washington, D.C.: USAID, December 1999.

van de Ruit, Catherine, Julian May and Benjamin Roberts. *A Poverty Assessment of the Small Enterprise Foundation on Behalf of CGAP.* University of Natal, 2001. www.cgap.org/assets/images/SEF%20final%20report.pdf.

van Greuning, Hennie, Joselito Gallardo, and Biiki Randhawa, *A Framework for Regulating Microfinance Institutions.* Washington, D.C.: World Bank, February 1999.

Vogel, Robert C., T. Fitzgerald. "Moving Towards Risk-Based Supervision in Developing Economies." *Consulting Assistance on Economic Reform CAER II Discussion Paper no. 66,* 2000.

Vor der Bruegge, Ellen, Joan E. Dickey, and Christopher Dunford. "Cost of Education in the Freedom from Hunger Version of *Credit with Education* Implementation." *Freedom from Hunger Research Paper no. 6,* Davis, Calif.: Freedom from Hunger, 1999.

Watershed Organization Trust (WOTR). "WOTR Micro Finance Summary Information" and "Results: Individual Interviews." Submitted to Opportunity International, October 2001.

Whitehead, Ann and Matthew Lockwood. "Gendering Poverty: A Review of Six World Bank African Poverty Assessments." *Development and Change* 30 (1999): 525–55.

WOCCU. "WOCCU Philippines CUES Quarterly Project Report." July–September 2001.

Woller, Gary. "Reassessing the Financial Viability of Village Banking: Past Performance and

Future Prospects," *Microbanking Bulletin 5* (September 2000): 3–8.

Women's Entrepreneurship Development Trust Fund (WEDTF). *Information on Microfinance and Empowerment of Women.* Zanzibar, Tanzania: WEDTF, 2001.

Women's World Banking (WWB). *Country Scorecard on Financial Systems that Work for the Majority.* New York, N.Y.: WWB, 2000.

———. *The Missing Links: Financial Systems That Work for the Majority.* New York, N.Y.: WWB, 1995.

Working Women's Forum (WWF). *Social Platform through Social Innovations: A Coalition with Women in the Informal Sector.* Chennai, India: Working Women's Forum, 2000.

World Bank. *Engendering Development: Through Gender Equality in Rights, Resources, and Voice—Summary.* Washington, D.C.: World Bank, 2001. www.worldbank.org/gender/prr/engendersummary.pdf.

———. *World Development Report 2000–2001.* Washington, D.C.: World Bank, 2001.

World Council for Credit Unions (WOCCU). "WOCCU Philippines CUES Quarterly Project Report." July–September 2001.

World Relief Rwanda. "Impact Assessment of TF UK Clients in the World Relief Rwanda URWEGO Program." World Relief Rwanda, 1999.

WOTR. "WOTR Micro Finance Summary Information" and "Results: Individual Interviews." Submitted to Opportunity International, October 2001.

Wright, Graham. "Examining the Impact of Microfinance Services—Increasing Income or Reducing Poverty?" *Small Enterprise Development* 10, no. 1 (1999).

Wright, Graham A. N. Deborah Kasente, Germina Ssemogerere, and Leonard Mutesasira (1999). "Vulnerability, Risks, Assets and Empowerment—The Impact of Microfinance on Poverty Alleviation." MicroSave-Africa and Uganda Women's Finance Trust, 1999. www.undp.org/sum/MicroSave/ftp_downloads/UWFTstudyFinal.pdf.

Wright, Graham A. N. et al. "Vulnerability, Risks, Assets and Empowerment—The Impact of Microfinance on Poverty Alleviation." Paper contributed to *World Development Report* 2001.

Wright, Jamie. Report on focus-group discussions with ADAPTE loan officers. Costa Rica, 2001.

Yawe, Agnes. "Engendering Microfinance Services: Beyond Access." Paper presented at the Feminisation of Debt workshop in London, March 2002. www.oneworldaction.org.

Yeung, Tomas Au. "NPLs of Taiwan Banks Estimated to Reach 18%" *The China Post*, 25 April 2002.

Young, K. "Household Resource Management." In L. Ostergaard, ed. *Gender and Development: A Practical Guide*, London: Routledge, 1992.

Yunus, Muhammad, *Grameen Bank II: Designed to Open New Possibilities.* Grameen Foundation USA, June 2002. www.gfusa.org/monthly/june/news.shtml.

Zafar, Roshaneh. "Microfinance and the Empowerment of Women: The Experience of Kashf Foundation, Pakistan." Paper presented at the Microcredit Summit, Meeting of Councils, New Delhi, India, 1–5 February 2001.

Zdrojewki, Nicole. "Exploring Empowerment: A Microethnography of Women's Self-Help Groups in Villupuram, Tamil Nadu." Washington, D.C.: George Washington University, 2001.

Zeller, Manfred and Manohar Sharma. "Rural Finance and Poverty Alleviation." *Food Policy Report.* Washington, D.C.: International Food Policy Research Institute, 1998.

Index

About the Authors

Sam Daley-Harris

SAM DALEY-HARRIS is President and founder of RESULTS Educational Fund, a 501(c)(3) organization dedicated to mass educational strategies to generate the will to end world hunger. RESULTS Educational Fund organized the February 1997 Microcredit Summit held in Washington, D.C. The Summit was attended by more than 2,900 participants from 137 countries and launched a nine-year campaign to reach 100 million of the world's poorest families, especially the women of those families, with credit for self-employment and other financial and business services by 2005.

Daley-Harris is also founder and President of RESULTS, an international citizens' lobby dedicated to creating the political will to end hunger and poverty. He is author of *Reclaiming Our Democracy: Healing the Break Between People and Government*, about which Jimmy Carter said, "[Daley-Harris] provides a road map for global involvement in planning a better future."

Daley-Harris lives in Washington, D.C., with his wife Shannon, who is a consultant with the Religious Affairs Division of the Children's Defense Fund. Their son Micah was born in May 1998 and their daughter Sophie was born in May 2001.

Anton Simanowitz

ANTON SIMANOWITZ is Project Coordinator of the ImpAct Programme (Improving Impact of Development Finance on Poverty, Action Research Programme), based at the University of Sussex, United Kingdom.

From 1994 until April 2000 he was based in rural South Africa, working for three years with the Small Enterprise Foundation (SEF), an MFI actively working with the poorest women, in the poorest province of the country.

At SEF Simanowitz focused on developing operational methodology for identifying, effectively working with, and achieving long-term positive impact. Part of this process involved developing an impact assessment and monitoring system, integrated into SEF's management information systems

Christopher Dunford

CHRISTOPHER DUNFORD is President of Freedom From Hunger, which works in fourteen countries to bring innovative and sustainable self-help solutions to the fight against chronic hunger and poverty. Dr. Dunford, who holds a Ph.D. in Ecology and Sociology, joined Freedom from Hunger in 1984. In 1986, Dr. Dunford conducted a study of U.S. poverty and health and developed a new programming strategy for Freedom From Hunger in the United States. Dr. Dunford is one of the three chief architects in the design and implementation of Freedom From Hunger's Credit with Education strategy.

John K. Hatch

JOHN HATCH is an ex-Peace Corps Volunteer, Fulbright scholar, Ph.D. in Economic Development from the University of Wisconsin (1973), consultant, inventor of the microcredit methodology known as "Village Banking" in 1983, founder of FINCA International (1984), and has personally built three village banking programs in Bolivia (1984–86), El Salvador (1989–92), and Guatemala (1993–96). He can be contacted at jhatch@villagebanking.org.

Amanda Penn

AMANDA PENN graduated cum laude from with a B.A. in Political Science from Binghamton University (1998) and holds an M.A. in International Affairs from The George Washington University (2002), where she specialized in Development. She can be contacted at heiwa@gwu.edu.

Sara R. Levine

SARA LEVINE holds a B.A. in American Studies from Yale University (1995) and an M.A. in International Affairs from The George Washington University (2002), where she specialized in Development and Microfinance (2002). She can be contacted at levoon@gwu.edu.

Susy Cheston

SUSY CHESTON was named Executive Director Emeritus of the Women's Opportunity Fund by the board of directors in 2001. In the same year, she assumed the position of Senior Vice President for Policy and Research for the Opportunity International Network. The founding executive director of the Women's Fund, Susy designed and implemented its pilot project in El Salvador in 1991 and 1992. Ms. Cheston oversaw the expansion of the Women's Opportunity Fund into twenty countries, through a financially sustainable "beyond credit" poverty-lending model called Trust Banks. Among the contributions the Women's Opportunity Fund has made to the industry is the Trust Bank Manual, a product of best practice exchanges among practitioners, available in English, Spanish, Indonesian and Russian. Other training and technical assisstance tools are also available at publications@opportunity.org.

She has spoken in Australia, Brazil, Ivory Coast, New Zealand, the United States, and Zimbabwe on microenterprise development and poverty issues and has been featured on National Public Radio's "All Things Considered," on CNN, and in a number of other broadcasts and publications. Throughout the 1980s, Susy worked in broadcasting in St. Louis and Boston. She has a B.A. in music and an M.A. in communications.

Lisa Kuhn

LISA KUHN is Program Analyst and Gender Advisor in the Policy and Research Division of the Opportunity International Network. Her work includes product development, research on emerging best practices on a variety of issues, and development of policy and tools to promote gender equity and sensitivity. She previously developed policy documents on microfinance for FINCA International and also worked with the Microcredit Summit Secretariat. She received her M.S. in Foreign Service from Georgetown University and her B.A. cum laude in Latin American Relations and Romance Languages from DePauw University.

David S. Gibbons

DAVID GIBBONS has been in microfinance for the poor in Asia for fourteen years. Amanah Ikhtiar Malaysia, the first international replication of Grameen banking for the poor, was the first step. It attracted attention and soon there were GB-type MFIs in several countries. In 1991, they formed CASHPOR, the Asian network for Credit and Savings for the Hardcore Poor of which Gibbons became Executive Trustee in 1993. CASHPOR member outreach to the poor is now just over 300,000 active savers of whom more than 282,000 are active loan clients with total loans outstanding of more than US$56 million. In 1997, Gibbons started a fast-track, commercial adaptation of GB in India. Called CASHPOR India, it is on target to reach 18,000 poor women and financial self-sufficiency by 2002. In addition to his work on the ground, Gibbons has written several books and training manuals on the international replication/adaptation of Grameen banking for the poor.

Jennifer W. Meehan

JENNIFER MEEHAN worked at The Chase Manhattan Bank (now JP Morgan Chase) before joining CASHPOR, the Asian Network of Grameen Bank Adaptors, as Financial Advisor in June 1998. Today, she provides consulting services to CASHPOR, the Calvert Social Investment Foundation, and Swayam Krishi Sangam, among others. She serves on the Editorial Board of CASHPOR's quarterly newsletter and on the Management Board of the Aavishkaar India Micro Venture Capital Fund, a newly launched social venture capital fund to finance rural innovations in India. She graduated summa cum laude from The George Washington University with a degree in International Economics.

Women's World Banking

WOMEN'S WORLD BANKING (WWB) is a global network of over fifty microfinance institutions and banks in thirty-four countries that provide microlending services to over 10 million poor women and men and savings services to millions more. Together, WWB network members aim to change the way the world works by connecting poor women to economic and financial systems locally and globally.

Poor women are at the center of what the WWB network does. The network reaches poor women by providing and organizing support to its member organizations, which in turn offer direct services to these women. In practical terms this means creating the possibility for a low-income woman to build her business and assets, improve her living conditions, keep her family well-fed and healthy, educate her children, develop respect at home and in her community, and secure a political voice.

WWB has been a leader in building a global consensus on performance standards for the microfinance industry, and in shaping policies and financial systems for the world's poor majority. By helping network members get what they need to succeed, and by helping shape financial systems and industry standards, WWB seeks to reduce the gap between the hundreds of millions of poor women who require financial services, and those who currently receive microloans.

Also from Kumarian Press...

The Commercialization of Microfinance: Balancing Business and Development
Edited by Deborah Drake and Elisabeth Rhyne

Defying the Odds: Banking for the Poor
Eugene Versluysen

Mainstreaming Microfinance
How Lending to the Poor Began, Grew and Came of Age in Bolivia
Elisabeth Rhyne

The New World of Microenterprise Finance
Building Healthy Financial Institutions for the Poor
Edited by María Otero and Elisabeth Rhyne

Visit Kumarian Press at **www.kpbooks.com** or
call **toll-free 800.289.2664** for a complete catalog.

 Kumarian Press, located in Bloomfield, Connecticut, is a forward-looking, scholarly press that promotes active international engagement and an awareness of global connectedness.